D1373862

West Indian Literature:
An Index to Criticism,
1930-1975

A
Reference
Publication
in
Latin American
Studies

William V. Jackson
Editor

West Indian Literature: An Index to Criticism, 1930-1975

JEANNETTE B. ALLIS

G.K.HALL &CO.

70 LINCOLN STREET, BOSTON, MASS.

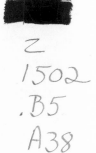

Z
1502
.B5
A38

INDIANA
UNIVERSITY LIBRARY

MAY   4 1982

NORTHWEST

Copyright © 1981 by Jeannette B. Allis

Library of Congress Cataloging in Publication Data

Allis, Jeannette B
  West Indian literature.

  Includes bibliographical references.
  1. West Indian literature (English)—History
and criticism—Bibliography.   I.   Title.
Z1502.B5A38   [PR9210]   016.820′9′9729
ISBN 0-8161-8266-3   80-24587

This publication is printed on permanent/durable acid-free paper
MANUFACTURED IN THE UNITED STATES OF AMERICA

FOR CLAYTON

AND FOR C. F. B.

Contents

THE AUTHOR: Jeannette B. Allis is Documents Librarian at the Public Library in St. Thomas, U.S. Virgin Islands. She graduated from New York University in 1965 and has recently received a Masters of Philosophy in West Indian Literature at the University of the West Indies. Her publications include numerous articles on the history and development of West Indian literature.

Periodicals and Newspapers Indexed

Imprint and volumes indexed are included with each citation.

A.S.A.W.I. BULLETIN (African Studies Association of the West
    Indies). Jamaica, University of the West Indies, no. 1,
    December 1967-.
        Indexed: nos. 1-6; 1967-1973.

ANTIOCH REVIEW. Yellow Springs, Ohio, Antioch Review, Inc., v. 1,
    Spring 1941-.
        Indexed: v. 1-31; 1941-1971.

ARIEL. Calgary, Canada, University of Calgary Press, v. 1, no. 1,
    January 1970-.
        Formerly A REVIEW OF ENGLISH LITERATURE.
        Indexed: v. 1-7; 1970-1976

THE BAJAN. Bridgetown, Barbados, Carib Publicity Co., Ltd., v. 1,
    no. 1, September 1953-v. 7, no. 4, December 1959.
        Superceded by THE BAJAN AND SOUTH CARIBBEAN.
        Indexed: complete.

THE BEACON. Port of Spain, Trinidad, Beacon Co., v. 1, no. 1,
    March 1931-v. 4, no. 1, November 1939.
        Indexed: complete.

BIM. Barbados, Coles Printery Ltd., v. 1, no. 1, December 1942-
        Indexed: v. 1-16; 1942-1977.

BLACK ACADEMY REVIEW. Bloomfield, New Jersey, Black Academy Press,
    v. 1, no. 1, 1970-.
        Indexed: v. 1-2; 1970-1971.

BLACK IMAGES. Toronto, Black Images, Inc., v. 1, no. 1, January
    1972-.
        Indexed: v. 1-3; 1972-1975.

BLACK ORPHEUS, A Journal of African and Afro-American Literature,
    Ibadan, Nigeria, no. 1, September 1957-no. 22, August 1967.

Indexed: complete.

BLACK SCHOLAR. Sausalito, California, Black World Foundation, v. 1, no. 1, November 1969-.
Indexed: v. 1-5; 1969-1974.

BLACK WORLD. Chicago: Johnson Publishing Co., v. 19, 1970-1976.
Formerly NEGRO DIGEST, 1942-1970.
Indexed: complete.

BOOKS ABROAD, An International Literary Quarterly, Norman, Oklahoma, Oklahoma University Press, v. 1, no. 1, 1927-.
Indexed: v. 36-48; 1962-1974.

CARIBBEAN CONTACT. Bridgetown, Barbados, Caribbean Contact, Ltd., v. 1, January 1973-.
Indexed: v. 1-5, no. 5: 1973-1977.

CARIBBEAN QUARTERLY. Kingston, Jamaica, University of the West Indies, v. 1, no. 1, April 1949-.
Indexed: v. 1-21; 1949-1975.

CARIBBEAN REVIEW. Miami, Florida, Caribbean Review, Inc., v. 1, no. 1; Spring 1969-
Indexed: v. 1-6; 1969-1975.

CARIBBEAN STUDIES. Rio Piedras, Puerto Rico, Institute of Caribbean Studies, v. 1, no. 1, April 1961-
Indexed: v. 1-13; 1961-1974.

CONTEMPORARY LITERATURE. Madison, Wisconsin, Wisconsin University Press, v. 9, no. 1, Winter 1968-
Formerly WISCONSIN STUDIES IN CONTEMPORARY LITERATURE.
Indexed: v. 9-15; 1968-1974.

CORLIT (Corinth Teachers Literary Group). California, Trinidad, no. 1, December 1973-
Indexed: no. 1-v. 2, nos. 1 2; 1973-1975.

THE CRITICAL QUARTERLY. Hull, England, Hull University, v. 1, no. 1, Spring 1959-
Indexed: v. 1-16; 1959-1974.

THE CRITICAL SURVEY, Journal of the Critical Quarterly Society, Hull, England, Critical Quarterly Society, v. 1, no. 1, Autumn 1962-v. 5, no. 4, Summer 1972.
Indexed: complete.

DAEDALUS, Journal of the American Academy of Arts and Sciences, Boston, Mass., American Academy of Arts and Sciences, v. 1,

May 1946-.
Indexed: v. 89-103; 1960-1974.

DALHOUSIE REVIEW. Halifax, Nova Scotia, Dalhousie University Press,
v. 1, April 1921-.
Indexed: v. 40-55; 1960-1975.

FLAMBEAU. Kingstown, St. Vincent, Kingstown Study Group, no. 1,
June 1965-no. 9, July 1968.
Indexed: complete.

FREEDOMWAYS. New York, Freedomways Associates, v. 1, 1961-.
Indexed: v. 1-15; 1961-1975.

HUMANITIES ASSOCIATION REVIEW. Ontario, Canada, Humanities
Association of Canada, v. 1, March 1951-
Indexed: v. 24-26; 1973-1975.

JAMAICA AND WEST INDIAN REVIEW. Kingston, Jamaica, Arawak Press,
Ltd., New Series, v. 1, no. 1, 1963-.
Formerly WEST INDIAN REVIEW.
Indexed: 1963-1974.

JAMAICA JOURNAL, Quarterly of the Institute of Jamaica, Kingston,
Jamaica, Institute of Jamaica, v. 1, no. 1, December 1967-.
Indexed: v. 1-9; 1967-1975.

JOHN O'LONDON'S, For Books and the Arts, London, v. 1, no. 1,
October 1959-v. 7, no. 169, December 1962.
Indexed: complete.

JOURNAL OF BLACK STUDIES. Beverly Hills, California, Sage Press,
v. 1, no. 1, 1970-.
Indexed: v. 1-5; 1970-1974.

JOURNAL OF COMMONWEALTH LITERATURE. London, University of Leeds
and Heinemann Educational Books, Ltd., no. 1, September 1965-.
Indexed: no. 1-v. 10, no. 1; 1965-1975.

KAIE, Official Organ of the National History and Arts Council,
Georgetown, Guyana, National History and Arts Council, no. 1,
October 1965-1973.
Indexed: complete.

KAIRI. Port-of-Spain, Trinidad, Creative Printing, Ltd., no. 1,
1974-.
Indexed: no. 1, 1974-Annual Issue 1976.

KYK-OVER-AL. British Guiana, British Guiana Writers Association,
v. 1, no. 1, December 1945-v. 9, no. 27, December 1960.
Indexed: complete.

LIFE AND LETTERS TODAY. London, v. 24, no. 29, January 1940-v. 65, no. 154, June 1950.
    Indexed:

LINK. Castries, St. Lucia, v. 1, no. 1, July/September 1968-.
    Indexed: v. 1-2; 1968-1970.

THE LISTENER. London, British Broadcasting Co., v. 1, 1929-.
    Indexed:

THE LITERARY CRITERION. Mysore, India, Geetha Book House, v. 1, no. 1, 1952-.
    Indexed: v. 1-12; 1952-1975.

LITERARY HALF-YEARLY. Mysore, India, Mysore University Press, v. 1, no. 1, 1960-.
    Indexed: v. 1-16; 1960-1975.

LONDON MAGAZINE, A Monthly Review of Literature, London, v. 1, no. 1, February 1954-.
    Indexed: v. 1-14; 1954-1975.

LONDON OBSERVER. London, 1791-.
    Indexed: 1950-1974.

MOKO. Trinidad, no. 1, October 28, 1968-July 20, 1973.
    Indexed: complete.

NEGRO DIGEST. Chicago: Johnson Publishing Co., v. 1, 1942-v. 19, 1970.
    Superceded by BLACK WORLD, 1970-1976.
    Indexed: complete.

NEW LETTERS. Missouri, Kansas, Missouri University Press, v. 38, no. 1, Fall 1971-.
    Continues THE UNIVERSITY REVIEW.
    Indexed: v. 38-42; 1971-1975.

NEW STATESMAN. London, Statesman and Nation Publishing Company, v. 1, no. 1, April 1913-.
    Indexed: v. 19-88; 1940-1974.

THE NEW VOICES. Diego Martin, Trinidad, The New Voices, v. 1, no. 1, 1973-.
    Indexed: v. 1-4, 1973-1976.

NEW WORLD (FORTNIGHTLY). Georgetown, Guyana, New World Associates, v. 1, no. 1, January 1965-no. 50, 1967.
    Indexed: complete.

NEW WORLD QUARTERLY. Mona, Jamaica, New World Group, v. 1, March

1963-v. 5, no. 4,
    Indexed: complete.

NEW YORK REVIEW OF BOOKS. New York, NYREV, Inc., v. 1, no. 1,
    1963-.
        Indexed: v. 1-18; 1963-1972.

NEW YORK TIMES. New York, 1851-.
    Indexed: 1949-1976.

NOVEL, A Forum on Fiction, Providence, Rhode Island, Brown
    University Press, v. 1, no. 1, Fall 1967-.
        Indexed: v. 1-8; 1967-1974.

NOW. St. Ann, Jamaica, no. 1, Spring 1973-.
    Indexed: nos. 1-4/5; 1973-1974.

PHYLON, The Atlanta University Review of Race and Culture, Atlanta,
    Georgia, Atlanta University Press, v. 1, no. 1, 1940-.
        Indexed: v. 1-35; 1940-1974.

PRESENCE AFRICAINE. Paris, Nouvelle Societe Presence Africaine,
    no. 1, 1947-.
        Indexed: nos. 1-85; 1947-1974.

PUBLIC OPINION. Kingston, Jamaica, June 1937-.
    Indexed: 1937-1971 (lacking 1943-1945).

QUEENS QUARTERLY. Kingston, Canada, Queens University Press,
    v. 1, 1907-.
        Indexed: v. 60-81; 1953-1974.

RACE, The Journal of the Institute of Race Relations, London, The
    Institute, v. 1, no. 1, November 1959-.
        Indexed: v. 1-14; 1959-1973.

REVIEW OF ENGLISH LITERATURE. Leeds, England, University of
    Leeds Press, v. 1, no. 1, January 1960-v. 8, no. 4, 1967.
        Superceded by ARIEL, 1970-.
        Indexed:

REVISTA/REVIEW INTERAMERICANA. Hato Rey, Puerto Rico, Inter-
    American University Press, v. 1, no. 1, Spring 1971-.
        Indexed: v. 1-4; 1971-1974.

SAVACOU. Mona, Jamaica, Caribbean Artists Movement, v. 1, no. 1,
    June 1970-.
        Indexed: v. 1-no. 11/12; 1970-1975.

SOUTHERN REVIEW, An Australian Journal of Literary Studies,

Adelaide, Australia, University of Adelaide. v. 1, no. 1,
    Indexed: v. 1-8; 1965-1975.

SPECTATOR. London, 1828-.
    Indexed: v. 186-230; 1951-1974.

STUDIES IN BLACK LITERATURE. Fredericksburg, Virginia, v. 1, no. 1,
    Spring 1970-.
    Indexed: v. 1-4; 1970-1973.

STUDIES IN THE NOVEL. Denton, Texas, North Texas State University,
    v. 1, no. 1, Spring 1969-.
    Indexed: v. 1-6; 1969-1974.

SUNDAY GLEANER. Kingston, Jamaica, Gleaner Co., Ltd., December 10,
    1939-.
    Indexed: 1939-1976.

SUNDAY GLEANER MAGAZINE. Kingston, Jamaica, Gleaner Co., Ltd.,
    March 21, 1963-.
    Indexed: 1963-1976.

SUNDAY GUARDIAN. Port-of-Spain, Trinidad,
    April 1952-.
    Indexed: 1952-1973.

SUNDAY GUARDIAN MAGAZINE. Port-of-Spain, Trinidad. January 1966-.
    Indexed: 1966-1972.

TAMARACK REVIEW. Toronto, Canada,
    no. 1, Autumn 1956-.
    Indexed: nos. 1-64; 1956-1974.

TAPIA. Tunapuna, Trinidad, and Tobago, Tapia House Publishing Co.,
    no. 1, September 1969-.
    Indexed: no. 1-v. 7, no. 16; 1969-April 1977.

TEXAS STUDIES IN LANGUAGE AND LITERATURE. Austin, Texas,
    University of Texas Press, v. 1, no. 1, Spring 1959-.
    Indexed: v. 1-16; 1959-1975.

THE TIMES. London, 1788-.
    Indexed: 1953-1974.

TIMES LITERARY SUPPLEMENT. London, 1902-.
    Indexed: no. 2,509-3,254; 1950-1964.

TRANSITION, A Journal of the Arts, Culture and Society, Kampala,
    Uganda, v. 1, no. 1, 1961-v. 7, no. 37, 1968.
    Indexed: complete.

VOICES. Port-of-Spain, Trinidad,
   v. 1, no. 1, 1964-.
     Indexed: v. 1-2; 1964-1969.

THE WEST INDIAN REVIEW. Kingston, Jamaica, Arawak Press, Ltd.,
   v. 1, no. 1, September 1934-1962.
     Superceded by JAMAICA AND WEST INDIAN REVIEW, 1963.
     Indexed: complete.

WORLD LITERATURE WRITTEN IN ENGLISH. Arlington, Texas, University
   of Texas at Arlington, no. 19/20, April 1971-.
     Indexed: no. 19-v. 16; 1971-April 1977.

ZUKA, Journal of East African Creative Writing, Nairobi, Kenya,
   Oxford University Press, East African Branch, no. 1, September
   1967-19   (suspended).
     Indexed: nos. 1-6; 1967-1972.

Essay Collections Indexed

Literary articles appearing in these collections have been analyzed similarly to periodical and newspaper articles. Titles have not been abbreviated in citations.

The Black Writer in Africa and the Americas. Ed. Lloyd W. Brown. Los Angeles: Hennessey and Ingalls, 1973.

Iouanaloa: Recent Writing From St. Lucia. Ed. Edward Brathwaite. Castries, St. Lucia: Department of Extra Mural Studies, 1963.

Is Massa Day Dead: Black Moods in the Caribbean. Ed. Orde Coombs. New York: Doubleday, 1974.

The Islands in Between: Essays on West Indian Literature. Ed. Louis James. London: Oxford University Press. 1968.

New Beacon Reviews: Collection One. Ed. John La Rose. London: New Beacon Books, 1968.

Abbreviations

Titles consisting of three or more words have been abbreviated. All others have been cited in full.

ASAWI	ASAWI BULLETIN
BAJAN	THE BAJAN AND SOUTH CARIBBEAN
BAR	BLACK ACADEMY REVIEW
HAR	HUMANITIES ASSOCIATION REVIEW
JBS	JOURNAL OF BLACK STUDIES
JCL	JOURNAL OF COMMONWEALTH LITERATURE
JLW	JOHN O'LONDON'S WEEKLY
LL	LIFE AND LETTERS
LSO	LONDON SUNDAY OBSERVER
NWF	NEW WORLD (FORTNIGHTLY)
NWQ	NEW WORLD QUARTERLY
NYRB	NEW YORK REVIEW OF BOOKS
NYT	NEW YORK TIMES
REL	REVIEW OF ENGLISH LITERATURE
RRI	REVISTA/REVIEW INTERAMERICANA
SBL	STUDIES IN BLACK LITERATURE
SGM	SUNDAY GLEANER MAGAZINE
SIN	STUDIES IN THE NOVEL

TGM   SUNDAY GUARDIAN MAGAZINE

TLS   TIMES LITERARY SUPPLEMENT

TSLL   TEXAS STUDIES IN LANGUAGE AND LITERATURE

WIR   WEST INDIAN REVIEW

WLWI   WORLD LITERATURE WRITTEN IN ENGLISH

Preface

Increased access to critical materials on West Indian literature dictated both the selection of items to be indexed as well as their arrangement. Although an effort was made to be as comprehensive as possible, particularly in the case of West Indian journals and newspapers, unfortunately, at least two major newspapers, the Barbados Advocate and the Guyana Graphic, were not available to the compiler.

While most of the items indexed are internationally known and should be available in major Latin American and Commonwealth collections in libraries in the United States, Great Britain, and Canada, some of the journals and newspapers from the West Indies may only be available in the West Indies itself. The user is directed to the West India Reference Collection (National Library) at the Institute of Jamaica, the University of the West Indies, or the publishing companies, for further information about specifically local publications such as Public Opinion, Flambeau, New Voices, Kairi, Corlit, and Link. Fortunately, a number of out-of-print journals such as the Beacon and Kyk-over-al, as well as back issues of Bim, have recently become available in reprint editions.

Collections of essays on West Indian literature were also indexed if the essays were written by several critics. Books dealing solely with one author have been included under the author's name. Books covering more general topics (e.g., Ramchand, The West Indian Novel and Its Background) are included in a bibliography in the Appendix, which also consolidates all the monographs appearing throughout the main work.

The limit of 1975 was set when this project was initiated; however, the increasing interest in West Indian literature has created a profusion of books and articles since that date. Some of these have been included in the index and in the appendix. It was felt that additional citations, in spite of the date limitation, could only enhance the work as a whole.

Part I of the index is an alphabetical listing by the author. The author's birthplace and dates are given (where known) next to his name. Citations concerning his work in general are listed immediately following in the section headed General. Citations dealing with specific titles are listed in publication order of the titles and are alphabetical under each title. Works by an author with no critical citations are listed with their publication dates (date of first publication) in the section headed Other Works.

Part II is an alphabetical listing by the name of the critic. Citations are listed chronologically under the critic's name. Where the work or author under consideration is not self-evident, this is given in parentheses.

Part III is a chronological and annotated listing of articles dealing generally with West Indian literature. Names of specific authors are included in the annotations and cross-referenced into the Author section of the index. Articles are listed by year and chronologically within each year. Only those years are listed for which articles were found.

This index includes reviews of novels, poetry, and collections of short stories. Reviews or articles on drama have been included only when the author is also a poet or a novelist, and only when the play is treated as a piece of literature rather than as a performance.

In order to be as comprehensive and as objective as possible, this index has been nonselective, making no critical distinction between a three-line and a three-page review, and making no judgments as to quality or merit. That task is left to the future users of this index.

The following work is a modified version of part of a thesis toward the degree of Master of Philosophy submitted to the University of the West Indies. I am indebted to my thesis advisor, Dr. Edward Baugh, of the Department of English at the Mona campus of the university for his patience, understanding, and good advice. I am also grateful to the Department of English as a whole for the grant which enabled me to complete my research.

This research would have been impossible without the excellent library collections in which I was fortunate enough to work. I am particularly grateful to the library staffs of the West India Reference Collection at the Institute of Jamaica, the University of the West Indies at Mona and Barbados, the Schomburg Institute of the New York Public Library, Columbia University, the College of the Virgin Islands, and to my colleagues at the Enid M. Baa Library and Archives in St. Thomas, U.S. Virgin Islands.

I would especially like to thank Mr. Calvin F. Bastian, whose constant encouragement strengthened my determination to complete

Preface

this book, and Dr. Anne Passmore-Rowe, who helped make the year spent in Jamaica a most pleasurable and productive one. Thanks also to my mother, Naomi Marie Braunsberg, for her typing assistance and moral support.

Finally, I wish to thank my son, Clayton Paul Allis, whose understanding and loyalty have been more than any mother (or researcher) has a right to expect.

J.B.A.
St. Thomas
1979

Prefacio

La disponibilidad de materias críticas sobre la literatura antillana determinó tanto la sellección de citas como su colocación. Hemos tratado de lograr un máximo de comprehsividad, especialmente con respecto a los periódicos y revistas antillanos. Sin embargo, el compilador desgraciadamente no pudo conseguir al menos dos periódicos importantes: el Advocate de Barbados y el Graphic de Guyana.

La mayoría de las publicaciones son conocidas internacionalmente y deben de estar disponibles en las colecciones principales latinoamericanas e inglesas de bibliotecas en los Estados Unidos, Inglaterra y el Canadá. Algunos periódicos y revistas, sin embargo, se encontrarán solamente en las Antillas mismas. En tal caso hay que consultar la West Indies Reference Collection (National Library) en el Institute of Jamaica, the University of the West Indies o los editoriales para conseguir más información sobre publicaciones regionales específicas, como Public Opinion, Flambeau, New Voices, Kairi, Corlit y Link. Felizmente, varias revistas ya agotadas, como The Beacon, y Kyk-over-al, y números viejos de Bim se han hecho disponibles recientemente en reimpresiones.

Incluídas son las colecciones de ensayos sobre literatura an antillana con tal que dichos ensayos fueran escritos por varios individuos. Los libros que tratan exclusivamente de un autor quedan inclusos bajo el nombre del autor. Los libros de temas más generales (v. gr., Ramchand, The West Indian Novel and Its Background) se encontraran en la bibliografía del apéndice, el cual también reune todas las monografías citadas en el texto.

Al comenzar este proyecto, decidimos limitar el contenido a materias publicadas hasta el año 1975. Pero el creciente interés en la literatura antillana ha resultado en una profusión de libros y artículos publicados después de esta fecha. Algunas se han incluído en el índice y en el apéndice. Es la opinión del compilador que, a pesar de la fecha determinada, las citas adicionales sólo pueden enriquecer el libro.

La Parte I del índice es una lista alfabética correspondiente a los autores. El lugar y la fecha de nacimiento, cuando sean conocidos, aparecen al lado del nombre del autor. Se encontrará citas sobre su obra en general en la sección siguiente, titulada "General". Las citas que tratan de obras específicas quedan registradas alfabéticamente, según la fecha de publicación (primera (primeras ediciones), en la sección "Other Works".

La Parte II es una lista alfabética correspondiente a los críticos. Las citas aparecen cronológicamente dabajo del nombre del crítico. En el caso de que la obra o autor tratado no sea evidente, la información se da entre parentesis.

La Parte III es una lista cronológica y anotada de artículos que tratan generalmente de la literatura antillana. Los nombres de autores específicos se incluyen en las anotaciones, con referencias a las citas correspondientes en la Parte I. Los articulos se registran cronológicamente. Se notan sólo los años en que aparece un artículo.

Este índice incluye reseñas de novelas, poemas y collecciones de cuentos. Las reseñas o artículos sobre obras dramáticas sólo se incluyen en el caso de que el autor sea también novelista o poeta y sólamente si la pieza es considerada críticamente como obra de literatura en vez de una producción específica.

Para lograr un máximo de comprensividad y objectividad, este índice no es selectivo; es decir, no hace distinciones críticas entre reseñas de tres líneas y de tres páginas. Tampoco hace juicios de calidad artística. Tel tarea queda en manos de los que se aprovechen de este índice.

Introduction

The literature of the West Indies--the geographical region
which includes those islands in the Caribbean Sea which were former
British possessions (now independent nations) and Guyana on the
South American mainland--is a comparatively recent regional
phenomenon. However, even before the first wave of West Indian
novelists migrated to Great Britain in the 1940s and rapidly
established literary reputations, literary activity was very much
in evidence.

Critical articles, book reviews, essays, and commentary on
literature and aesthetics in journals and newspapers from the West
Indies as well as other areas during the critical period of
1930-1975 make it possible to trace the growth and development of
a literary movement in the West Indies--a movement that continues
to grow and define itself. The critical voices from outside the
West Indies as well as those from within have both contributed to
this process. Without the insistently self-confident critical
voices from outside, West Indian critics might not have reacted so
quickly and so violently to the necessity of stating their own
aesthetic terms and defining their own cultural context.

Trinidadian critic Kenneth Ramchand defines West Indian
literature as works written by native West Indians, and considers
Becka's Buckra Baby, written in 1903 by Jamaican Tom Redcam (Tom
McDermott), the first West Indian novel. During the first half of
the twentieth century a number of West Indian novels appeared.
Authors H. G. de Lisser, Claude McKay, W. Adolphe Roberts, C. L. R.
James, and Alfred Mendes all attempted to express a West Indian
way of life. Poetry was being published by West Indian magazines
such as The Quarterly and The Forum and even by the British magazine
Life and Letters. Most of these efforts, however, were the
expressions of individuals rather than of a movement, and it was
not until the 1930s that West Indians began to make a concerted
effort to produce a literature that expressed a West Indian point
of view. The growing interest in nationalism encouraged by
journals such as the Beacon (Trinidad) and Public Opinion (Jamaica)
was inevitably translated into aesthetic terms. An editorial in
the Beacon in 1933 points the way toward a nationalization of the

artistic spirit:

> It is important, moreover, that we break away as far
> as possible from the English tradition; and the fact
> that some of us are still slaves to Scott and Dickens
> is merely because we lack the necessary artistic
> individuality and sensibility in order to see how
> incongruous that tradition is with the West Indian
> scene and spirit . . . a love for the fine word or
> sentence is nothing to be ashamed of but the fact
> remains that the sooner we throw off the veneer of
> culture that our colonization has brought us, the
> better for our artistic aims.[1]

The literary journals Bim in Barbados in 1942, and Kyk-over-al
in Guyana in 1945 provided a much-needed publishing outlet for
young writers in the West Indies. In London, the BBC radio program "Caribbean Voices" offered financial support to those West
Indian writers who migrated toward the publishing houses of Great
Britain.

The self-exile of many West Indian writers to Great Britain
and North America in the late 1940s and 1950s created an unusual
situation in which the artistic spokesmen for an area were operating
not only at a great distance from that area, but for an audience of
whom very few were their own countrymen. There were--and continue
to be--many reasons for this exile. First, the overriding prac-
tical one of the lack of publishing houses; second, the lack of a
reading public in the West Indies; third, the lack of an opportunity
to practice one's craft and make a living at the same time. London,
New York, or Toronto offered opportunities for book reviewing,
journalism, or publication of stories and poems in magazines. The
radio program "Caribbean Voices" has already been mentioned. This
was a weekly program beamed to the West Indies, on which West
Indian writers in London would give readings and engage in literary
discussion. In 1953 its director, an Englishman, Henry Swanzy,
described it thus: "the main value of a programme like Caribbean
Voices is to provide an outlet for writers who would otherwise be
mute, a means of inter-communication with like minds, and, if
anything so sordid can be mentioned, money."[2]

Great Britain as the "mother country," as the traditional pur-
veyor of education, as the ultimate cultural standard for its
colonies, exerted a strong psychological attraction for the West
Indian writer who needed the metropolitan stamp of approval.
Indeed, West Indian readers often geared their own reactions to a
new West Indian novel by the response from the London reviews.

For the most part, these writers of the 1950s and early 1960s
were novelists and included Edgar Mittelholzer, George Lamming,

Introduction

Samuel Selvon, V. S. Naipaul, Michael Anthony, Wilson Harris, Jan
Carew, Andrew Salkey, and others. All of these writers, with the
exception of Mittelholzer, are still living. All are still writing
and are very much an active part of the West Indian literary scene.
All except Anthony are still living outside their homelands.

In the 1970s the publishing situation in the West Indies is
still woefully inadequate (most of the publishing houses are
branches of British companies) and though the audience is growing
and literary opportunities exist, it is still difficult for a
writer to make a living in the West Indies. A number of writers,
by combining writing with other activities, such as teaching, do,
however, and more complex reasons have been suggested to explain the
self-imposed exile of many writers and artists. Novelists George
Lamming and Jan Carew postulate an inward psychological exile that
the West Indian, and, in particular, the West Indian artist, is prey
to by the very conditions of his birth. Lamming explains:

> First isolated by a lack of common idiom, this
> humanity made a bid for possession of the language,
> exposed utterly and naked to the process of being
> possessed by all the conceptual and poetic
> possibilities of the language that would become
> their new possession. Supervising this complexity
> of learning to be a new man in a new place, was an
> authority whose home was elsewhere, be it England
> or France. Hence the additional isolation increased
> further by the arrangement whereby islands under
> the same European powers were breeding political
> institutions which represented different stages of
> development.... And feeding on this spiritual swamp
> was the inevitable virus of class, breeding another
> fiction of distance within the same islands.
>   This political isolation of territories, matched
> by an inward exile in each, found a common and con-
> tradictory frame of reference. Deprived of the
> reservoir of history each had in common with the other,
> all in their different ways entered into a psychology
> of expectations whose melancholy rewards had to be
> sought outside.[3]

Jan Carew, from Guyana, carries this concept of inner exile
existing at many levels further, to apply directly to the West
Indian artist:

> The West Indian was subjected to successive waves
> of alienation from his parent culture, and it did not
> matter whether this culture was European, African,
> Asian or Amerindian; and this perhaps laid the basis
> for a permanent state of exile. It was as though he

(West Indian man) by first achieving a state of
absolute anonymity, could come closer to the human
self that he was.[4]

Carew maintains that the West Indian had to learn to function
in conventional structures without the benefit of the conventions
of history. He concludes that, "in order to understand the nature
of the dilemma confronting the West Indian artist in exile, one
must first understand the state of exile that has existed for cen-
turies in West Indian society itself."[5]

This psychic need for context, for tradition, for stability, for
identity, drove the West Indian writers into exile. Only by
counterbalancing themselves against the ordered systems of Western
culture could they begin to find their own. Only by seeing what
they were not could they begin to know what they were. The oft-
quoted incident near the end of Lamming's In the Castle of My Skin
where Trumper returns from the United States with his newfound
identity of Blackness and tries to explain this to the hero, "G,"
illustrates the situation of the West Indian leaving to discover
himself within a wider context. The implication that "G" can only
understand this by leaving also, further illustrates the dilemma
that West Indians must face. In the Castle of My Skin was written
by the migrant Lamming in 1953. Today, however, West Indians are
attempting to solve Lamming's dilemma by constructing a West Indian
cultural framework at home.

To this end, a number of West Indian writers have chosen to
make the West Indies their base. Derek Walcott and Edward
Brathwaite, for example, have both sojourned abroad but primarily
identify themselves with St. Lucia/Trinidad and Barbados/Jamaica,
respectively. Interestingly enough, it is primarily the poets who
have chosen to remain in their homeland, while the novelists often
work abroad.

Although West Indian literature as an identifiable regional
body is barely thirty years old, it can already boast several
generations of writers. Those writers who went into exile in the
1950s and early 1960s comprise an older generation in terms of
their philosophical approach. Many writers, such as Mervyn Morris
and Edward Brathwaite, left, only to return. Finally, there are
those writers who have chosen not to leave at all: Earl Lovelace,
Malik, Robert Lee, Bruce St. John, and increasingly many others.

The coming of independence for many Caribbean nations has
drawn diverse elements together and discarded those no longer
applicable. The 1970s have seen the growth of a cohesive regional
literature which is being assessed by West Indian critics in a West
Indian context.

xxx

Introduction

With the writers choosing to define themselves within their homeland, the critics have likewise followed suit. West Indian critics such as Gordon Rohlehr, Michael Gilkes, Victor Questel, Edward Baugh, Edward Brathwaite, Mervyn Morris, and Kenneth Ramchand have settled down to the task of constructing an aesthetic matrix from this diverse and abundant material.

Critical development, going hand in hand with literary growth, has been characterized by gradual rejection of external influences in favor of a regional criticism for a regional literature, and by the recognition of the importance of cultural context. Writing by West Indian critics has been generally informed by a close bond among the critic, the writer, and the writer's frame of reference; while writing by non-West Indian critics has often been characterized by a psychic as well as physical distance separating him from the writer's world. The internal critic has been interpreting a culture through an art form, while the external critic tends to analyze an art form from a predetermined cultural bias. While the internal critic has been identifying relevant aesthetic standards for literary interpretation, the external critic imposes his own aesthetic model on what he finds.

While some subjectivity in literary criticism is unavoidable, surely the depth and the degree can be monitored and controlled. It is the critic's responsibility to recognize his own prejudices and to take them into account so that he can counterbalance them, compensate for them, or admit them openly to his readers. In the case of West Indian literature, it would seem that non-West Indian critics have, for the most part, been unaware of, or uninterested in, the subtle cultural biases interfering between themselves and the literature. On the other hand, the West Indian critic has also to some extent been burdened down by a personal involvement in an ongoing cultural process which has greatly influenced his critical appraisals.

For the external critic, the historical relationship that his country has had with the West Indies has tended to affect his point of view toward the literature. For example, a British critic, working from the background of a colonial relationship, evaluates V. S. Naipaul in quite different terms than does an Indian critic for whom Naipaul is a woefully erring cousin. Similarly, a black American critic might very well base his assessment of Naipaul on the grounds of racial sympathies.

In addition, the external critic has been generally guided by European literary traditions and its aesthetic standards. In general, West Indian literature has not been seen as the expression of a distinct culture, but rather as the extension of Western literature. However, one cannot fairly assess the literature of one culture from the viewpoint of another.

It is often more to the point, then, for the West Indian critic
to evaluate the writing of his own area. As has been pointed out
by the Canadian critic Desmond Pacey in discussing Canadian
criticism,

> subtle nuances in literature are possible only when
> the reader and the writer participate in the same
> process of living ... [for example] the homogenized
> culture of mid-twentieth century America makes it
> possible for writers like John Updike or John O'Hara to
> work in terms of lights and shadow of implications,
> where a great deal can be suggested by the mere mention
> of a detail of dress or manner and even linguistic
> peculiarities.[6]

Unfortunately, the issue has been further complicated by the
fact that West Indian critics themselves must to some extent un-
learn and reject the European idiom in favor of a West Indian
aesthetic which they must recognize and construct.

"Our work has been to integrate, not to separate,"[7] Gordon
Rohlehr said in a 1975 issue of Bim, speaking of the many oral and
written artistic expressions in the West Indies which the critic
must fuse into an aesthetic whole. However, as Jamaican critic
Sylvia Wynter has pointed out, British literary critics and West
Indian critics with British propensities were, for many years, the
arbiters of literary taste in the West Indies. The West Indian
critics "mediated"[8] themselves until, according to Wynter, they had
compromised their own cultural instincts almost to nonexistence.

For example, a full appreciation of Jamaican novelist Roger
Mais cannot necessarily be gained by comparing him only to British
authors, nor will an analysis of his style in terms of the
Victorian novel do much beyond revealing considerable overwriting.
By shifting the cultural context, however, and seeing his best-
known work, The Hills Were Joyful Together, in terms of the
Kingston "yard" as Jean D'Costa does in her essay on Mais in The
Islands in Between[9] or, by analyzing Mais's work Brother Man within
the context of the "jazz" novel, as Edward Brathwaite has done in
his essay, "Jazz and the West Indian novel," it becomes possible to
see Mais from an entirely new perspective:

> The "jazz novel," in the normal course of things will
> hardly be an "epic." Dealing with a specific clearly-
> defined, folk-type community, it will try to express
> the essence of this community through its form. It
> will absorb its rhythms from the people of this
> community; and its concern will be for the community
> as a whole, its characters taking their place in that
> community, of which they are felt and seen to be an
> integral part.... We are not here trying to say what

> anybody should or should not write. We are
> striving towards a way of <u>seeing</u> what they write
> and relating it to our indigenous experience.[10]

Establishing the concept of a "jazz" novel enables Brathwaite
to approach <u>Brother Man</u> from a fresh angle. Form, structure, syn-
tax, and language are all given new meaning as they are defined in
this context. Finding that traditional Western standards could
not do sufficient justice in evaluating Mais because Mais himself
was reaching for a new form, Brathwaite experimented with super-
imposing a different aesthetic model from the more closely
connected culture of black America, and applying a musical idiom
to literature. The result allows him to reveal aspects of Mais
that might otherwise be dismissed. Mais's strengths and weaknesses
can perhaps be more fairly assessed in terms of this new aesthetic,
which seems to be closer to the spirit of his work.

Here, the non-West Indian could be hampered by his inability or
unwillingness to make a cultural leap and sympathize with the framework that the artist is working in. On the other hand, the West
Indian critic has often been hampered by his involvement in the
literary production, by his tendency to make the art form carry too
much of a cultural load, or by his unwillingness to disengage. In
his concern with "elucidating the relevance of West Indian litera--
ture to West Indian life,"[11] he assumes an intellectual and
societal responsibility that can also become a burden.

The search for a viable context lies at the heart of the West
Indian writer's problem, a problem that has been recognized by
artist and critic alike.

> In all societies, the artist is an embodiment of his
> culture and society. He functions within the frame-
> work of his heritage, and through his labors, he adds,
> enriches and further defines that background. The
> picture is an entirely different one for the West
> Indian.... No one living in the West Indies is
> indigenous to the area.... Our cities, parks, public
> buildings, places of worship have nothing whatever to
> do with the Caribs and the Arawaks; they are bits and
> scraps of Spain, England, Scotland, Wales and Ireland
> all held together by the English language. The West
> Indian artist, therefore, came to define himself, not
> in terms of his original ancestry, not in terms of the
> people indigenous to his geography, but in terms of
> something else and the way in which he sees himself in
> relation to that something else.[12]

In the quest for a valid context, for an identity, it is evident that the colonial history of the West Indies, a history of

slavery and exploitation, has not lent itself to positive cultural
development and has, in fact, been the major contributor to
cultural ambiguity. In the relationship of master and slave, the
Western culture of the master engulfed to a large extent the
African one of the slave. The lack of a written tradition and a
common language, as well as the condition of slavery itself, all
worked toward fragmentation of African heritage, and "they [the
African slaves] could offer no lasting opposition to the dominant
Western heritage as represented in the learning of Europe."[13]

Faced with a number of cultural options, some more apparent
than others, it has been the task of the West Indian intellectual
to accept or reject them in terms of the unique context of the West
Indies. It is suggested that the critic, as well as the artist
educated under a British system and inculcated with Western values
from childhood (for documentation of this one need look no further
than George Lamming's In the Castle of My Skin,) must pass through
the fire--the fire of self-realization and self-identification--to
emerge with the West Indies in the center of his vision. In his
partially autobiographical essay "Timheri" Edward Brathwaite sums
up the situation thus:

> The problem of and for West Indian artists and intellec-
> tuals is that having been born and educated within this
> fragmented culture, they start out in the world without
> a sense of "wholeness." ... Disillusion with the frag-
> mentation leads to a sense of rootlessness. The ideal
> does not and cannot correspond to perceived and inherited
> reality. The result: dissociation of the sensibility.
> The main unconscious concern of many of the most
> articulate West Indian intellectuals and artists in the
> early post-colonial period was a description and analysis
> of this dissociation.... The second phase of West
> Indian and Caribbean artistic life, on which we are now
> entering, having become conscious of the problem, is
> seeking to transcend and heal it.[14]

Commitment to this process has already brought the West Indian
critic to a discovery of new forms, new ways of seeing and
evaluating, and has opened up a myriad of possibilities within a
framework constructed partially by the critic himself. Brathwaite
and the jazz novel have already been mentioned. Trinidadian critic
Gordon Rohlehr, in his exploration of Caribbean rhythms, has noted
that "it seems to me that there is in the spoken language of
Trinidad a potential of rhythmic organization which our poets have
not yet discovered."[15] He has since found these rhythms in the
poetry being written in the Caribbean today. Guyanese novelist
Wilson Harris has tried to shape his novels to fit the consciousness
of Caribbean man. Critic Michael Gilkes finds that Harris's novels

illustrate what must be considered as perhaps the
most remarkable and original aspect of West Indian
writing; one in which the condition of cultural and
racial admixture itself becomes the "complex womb"
of a new wholeness of vision. A creative attempt is
made to heal the divided psyche of Caribbean Man by
looking inwards.[16]

Stephen Henderson, a black American critic, defines the problems
of identifying and creating an aesthetic for black American
literature in a statement that could as well apply to the West
Indies:

Art, of course, including literature, does not exist
in a vacuum, and reflects--and helps to shape--the
lives of those who produce it. It is able to do these
things, moreover, because of the special heightening
and refining of experience that is characteristic of
art. Literature, accordingly, is the verbal organization of experience into beautiful forms, but what
is meant by "beautiful" and by "forms" is to a
significant degree dependent upon a people's way of life,
their needs, their aspirations, their history--in
short, their culture. Ultimately the "beautiful"
is bound up with the truth of a people's history, as
they perceive it themselves, and if their vision is
clear, its recording just, others may perceive that
justness too ... they may even share in the general
energy, if not in the specific context of that vision.[17]

NOTES

1. Beacon, 2, no. 12 (June 1933), 3.

2. H. L. V. Swanzy, "Caribbean Voices, Prolegomena to a West Indian Culture." Caribbean Quarterly, 1, no. 2 (1949), 28.

3. George Lamming, "The West Indian People," New World Quarterly, 2, no. 2 (Croptime 1966), 67.

4. Jan Carew, "An Artist in Exile--From the West Indies." New World Fortnightly, 1, nos. 27 and 28 (November 12, 1965), 25.

5. Carew, p. 25.

6. Desmond Pacey, Essays in Candian Criticism, 1938-1968 (Toronto: Ryerson Press, 1969), p. 25.

7. Gordon Rohlehr, "A Carrion Time," Bim, 15, no. 58 (June 1975), 105.

8. In her two-part article in Jamaica Journal, "We Must Learn to Sit Down Together and Talk about a Little Culture; Reflections on West Indian Writing and Criticism," 2, no. 4 (December 1968), 23-32; 3, no. 1 (March 1969), 27-42.

9. Jean Creary D'Costa, "A Prophet Armed, the Novels of Roger Mais," in The Islands in Between, ed. Louis James (London: Oxford University Press, 1968), pp. 50-63.

10. Edward Brathwaite, "Jazz and the West Indian Novel, pt. 3," Bim, 12, no. 46 (January-June 1968), 124.

11. Edward Baugh, "Towards a West Indian Criticism," Caribbean Quarterly, 14, nos. 1 and 2 (March-June 1968), 141.

12. Ismith Khan, "Dialect in West Indian Literature," in The Black Writer in Africa and the Americas, ed. Lloyd W. Brown (Los Angeles: Hennessey and Ingalls, 1973), p. 153.

13. Peter Blackman, "Is There a West Indian Literature," Life and Letters, 59, no. 135 (1948), 98.

14. Edward Brathwaite, "Timehri," in Is Massa Day Dead?, ed. Orde Coombs (New York: Anchor Books, 1974), p. 30.

15. Gordon Rohlehr, "Sparrow and the Language of the Calypso," Savacou, no. 2 (September 1970), p. 99.

16. Michael Gilkes, Racial Identity and Individual Consciousness in the Caribbean Novel (Georgetown, Guyana: National History and Arts Council, 1975), p. 44.

17. Stephen Henderson, Understanding the New Black Poetry (New York: William Morrow, 1973), p. 4.

Part I
Index of Authors

ABRAHAMS, PETER. South Africa/Jamaica, 1919-

General

   Griffiths, Gareth. "The Language of Disillusion in the
      African Novel." COMMON WEALTH: PAPERS DELIVERED AT THE
      CONFERENCE OF COMMONWEALTH LITERATURE, AARHUS UNIVERSITY,
      APRIL 26-30, 1971. Aarhus, Denmark: Aarhus University,
      1971, pp. 62-65.

   Ogungbesan, Kolawole. "The Political Novels of Peter
      Abrahams." PRESENCE AFRICAINE, no. 83, 1972, pp. 33-50.
      Also appears in PHYLON, v. 34, December 1973, pp. 419-
      432.

   Panton, George. "Peter Abrahams. Our Distinguished
      Immigrant." SUNDAY GLEANER, March 23, 1975, p. 23.

   Wade, Michael. "The Novels of Peter Abrahams." CRITIQUE,
      v. 11, no. 1, 1968, pp. 82-95.

   Wade, Michael. PETER ABRAHAMS. London: Evans, 1972

THE PATH OF THUNDER (1948)

   Jefferson, Miles M. Review. PHYLON, v. 9, 1948, pp. 188-
      189.

   Laski, Marghanita. Review. LSO, March 9, 1952, p. 7.

WILD CONQUEST (1950)

   Anon. Review. TLS, no. 3102, August 11, 1961, p. 522.

   Carew, Jan. "African Literature--From the Breath of Gods."
      NYT, April 2, 1972, Section 7, p. 7.

   Hale, Lionel. Review. LSO, June 24, 1951, p. 7.

Abrahams, Peter

> Jackson, Blyden. Review. PHYLON, v. 11, 1950, pp. 290-291.
>
> Panton, George. Review. SUNDAY GLEANER, November 6, 1966, p. 4.

RETURN TO GOLI (1953)

> Sachs, Solly. "A Tragic Homecoming." LSO, June 21, 1953, p. 10.

TELL FREEDOM (1954)

> Anon. "Growing Up in Johannesburg." THE TIMES (London), June 9, 1954, p. 8.
>
> Hopkinson, Tom. "Dark Beginnings." LSO, June 20, 1954, p. 9.
>
> Jackson, Blyden. Review. PHYLON, v. 15, 1954, pp. 410-411.
>
> Prescott, Orville. Review. NYT, August 9, 1954, p. 15.
>
> Stern, James. "Days of Agony, Minutes of Fun." NYT, August 8, 1954, Section 7, p. 1.

MINE BOY (1955)

> Anon. Review. BAJAN, v. 2, no. 9, May 1955, p. 28.
>
> Anon. Review. PUBLIC OPINION, June 14, 1940, pp. 7, 13.
>
> Reinhardt, John E. Review. PHYLON, v. 16, 1955, pp. 476-477.
>
> Rodman, Selden. "A Search for a Place in the Sun." NYT, June 12, 1955, Section 7, p.5.

A WREATH FOR UDOMO (1956)

> Anon. Review. SPECTATOR, v. 196, May 11, 1956, p. 665.
>
> Anon. Review. TLS, no. 2829, May 18, 1956, p. 295.
>
> Clark, Edward. Review. PHYLON, v. 18, 1957, pp. 97-98.
>
> Lash, John S. Review. PHYLON, v. 17, 1956, pp. 296-297.
>
> Lewis, Primula. "Politics and the Novel; an Appreciation of

Abrahams, Peter

A WREATH FOR UDOMO and THIS ISLAND NOW by Peter
Abrahams." ZUKA, no. 2, May 1968, pp. 41-47.

el Mukrane, Hadj. Review (French). PRESENCE AFRICAINE,
no. 17-18, 1958, pp. 238-239.

Prescott, Orville. Review. NYT, May 25, 1956, p. 21.

Pritchett, V. S. Review. NEW STATESMAN, v. 56, October 4,
1958, pp. 468-469.

Richardson, E. C. "Abraham's New Novel Is a Must."
SUNDAY GUARDIAN (Trinidad), December 7, 1958, p. 22.

Richardson, Maurice. Review. NEW STATESMAN, v. 51, May 12,
1956, pp. 543-544.

Sampson, Anthony. "An African Story." LSO, May 6, 1956,
p. 17.

Stern, James. "If Exiles Return." NYT, May 20, 1956,
Section 7, p. 5.

Wickham, John. Review. BIM, v. 7, no. 25, July-December
1957, pp. 59-61.

A NIGHT OF THEIR OWN (1965)

Anon. Review. THE TIMES (London), March 25, 1965, p. 15.

Hemmings, F. W. J. Review. NEW STATESMAN, v. 69, March 26,
1965.

Jacobson, Dan. Review. LSO, March 28, 1965, p. 26.

Panton, George. "Vivid Story of South Africa's Troubles."
SUNDAY GLEANER, April 4, 1964, p. 4.

Zuckerman, Ruth V. H. Review. BOOKS ABROAD, v. 40, no. 1,
Winter 1966, p. 116.

THIS ISLAND NOW (1967)

Anon. "Growing Pains." TLS, no. 3,373, October 20, 1966,
p. 964.

Anon. "Past Imperfect, Present Continuous, Future Perfect?"
CARIBBEAN CONTACT, v. 2, no. 1, 1974, p. 2.

Alexander, Lorrimer

>   Anon. Review. BAJAN, no. 163, March 1967, p. 28.
>
>   Anon. Review. THE TIMES (London), September 29, 1966, p. 16.
>
>   Baugh, Edward. Review. BIM, v. 11, no. 44, January-June 1967, pp. 298-299.
>
>   Lewis, Primula. "Politics and the Novel; an Appreciation of A WREATH FOR UDOMO and THIS ISLAND NOW by Peter Abrahams." ZUKA, no. 2, May 1968, pp. 41-47.
>
>   Morris, Mervyn. Review. PUBLIC OPINION, November 4, 1966, p. 3.
>
>   Ogungbesan, Kolawole. "The Politics of THIS ISLAND NOW." JCL, v. 8, no. 1, 1973, pp. 33-41.
>
>   Panton, George. "Our Country--Past and Future." SUNDAY GLEANER, October 23, 1966, p. 4.
>
>   Wynter, Sylvia. "The Instant Novel Now." NWQ, v. 3, no. 3, High Season 1967, pp. 78-81
>
>   Zuckerman, Ruth V. H. Review. BOOKS ABROAD, v. 41, no. 4, Autumn 1967, pp. 487-488.

ALEXANDER, LORRIMER. Guyana

General

>   Brathwaite, Edward. "Jazz and the West Indian Novel, Part II." BIM, v. 12, no. 45, July-December 1967, pp. 39-51.

ALLFREY, PHYLLIS SHAND. Dominica, 1900-

General

>   Carr, Bill. "The West Indian Novelist: Prelude and Context." CARIBBEAN QUARTERLY, v. 11, nos. 1 and 2, March and June 1965, pp. 71-84.
>
>   Davies, Barrie. "Neglected West Indian Writers, no. 1, Phyllis Allfrey, THE ORCHID HOUSE." WLWE, v. 11, no. 2, November 1972, pp. 81-83.
>
>   Ramchand, Kenneth. "Terrified Consciousness." JCL, no. 7, July 1969, pp. 8-19.

Anthony, Michael

THE ORCHID HOUSE   (1953)

> Anon. "Local Colour."   THE TIMES (London), July 11, 1953,
>   p. 8.

> Anon. Review. BAJAN, v. 1, no. 12, August 1954, p. 21.

> Anon. "Some WI Novels Face Neglect in West Indies."
>   SUNDAY GUARDIAN (Trinidad), February 5, 1961, p. 4.

> Laski, Marghanita. Review. LSO, July 19, 1953, p. 8.

Other Works

IN CIRCLES, POEMS   (1940)

PALM AND OAK   (1973)

ANTHONY, MICHAEL, Trinidad, 1932–

General

> Anthony, Michael. "Growing Up with Writing: A Particular
>   Experience." JCL, no. 7, July 1969, pp. 80–87.
>   Also appears in SAVACOU, no. 2, September 1970, pp. 61–66.

> Anthony, Michael. "The Return of a West Indian Writer"
>   (interview). BIM, v. 14, no. 56, January–June 1973,
>   pp. 212–218.

> Brathwaite, Edward. "West Indian Prose Fiction in the
>   Sixties: A Survey." CRITICAL SURVEY, v. 3, Winter 1967,
>   pp. 169–174. Also appears in BIM, v. 12, no. 47, July–
>   December 1968, pp. 157–167, and with additional material
>   in BLACK WORLD, v. 20, no. 11, September 1971, pp. 14–29.

> Brown, Wayne. "I Feel a Lot of Gratitude to Naipaul"
>   (interview). SUNDAY GUARDIAN (Trinidad), July 25, 1970,
>   p. 17.

> Brown, Wayne. "On Art, Artists and the People." SUNDAY
>   GUARDIAN (Trinidad), August 9, 1970, p. 10.

> Brown, Wayne. "The Possibilities for West Indian Writing."
>   SUNDAY GUARDIAN (Trinidad), November 22, 1970, p. 21.

> Clarke, Austin. "Some Speculations as to the Absence of
>   Racial Vindictiveness in West Indian Literature." THE

Anthony, Michael

>   BLACK WRITER IN AFRICA AND THE AMERICAS (edited by Lloyd
>   W. Brown). Los Angeles: Hennessey and Ingalls, 1973,
>   pp. 165-194.

>   Drayton, Arthur D. "The European Factor in West Indian
>   Literature." LITERARY HALF-YEARLY, v. 11, no. 1, 1970,
>   pp. 71-94.

>   Gonzalez, Anson. "The Man from the South, Michael Anthony."
>   TRINIDAD AND TOBAGO LITERATURE ON AIR, Trinidad:
>   National Cultural Council, 1973, pp. 83-91.

>   James, C. L. R. "Discovering Literature in Trinidad: the
>   Nineteen-Thirties." JCL, no. 7, July 1969, pp. 73-80.
>   Also appears in SAVACOU, no. 2, September 1970, pp. 54-60.

>   James, Louis. "The Sad Initiation of Lamming's 'G.' ..."
>   COMMON WEALTH: PAPERS DELIVERED AT THE CONFERENCE OF
>   COMMONWEALTH LITERATURE, AARHUS UNIVERSITY, APRIL 26-30,
>   1971. Aarhus, Denmark: Aarhus University, 1971.

>   Lacovia, R. M. "Caribbean Literature, a Brave New World."
>   BLACK IMAGES, v. 1, no. 1, Spring 1972, pp. 15-22.

>   Lacovia, R. M. "Caribbean Literature in English." BAR,
>   v. 2, nos. 1 and 2, 1971, pp. 109-125.

>   Ramchand, Kenneth. "History and the Novel: A Literary
>   Critic's Approach." SAVACOU, v. 1, no. 5, June 1971,
>   pp. 103-113.

>   Sander, Reinhard. "The Homesickness of Michael Anthony;
>   The Predicament of a West Indian Exile." LITERARY HALF-
>   YEARLY, v. 16, no. 1, January 1975, pp. 95-124.

THE GAMES WERE COMING (1963)

>   Anon. Review. THE TIMES (London), November 21, 1963, p. 18.

>   Anon. Review. TLS, no. 3223, December 5, 1963, p. 1017.

>   Drayton, Arthur D. Review. BLACK ORPHEUS, no. 15, 1964,
>   p. 61.

>   Levin, Martin. Review. NYT, April 14, 1968, Section 7,
>   p. 31.

>   Marshall, Harold. Review. BIM, v. 10, no. 38, January-June

Anthony, Michael

1964, p. 145.

McGinness, Frank, "West Indian Windfall." LONDON MAGAZINE,
v. 7, no. 1, April 1967, pp. 117-120.

Moynahan, Julian. Review. LSO, November 17, 1963, p. 24.

Panton, George. "New Caribbean Voices." SUNDAY GLEANER,
December 15, 1963, p. 14.

Wynter, Sylvia. Review. CARIBBEAN STUDIES, v. 9, no. 4,
January 1970, pp. 111-118.

THE YEAR IN SAN FERNANDO   (1965)

Anon. Review, BAJAN, v. 12, no. 11, July 1965, p. 29.

Anon. Review. LSO, February 21, 1965, p. 27.

Arthur, Kevyn. Review. BIM, v. 11, no. 41, June-December
1965, pp. 70-71.

Edwards, Paul, and Kenneth Ramchand. "The Art of Memory:
Michael Anthony's THE YEAR IN SAN FERNANDO." JCL, no. 7,
July 1969, pp. 59-72.

King, Eric. Review. CARIBBEAN QUARTERLY, v. 16, no. 4,
December 1970, 87-91.

Luengo, Anthony. "Growing Up in San Fernando: Change and
Growth in Michael Anthony's THE YEAR IN SAN FERNANDO."
ARIEL, v. 6, no. 2, April 1975, pp. 81-95.

Macmillan, M. "Language and Change." JCL, no. 1, September
1965, p. 175.

Panton, George. "W.I. Novels--And a Lecture on Them,"
SUNDAY GLEANER, August 8, 1965, p. 4.

Walcott, Derek. "Just the Way It Was." SUNDAY GUARDIAN
(Trinidad), March 14, 1965, p. 8.

GREEN DAYS BY THE RIVER   (1967)

Anon. Review. BAJAN, no. 166, June 1967, p. 28. Also
appears in BIM, v. 12, no. 45, July-December 1967, p. 68.

Anon. Review. THE TIMES (london), February 2, 1967, p. 16.

Arthur, William Seymour

> McGuinness, Frank. "West Indian Windfall," LONDON MAGAZINE,
> v. 7, no. 1, April 1967, pp. 117-120.

> Panton, George. Review. SUNDAY GLEANER, March 26, 1967,
> p. 4.

> Subrami. Review. WLWE, no. 19, April 1971, p. 84.

> Vansittart, Peter. Review. SPECTATOR, v. 218, February 3,
> 1967, p. 141.

> Wynter, Sylvia. Review. CARIBBEAN STUDIES, v. 9, no. 4,
> January 1970, pp. 111-118.

SANDRA STREET AND OTHER STORIES (1973)

> Phelps, Karen. "Back to Childhood." SUNDAY GUARDIAN
> (Trinidad), April 8, 1973, p. 7.

> Questel, Victor. "Look and Listen." TAPIA, v. 3, no. 32,
> 1973, p. 11.

CRICKET IN THE ROAD (1973)

> C. L. [Cedric Lindo]. Review. SUNDAY GLEANER, February
> 24, 1974, p. 23.

Other Works

STREETS OF CONFLICT (1975)

ARTHUR, WILLIAM SEYMOUR. Barbados,

NO IDLE WINDS

> Lamming, George. Review. BIM, v. 6, no. 22, June 1955,
> pp. 132-133.

Other Works

WHISPERS OF THE DAWN

MORNING GLORY

AUSTIN, LEO I. Barbados,

POEMS (1955)

Baugh, Edward C.

Harris, Wilson. Review. KYK-OVER-AL, v. 6, no. 20, Mid-
      year 1955, pp. 205-206.

Lamming, George. Review. BIM, v. 6, no. 22, June 1955,
      pp. 132-133.

BARRETT, (LINDSAY) ESEOGHENE. Jamaica, 1941-.

   General

      Brathwaite, Edward. "West Indian Prose Fiction in the
         Sixties." BLACK WORLD, v. 20, no. 11, September 1971,
         pp. 14-29.

      Maxwell, Marina. "Towards a Revoluation in the Arts,"
         SAVACOU, no. 2, September 1970, pp. 19-32.

   SONG FOR MUMU   (1967)

      Baugh, Edward. Review. CARIBBEAN QUARTERLY, v. 13, no. 4,
         December 1967, pp. 53-54.

      Panton, George. Review. SUNDAY GLEANER, August 18, 1968,
         p. 4.

      Wall, Stephen. Review. LSO, December 10, 1967, p. 28.

   Other Works

   THE STATE OF BLACK DESIRE   (1966)

BASTIEN, ELIOT. Trinidad,

   General

      Anon. "The Pamphleteers. Natural Reformers in Our Society."
         SUNDAY GUARDIAN (Trinidad), April 25, 1965, pp. 4-5.

      Walcott, Derek. "Young Trinidadian Poets." SUNDAY
         GUARDIAN (Trinidad), June 19, 1966, p. 5.

   ANANCY STORY   (1972)

      Asein, S. O. "Bastien's ANANCY STORY: A Critique." BLACK
         IMAGES, v. 1, no. 2, Summer 1972, pp. 25-27.

BAUGH, EDWARD C. Jamaica, 1936-

Bell, Vera

SEVEN JAMAICAN POETS   (1971, edited by Mervyn Morris)

Forde, A. N.   Review.   BIM, v. 14, no. 54, January-June 1972, pp. 117.

C. L.   [Cedric Lindo].   "Worthy Examples of Our Poetry." SUNDAY GLEANER, May 23, 1971, p. 29.

Morrison, Hugh P.   Review.   CARIBBEAN QUARTERLY, v. 18, no. 4, December 1972, pp. 82-83.

BELL, VERA.   Jamaica,

General

Anon.   "Review of FOCUS . . . The Short Stories."   PUBLIC OPINION, December 18, 1948, pp. 10-11.

Brathwaite, Edward.   "The African Presence in Caribbean Literature."   DAEDALUS, v. 103, no. 2, Spring 1974, 73-109.

Brown, Wayne.   "Poetry of the Forties, Part 6: 'Ancestor on the Auction Black.'"   SUNDAY GUARDIAN (Trinidad), October 18, 1970, p. 6.

Dathorne, O. R.   "Africa in the Literature of the West Indies."   JCL, no. 1, September 1965, pp. 95-116.

Dathorne, O. R.   "The Theme of Africa in West Indian Literature."   BLACK ORPHEUS, no. 16, 1964, pp. 42-53.   Also appears in PHYLON, v. 26, no. 3, Fall 1965, pp. 253-276.

Oakley, Leo.   "Ideas of Patriotism and National Dignity in Some Jamaican Writings."   JAMAICA JOURNAL, v. 4, no. 3, September 1970, pp. 16-31.   Also appears in SUNDAY GLEANER, part 1, March 28, 1971, pp. 31, 34; part 2, April 4, 1971, p. 27; part 3, April 11, 1971, p. 25.

OGOG   (1971)

Panton, George.   Review.   SUNDAY GLEANER, July 18, 1971, p. 28.

BENNETT, ALVIN.   Jamaica, 1918-

GOD THE STONE BREAKER   (1964)

Bennett, Louise

Anon.   Review.   THE TIMES (London), July 16, 1964, p. 15.

Anon.   "Unlovable Jamaicans."   TLS, no. 3256, July 23, 1964,
p. 645.

Panton, George.   "Drop Pan--And All That."   SUNDAY GLEANER,
August 2, 1964, p. 4.

Other Works

BECAUSE THEY KNOW NOT (n.d.)

BENNETT, LOUISE.   Jamaica, 1919-

General

Baker, Peta-Anne.   "Louise Bennett-Coverley: A Poet of
Utterance."   CARIBBEAN CONTACT, v. 1, no. 8, August 1973,
p. 6.

Brathwaite, Edward.   "The African Presence in Caribbean
Literature."   DAEDALUS, v. 103, no. 2, Spring 1974, pp.
73-109.

Brathwaite, Edward.   "Jazz and the West Indian Novel."   BIM,
part 1, v. 11, no. 44, January-June 1967, pp. 275-284;
part 2, v. 12, no. 45, July-December 1967, pp. 39-51;
part 3, v. 12, no. 46, January-June 1968, pp. 115-126.

Dathorne, O. R.   "Africa in the Literature of the West
Indies."   JCL, no. 1, September 1965, pp. 95-116.

Dathorne, O. R.   "The Theme of Africa in West Indian
Literature."   BLACK ORPHEUS, no. 16, 1964, pp. 42-53.
Also appears in PHYLON, v. 26, Fall 1965, pp. 255-276.

James, Louis.   "Caribbean Poetry in English--Some Problems."
SAVACOU, no. 2, September 1970, pp. 78-86.

Morris, Mervyn.   "On Reading Louise Bennett, Seriously."
SUNDAY GLEANER, part 1, June 7, 1964, pp. 4, 23; part 2,
June 14, 1964, p. 4; part 3, June 21, 1964, p. 4; part 4,
June 28, 1964, p. 4.   Also appears in JAMAICA JOURNAL, v.
1, no. 1, December 1967, pp. 69-74.

Oakley, Leo.   "Ideas of Patriotism and National Dignity in
Some Jamaican Writings."   JAMAICA JOURNAL, v. 4, no. 3,

Bennett, Louise

> September 1970, pp. 16–31. Also appears in SUNDAY
> GLEANER, part 1, March 28, 1971, pp. 31, 34; part 2, April
> 4, 1971, p. 27; part 3, April 11, 1971, p. 25.

> Panton, George. "Our Well-known Well-loved Poet." SUNDAY
> GLEANER, August 11, 1974, p. 23.

> Rohlehr, Gordon. "The Folk in Caribbean Literature." TAPIA,
> part 2, v. 2, no. 12, December 24, 1972, pp. 8, 9, 15.

> Scott, Dennis. "Bennett on Bennett" (interview). CARIBBEAN
> QUARTERLY, v. 14, nos. 1 and 2, March–June 1968, pp. 97–
> 101.

> Wilmot, Cynthia. "It Happened in a Tramcar." SUNDAY
> GLEANER, November 27, 1955, p. 5.

ANANCY STORIES (1945)

> Lindo, Archie. "Louise Bennett's New Book." SUNDAY
> GLEANER, January 7, 1945, 1945, p. 4.

LAUGH WITH LOUISE (1961)

> Panton, George. Review. SUNDAY GLEANER, December 10, 1961,
> p. 14.

JAMAICA LABRISH (1966)

> Anon. "Jamaica Talk." TLS, no. 3381, December 15, 1966,
> p. 1173.

> Morris, Mervyn. Review. PUBLIC OPINION, November 25, 1966,
> p. 5.

> Nettleford, Rex. "Notes and Introduction." JAMAICA LABRISH.
> Kingston, Jamaica: Sangster's Bookshop, 1966, pp. 9–24.

> Panton, George. "A Literary Event." SUNDAY GLEANER,
> December 4, 1966, p. 4.

Other Works

DIALECT VERSES (1942)

JAMAICAN HUMOR IN DIALECT (1943)

Braithwaite, E. R.

JAMAICAN DIALECT POEMS (1948)

MIS LULU SEZ: A COLLECTION OF DIALECT POEMS (1949)

BRAITHWAITE, E. R. Guyana, 1922–

General

> Birbalsingh, F. M. "To John Bull, with Hate." CARIBBEAN
> QUARTERLY, v. 14, no. 4, September 1968, pp. 74-81.

> Salkey, Andrew. "Why Braithwaite's Return to Writing was
> Not Easy" (interview). SUNDAY GUARDIAN (Trinidad),
> October 8, 1972, p. 6.

> Seymour, A. J. "The Novel in Guyana." KAIE, no. 4, July
> 1967, pp. 59-63.

> Sparer, Joyce L. "Attitudes towards 'Race' in Guyanese
> Literature." CARIBBEAN STUDIES, v. 8, no. 2, July 1968,
> pp. 23-63.

> Swire, Myrthe. "E. R. Braithwaite, Controversial as Ever
> But with Subdued Anger." SUNDAY GLEANER, June 12, 1966,
> p. 4.

TO SIR WITH LOVE (1959)

> Akanji, Sangodare. Review. BLACK ORPHEUS, no. 6, November
> 1959, pp. 51-52.

> Allsopp, Joy. Review. KYK-OVER-AL, v. 9, no. 26, December
> 1959, pp. 56-57.

> Anon. "Apples for the Teacher." TLS, no. 2979, April 3,
> 1959, p. 194.

> Anon. Review. NEW STATESMAN, v. 57, March 28, 1959, pp.
> 454.

> Croft, Michael. "Classroom War." LSO, March 29, 1959, p.
> 15.

> Jennings, Elizabeth. Review. LONDON MAGAZINE, v. 6, no. 10,
> October 1959, pp. 67-68.

> Panton, George. Review. SUNDAY GLEANER, May 10, 1959, p. 4.

13

Braithwaite, E. R.

 Ramchand, Kenneth. "Decolonization in West Indian Literature." TRANSITION, v. 5, no. 22, 1965, pp. 48-49.

 Ramchand, Kenneth. "The Myth of TO SIR WITH LOVE." VOICES,
  v. 1, no. 5, December 1965, pp. 13-20.

 Wain, John. "Outlander among London Savages." NYT, May 1,
  1960, Section 7, p. 6.

PAID SERVANT (1962)

 Anon. Review. JLW, v. 7, December 1962, p. 520.

 Anon. Review. NEW STATESMAN, v. 64, October 19, 1962,
  p. 536.

 Anon. Review. TLS, November 16, 1962, p. 866.

 Anon. "West Indian Angle." THE TIMES (London), October 25,
  1962, p. 15.

 Biram, Brenda M. Review. NEGRO DIGEST, v. 18, no. 6, 1969,
  pp. 92-93.

 Hope, Francis. Review. LSO, October 28, 1962, p. 27.

 Hudson, Jo. Review. FREEDOMWAYS, v. 8, Third Quarter 1968,
  pp. 275-276.

 Panton, George. "Sequel to 'With Love.'" SUNDAY GLEANER,
  January 20, 1963, p. 14.

 Showers, Paul. Review. NYT, May 19, 1968, Section 7, p. 40.

A KIND OF HOMECOMING (1963)

 Anon. Review. THE TIMES (London), June 27, 1963, p. 15.

 Anon. Review. TLS, no. 3203, July 19, 1963, p. 530.

 Brucker, Milton. "A Mixed Bag of Impressions Datelined
  West Africa." NYT, August 5, 1962, Section 7, p. 3.

 Davidson, Basil. Review. NEW STATESMAN, v. 65, June 21,
  1963, pp. 940.

 Je'sman, Czeslaw. Review. RACE, v. 5, no. 1, July 1963,

pp. 95-96.

Panton, George. Review. SGM, July 7, 1963, p. 9.

CHOICE OF STRAWS (1965)

Anon. Review. BAJAN, no. 155, July 1966, p. 30.

Anon. Review. LSO, October 24, 1965, p. 28.

Kettle, Arnold. "Two West Indian Novelists." JCL, no. 2,
December 1966, pp. 173-175.

Panton, George. "Black and White in England." SUNDAY
GLEANER, November 7, 1965, p. 4.

RELUCTANT NEIGHBORS (1971)

Coombs, Orde. Review. NYT, September 17, 1972, Section 7,
p. 4.

McGlashan, Colin. Review. NEW STATESMAN, v. 84, October 20,
1971, p. 558.

Panton, George. Review. SUNDAY GLEANER, October 29, 1972,
p. 37.

HONORARY WHITE (1975)

Anon. "Experiences in South Africa." SUNDAY GLEANER,
December 7, 1975, p. 25.

Dondy, Farrukh. "Little Ventured, Little Gained." TAPIA,
v. 5, no. 41, October 1975, p. 8.

Mphahlele, Ezekiel. Review. NYT, July 13, 1975, Section 7,
p. 18.

BRATHWAITE, EDWARD KAMAU. Barbados, 1930-

General

Brown, Lloyd W. "The Calypso Tradition in West Indian
Literature." BAR, v. 2, nos. 1 and 2, 1971, pp. 127-143.

Brown, Wayne. "On Art, Artists, and the People." SUNDAY
GUARDIAN (Trinidad), August 9, 1970, p. 10.

West Indian Literature

Brathwaite, Edward Kamau

Clarke, Austin. "Some Speculations as to the Absence of Racial Vindictiveness in West Indian Literature." THE BLACK WRITER IN AFRICA AND THE AMERICAS, Los Angeles: Hennessey and Ingalls, 1973, pp. 165-194.

D'Costa, Jean. "Poetry Review: The Poetry of Edward Brathwaite." JAMAICA JOURNAL, v. 2, no. 3, September 1968, pp. 24-28.

Derrick, Anthony. "An Introduction to Caribbean Literature." CARIBBEAN QUARTERLY, v. 15, nos. 2 and 3, June-September 1969, pp. 65-78.

Drayton, Arthur D. "The European Factor in West Indian Literature." LITERARY HALF-YEARLY, v. 11, no. 1, 1970, pp. 71-94.

Grant, Damian. "Emerging Image: The Poetry of Edward Brathwaite." CRITICAL QUARTERLY, v. 12, Summer 1970, pp. 186-193.

Harris, Wilson. "History, Fable and Myth in the Caribbean and Guianas." CARIBBEAN QUARTERLY, v. 16, no. 2, June 1970, pp. 1-32.

Ismond, Patricia. "Walcott vs. Brathwaite." CARIBBEAN QUARTERLY, v. 17, nos. 3 and 4, September-December 1971, pp. 54-70.

James, Louis. "Caribbean Poetry in English--Some Problems." SAVACOU, no. 2, September 1970, pp. 78-86.

James, Louis. "Islands of Man, Reflections on the Emergence of a West Indian Literature." SOUTHERN REVIEW, v. 2, 1966, pp. 150-163.

Kemoli, Arthur. "The Theme of 'The Past' in Caribbean Literature." WLWE, v. 12, November 1973, pp. 304-325.

Lacovia, R. M. "Caribbean Literature in English: 1949-1970. BAR, v. 2, nos. 1 and 2, 1971, pp. 109--125.

Maxwell, Marina. "Towards a Revolution in the Arts." SAVACOU, no. 2, September 1970, pp. 19-32.

Moore, Gerald. "Use Men Language." BIM, v. 15, no. 57, March 1974, pp. 69-76.

16

Brathwaite, Edward Kamau

Panton, George. "Edward Kamau Brathwaite. Poet, Historian, and Playwright." SUNDAY GLEANER, December 15, 1974, p. 27.

Questel, Victor. "Their Tragic Destiny." TAPIA, v. 6, no. 20, May 16, 1976, pp. 4, 11.

Ramsaran, J. A. "The 'Twice-Born' Artist's Silent Revolution." BLACK WORLD, v. 20, no. 7, May 1971, pp. 58-67.

Rohlehr, F. Gordon. "Afterthoughts." TAPIA, no. 23, December 1971, pp. 8, 13. Also appears in BIM, v. 14, no. 56, January-June 1973, pp. 227-232.

Rohlehr, F. Gordon. "The Carrion Time." TAPIA, v. 4, no. 24, June 1974, pp. 5-8, 11. Also appears in BIM, v. 15, no. 58, June 1975, pp. 92-109.

Rohlehr, F. Gordon. "The Creative Writer and West Indian Society." KAIE, no. 11, August 1973, pp. 48-77.

Rohlehr, F. Gordon. "West Indian Poetry: Some Problems of Assessment." TAPIA, no. 20, August 29, 1971, pp. 11-14. Also appears in BIM, part. 1, v. 14, no. 54, January-June 1972, pp. 80-88; part 2, v. 14, no. 55, July-December 1972, pp. 134-144.

Walcott, Derek. "Sentimental Journeys...." SUNDAY GUARDIAN (Trinidad), August 15, 1965, p. 7.

Walmsley, Anne. "Dimensions of Song, a Comment on the Poetry of Derek Walcott and Edward Brathwaite." BIM, v. 13, no. 51, July-December 1970, pp. 152-167.

FOUR PLAYS FOR PRIMARY SCHOOLS (1964)

Marshall, Harold. Review. BIM, v. 10, no. 41, June-December 1965, pp. 71-72.

Panton, George. "Little Plays for Little Children." SUNDAY GLEANER, December 13, 1964, p. 4.

ODALE'S CHOICE (1967)

Panton, George. Review. SUNDAY GLEANER, November 12, 1967, p. 4.

17

Brathwaite, Edward Kamau

RIGHTS OF PASSAGE (1967)

Anon. Review. TLS, no. 3390, February 16, 1967, p. 127.

Baugh, Edward. Review. BIM, v. 12, no. 45, July–December 1967, pp. 66–68.

Charles, Pat. Review. LINK, v. 1, no. 1, July–September 1968, pp. 32–34.

Cox, C. B. Review. SPECTATOR, v. 218, March 24, 1967, p. 343.

Cox, C. B. Review. CRITICAL SURVEY, v. 3, Summer 1967, p. 107.

Foakes, R. A. "Caribbean Poetry." JCL, no. 6, January 1969, pp. 147–150.

James, Louis. Review. CARIBBEAN QUARTERLY, v. 13, no. 1, March 1967, pp. 38–41.

Moore, Gerald. "West Indian Poet." TRANSITION, v. 7, no. 32, pp. 62–63.

Morris, Mervyn. "Niggers Everywhere." NWQ, v. 3, no. 4, Cropover 1967, pp. 61–65.

Panton, George. Review. SUNDAY GLEANER, March 12, 1967, p. 4.

Rohlehr. F. Gordon. Review. MOKO, no. 12, April 9, 1969, p. 2.

Scott, Dennis. "The Poem of Exile." PUBLIC OPINION, March 31, 1967, p. 7.

Symons, Julian. Review. NEW STATESMAN, v. 73, April 7, 1967, p. 479.

Walcott, Derek. "Tribal Flutes." SGM, March 19, 1967, pp. 2–3.

MASKS (1968)

Anon. "MASKS and Edward Brathwaite." SUNDAY GLEANER, February 9, 1969, p. 4.

Brathwaite, Edward Kamau

Anon. Review. SUNDAY GLEANER, July 21, 1968, p. 4.

Baugh, Edward. Review. BIM, v. 12, no. 47, July-December 1968, pp. 209-211.

Moore, Gerald. "Confident Achievement." JCL, no. 7, July 1969, pp. 122-124.

Risden, Winnifred. Review. CARIBBEAN QUARTERLY, v. 14, nos. 1 and 2, pp. 145-147.

Roach, Eric. "MASKS--A Homecoming with a Taste of Aloes." SUNDAY GUARDIAN (Trinidad), October 12, 1968, p. 6.

Rohlehr, F. Gordon. Review. MOKO, no. 12, April 9, 1969, p. 2.

ISLANDS (1969)

Anon. Review. BAJAN, no. 197, January 1970, pp. 18-19.

Brown, Wayne. "W. I. Literature of the Past Year." SUNDAY GUARDIAN (Trinidad), August 30, 1970, p. 5.

Moore, Gerald. Review. BIM, v. 13, no. 51, January-June 1970, pp. 186-189.

Morris, Mervyn. "New Poetry by Brathwaite and Walcott." SUNDAY GLEANER, November 30, 1969, p. 4.

Rohlehr, F. Gordon. "The Historian as Poet." LITERARY HALF-YEARLY, v. 11, no. 2, 1970, pp. 171-178.

Rohlehr, F. Gordon. Review. CARIBBEAN QUARTERLY, v. 16, no. 4, December 1970, pp. 29-35.

THE ARRIVANTS (1973)

Asein, Samuel O. "The Concept of Form: A Study of Some Ancestral Elements in Brathwaite's Triology." ASAWI BULLETIN, no. 4, December 1971, pp. 9-38.

C. L. [Cedric Lindo]. "Poetic Bridge to Africa." SUNDAY GLEANER, January 30, 1974, p. 26.

Lewis, Maureen Warner. "Odemankoma Kyerema Se...." CARIBBEAN QUARTERLY, v. 19, no. 2, June 1973, pp. 51-99.

Brathwaite, Edward Kamau

> Morris, Mervyn. "This Broken Ground, Edward Brathwaite's
> Trilogy of Poems." NWQ, v. 5, no. 3, High Season 1972,
> pp. 14-26.
>
> Rohlehr, F. Gordon. "Islands." CARIBBEAN STUDIES, v. 10,
> no. 4, January 1971, pp. 173-202.

DAYS AND NIGHTS (1976)

> Anon. Review. SUNDAY GLEANER, February 1, 1976, p. 8.

OTHER EXILES (1977)

> Anon. Review. SUNDAY GLEANER, February 22, 1977, p. 20.
>
> Ramchand, Kenneth. "The Pounding in His Dark; Edward
> Brathwaite's Other Poetry." TAPIA, v. 7, no. 1, January
> 2, 1977, pp. 6-8.

BROWN, WAYNE. Trinidad, 1944-

General

> James, Louis. "Islands of Man, Reflections on the Emergence
> of a West Indian Literature." SOUTHERN REVIEW, v. 2,
> 1966, pp. 150-163.
>
> McFarlane, Basil. "The Century of Exile, Basil McFarlane
> Speaks with Wayne Brown." JAMAICA JOURNAL, v. 7, no. 3,
> September 1975, pp. 38-44.
>
> Panton, George. "The Poet Who Became a Biographer." SUNDAY
> GLEANER, March 21, 1976, p. 8.
>
> Rohlehr, F. Gordon. "A Carrion Time." TAPIA, v. 4, no. 24,
> June 1974, pp. 5-8, 11. Also appears in BIM, v. 15, no.
> 58, June 1974, pp. 92-109.

ON THE COAST (1973)

> Anon. "Coming to Terms with Major Issues of Modern W.I."
> SUNDAY GUARDIAN (Trinidad), February 25, 1973, p. 9.
>
> Brown, Stewart. Review. NOW, no. 2, Summer 1973, pp. 47-50.
>
> Carey, John. Review. LONDON MAGAZINE, New Series, v. 13,
> no. 2, June-July 1973, pp. 120-121.

Johnson, Lee S. B. Review. CARIBBEAN QUARTERLY, v. 18, no. 4. 1972, pp. 84-86.

Morris, Mervyn. "Below the Surface." SUNDAY GLEANER, September 16, 1973, p. 31.

Nyabonyo, Virginia Simmons. Review. BOOKS ABROAD, v. 48, no. 1, Winter 1974, p. 204.

CAMPBELL, FESTUS AMTAC. Jamaica, 1951–

IN PORTLAND'S VALLEY OF BEAUTY (1974)

Anon. "Jamaica." SUNDAY GLEANER, September 15, 1974, p. 27.

CAMPBELL, GEORGE. Jamaica, 1915–

General

Anon. "Fellowships." SGM, January 15, 1967, pp. 8-9.

Asein, S. O. "The 'Protest' Tradition in West Indian Poetry, from George Campbell to Martin Carter." JAMAICA JOURNAL, v. 6, no. 2, June 1972, pp. 40-45.

Bennett, Wycliffe. "The Jamaican Poets." LL, v. 57, no. 128, April 1948, pp. 58-61.

Brathwaite, Edward. "The African Presence in Caribbean Literature." DAEDALUS, v. 103, no. 2, Spring 1974. pp. 73-109.

Brown, Wayne. "Poetry of the Forties, Part 3: The Dilemma." SUNDAY GUARDIAN (Trinidad) October 4, 1970, p. 11.

Brown, Wayne. "Poetry of the Forties, Part 5: The Mulatto Question." SUNDAY GUARDIAN (Trinidad), October 11, 1970, p. 11.

Coulthard, G. R. "The Coloured Woman in Caribbean Poetry (1800-1960)." RACE, v. 2, no. 2, May 1961, pp. 53-61.

Dathorne, O. R. "Africa in the Literature of the West Indies." JCL, no. 1, September 1965, pp. 95-116.

Derrick, Anthony. "An Introduction to Caribbean Literature." CARIBBEAN QUARTERLY, v. 15, nos. 2 and 3, June-September

Campbell, George

1969, pp. 65-78.

Drayton, Arthur D. "The European Factor in West Indian
    Literature." LITERARY HALF-YEARLY, v. 11, no. 1, 1970,
    pp. 71-94.

Fuller, Roy. "Caribbean Poetry." SUNDAY GLEANER (Jamaica)
    June 13, 1948, p. 9.

Keane, E. McG. "Some Religious Attitudes in West Indian
    Poetry." BIM, part 1, v. 4, no. 15, December 1951,
    pp. 169-174; part 2, v. 4, no. 16, June 1952, pp. 266-271.

McFarlane, Basil. "On Jamaican Poetry." KYK-OVER-AL, v. 3,
    no. 13, Year End 1951, pp. 207-209.

Oakley, Leo. "Ideas of Patriotism and National Dignity in
    Some Jamaican Writings." JAMAICA JOURNAL, v. 4, no. 3,
    1970, 16-21. Also appears in SUNDAY GLEANER (Jamaica,
    part 1, March 28, 1971, pp. 31, 34; part 2, April 4, 1971,
    p. 27; part 3, April 11, 1971, p. 27.

St. John, Orford. "Perspective on FOCUS." WIR, v. 1, no.
    11/12, December 1956, p. 83. Seymour, A. J. "The
    Literary Adventure of the West Indies." KYK-OVER-AL, v.
    2, no. 10, April 1950, entire issue.

Seymour, A. J. "The Literary Adventure of the West Indies."
    KYK-OVER-AL, v. 2, no. 10, April 1950, entire issue.

Swanzy, Henry. "Caribbean Voices, Prolegomena to a West
    Indian Culture." CARIBBEAN QUARTERLY, v. 1, no. 2,
    September 1962, pp. 21-28. Reprinted in CARIBBEAN
    QUARTERLY, v. 8, no. 2, 1962, pp. 121-128.

Walcott, Derek. "A New Poet, Jamaican." SUNDAY GUARDIAN
    (Trinidad), June 20, 1965, p. 6.

Walcott, Derek. "The Poetry of George Campbell." PUBLIC
    OPINION, July 20, 1957, p. 7.

D. W. [Derek Walcott], "West Indian Writing." PUBLIC
    OPINION, January 26, 1957, p. 7.

A PLAY WITHOUT SCENERY (1940, drama)

Bell, Vera. Review. PUBLIC OPINION, March 29, 1940, p. 7.

FIRST POEMS (1949)

McFarlane, Basil. "George Campbell: The Road We Travel." PUBLIC OPINION, March 22, 1947, p. 7.

Other Works

CRY FOR HAPPY (1958)

CAMPBELL, OWEN. St. Vincent,

General

   Brathwaite, Edward. "Sir Galahad and the Islands." BIM, v. 7, no. 25, July-December 1957, pp. 8-16. Also appears in IOUANALOA, RECENT WRITING FROM ST. LUCIA. Castries, St. Lucia: Department of Extra and Mural Studies, 1963, pp. 50-59.

CARBERRY, H. D. Jamaica, 1921-

General

   Drayton, Arthur D. "The European Factor in West Indian Literature." LITERARY HALF-YEARLY, v. 11, no. 1, 1970, pp. 71-94.

   Hearne, John. "Barren Treasury." PUBLIC OPINION, November 11, 1950, pp. 6 and 8.

   James, Louis. "Caribbean Poetry in English--Some Problems." SAVACOU, no. 2, September 1970, pp. 78-86.

   Keane, E. McG. "Some Religious Attitudes in West Indian Poetry." BIM, part 1, v. 4, no. 15, December 1951, pp. 169-174; part 2, v. 4, no. 16, June 1952, pp. 266-271.

   Seymour, A. J. "Nature Poetry in the West Indies." KYK-OVER-AL, v. 3, no. 11, October 1950, pp. 39-47.

   Walcott, Derek. "Some Jamaican Poets." PUBLIC OPINION, part 1, August 3, 1957, p. 7; part 2, August 10, 1957, p. 7.

CAREW, JAN. Guyana, 1922-

General

   Amis, Kingsley. "Fresh Winds from the West." SPECTATOR, v. 200, May 2, 1958, pp. 565-566.

Carew, Jan

Brown, Lloyd W. "The Crisis of Black Identity in the West
Indian Novel." CRITIQUE, v. 11, no. 3, 1969, pp. 97-112.

Cartey, Wilfred. "The Rhythm of Society and Landscape."
NWQ, Guyana Independence Issue, 1966, pp. 97-104.

Maes-Jelinek, Hena. "The Myth of El Dorado in the Caribbean
Novel." JCL, v. 6, no. 1, June 1971, pp. 113-127.

Ramchand, Kenneth. "Dialect in West Indian Fiction."
CARIBBEAN QUARTERLY, v. 14, nos. 1 and 2, March-June 1968,
pp. 27-42. Also appears in his THE WEST INDIAN NOVEL AND
ITS BACKGROUND. London: Faber and Faber, 1970, pp. 96-
116.

Rickards, Colin. "Jan Carew to Return Home." SUNDAY
GLEANER, June 19, 1966, p. 4.

Seymour, A. J. "The Novel in Guyana." KAIE, no. 4, July
1967, pp. 59-63.

Sparer, Joyce L. "Attitudes towards 'Race' in Guyanese
Literature." CARIBBEAN STUDIES, v. 8, no. 2, July 1968,
pp. 23-63.

Wynter, Sylvia. "Strangers at the Gate, Caribbean Novelists
in Search of Identity." SUNDAY GLEANER, January 18, 1959,
p. 14.

BLACK MIDAS (1958)

Anon. Review. THE TIMES (London), March 27, 1958, p. 13.

Anon. Review. TLS, no. 2929, April 18, 1958, p. 202.

Goyden, William. "Splendor Was the Spoiler." NYT,
September 17, 1958, Section 17, p. 39.

Newby, P. H. Review. LONDON MAGAZINE, v. 5, no. 11,
November 1958, pp. 82-84.

Panton, George. "Pork Knockers of British Guiana." SUNDAY
GLEANER, May 4, 1958, p. 11.

Seymour, A. J. Review. KYK-OVER-AL, v. 8, no. 24, December
1958, pp. 86-87.

Index of Authors

Carew, Jan

THE WILD COAST (1958)

Anon. Review. THE TIMES (London), November 27, 1958, p. 13.

Anon. Review. TLS, no. 2964, December 19, 1958, p. 733.

Anon. "Tengar Is Another Ocean Shark." SUNDAY GUARDIAN (Trinidad), January 11, 1959, p. 22.

Aragbabalu, Omidiji. Review. BLACK ORPHEUS, no. 7, June 1960, pp. 63-64.

Jackman, Oliver. Review. BIM, v. 8, no. 29, June-December 1959, pp. 64-67.

Naipaul, V. S. Review. NEW STATESMAN, v. 56, December 6, 1958, pp. 826-827.

Nicholson, Geoffrey. Review. SPECTATOR, v. 201, November 28, 28, 1958, p. 787.

Panton, George. "Journalistic Description of the Unfamiliar." SUNDAY GLEANER, January 18, 1959, p. 14.

Rees, Goronwy. Review. LISTENER, v. 60, December 18, 1958, p. 1046.

THE LAST BARBARIAN (1961)

Anon. Review. THE TIMES (London), March 30, 1961, p. 15.

Anon. Review. TLS, no. 3085, April 14, 1961, p. 237.

Collymore, Frank. Review. BIM, v. 9, no. 34, January-June 1962, pp. 149-150.

Grigson, Geoffrey. Review. SPECTATOR, v. 206, March 31, 1961.

Panton, George. Review. SUNDAY GLEANER, November 25, 1962, 1962, p. 14.

Rickards, Colin. "Carew's Latest Not His Best." SUNDAY GLEANER, August 6, 1961, p. 14.

Sanford, Antonia. Review. JLW, v. 4, March 1961, p. 354.

Walcott, Derek. "Really Good W.I. Novel Needed Now."

Carr, Ernest J.

      SUNDAY GUARDIAN (Trinidad), April 30, 1961, p. 7.

    Wyndham, Francis. Review. LSO, March 26, 1961, p. 30.

MOSCOW IS NOT MY MECCA (1964)

    Anon. Review. BAJAN, v. 12, no. 8, April 1965, p. 30.

    Brophy, Brigid. Review. NEW STATESMAN, v. 68, November 6, 1964, pp. 703.

    Gradussov, Alex. Review. BIM, v. 11, no. 43, July-December 1966, pp. 224-225.

    Panton, George. "Race Prejudice in Moscow." SUNDAY GLEANER, November 29, 1964, p. 4.

    Walcott, Derek. "Dialect and Dialectic." SUNDAY GUARDIAN, (Trinidad), November 22, 1964, p. 18.

UNIVERSITY OF HUNGER (1966, drama)

    Jardine, Monica. Review. NWF, v. 1, no. 48, September 19, 1966, pp. 23-25.

THE THIRD GIFT (1975)

    Agard, John. Review. CARIBBEAN CONTACT, v. 2, no. 10, January 1975, p. 3.

Other Works

GREEN WINTER (1968)

CRY, BLACK POWER (1973)

CARR, ERNEST J. Trinidad,

General

    Keane, E. McG. "Some Religious Attitudes in West Indian Poetry." BIM, part 1, v. 4, no. 15, December 1951, pp. 169-174; part 2, v. 4, no. 16, June 1952, pp. 266-271.

    Pearse, Andrew. "West Indian Themes." CARIBBEAN QUARTERLY, V. 2, no. 2, September 1952, pp. 12-23.

CARTER, MARTIN. Guyana, 1927–

General

    Anon. "The Miniature Poets." KYK-OVER-AL, v. 5, no. 15,
      Year-End 1952, pp. 84–86.

    Asein, S. O. "The 'Protest' Tradition in West Indian Poetry,
      from George Campbell to Martin Carter." JAMAICA JOURNAL,
      v. 6, no. 2, June 1972, pp. 40–45.

    Brathwaite, Edward. "KYK-OVER-AL, and the Radicals." NWQ,
      Guyana Independence Issue, 1966, pp. 55–57.

    Carew, Jan. "British West Indian Poets and Their Culture."
      PHYLON, v. 14, 1953, pp. 71–73.

    Carter, Martin. "A Guyanese Poet in Cardiff" (interview).
      KAIE, no. 2, May 1966, pp. 18–21.

    Dathorne, O. R. "Africa in the Literature of the West
      Indies." JCL, no. 1, September 1965, pp. 95–116.

    Dathorne, O. R. "The Theme of Africa in West Indian
      Literature." BLACK ORPHEUS, no. 16, 1964, pp. 42–53.
      Also appears in PHYLON, v. 26, Fall 1965, pp. 255–276.

    James, Louis. "Caribbean Poetry in English--Some Problems."
      SAVACOU, no. 2, September 1970, pp. 78–86.

    James, Louis. "The Necessity of Poetry." NWQ, Guyana
      Independence Issue, 1966, pp. 111–115.

    McDonald, Ian. Introduction to "Jail Me Quickly--Five Poems
      by Martin Carter." NWF, v. 1, no. 34, February 18, 1966,
      pp. 19–20.

    Moore, Gerald. "Use Men Language." BIM, v. 15, no. 57,
      March 1974, pp. 69–76.

    Rohlehr, F. Gordon. "Afterthoughts." TAPIA, no. 23,
      December 26, 1971, pp. 8, 13. Also appears in BIM, v. 14,
      no. 56, January–June 1973, pp. 227–232.

    Rohlehr, F. Gordon. "The Creative Writer and West Indian
      Society." KAIE, no. 11, August 1973, pp. 48–77.

Cartey, Wilfred

> Rohlehr, F. Gordon. "West Indian Poetry: Some Problems of Assessment." TAPIA, no. 20, August 29, 1971, pp. 11-14. Also appears in BIM, part 1, v. 14, no. 54, January-June 1972, pp. 80-88; part 2, v. 14, no. 55, July-December 1972, pp. 134-144.

> Sparer, Joyce. L. "Attitudes towards 'Race' in Guyanese Literature." CARIBBEAN STUDIES, v. 8, no. 2, July 1968, pp. 23-63.

> Walcott, Derek. "Fellowships." SGM, January 15, 1967, pp. 8-9.

POEMS OF RESISTANCE (1954)

> King, C. G. O. "Martin Carter--Voice of Resistance." SUNDAY GLEANER, August 9, 1964, p. 4.

> Walcott, Derek. "Too Much of the Wrong Subject." SUNDAY GUARDIAN (Trinidad), June 14, 1964, p. 6.

POEMS OF SUCCESSION (1977)

> Lowhar, Syl. "Carter's 'Resistance' and 'Succession.'" CARIBBEAN CONTACT, v. 5, no. 5, August 1977, p. 7.

CARTEY, WILFRED. Trinidad, 1931-

HOUSE OF BLUE LIGHTNING (1973)

> Roach, Eric. Review. SUNDAY GUARDIAN (Trinidad), September 16, 1973, p. 15.

CHARLES, FAUSTIN. Trinidad, 1944.

General

> Brown, Wayne. "New W.I. Writers of the Past Year." SUNDAY GUARDIAN (Trinidad), September 6, 1970, p. 8.

> Moore, Gerald. "Use Men Language." BIM, v. 13, no. 52, January-June 1971, pp. 252-255.

THE EXPATRIATE--POEMS 1963-68 (1969)

> Brathwaite, Edward K. Review. CARIBBEAN QUARTERLY, v. 16, no. 2, June 1970, pp. 65-69. Also appears in BIM, v. 13,

no. 52, January–June 1971, pp. 252–255.

Brown, Wayne. "An Exciting Trinidad Poet." SUNDAY GUARDIAN (Trinidad), August 2, 1970, p. 15.

Other Works

CRAB TRACK (1973)

CLARKE, A. M. Trinidad

General

Dathorne, O. R. "Africa in the Literature of the West Indies." JCL, no. 1, September 1965, pp. 95–116.

Dathorne, O. R. "The Theme of Africa in West Indian Literature." BLACK ORPHEUS, no. 16, 1964, pp. 42–53. Also appears in PHYLON, v. 26, Fall 1965, pp. 255–276.

CLARKE, AUSTIN. Barbados, 1932–

General

Brown, Lloyd W. "The American Image in British West Indian Literature." CARIBBEAN STUDIES, v. 11, no. 1, April 1971, pp. 30–45.

Brown, Lloyd W. "Beneath the North Star: The Canadian Image in Black Literature." DALHOUSIE REVIEW, v. 50, no. 3, Autumn 1970, pp. 317–329.

Brown, Lloyd W. "The Calypso Tradition in West Indian Literature." BAR, v. 2, nos. 1 and 2, 1971, pp. 127–143.

Brown, Lloyd W. "The Crisis of Black Identity in the West Indian Novel." CRITIQUE, v. 11, no. 3, 1969, pp. 97–112.

Brown, Lloyd W. "The West Indian Novel in North America: A Study of Austin Clarke." JCL, no. 9, July 1970, pp. 89–103.

MacCulloch, Clare. "Look Homeward, Bajan; A Look at the Work of Austin Clarke, A Barbadian Expatriate as Seen by an Outsider." BIM, v. 14, no. 55, July–December 1972, pp. 179–182.

Clarke, Austin

     Ramchand, Kenneth. "Dialect in West Indian Fiction."
        CARIBBEAN QUARTERLY, v. 14, nos. 1 and 2, March-June 1968,
        pp. 27-42. Also appears in his THE WEST INDIAN NOVEL AND
        ITS BACKGROUND. London: Faber and Faber, 1970, pp. 96-
        116.

     Tyrwhitt, Janice. "Clarke Closes In." TAMARACK REVIEW, no.
        38, Winter 1968, pp. 89-91.

SURVIVORS OF THE CROSSING (1964)

     Anon. Review. THE TIMES (London), October 8, 1964, p. 15.

     Anon. Review. TLS, no. 3268, October 15, 1964, p. 933.

     Arthur, Kevyn Alan. Review. BIM, v. 10, no. 40, January-
        June 1965, pp. 291-292.

     Panton, George. "Bacchanal and Cane." SUNDAY GLEANER,
        November 1, 1964, p. 4.

AMONGST THISTLES AND THORNS (1965)

     Anon. Review. THE TIMES (London), July 1, 1965, p. 15.

     Panton, George. Review. SUNDAY GLEANER, August 22, 1965,
        p. 4.

     Walcott, Derek. "A Bajan Boyhood." SUNDAY GUARDIAN
        (Trinidad), September 5, 1965, p. 8.

THE MEETING POINT (1965)

     Anon. "Barbados in Toronto." TLS, no. 3402, May 11, 1967,
        p. 404.

     Anon. Review. BAJAN, no. 168, August 1967, p. 26.

     Anon. Review. THE TIMES (London), May 18, 1967, p. 15.

     Dalt, Gary Michael. Review. TAMARACK REVIEW, no. 45,
        Autumn 1967, pp. 117-120.

     Marshall, Harold. Review. BAJAN, no. 226, August 1972,
        pp. 33-36.

     Panton, George. Review. SUNDAY GLEANER, July 2, 1967, p. 4.

Collymore, Frank A.

Wall, Stephen. Review. LSO, May 7, 1967, p. 27.

WHEN HE WAS FREE AND YOUNG AND USED TO WEAR SILKS (1971)

Jeffers, Keith. "Clarke: Promise and Insight with Flaws."
BLACK IMAGES, v. 1, no. 1, January 1972, p. 14.

McNamara, Eugene. Review. QUEENS QUARTERLY, v. 79, no. 1,
Spring 1972, p. 120.

Marshall, Harold. Review. BIM, v. 14, no. 54, January-June
1972, pp. 113-116.

THE BIGGER LIGHT (1975)

Gosine, Vishnu. Review. CORLIT, v. 2, nos. 1-2, April-July
1975, p. 47.

Levin, Martin. Review. NYT, February 16, 1975, Section 7,
p. 12.

Other Works

STORM OF FORTUNE (1972)

THE PRIME MINISTER (1977)

COLLYMORE, FRANK A. Barbados, 1893-1980

General

Anon. "Three Evenings with Six Poets." KYK-OVER-AL, v. 3,
no. 13, pp. 214-220.

Anon. "Tribute to Frank Collymore." SAVACOU, 7/8, January/
June 1973, entire issue, 156 pp.

Baugh, Edward. "Frank Collymore and the Miracle of BIM."
NWQ, Barbados Independence Issue, v. 3, nos. 1 and 2, Dead
Season 1966-Croptime 1967, pp. 129-133.

Keane, E. McG. "Some Religious Attitudes in West Indian
Poetry." BIM, part 1, v. 4, no. 15, December 1951, pp.
169-174; part 2, v. 4, no. 16, June 1952, pp. 266-271.

Mills, Therese. "BIM's Grand Old Man Retires." SUNDAY
GUARDIAN (Trinidad), July 8, 1973, p. 7.

Collymore, Frank A.

> Owens, R. J. "West Indian Poetry." CARIBBEAN QUARTERLY, v. 7, no. 3, December 1961, pp. 120-127.

> Seymour, A. J. "The Literary Adventure of the West Indies." KYK-OVER-AL, v. 2, no. 10, April 1950, entire issue, 40 pp.

> Seymour, A. J. "Nature Poetry in the West Indies." KYK-OVER-AL, v. 3, no. 11, October 1950, pp. 39-47.

> Wickham, John. "Colly--A Profile." BAJAN, no. 231, January 1973, pp. 12, 14, 16-17.

FLOTSAM (1943)

> Swanzy, Henry. Review. BIM, v. 3, no. 9, 1948, pp. 77-79.

COLLECTED POEMS (1959)

> Anon. Review. BAJAN, v. 7, no. 6, February 1960, pp. 28-29.

> Anon. Review. BIM, v. 8, no. 30, January-June 1960, pp. 137-139.

> Panton, George. "Through the Poet's Eye." SUNDAY GLEANER, January 3, 1960, p. 14.

Other Works

THIRTY POEMS (1944)

BENEATH THE CASUARINAS (1945)

RHYMED RUMINATIONS ON THE FAUNA OF BARBADOS (1969)

D'COSTA, JEAN. Jamaica,

SPRAT MORRISON (1972)

> G. P. [George Panton]. "Entertaining Story of a Young Jamaican Boy." SUNDAY GLEANER, December 10, 1972, p. 47.

ESCAPE TO LAST MAN PEAK (1975)

> Anon. "Good Adventure Story for Children." SUNDAY GLEANER, November 23, 1975, p. 23.

DATHORNE, OSCAR RONALD.   Guyana, 1934-

General

    Cartey, Wilfred.   "The Rhythm of Society and Landscape."
    NWQ, Guyana Independence Issue, 1966, pp. 97-104.

    Dathorne, O. R.   "Africa in the Literature of the West
    Indies."   JCL, no. 1, September 1965, pp. 95-116.

    Dathorne, O. R.   "The Theme of Africa in West Indian Litera-
    ture."   BLACK ORPHEUS, no. 16, 1964, pp. 42-53.   Also
    appears in PHYLON, v. 26, Fall 1965, pp. 255-276.

    Derrick, Anthony.   "An Introduction to Caribbean Literature."
    CARIBBEAN QUARTERLY, v. 15, nos. 2 and 3, June-September
    1969, pp. 65-78.

    Kemoli, Arthur.   "The Theme of 'The Past' in Caribbean
    Literature."   WLWE, v. 12, no. 2, November 1973, pp. 304-
    325.

    Seymour, A. J.   "The Novel in Guyana."   KAIE, no. 4, July
    1967, pp. 59-63.

    Sparer, Joyce L.   "Attitudes towards 'Race' in Guyanese
    Literature."   CARIBBEAN STUDIES, v. 8, no. 2, July 1968,
    pp. 23-63.

DUMPLINGS IN THE SOUP   (1963)

    Anon.   Review.   NEW STATESMAN, v. 65, April 5, 1963, p. 497.

    Anon.   Review.   TLS, no. 3189, April 12, 1963, p. 253.

    Banham, Martin.   Review.   BOOKS ABROAD, v. 39, no. 1,
    Winter 1965, pp. 111-112.

    Marshall, Harold.   Review.   BIM, v. 10, no. 39, July-
    December 1964, pp. 226-227.

THE SCHOLAR MAN   (1964)

    Aragbabalu, Omidjii.   Review.   BLACK ORPHEUS, no. 18,
    October 1965, pp. 62-63.

    Brathwaite, Edward.   Review.   BIM, v. 10, no. 41, June-

Dathorne, Oscar Ronald

      December 1965, pp. 68-69.

      Panton, George. "Search for Identity." SUNDAY GLEANER, September 27, 1964, p. 4.

      Povey, J. F. Review. BOOKS ABROAD, v. 39, no. 4, Autumn 1965, p. 483.

      Salvesen. Review. NEW STATESMAN, v. 68, September 11, 1964, p. 366.

DAWES, NEVILLE. Jamaica, 1926-

General

      Brathwaite, Edward. "Jazz and the West Indian Novel." BIM, part 1, v. 11, no. 44, January-June 1967, pp. 275-284; part 2, v. 12, no. 45, July-December 1967, pp. 39-51; part 3, v. 12, no. 46, January-June 1968, pp. 115-126.

      Brathwaite, Edward. "Roots." BIM, v. 10, no. 37, July-December 1963, pp. 10-21.

      Carr, W. I. "Reflections on the Novel in the British Caribbean." QUEENS QUARTERLY, v. 70, Winter 1963, pp. 585-597.

      Seymour, A. J. "The Novel in the British Caribbean, Part 3." BIM, v. 11, no. 44, January-June 1967, pp. 238-242.

THE LAST ENCHANTMENT (1960)

      Anon. Review. THE TIMES (London), July 14, 1960, p. 15.

      Anon. Review. TLS, no. 3060, October 21, 1960, p. 485.

      Brathwaite, Edward K. Review. BIM, v. 9, no. 33, July-December 1961, pp. 74-75.

      Lamming, George. Review. RACE, v. 2, no. 2, May 1961, p. 92.

      McFarlane, Basil. "Jamaican Novel, A Review, THE LAST ENCHANTMENT." JAMAICA JOURNAL, v. 9, nos. 2 and 3, 1975, pp. 51-52.

      Panton, George. "Have We Really Solved the Race Problem?"

de Lisser, Herbert G.

SUNDAY GLEANER, March 19, 1961, p. 14.

Walcott, Derek. "New Novel by Dawes Sticks to Formula."
SUNDAY GUARDIAN (Trinidad), September 11, 1960, p. 5.

DE BOISSIERE, RALPH. Trinidad,

General

Birbalsingh, F. M. "The Novels of Ralph de Boissiere." JCL,
no. 9, July 1970, pp. 104-108.

Rawlins, Randolph. "Migrants with Manuscripts, Social Background of the West Indian Novel." BLACK ORPHEUS, no. 4,
1958, pp. 46-50.

Seymour, A. J. "The Novel in the British Caribbean, Part 3."
BIM, v. 11, no. 44, January-June 1967, pp. 238-242.

Wickham, John. "West Indian Writing." BIM, v. 13, no. 50,
January-June 1970, pp. 68-80.

Works

CROWN JEWEL   (1952)

RUM AND COCA-COLA   (1956)

NO SADDLES FOR KANGAROOS, A NOVEL   (1964)

DE LISSER, HERBERT G.   Jamaica, 1878-1944

General

R.L.C.A.   [Aarons, R. L. C.].   "Remembering H. G. de Lisser."
SUNDAY GLEANER, June 9, 1974, p.22.

Anon.   Tribute to the Late H. George de Lisser." SUNDAY
GLEANER, June 11, 1944, p. 4.

Dathorne, O. R.   "Africa in the Literature of the West
Indies." JCL, no. 1, September 1965, pp. 95-116.

Dathorne, O. R.   "The Theme of Africa in West Indian
Literature." BLACK ORPHEUS, no. 16, 1964, pp. 42-53.   Also
appears in PHYLON, v. 26, Fall 1965, pp. 255-276.

de Lisser, Herbert G.

Dewar, Lilian. "Jamaica in the Novel." KYK-OVER-AL, v. 3, no. 12, pp. 108-113.

Drayton, Arthur D. "The European Factor in West Indian Literature." LITERARY HALF-YEARLY, v. 11, no. 1, 1970, pp. 71-94.

Jacobs, H. P. "The Era of New Eras." PUBLIC OPINION, March 4, 1939, p. 3.

Panton, George. "The Arch Conservative Who Was Also a Pioneer." SUNDAY GLEANER, July 14, 1974, p. 31.

Panton, George. "West Indies--Past and Present." SUNDAY GLEANER, November 30, 1958, p. 18.

Ramchand, Kenneth. "Dialect in West Indian Fiction." CARIBBEAN QUARTERLY, v. 14, nos. 1 and 2, March-June 1968, pp. 27-42. Also appears in his THE WEST INDIAN NOVEL AND ITS BACKGROUND. London: Faber and Faber, 1970, pp. 96-116.

Ramchand, Kenneth. "History and the Novel: A Literary Critics Approach." SAVACOU, v. 1, no. 5, June 1971, pp. 103-113.

Rickards, Colin. "H. G. de Lisser Rides Again." SUNDAY GLEANER, September 17, 1961, p. 14.

Roberts, W. Adolphe. "Caribbean Literature: The British Possessions." WIR, v. 4, no. 42, April 25, 1953, pp. 16-17.

Wynter, Sylvia. "Novel and History, Plot and Plantation." SAVACOU, v. 1, no. 5, June 1971, pp. 95-102.

JANE'S CAREER: A STORY OF JAMAICA (1914)
(JANE: A STORY OF JAMAICA, 1913)

Anon. "A Black Heroine of Fifty Years Ago." SUNDAY GLEANER, July 20, 1975, p. 23.

Cooke, Michael G. "West Indian Picaresque." NOVEL, v. 7, no. 1, FALL 1973, pp. 93-96.

Figueroa, John. "JANE'S CAREER." WLWE, v. 12, April 1973, pp. 97-105.

Dizzy, Ras

THE WHITE WITCH OF ROSEHALL   (1929)

   Ramchand, Kenneth. "Decolonization in West Indian Litera-
      ture." TRANSITION, v. 5, no. 22, 1965, pp. 48-49.

UNDER THE SUN: A JAMAICAN COMEDY   (1937)

   Hill, Frank. Review. PUBLIC OPINION, October 30, 1937,
      p. 9.

PSYCHE   (1953)

   C. G. "Stories of Old Jamaica." SUNDAY GLEANER, June 24,
      1973, p. 47.

   Chapman, Esther. Review. WIR, v. 4, no. 20, September 13,
      1952, p. 12.

MORGAN'S DAUGHTER   (1953)

   Black, Clinton V. "Buccaneer Blood." PUBLIC OPINION,
      August 15, 1953, p. 5.

   C. G. "Stories of Old Jamaica." SUNDAY GLEANER, June 24,
      1973, p. 47.

THE CUP AND THE LIP   (1956)

   Anon. "English Views on a Jamaican Book." SUNDAY GLEANER,
      July 22, 1956, p. 9.

ARAWAK GIRL   (1958)

   R. R. "Why Did the West Indian Novel Arise in Jamaica?"
      PUBLIC OPINION, December 20, 1958, p. 9.

Other Works

SUSAN PROUDLEIGH   (1915)

TRIUMPHANT SQUALITONE: A TROPICAL EXTRAVAGANZA   (1917)

REVENGE, A TALE OF OLD JAMAICA   (1919)

DIZZY, RAS. Jamaica, 1934/5-

General

Dizzy, Ras

    Moore, Gerald. "Use Men Language." BIM, v. 15, no. 57, March 1974, pp. 69-76.

    Owens, J. V. "Literature on the Rastafari: 1955-1974, A Review." SAVACOU, no. 11/12, September 1975, pp. 86-105.

DRAYTON, GEOFFREY. Barbados, 1924-

General

    Dathorne, O. R. "Africa in the Literature of the West Indies." JCL, no. 1, September 1965, pp. 95-116.

    Dathorne, O. R. "The Theme of Africa in West Indian Literature." BLACK ORPHEUS, no. 16, 1964, pp. 42-53. Also appears in PHYLON, v. 26, Fall 1965, pp. 255-276.

    Ramchand, Kenneth. "Terrified Consciousness." JCL, no. 7, July 1969, pp. 8-19. Also appears in his THE WEST INDIAN NOVEL AND ITS BACKGROUND. London: Faber and Faber, 1970, pp. 233-236.

THREE MERIDIANS (1950)

    Anon. Review. CARIBBEAN QUARTERLY, v. 2, no. 1, April 1950, p. 45.

    Harrison, John. Review. BIM, v. 4, no. 14, June 1951, pp. 144-145.

CHRISTOPHER (1959)

    Anon. Review. THE TIMES (London), February 5, 1959, p. 13.

    Anon. Review. TLS, no. 2973, February 13, 1959, p. 81.

    Davies, Barrie. Review. WLWE, v. 12, April 1973, pp. 119-121.

    Forde, A. N. Review. BIM, v. 8, no. 29, June-December 1959, p. 64.

    Panton, George. "The Brighter Side." SUNDAY GLEANER, June 28, 1959, p. 14.

ZOHARA (1961)

Anon. Review. BAJAN, v. 9, no. 2, October 1961, p. 29.

Anon. "Superstition in Spain." SUNDAY GLEANER, April 22, 1962, p. 14.

Brooke-Rose, Christine. Review. LSO, August 13, 1961, p. 20.

Marshall, Harold. Review. BIM, v. 9, no. 34, January-June 1962, p. 152.

Walcott, Derek. Review. SUNDAY GUARDIAN (Trinidad), November 12, 1961, p. 26.

EMTAGE, JAMES B. Barbados,

General

Ramchand, Kenneth. "Terrified Consciousness." JCL, no. 7, July 1969, pp. 8-19. Also appears in his THE WEST INDIAN NOVEL AND ITS BACKGROUND. London: Faber and Faber, 1970, pp. 223-236.

BROWN SUGAR, A VESTIGIAL TALE (1966)

Morris, Mervyn. Review. PUBLIC OPINION, May 1967, p. 5.

Panton, George. Review. SUNDAY GLEANER, July 24, 1966, p. 4.

ESCOFFERY, GLORIA. Jamaica, 1923-

General

Walcott, Derek. "Sentimental Journeys. . . ." SUNDAY GUARDIAN (Trinidad), August 15, 1965, p. 7.

Works

LANDSCAPE IN THE MAKING (1926)

FERGUSON, MERRILL. Jamaica,

THE VILLAGE OF LOVE (1960)

Anon. "New Jamaican Author." SUNDAY GLEANER, January 24, 1960, p. 10.

Figueroa, John J.

      Charles, Pat. Review. IOUANALOA, RECENT WRITING FROM ST.
      LUCIA. Castries, St. Lucia: Department of Extra and
      Mural Studies, 1963, pp. 66-68.

      Rickards, Colin. "New Novelist Chooses Mythical West Indian
      Island." SUNDAY GUARDIAN (Trinidad), April 23, 1961, p.
      4.

      Walcott, Derek. "Novel with an Awkward Sincerity." SUNDAY
      GUARDIAN (Trinidad), March 26, 1961, p. 11.

FIGUEROA, JOHN J. Jamaica, 1920-

   General

      St. John, Orford. "Perspective on FOCUS." BIM, v. 10, no.
      37, July-December 1963, pp. 63-65.

   LOVE LEAPS HERE (1962)

      Forde, A. N. Review. BIM, v. 10, no. 37, July-December
      1963, pp. 63-65.

      Morris, Mervyn. Review. CARIBBEAN QUARTERLY, v. 9, nos. 1
      and 2, 1963, pp. 91-95.

      Walcott, Derek. "Lazy at Times But Honest." SUNDAY
      GUARDIAN (Trinidad), January 27, 1963, p. 5.

FORDE, A. N. Barbados, 1923-

   General

      Pearse, Andrew. "West Indian Themes." CARIBBEAN QUARTERLY,
      v. 2, no. 2, September 1952, pp. 12-23.

   Works

   CANES BY THE ROADSIDE

FOSTER, MICHAEL. Barbados, 1945-1965

   General

      Walcott, Derek. "Sentimental Journeys. . . ." SUNDAY
      GUARDIAN (Trinidad), August 15, 1965, p. 7.

Gonzalez, Anson

THINGS (1965)

    Massiah, E. B. B. Review. BIM, v. 11, no. 42, January-
       June 1966, pp. 141--143.

FRASER, FITZROY. Jamaica, 1936-

  <u>General</u>

    Harrison, John. "From the West Indies" (transcript of a
       radio talk given in Suva, Fiji). BIM, v. 10, no. 37,
       July-December 1963, pp. 62-63.

  THE COMING OF THE HARVEST (1958)

    Chapman, Esther. Review. WIR, v. 4, no. 3, March 1959,
       p. 61.

    Panton, George. Review. SUNDAY GLEANER, December 21, 1958,
       p. 14.

  WOUNDS IN THE FLESH (1962)

    Anon. Review. THE TIMES (London), March 15, 1962, p. 15.

    Anon. Review. TLS, March 30, 1962, p. 221.

    Butler, Rupert. Review. JLW, v. 6, April 1962, p. 384.

    Panton, George. "New Author--Jamaican." SUNDAY GLEANER,
       April 1, 1962, p. 14.

    Rickards, Colin. "New Jamaican Author Has Hint of Naipaul."
       SUNDAY GUARDIAN (Trinidad), April 8, 1962, p. 17.

    Walcott, Derek. "Jamaican Lucky Jim Nurses a Grudge."
       SUNDAY GUARDIAN (Trinidad), July 15, 1962, p. 9.

  <u>Other Works</u>

  MONOLOGUE (1960)

GONZALEZ, ANSON. Trinidad,

  <u>General</u>

    Fraser, Alfred. "The Experience of the 70's." NEW VOICES,

Gray, Cecil

v. 1, no. 2, 1973, pp. 33-35.

Rohlehr, F. Gordon. "Afterthoughts." TAPIA, no. 23, December 1971, pp. 8, 13. Also appears in BIM, v. 14, no. 56, January-June 1973, pp. 227-232.

Rohlehr, F. Gordon. "West Indian Poetry: Some Problems of Assessment." TAPIA, no. 20, August 1971, pp. 11-14. Also appears in BIM, part 1, v. 14, no. 54, January-June 1972, pp. 80-88; part 2, v. 14, no. 55, July-December 1972, pp. 134-144.

SCORE (1972, with Victor Questel)

Brown, Stewart. Review. NOW, no. 2, Summer 1973, pp. 9-12.

Hackett, Winston. "Survival." TAPIA, part 1, v. 5, no. 34, August 1975, pp. 4-5, 9; part 2, v. 5, no. 36, August 1975, pp. 6-7.

THE LOVE SONG OF BOYSIE B AND OTHER POEMS (1974)

Questel, Victor. "The Price of Selfhood." NEW VOICES, v. 2, no. 4, June 1974, pp. 11-14.

Questel, Victor. "Stripping of the Masks." TAPIA, v. 4, no. 10, March 1974, pp. 6-8.

GRAY, CECIL. Trinidad,

General

Pearse, Andrew. "West Indian Themes." CARIBBEAN QUARTERLY, v. 2, no. 2, September 1952, pp. 12-23.

HARRIS, WILSON. Guyana, 1921-

General

Adler, Joyce Sparer. "Wilson Harris and the Twentieth Century Man." NEW LETTERS, v. 40, no. 1, Fall 1973, pp. 49-61.

Agard, John. "World of Caribbean Artists: The Shame of It All." CARIBBEAN CONTACT, v. 3, no. 2, May 1975, p. 9.

Anon. "The Miniature Poets." KYK-OVER-AL, v. 5, no. 15,

Harris, Wilson

Year-end 1952, pp. 84-86.

Brathwaite, Edward. "The African Presence in Caribbean Literature." DAEDALUS, v. 103, no. 2, Spring 1974, pp. 73-109.

Brathwaite, Edward. "The Controversial Tree of Time." BIM, v. 8, no. 30, January-June 1960, pp. 104-114.

Brathwaite, Edward. "Jazz and the West Indian Novel." BIM, part 1, v. 11, no. 44, January-June 1967, pp. 275-284; part 2, v. 12, no. 45, July-December 1967, pp. 39-51; part 3, v. 12, no. 46, January-June 1968, pp. 115-126.

Brathwaite, Edward. "KYK-OVER-AL and the Radicals." NWQ, Guyana Independence Issue, 1966, pp. 55-57.

Brathwaite, Edward. "Timehri." SAVACOU, no. 2, September 1970, pp. 35-44. Also appears in IS MASSA DAY DEAD? New York: Doubleday, 1974, pp. 29-44.

Brathwaite, Edward. "West Indian Prose Fiction in the Sixties, a Survey." CRITICAL SURVEY, v. 3, Winter 1967, pp. 169-174. Also appears in BIM, v. 12, no. 47, July-December 1968, pp. 157-165, and SUNDAY GLEANER, part 1, March 8, 1970, p. 27; part 2, March 15, 1970, p. 27.

Brown, Lennox. "Wilson Harris Ahead" (interview). SUNDAY GUARDIAN (Trinidad), May 30, 1971, pp. 6, 19.

Carew, Jan. "British West Indian Poets and Their Culture." PHYLON, v. 14, 1953, pp. 71-73.

Dathorne, O. R. "Africa in the Literature of the West Indies." JCL, no. 1, September 1965, pp. 95-116.

Dathorne, O. R. "The Theme of Africa in West Indian Literature." BLACK ORPHEUS, no. 16, 1964, pp. 42-53.

Derrick, A. "An Introduction to Caribbean Literature." CARIBBEAN QUARTERLY, v. 15, nos. 2 and 3, June-September 1969, pp. 65-78.

Drayton, Arthur D. "The European Factor in West Indian Literature." LITERARY HALF-YEARLY, v. 11, no. 1, 1970, pp. 71-94.

West Indian Literature

Harris, Wilson

Gilkes, Michael. WILSON HARRIS AND THE CARIBBEAN NOVEL. London: Longman Caribbean, 1975.

Hearne, John. "El Dorado of the Soul." PUBLIC OPINION, April 6, 1963, p. 12.

Hearne, John. "The Fugitive in the Forest: A Study of Four Novels by Wilson Harris." JCL, no. 4, December 1967, pp. 99-112. Also appears in THE ISLANDS IN BETWEEN. London: Oxford University Press, 1968, pp. 140-153.

Howard, W. J. "Wilson Harris and the 'Alchemical Imagination.'" LITERARY HALF-YEARLY, v. 11, no. 2, 1970, pp. 17-26.

Howard, W. J. "Wilson Harris 'Guiana Quartet' from Personal Myth to National Identity." ARIEL, v. 1, no. 1, January 1970, pp. 46-60.

Irish, J. A. George. "Magical Realism: A Search for Caribbean and Latin American Roots." RRI, v. 4, no. 3, Fall 1974, pp. 411-421.

James, C. L. R. "Home Is Where They Want to Be." TGM, February 14, 1965, pp. 4-5.

James, Louis. "Caribbean Poetry in English--Some Problems." SAVACOU, no. 2, September 1970, pp. 78-86.

James, Louis. "Islands of Man, Reflections on the Emergence of a West Indian Literature." SOUTHERN REVIEW, v. 2, no. 2, 1966, pp. 150-163.

James, Louis. "The Necessity of Poetry." NWQ, Guyana Independence Issue, 1966, pp. 111-115.

Kemoli, Arthur. "The Theme of 'The Past' in Caribbean Literature." WLWE, v. 12, November 1973, pp. 304-325.

Lacovia, R. M. CARIBBEAN AESTHETICS: A PROLEGOMENON. BLACK IMAGES, v. 2, no. 2, Black Images Monograph no. 1, 1973, 47 pp.

Lacovia, R. M. "Caribbean Literature in English: 1949-1970." BAR, v. 2, nos. 1 and 2, 1971, pp. 109-125.

Maes-Jelinek, Hena. "The Myth of El Dorado in the Caribbean

Novel." JCL, v. 6, no. 1, June 1971, pp. 113-127.

Maxwell, Marina. "Towards a Revoluation in the Arts."
    SAVACOU, no. 2, September 1970, pp. 19-32.

Mohr, Eugene V. "West Indian Fiction Is Alive and Well."
    CARIBBEAN REVIEW, v. 5, no. 4, Winter 1973, pp. 23-29.

Moss, John G. "William Blake and Wilson Harris: The
    Objective Vision." JCL, v. 9, no. 3, April 1975, pp. 29-
    40.

Munro, Ian, and Reinhard Sander, eds. "Interview with Wilson
    Harris." KAS-KAS: INTERVIEWS WITH THREE CARIBBEAN
    WRITERS IN TEXAS. Austin, Texas: African and
    Afro-American Research Institute, 1972, pp. 43-55.

Nettleford, Rex. "Caribbean Perspectives--The Creative
    Potential and the Quality of Life." CARIBBEAN QUARTERLY,
    v. 17, nos. 3 and 4, September-December 1971, pp. 120-121.

Page, Malcolm. "West Indian Writers." NOVEL, v. 3, no. 2,
    Winter 1970, pp. 167-172.

Ramchand, Kenneth. "Aborigines, Their Role in West Indian
    Literature." JAMAICA JOURNAL, v. 3, no. 4, December 1969,
    pp. 51-54. Also appears as "The Significance of the
    Aborigines in Wilson Harris' Fiction." LITERARY HALF-
    YEARLY, v. 11, no. 2, 1970, pp. 7-16.

Ramchand, Kenneth. "Dialect in West Indian Fiction."
    CARIBBEAN QUARTERLY, v. 14, nos. 1 and 2, March-June 1968,
    pp. 27-42. Also appears in his THE WEST INDIAN NOVEL AND
    ITS BACKGROUND. London: Faber and Faber, 1970, pp. 96-
    116.

Ramchand, Kenneth. "The Dislocated Image." NWQ, Guyana
    Independence Issue, 1966, pp. 107-110.

Ramchand, Kenneth. "Wilson Harris, Caribbean Genius."
    SUNDAY GLEANER, January 11, 1970, pp. 4, 18.

Ramsaran, J. A. "The Social Groundwork of Politics in Some
    West Indian Novels." NEGRO DIGEST, v. 18, no. 10, August
    1969, pp. 71-77.

Rohlehr, F. Gordon. "The Creative Writer and West Indian

Harris, Wilson

Society." KAIE, no. 11, August 1973, pp. 48-77.

Scott, Dennis. "Novels of Wilson Harris Reveal Guyanese History." SUNDAY GLEANER, February 22, 1970, pp. 4, 10.

Seymour, A. J. "The Novel in Guyana." KAIE, no. 4, July 1967, pp. 59-63.

Seymour, A. J. "The Novels of Wilson Harris." BIM, v. 10, no. 38, January-June 1964, pp. 139-141.

Sparer, Joyce L. "The Art of Wilson Harris." NEW BEACON REVIEWS: COLLECTION ONE. London: New Beacon Books, 1968 1968, pp. 22-30.

Sparer, Joyce L. "Attitudes towards 'Race' in Guyanese Literature." CARIBBEAN STUDIES, v. 8, no. 2, July 1968, pp. 23-63.

Walcott, Derek. "Analyzing Wilson Harris." TGM, May 30, 1965, pp. 8, 14.

Walcott, Derek. "The Gift of Comedy." TGM, October 22, 1967, pp. 2-3.

Walcott, Derek. "Tracking Mr. Wilson Harris." SUNDAY GUARDIAN (Trinidad), April 24, 1966, p. 9.

Wynter, Sylvia. "We Must Learn to Sit Down Together and Talk About a Little Culture; Reflections on West Indian Writing and Criticism, Part 2." JAMAICA JOURNAL, v. 3, no. 1, March 1969, pp. 27-42.

FETISH (1951)

Seymour, A. J. Review. KYK-OVER-AL, v. 3, no. 13, Year-end 1951, p. 248.

ETERNITY TO SEASON (1954)

Seymour, A. J. Review. BIM, v. 6, no. 22, June 1955, pp. 133-135.

PALACE OF THE PEACOCK (1960)

Anon. "Exploring in Depth." TLS, no. 3057, September 30, 1960, p. 625.

Index of Authors

Harris, Wilson

Anon. Review. BIM, v. 9, no. 32, July-December 1961, p. 76.

Anon. Review. THE TIMES (London), September 1, 1960, p. 13.

Brahms, F. "A Reading of Wilson Harris's PALACE OF THE PEACOCK. NEW LETTERS, v. 40, no. 1, Fall 1973.

Bryden, Ronald. Review. SPECTATOR, v. 205, September 23, 1960, p. 454.

Maes-Jelinek, Hena. "The True Substance of Life: Wilson Harris's PALACE OF THE PEACOCK." COMMON WEALTH: PAPERS DELIVERED AT THE CONFERENCE OF COMMONWEALTH LITERATURE, AARHUS UNIVERSITY April 26-30, 1971. Aarhus, Denmark: Aarhus University, 1971.

Panton, George. "B. G. Conundrum." SUNDAY GLEANER, October 2, 1960, p. 14.

Rickards, Colin. "Caribbean Bookshelf." SUNDAY GLEANER, May 18, 1969, p. 4.

Seymour, A. J. Review. KYK-OVER-AL, v. 9, no. 27, December 1960, pp. 142-144.

Walcott, Derek. "A Work of Power and Imagination." SUNDAY GUARDIAN (Trinidad), October 16, 1960, p. 5.

THE FAR JOURNEY OF OUDIN (1961)

Anon. Review. TLS, no. 3112, October 20, 1961, p. 756.

Panton, George. "Social Problems of Independence." SUNDAY GLEANER, November 5, 1961, p. 14.

Sealy, Karl. Review. BIM, v. 9, no. 35, July-December 1962, pp. 223-224.

THE WHOLE ARMOUR (1962)

Anon. Review. TLS, no. 3158, September 7, 1962, p. 669.

Hench, Michael M. "The Fearful Symmetry of THE WHOLE ARMOUR ARMOUR." RRI, v. 4, no. 3, Fall 1974, pp. 446-551.

Panton, George. "Mystical West Indian Writer." SUNDAY GLEANER, November 4, 1962, p. 14.

THE SECRET LADDER (1963)

47

Harris, Wilson

    Anon. "Journey's End." TLS, no. 3181, February 15, 1963,
      p. 105.

    Anon. Review. THE TIMES (London), February 14, 1963, p. 15.

    Burgess, Anthony. Review. LSO, February 10, 1963, p. 18.

    Dathorne, O. R. Review. BLACK ORPHEUS, no. 14, February 1
      1964, pp. 61-62.

    Panton, George. "Two West Indian Writers." SGM, May 26,
      1963, p. 13.

HEARTLAND (1964)

    Anon. Review. TLS, no. 3264, September 17, 1964, p. 864.

    Panton, George. "More Seeking by West Indians." SUNDAY
      GLEANER, October 4, 1964, p. 4.

THE EYE OF THE SCARECROW (1965)

    Anon. Review. BAJAN, no. 154, June 1966, p. 31.

    Anon. Review. SUNDAY GLEANER, December 26, 1965, p. 4.

    Anon. Review. THE TIMES (London), November 25, 1965, p. 15.

    Burgess, Anthony. Review. SPECTATOR, v. 215, December 3,
      1965.

    Gool, Reshard. "To Harris with Love." NWQ, v. 3, no. 4,
      Cropover 1967, pp. 73-75.

    Walcott, Derek. "The Explorer Is in Danger of Disappearing."
      SUNDAY GUARDIAN (Trinidad), February 27, 1966, p. 8.

    Wardle, Irving. Review. LSO, November 28, 1965, p. 28.

THE WAITING ROOM (1967)

    Coleman, John. Review. LSO, May 21, 1967, p. 27.

    Panton, George. Review. SUNDAY GLEANER, July 9, 1967, p. 4.

    Sparer, Joyce L. Review. CARIBBEAN QUARTERLY, v. 14, nos.
      1 and 2, March-June 1968, pp. 148-151.

Index of Authors

Harris, Wilson

Wilding, Michael. Review. LONDON MAGAZINE, New Series, v. 7, no. 5, August 1967, p. 95.

TUMATUMARI (1968)

Alder, Joyce Sparer. "TUMATUMARI and the Imagination of Wilson Harris." JCL, no. 7, July 1969, pp. 20-31.

Anniah Gowda, H. H. "Wilson Harris's TUMATUMARI." LITERARY HALF-YEARLY, v. 11, no. 1, 1970, pp. 31-38.

Graham, Kenneth. Review. LISTENER, v. 80, September 5, 1968, pp. 313.

Moore, Gerald. Review. BIM, v. 13, no. 51, July-December 1970, pp. 193-194.

Panton, George. Review. SUNDAY GLEANER, October 13, 1968, p. 4.

Russell, D. W. "The Dislocating Act of Memory: An Analysis of Wilson Harris's TUMATUMARI." WLWE, v. 13, November 1974, pp. 237-249.

Tindall, Gillian. Review. NEW STATESMAN, v. 76, September 6, 1968, pp. 292.

Wall, Stephen. Review. LSO, September 15, 1968, p. 29.

ASCENT TO OMAI (1970)

Anon. Review. NEW STATESMAN, v. 79, February 28, 1970, pp. 300.

Anon. Review. SUNDAY GLEANER, March 8, 1970, p. 27.

Brown, Wayne. "West Indian Literature of the Past Year." SUNDAY GUARDIAN (Trinidad), August 30, 1970, p. 5.

Cole, Barry. Review. SPECTATOR, v. 224, February 21, 1970, pp. 246.

Gilkes, Michael. "The Art of Extremity: A Reading of Wilson Harris's ASCENT TO OMAI." CARIBBEAN QUARTERLY, v. 17, nos. 3 and 4, September-December 1971, pp. 83-90. Also appears in LITERARY HALF-YEARLY, v. 15, no. 1, January 1974, pp. 120-133.

Harris, Wilson

    Maes-Jelinek, Hena. "ASCENT TO OMAI." LITERARY HALF-YEARLY,
       v. 13, no. 1, January 1972, pp. 1-8.

    Moss, John G. Review. WLWE, no. 19, April 1971, pp. 84-85.

    Munro, Ian H. "The Manuscript of ASCENT TO OMAI." NEW
       LETTERS, v. 40, no. 1, Fall 1973, pp. 37-48.

    Ramchand, Kenneth. "Before the People Became Popular. . . ."
       CARIBBEAN QUARTERLY, v. 18, no. 4, 1972, pp. 70-73.

    Salkey, Andrew. "The Sieve of Tradition." MOKO, no. 46,
       November 13, 1970, p. 9.

THE SLEEPERS OF RORAIMA (1970)

    Anniah Gowda, H. H. "Civilization through Fables." LITERARY
       HALF-YEARLY, v. 14, no. 1, January 1973, pp. 169-174.

    Boxill, Anthony. Review. WLWE, April 1971, no. 19, pp. 86-
       87.

    Garioch, Robert. Review. LISTENER, v. 84, September 17,
       1970, pp. 383.

    James, Louis. "The Sad Initiation of Lamming's 'G.'. . ."
       COMMON WEALTH: PAPERS DELIVERED AT THE CONFERENCE OF
       COMMONWEALTH LITERATURE, AARHUS UNIVERSITY, APRIL 26-30,
       1971. Aarhus, Denmark: Aarhus University, 1971, pp. 62-
       65.

    C. L. [Cedric Lindo]. Review. SUNDAY GLEANER, October 18,
       1970, p. 27.

    Maes-Jelinek, Hena. "Natural and Psychological Landscapes."
       JCL, v. 7, no. 1, June 1971, pp. 117-120.

THE AGE OF THE RAINMAKERS (1971)

    Anniah Gowda, H. H. "Civilization through Fables."
       LITERARY HALF-YEARLY, v. 14, no. 1, January 1973, pp.
       169-174.

    Maes-Jelinek, Hena. "Natural and Psychological Landscapes."
       JCL, v. 7, no. 1, June 1971, pp. 117-120.

    Panton, George. Review. SUNDAY GLEANER, June 6, 1971, p. 29.

BLACK MARSDEN   (1972)

Adams, Rolston. "A Pursuit of Archetypes of Culture. . . ."
CARIBBEAN QUARTERLY, v. 19, no. 4, December 1973,
pp. 53-55.

Bailey, Paul. Review. LONDON MAGAZINE, New Series, v. 12,
no. 6, February/March 1973, p. 160.

Gilkes, Michael. "A Double Vision--A Tabula-Rasa
Comedy. . . ." CARIBBEAN QUARTERLY, v. 19, no. 4,
December 1973, pp. 57-59.

Gilkes, Michael. "Magical Reality." JCL, v. 9, no. 1,
August 1974, pp. 77-79.

Johnson, B. S. Review. NEW STATESMAN, v. 84, December 1,
1972, pp. 832.

C. L. [Cedric Lindo]. "A Scottish Wilson Harris Puzzle."
SUNDAY GLEANER, December 10, 1972, p. 47.

Thwaite, Anthony. Review. LSO, November 26, 1972, p. 35.

Waugh, Auberon. Review. SPECTATOR, v. 227, December 23,
1972, pp. 1008-1009.

COMPANIONS OF THE DAY AND NIGHT   (1975)

Beasley, W. Conger, Jr. Review. NEW LETTERS, v. 42, no. 1,
Fall, 1975, pp. 114-115.

Gilkes, Michael. "An Infinite Canvas: Wilson Harris's
COMPANIONS OF THE DAY AND NIGHT." WLWE, v. 15, April
1976, pp. 161-173.

HEARNE, JOHN. Jamaica, 1926-

General

Anon. "The Caribbean Mixture, Variations and Fusions in
Race and Style." TLS, no. 3154, August 10, 1962, p. 578.

Anon. "John Hearne, Best of the Younger Set." SUNDAY
GLEANER, Independence Supplement, July 28, 1962, pp. 44
and 45.

Hearne, John

Birbalsingh, Frank M. "Escapism in the Novels of John
Hearne." CARIBBEAN QUARTERLY, v. 16, no. 1, March 1970,
pp. 28-38.

Brathwaite, Edward. "The New West Indian Novelists." BIM,
part 1, v. 8, no. 31, July-December 1960, pp. 199-210;
part 2, v. 8, no. 32, January-June 1961, pp. 271-280.

Brathwaite, Edward. "Roots." BIM, v. 10, no. 37, July-
December 1963, pp. 10-21.

Carr, Bill. "Reflections on the Novel in the British
Caribbean." QUEENS QUARTERLY, v. 70, Winter 1963,
pp. 585-597.

Carr, Bill. "The Unreal World of Mr. Hearne." SUNDAY
GLEANER, August 27, 1961, p. 14.

Cartey, Wilfred. "The Novels of John Hearne." JCL, no. 7,
July 1969, pp. 45-58.

Dathorne, O. R. "Africa in the Literature of the West In
Indies." JCL, no. 1, September 1965, pp. 95-116.

Dathorne, O. R. "Africa in West Indian Literature." BLACK
ORPHEUS, no. 16, 1964, pp. 42-53. Also appears under
title "The Theme of Africa in West Indian Literature,"
in PHYLON, v. 26, Fall 1965, pp. 255-276.

Davies, Barrie. "The Seekers. The Novels of John Hearne."
THE ISLANDS IN BETWEEN. London: Oxford University Press,
1968, pp. 109-120.

Figueroa, John J. "John Hearne, West Indian Writer." RRI,
v. 2, no. 1, Spring 1972, pp. 72-79.

Lacovia, R. M. "Caribbean Literature in English." BAR, v.
2, nos. 1 and 2, 1971, pp. 109-125.

Lacovia, R. M. "English Caribbean Literature, A Brave New
World." BLACK IMAGES, v. 1, no. 1, January 1972, pp.
15-22.

Panton, George. "John Hearne, Accurate Portrayer of the
Middle-Class." SUNDAY GLEANER, March 9, 1975, pp. 23, 24.

Ramchand, Kenneth. "Dialect in West Indian Fiction."

Index of Authors

Hearne, John

CARIBBEAN QUARTERLY, v. 14, nos. 1 and 2, March–June 1968, pp. 27–42. Also appears in his THE WEST INDIAN NOVEL AND ITS BACKGROUND. London: Faber and Faber, 1970, pp. 96–116.

Seymour, A. J. "A Letter to John Hearne." KYK-OVER-AL, v. 8, no. 24, December 1958, pp. 78–81.

Seymour, A. J. "The Novel in the British Caribbean, Part 3." BIM, v. 11, no. 44, January–June 1967, pp. 238–242.

Walcott, Derek. "Neo-Realism Parallel Noted in West Indian Novels." SUNDAY GUARDIAN (Trinidad), April 24, 1960, p. 7.

Walcott, Derek. "Novelist Hearne Possesses Neat Disciplined Style." SUNDAY GUARDIAN (Trinidad), September 3, 1961, p. 7.

Wyndham, Francis. "The New West Indian Writers." BIM, v. 7, no. 28, January–June 1959, pp. 188–190.

Wynter, Sylvia. "Strangers at the Gate, Caribbean Novelists in Search of Identity." SUNDAY GLEANER, January 18, 1959, p. 14.

Wynter, Sylvia. "We Must Learn to Sit Down Together and Talk About a Little Culture; Reflections on West Indian Writing and Criticism, Part 2." JAMAICA JOURNAL, v. 3, no. 1, March 1969, pp. 27–42.

VOICES UNDER THE WINDOW (1955)

Anon. Review. BIM, v. 6, no. 23, 1955, pp. 206–207.

Black, Anna. "We Die Alone." PUBLIC OPINION, October 15, 1955, p. 5.

Clark, Edward. Review. PHYLON, v. 18, 1957, pp. 97–98.

Maclaren-Ross, J. Review. LISTENER, V. 54, 1955, p. 391.

Morris, Mervyn. "Pattern and Meaning in VOICES UNDER THE WINDOW." JAMAICA JOURNAL, v. 5, no. 1, March 1971, pp. 53–56.

Panton, George. Review. SUNDAY GLEANER, March 18, 1973,

Hearne, John

    p. 35.

  Quigley, Isabel. Review. SPECTATOR, v. 195, September 16, 1955, pp. 374.

STRANGER AT THE GATE (1956)

  Allan, Greig. Review. BIM, v. 6, no. 24, 1956, pp. 271-272.

  Anon. Review. SPECTATOR, v. 196, May 11, 1956, p. 665.

  Anon. Review. TLS, no. 2830, May 25, 1956, p. 309.

  Cawley, John Alpha. "Jamaican Novelist with Fire in His Heart." PUBLIC OPINION, May 26, 1956, p. 6.

  Chapman, Esther. "John Hearne's Second Novel." WIR, v. 1, no. 7, July 1956, p. 9.

  Richardson, Maurice. Review. NEW STATESMAN, v. 51, May 12, 1956, p. 544.

THE FACES OF LOVE (1957)

  Anon. Review. SUNDAY GUARDIAN (Trinidad), May 12, 1957, p. 7.

  Bagley, John. Review. SPECTATOR, v. 198, April 26, 1957.

  Brathwaite, Edward. Review. BIM, v. 7, no. 25, July-December 1957, pp. 63-64.

  Bryden, Ronald. Review. LISTENER, v. 57, 1957, p. 726.

  Chapman, Esther. Review. WIR, v. 2, no. 6, June 1957, p. 68.

  Comfort, Alex. Review. NEW STATESMAN, v. 53, April 27, 1957, p. 548.

  Davenport, John. Review. LSO, April 28, 1957, p. 13.

  Pritchett, V. S. Review. NEW STATESMAN, v. 56, October 4, 1958, pp. 468-469.

  Ross, Angus. Review. PUBLIC OPINION, May 4, 1957, p. 7.

Wyndham, Francis. Review. LONDON MAGAZINE, v. 4, no. 8, August 1957, pp. 66-67.

THE AUTUMN EQUINOX (1959)

Akanji, Sangodare. Review. BLACK ORPHEUS, no. 8, 1960, pp. 53-54.

Anon. Review. THE TIMES (London), November 12, 1959, p. 15.

Anon. Review. TLS, no. 3015, December 11, 1959, p. 721.

Brathwaite, Edward. Review. BIM, v. 8, no. 31, July-December 1960, pp. 215-217.

Coleman, John. Review. SPECTATOR, v. 203, November 6, 1959, p. 641.

Gilbert, Morris. "Three Faces of Love on the Island of Cayuna." NYT, Section 7, November 19, 1961, p. 58.

Miller, Karl. Review. LSO, November 8, 1959, p. 23.

Newton, Duff. Review. JLW, v. 1, December 1959, p. 328.

West, Paul. Review. NEW STATESMAN, v. 58, November 14, 1959, p. 686.

THE LAND OF THE LIVING (1961)

Anon. Review. BAJAN, v. 9, no. 10, June 1962, p. 19.

Anon. Review. THE TIMES, (London), November 2, 1961, p. 16.

Anon. Review. TLS, no. 3117, November 24, 1961, p. 851.

Brooke-Rose, Christine. Review. LSO, November 5, 1961, p. 29.

Carr, Bill, Review. CARIBBEAN QUARTERLY, v. 8, no. 1, 1962, pp. 54-55.

Carr, Bill. "A View of John Hearne." PUBLIC OPINION, March 6, 1964, pp. 8-9.

Charles, Pat. Review. IOUANALOA, RECENT WRITING FROM ST. LUCIA. Castries, St. Lucia: Department of Extra-Mural

Heath, Roy A. K.

Studies, 1963, pp. 66-68.

Hoyte, Clyde. "Yes, Hearne Has Arrived." PUBLIC OPINION, November 25, 1961, p. 4.

Levin, Martin. Review. NYT, August 12, 1962, Section 7, p. 24.

Mayne, Richard. Review. NEW STATESMAN, v. 62, September 29, 1961, p. 440.

Panton, George. Review. SUNDAY GLEANER, November 26, 1961, p. 14.

Thompson, Ivy. "Who's Who in the West Indian Novel." CARIBBEAN CONTACT, v. 1, no. 5, April 1973, pp. 4, 18.

Walcott, Derek. "Love and Anguish on a Tropic Island." SUNDAY GUARDIAN (Trinidad), December 24, 1961, p. 7.

HEATH, ROY A. K. Guyana, 1926-

A MAN COME HOME (1975)

Anon. "Life in a Georgetown Yard." SUNDAY GLEANER, January 5, 1975, p. 27.

D'Costa, Jean. Review. JAMAICA JOURNAL, v. 9, nos. 2 and 3, 1975, pp. 53-58.

Hamner, Robert D. Review. WLWE, v. 15, April 1976, pp. 253-255.

HENDRIKS, ARTHUR LEMIERE. Jamaica, 1922-

General

Drayton, Arthur D. "The European Factor in West Indian Literature." LITERARY HALF-YEARLY, v. 11, no. 1, 1970, pp. 71-94.

King, Cameron. "A. L. Hendriks, Poetic Journey." SUNDAY GLEANER, part 1, March 6, 1966. p. 4; part 2, "Spiritual Exploration, Poetry of A. L. Hendriks." April 24, 1966, p. 4.

Oakley, Leo. "Ideas of Patriotism and National Dignity in

Hendriks, Arthur Lemiere

Some Jamaican Writings." JAMAICA JOURNAL, v. 4, no. 3,
September 1970, pp. 16-21. Also appears in SUNDAY
GLEANER, part 1, March 28, 1971, pp. 31, 34; part 2, April
4, 1971, p. 27; part 3, April 11, 1971, p. 25.

Panton, George. "The Businessman Poet." SUNDAY GLEANER,
June 16, 1974, p. 21.

Pearse, Andrew. "West Indian Themes." CARIBBEAN QUARTERLY,
v. 2, no. 2, 1951, pp. 12-23.

ON THIS MOUNTAIN AND OTHER POEMS   (1965)

Anon. Review. SUNDAY GLEANER, July 11, 1965, p. 4.

Morris, Mervyn. Review. BIM, v. 11, no. 43, July-December
1966, pp. 225-228.

Walcott, Derek. "A New Poet, Jamaican." SUNDAY GUARDIAN
(Trinidad), June 20, 1965, p. 6.

MUET   (1971)

Brown, Stewart. Review. NOW, v. 1, Spring 1973, pp. 25-27.

Forde, A. N. Review. BIM, v. 14, no. 55, July-December
1972, pp. 186-188.

C. L. [Cedric Lindo]. Review. SUNDAY GLEANER, March 5,
1972, p. 27.

THESE GREEN ISLANDS   (1971)

Forde, A. N. Review. BIM, v. 14, no. 55, July-December
1972, pp. 186-188.

C. L. [Cedric Lindo]. "Enjoyable Collection by a Jamaican
Poet." SUNDAY GLEANER, January 23, 1972, p. 25.

SEVEN JAMAICAN POETS   (1971, edited by Mervyn Morris)

Forde, A. N. Review. BIM, v. 14, no. 54, January-June
1972, p. 116.

C. L. [Cedric Lindo]. "Worthy Examples of Our Poetry."
SUNDAY GLEANER, May 23, 1971, p. 29.

Herbert, C. L.

Morrison, Hugh P. Review. CARIBBEAN QUARTERLY, v. 18, no. 4, December 1972, pp. 82-83.

MADONNA OF THE UNKNOWN NATION (1974)

S. B. "A Major Poetic Talent." SUNDAY GLEANER, September 1, 1974, p. 24.

HERBERT, C. L. Trinidad, 1927-

General

Brown, Wayne. "Poetry of the Forties, Part 3; The Dilemma." SUNDAY GUARDIAN (Trinidad), October 4, 1970, p. 11.

Fuller, Roy. "Caribbean Poetry." SUNDAY GLEANER, June 13, 1948, p. 9.

Swanzy, Henry. "Caribbean Voices, Prolegomena to a West Indian Culture." CARIBBEAN QUARTERLY, v. 1, no. 2, September 1949. Reprinted in v. 8, no. 2, June 1962, pp. 121-128.

HERCULES, FRANK. Trinidad.

General

Anon. "Writing Is an Instrument for Frank Hercules." SUNDAY GLEANER, August 25, 1968, pp. 4, 8.

WHERE THE HUMMINGBIRD FLIES (1961)

Panton, George. "Have We Really Solved the Race Problem?" SUNDAY GLEANER, March 19, 1961, p. 14.

I WANT A BLACK DOLL (1967)

Panton, George. "Colour It Black." SUNDAY GLEANER, May 21, 1967, p. 4.

HODGE, MERLE. Trinidad, 1944-

CRICK CRACK MONKEY (1970)

Brown, Wayne. "Close Down the Libraries Says This Teacher" (interview). SUNDAY GUARDIAN (Trinidad), November 1, 1970, p. 10.

Hopkinson, Abdur-Rahman (Slade)

Brown, Wayne. "Growing Up in Colonial T'dad." SUNDAY
GUARDIAN (Trinidad), June 28, 1970, pp. 6, 17.

Brown, Wayne. "New West Indian Writers of the Past Year."
SUNDAY GUARDIAN (Trinidad), September 6, 1970, p. 8.

Feld, Michael. Review. LONDON MAGAZINE, New Series, v. 10,
no. 2, May 1970, p. 104.

Harvey, Elizabeth. Review. WLWE, no. 19, April 1971, p. 87.

Hood, Stuart. Review. LISTENER, v. 83, March 19, 1970.

Jordon, Clive. Review. NEW STATESMAN, v. 79, March 1970,
p. 334.

Panton, George. Review. SUNDAY GLEANER, May 24, 1970, p.
31.

HOLLAR, CONSTANCE. Jamaica, 1880-1945

General

Mais, Roger. "Contemporary Jamaican Verse." PUBLIC OPINION,
November 4, 1939, p. 10.

Oakley, Leo. "Ideas of Patriotism and National Dignity in
Some Jamaican Writings." JAMAICA JOURNAL, v. 4, no. 3,
September 1970, pp. 16-21.

HO LUNG, RICHARD. Jamaica,

General

Moore, Gerald. "Use Men Language." BIM, v. 15, no. 57, 1
1974, pp. 69-76.

HOPKINSON, ABDUR-RAHMAN (SLADE). Guyana, 1934-

General

Anthony, Michael. "Conversation with Slade Hopkinson. . ."
(interview). SUNDAY GUARDIAN (Trinidad), August 9, 1970,
p. 13.

Gonzalez, Anson. "Our Theatre Is Looking Homeward. . . ."
TGM, August 27, 1972, pp. 28-29.

Hosein, Clyde

    Panton, George. "A True Caribbean Man." SUNDAY GLEANER, March 7, 1976, p. 8.

    Walcott, Derek. "BIM, Putting on the Style." SUNDAY GUARDIAN (Trinidad), September 18, 1966, p. 7.

    Walcott, Derek. "Sentimental Journeys. . . ." SUNDAY GUARDIAN (Trinidad), August 15, 1965, p. 7.

THE MAD WOMAN OF PAPINE (1977)

THE FRIEND (1977)

    Questel, Victor. Review. CARIBBEAN CONTACT, v. 5, no. 4, July 1977, p. 3.

Other Works

THE FOUR AND OTHER POEMS (1954)

THE ONLIEST FISHERMAN (play, 1957)

HOSEIN, CLYDE. Trinidad,

General

    Mackoon, Lindsay. "A Poet with Rare Vision." SUNDAY GUARDIAN (Trinidad), February 17, 1963, p. 10.

HUTCHINSON, LIONEL. Barbados,

MAN FROM THE PEOPLE (1970)

    Anon. "Panty Politics." TLS, no. 3541, January 8, 1970, p. 39.

    Anon. Review. BAJAN, no. 207, December 1970, p. 22.

    Anon. Review. LSO, January 11, 1970, p. 29.

    Panton, George. "The Naked Truth." SUNDAY GLEANER, August 17, 1969, p. 4.

    Wickham, John. Review. BIM, v. 13, no. 51, July-December 1970, pp. 192-193.

ONE TOUCH OF NATURE (1971)

Hunte, George. Review. BAJAN, no. 209, February 1971, p. 22.

C. L. [Cedric Lindo]. Review. SUNDAY GLEANER, February 7, 1971, p. 23.

INGRAM, KENNETH E. Jamaica, 1921-

General

   Seymour, A. J. "Nature Poetry in the West Indies." KYK-OVER-AL, v. 3, no. 11, October 1950, pp. 39-47.

JACKMAN, OLIVER. Barbados,

SAW THE HOUSE IN HALF (1974)

   Wickham, John. Review. BAJAN, no. 255, February 1975, p. 22.

JAMES, C. L. R. Trinidad, 1901-

General

   Brathwaite, Edward. "Timehri." SAVACOU, no. 2, 1970, pp. 35-44. Also appears in IS MASSA DAY DEAD. New York: Doubleday, 1974, pp. 29-42.

   Brathwaite, Edward. "West Indian Prose Fiction in the Sixties, A Survey." CRITICAL SURVEY, v. 3, 1967, pp. 169-174. Also appears in BIM, v. 12, no. 47, July-December 1968, pp. 157-165.

   Brown, Wayne. "On Art, Artists and the People." SUNDAY GUARDIAN (Trinidad), August 9, 1970, p. 10.

   Drayton, Arthur D. "The European Factor in West Indian Literature." LITERARY HALF-YEARLY, v. 11, no. 1, 1970, pp. 71-94.

   James, C. L. R. "Discovering Literature in Trinidad: The Nineteen-Thirties." JCL, no. 7, July 1969, pp. 73-80. Also appears in SAVACOU, no. 2, September 1970, pp. 54-60.

   Moore, Gerald. "Use Men Language." BIM, v. 15, no. 57, March 1974, pp. 69-76.

   Munro, Ian, and Reinhard Sander, eds. "Interview with

James, C. L. R.

C. L. R. James." KAS-KAS: INTERVIEWS WITH THREE CARIBBEAN
WRITERS IN TEXAS. Austin, Texas: African and
Afro-American Research Institute, 1972, pp. 43-55.

Rawlins, Randolph. "Migrants with Manuscripts, Social Background of the West Indian Novel." BLACK ORPHEUS, no. 4,
1958, pp. 46-50.

Roberts, W. Adolphe. "Caribbean Literature: The British
Possessions." WIR, v. 4, no. 42, April 25, 1953, pp. 16-
17.

Wickham, John. "West Indian Writing." BIM, v. 13, no. 50,
January-June 1970, pp. 68-80.

MINTY ALLEY (1936)

Anon. Review. TLS. no. 1813, October 31, 1936, p. 884.

Anon. "Trinidadian Literature Today and Yesterday." SUNDAY
GLEANER, October 17, 1971, p. 31.

Hodge, Merle. "Peeping Tom in the Nigger Yard." TAPIA, no.
25, April 2, 1972, pp. 11-12.

Wickham, John. Review. BIM, v. 14, no. 54, January-June
1972, pp. 111-113.

BEYOND A BOUNDARY (1963)

Anon. Review. TLS, no. 3199, June 21, 1963, p. 459.

Carr, Bill. "C. L. R. James' New Book." PUBLIC OPINION,
November 16, 1963, p. 16.

Carr, Bill. Review. PUBLIC OPINION, April 3, 1964, pp. 8-9.

Ross, Alan. "A Broad View of Cricket." LSO, June 2, 1963,
p. 19.

JERRY, BONGO. Jamaica,

General

Brathwaite, Edward. "The African Presence in Caribbean
Literature." DAEDALUS, v. 103, no. 2, Spring 1974, pp.
73-109.

Moore, Gerald. "Use Men Language." BIM, v. 15, no. 57, March 1974, pp. 69-76.

Rohlehr, F. Gordon. "Afterthoughts." TAPIA, no. 23, December 1971, pp. 8 and 13. Also appears in BIM, v. 14, no. 56, January-June 1973, pp. 227-230.

Rohlehr, F. Gordon. "The Carrion Time." TAPIA, v. 4, no. 24, June 1974, pp. 5-8, 11. Also appears in BIM, v. 15, no. 58, June 1975, pp. 92-109.

Rohlehr, F. Gordon. "West Indian Poetry: Some Problems of Assessment." TAPIA, no. 20, August 1971, pp. 11-14. Also appears in BIM, part 1, v. 14, no. 54, January-June 1972, pp. 80-88; part 2, v. 14, no. 55, July-December 1972, pp. 134-144 and under title "Some Problems of Assessment: A Look at New Expressions in the Arts of the Contemporary Caribbean." CARIBBEAN QUARTERLY, v. 17, nos. 3 and 4, September-December 1971, pp. 92-113.

JOHN, FRANK. Trinidad, 1941-

BLACK SONGS (1970)

Anon. Review. SUNDAY GLEANER, September 20, 1970, p. 29.

JOHNSON, LINTON KWESI. Jamaica, 1952-

DREAD BEAT AND BLOOD (1976)

Anon. Review. SUNDAY GLEANER, January 18, 1976, p. 8.

JONES, MARION PATRICK. Trinidad,

PAN BEAT (1973)

King, Lloyd. "A Call to Two Different Worlds." TAPIA, v. 3, no. 20, May 20, 1973, p. 4.

C. L. [Cedric Lindo]. "Readable Slice of Trinidadian Life." SUNDAY GLEANER, April 8, 1973, p. 35.

Other Works

J'OUVERT MORNING (1976)

KEANE, E. McG. St. Vincent, 1927-

Kempadoo, Peter

L'OUBLI   (1950)

  Anon. Review. CARIBBEAN QUARTERLY, v. 2, no. 1, April 1950,
    p. 46.

  Anon. Review. KYK-OVER-AL, v. 3, no. 11, October 1950, pp.
    74-77.

  Williams, Daniel. Review. BIM, v. 4, no. 13, 1950, pp. 69-
    71

KEMPADOO, PETER. See LAUCHMONEN

KENT, LENA (pseud. Lettice Ada King). Jamaica.

  General

  Mais, Roger. "Contemporary Jamaican Verse." PUBLIC OPINION,
    November 4, 1939, p. 10.

  Oakley, Leo. "Ideas of Patriotism and National Dignity in
    Some Jamaican Writings." JAMAICA JOURNAL, v. 4, no. 3,
    September 1970, pp. 16-21.

KHAN, ISMITH. Trinidad, 1925-

  General

  Brown, Lloyd W. "The Calypso Tradition in West Indian Litera-
    ture." BAR, v. 2, nos. 1 and 2, 1971, pp. 127-143.

  Davies, Barrie. "The Personal Sense of a Society--Minority
    View: Aspects of the 'East Indian' Novel in the West
    Indies." SIN, v. 4, no. 2, Summer 1972, pp. 284-295.

  Lacovia, R. M. "Ismith Khan and the Theory of Rasa." BLACK
    IMAGES, v. 1, nos. 3 and 4, Autumn-Winter 1972, pp. 23-27.

  Ramchand, Kenneth. "Obeah and the Supernatural in West
    Indian Literature." JAMAICA JOURNAL, v. 3, no. 2, June
    1969, pp. 52-54.

THE JUMBIE BIRD   (1961)

  Thompson, Ivy. "Who's Who in the West Indian Novel."
    CARIBBEAN CONTACT, v. 1, no. 5, April 1973, pp. 4, 18.

Walcott, Derek. "Third Trinidadian Novelist Makes His Bow." SUNDAY GUARDIAN (Trinidad), October 22, 1961, p. 5.

THE OBEAH MAN (1964)

Anon. Review. TLS, no. 3268, October 15, 1964, p. 933.

Blundell, M. S. Review. CARIBBEAN QUARTERLY, v. 11, nos. 1 and 2, March and June 1965, pp. 95-97.

Panton, George. "Bacchanal and Cane." SUNDAY GLEANER, November 1, 1964, p. 4.

LADOO, HAROLD SONNY. Trinidad, 1945-1973

General

Early, L. R. "The Two Novels of Harold Ladoo." WLWE, v. 15, April 1976, pp. 174-184.

Questel, Victor. "Their Tragic Destiny." TAPIA, v. 6, no. 20, May 16, 1976, pp. 4, 11.

NO PAIN LIKE THIS BODY (1972)

Espinet, Emile. Review. BLACK IMAGES, v. 2, no. 1, Spring 1973, pp. 60-62.

Questel, Victor. Review. KAIRI, no. 1, 1974, p. 8.

Questel, Victor. "Suffering, Madness or an Early Death." TAPIA, v. 4, no. 17, April 1974, pp. 5, 11.

YESTERDAYS (1974)

Laird, Christopher. "The Novel of Tomorrow, Today." KAIRI, no. 1, 1975, p. 12.

Such, Peter. Review. TAMARACK REVIEW, no. 63, 1974, pp. 78-80.

LAMMING, GEORGE. Barbados, 1927-

General

Aarons, R. L. C. "George Lamming--Novelist as Exile." SUNDAY GLEANER, part 1, February 8, 1976, pp. 23-31; part

Lamming, George

2, February 15, 1976, p. 8.

Anon. "The Caribbean Mixture, Variations and Fusions in Race and Style." TLS, no. 3154, August 10, 1962, p. 578.

Anon. "Caribbean Voices." TLS, no. 2788, August 5, 1955, pp. 16-17.

Anthony, Michael. "Lamming Sees TV in Caribbean as De-humanizing Innovation" (interview), SUNDAY GUARDIAN (Trinidad), August 16, 1970, pp. 1, 16.

Brathwaite, Edward. "Jazz and the West Indian Novel, Part 2." BIM, v. 12, no. 45, July-December 1967, pp. 39-51.

Brathwaite, Edward. "The New West Indian Novelist, Part 2." BIM, v. 8, no. 32, January-June 1961, pp. 271-274.

Brathwaite, Edward. "Roots." BIM, v. 10, no. 37, July-December 1963, pp. 10-21.

Brathwaite, Edward. "Sir Galahad and the Islands." BIM, v. 7, no. 25, July-December 1957, pp. 8-16. Also appears, with additional concluding note, under the same title in IOUANALOA, RECENT WRITING FROM ST. LUCIA. Castries, St. Lucia: Department of Extra Mural Studies, 1963.

Brathwaite, Edward. "Timehri." SAVACOU, no. 2, September 1970, pp. 35-44. Also appears in IS MASSA DAY DEAD? New York: Doubleday, 1974, pp. 29-44.

Brathwaite, Edward. "West Indian Prose Fiction in the Sixties, A Survey." CRITICAL SURVEY, v. 3, Winter 1967, pp. 169-174. Also appears in BIM, v. 12, no. 47, July-December 1968, pp. 157-165; SUNDAY GLEANER, part 1, March 8, 1970, p. 27; part 2, March 15, 1970, p. 27; part 3, March 22, 1970, p. 27; part 4, March 29, 1970, p. 27; BLACK WORLD, v. 20, no. 11, September 1971, pp. 14-29.

Brown, Lloyd W. "The American Image in British West Indian Literature." CARIBBEAN STUDIES, v. 11, no. 1, April 1971, pp. 30-45.

Brown, Lloyd W. "The Calypso Tradition in West Indian Literature." BAR, v. 2, nos. 1 and 2, 1971, pp. 127-143.

Brown, Lloyd W. "The Crisis of Black Identity in the West

Lamming, George

Indian Novel." CRITIQUE, v. 11, no. 3, 1969, pp. 97-112.

Brown, Wayne. "The First Generation of West Indian
   Novelists." SUNDAY GUARDIAN (Trinidad), June 7, 1970, pp.
   6, 11.

Brown, Wayne. "On Art, Artists, and the People." SUNDAY
   GUARDIAN (Trinidad), August 9, 1970, p. 10.

Brown, Wayne. "On Exile and the Dialect of the Tribe."
   SUNDAY GUARDIAN (Trinidad), November 8, 1970, p. 19.

Brown, Wayne. "The Possibilities for West Indian Writing."
   SUNDAY GUARDIAN (Trinidad), November 22, 1970, p. 21.

Carr, Bill. "Reflections on the Novel in the British
   Caribbean." QUEENS QUARTERLY, v. 70, Winter 1963, pp.
   585-597.

Carr, Bill. "The West Indian Novelist: Prelude and Context." CARIBBEAN QUARTERLY, March and June 1965, v.11,
   nos. 1 and 2, pp. 71-84.

Cartey, Wilfred. "Lamming and the Search for Freedom." NWQ,
   Barbados Independence Issue, v. 3, nos. 1 and 2, Dead
   Season 1966-Croptime 1967, pp. 121-128.

Clarke, Austin. "Some Speculations as to the Absence of
   Racialistic Vindictiveness in West Indian Literature."
   THE BLACK WRITER IN AFRICA AND THE AMERICAS. Los Angeles:
   Hennessey and Ingalls, 1973, pp. 165-194.

Dathorne, O. R. "Africa in the Literature of the West
   Indies." JCL, no. 1, September 1965, pp. 95-116.

Dathorne, O. R. "Africa in West Indian Literature." BLACK
   ORPHEUS, no. 16, October 1964, pp. 42-53. Also under
   title "The Theme of Africa in West Indian Literature."
   PHYLON, v. 26, Fall 1965, pp. 255-276.

Dawes, Neville. "Thoughts on West Indian Poetry." PUBLIC
   OPINION, January 3, 1953, p. 5.

Derrick, Anthony. "An Introduction to Caribbean Literature."
   CARIBBEAN QUARTERLY, v. 15, nos. 2 and 3, June-September
   1969, pp. 65-78.

West Indian Literature

Lamming, George

Diaz, Arturo Maldonaldo. "Place and Nature in George
Lamming's Poetry." RRI, v. 4, no. 3, Fall 1974, pp. 402-
410.

Drayton, Arthur D. "The European Factor in West Indian
Literature." LITERARY HALF-YEARLY, v. 11, no. 1, 1970,
pp. 71-94.

Fuller, Roy. "Caribbean Poetry." SUNDAY GLEANER, June 13,
1948, p. 9.

Gunter, Helmut. "George Lamming." BLACK ORPHEUS, no. 6,
November 1959, pp. 39-43.

Hall, Stuart M. "Lamming, Selvon and Some Trends in the
West Indian Novel." BIM, v. 6, no. 23, December 1955,
pp. 172-178.

Hamilton, Bruce. "New World of the Caribbean." BIM, v. 7,
no. 25, July-December 1957, pp. 53-55.

James, C. L. R. "Home Is Where They Want to Be." TGM,
February 14, 1965, pp. 4-5.

James, Louis. "The Sad Initiation of Lamming's 'G.'"
COMMON WEALTH: PAPERS DELIVERED AT THE CONFERENCE OF
COMMONWEALTH LITERATURE AT AARHUS UNIVERSITY, April 26-
30, 1971. Aarhus, Denmark: Aarhus University, 1971.

Keane, E. McG. "Some Religious Attitudes in West Indian
Poetry." BIM, part 1, v. 4, no. 15, December 1951, pp.
169-174; part 2, v. 4, no. 16, June 1952, pp. 266-271.

Kemoli, Arthur. "The Theme of 'The Past' in Caribbean
Literature." WLWE, v. 12, November 1973, pp. 304-325.

Lacovia, R. M. "Caribbean Literature in English." BAR,
v. 2, nos. 1 and 2, 1971, pp. 109-125.

Marr, N. J. "West Indian Literary Giants." SUNDAY
GLEANER, January 23, 1955, p.6.

Maxwell, Marina. "Towards a Revolution in the Arts."
SAVACOU, no. 2, September 1970, pp. 19-32.

Mohr, Eugene V. "West Indian Fiction Is Alive and Well."
CARIBBEAN REVIEW, v. 5, no. 4, 1973, pp. 23-29.

Lamming, George

Morris, Mervyn. "George Lamming, Author." PUBLIC OPINION, March 10, 1967, p. 7.

Morris, Mervyn. "The Poet as Novelist, The Novels of George Lamming." THE ISLANDS IN BETWEEN. London: Oxford University Press, 1968.

Munroe, Ian, and Reinhard Sander. "The Making of a Writer; A Conversation with the West Indian Writer George Lamming at the University of Texas, November 29, 1970." CARIBBEAN QUARTERLY, v. 17, nos. 3 and 4, September-December 1971, pp. 72-82.

Munroe, Ian, and Reinhard Sander, eds. "Interview with George Laminng." KAS-KAS; INTERVIEWS WITH THREE CARIBBEAN WRITERS IN TEXAS. Texas: African and Afro-American Research Institute, 1972, pp. 43-55.

Munroe, Ian; Sander, Reinhard; and Dean Beebe. "Writing and Publishing in the West Indies; An Interview with George Lamming." WLWE, no. 19, April 1971, pp. 17-22.

Page, Malcolm. "West Indian Writers." NOVEL, v. 3, no. 2, Winter 1970, pp. 167-172.

Pearse, Andrew C. "West Indian Themes." CARIBBEAN QUARTERLY, v. 2, no. 2, September 1951, pp. 12-23.

Questel, Victor. "Their Tragic Destiny." TAPIA, v. 6, no. 20, May 16, 1976, pp. 4, 11.

Ramchand, Kenneth. "Dialect in West Indian Fiction." CARIBBEAN QUARTERLY, v. 14, nos. 1 and 2, March-June 1968, pp. 27-42. Also appears in his THE WEST INDIAN NOVEL AND ITS BACKGROUND. London: Faber and Faber, 1970, pp. 96-116.

Ramchand, Kenneth. "History and the Novel: A Literary Critic's Approach." SAVACOU, v. 1, no. 5, June 1971, pp. 103-113.

Rawlins, Randolph. "Migrants with Manuscripts; Social Background of the West Indian Novel." BLACK ORPHEUS, no. 4, 1958, pp. 46-50.

Rohlehr, F. Gordon. "Afterthoughts." TAPIA, no. 23, December 26, 1971, pp. 8, 13. Also appears in BIM, v. 14,

Lamming, George

no. 56, January-June 1973, pp. 227-230.

Rohlehr, F. Gordon. "The Creative Writer and West Indian Society." KAIE, no. 11, August 1973, pp. 48-77. Also appears in TAPIA, part 1, v. 4, no. 31, August 1974, pp. 5-9; part 2, v. 4, no. 32, August 1974, pp. 6-7; part 3, v. 4, no. 33, August 1974, pp. 4-6; part 4, no. 35, August 1974, pp. 4-5,7.

Rohlehr, F. Gordon. "The Folk in Caribbean Literature, Part 1." TAPIA, v. 2, no. 11, December 17, 1972, pp. 7-8, 13-15.

Rohlehr, F. Gordon. "West Indian Poetry: Some Problems of Assessment." TAPIA, no. 20, August 1971, pp. 11-14; Also appears in BIM, part 1, v. 14, no. 54, January-June 1972, pp. 80-88; part 2, v. 14, no. 55, July-December 1972, pp. 134-144; and under title "Some Problems of Assessment: A Look at New Expression in the Arts of the Contemporary Caribbean." CARIBBEAN QUARTERLY, v. 17, nos. 3 and 4, 1971, pp. 92-113.

Seymour, A. J. "The Novel in the British Caribbean, Part 3." BIM, v. 11, no. 44, January-July 1967, pp. 238-242.

Swanzy, Henry. "Caribbean Voices, Prolegomena to a West Indian Culture." CARIBBEAN QUARTERLY, v. 1, no. 2, September 1962, pp. 21-28. Also appears in CARIBBEAN QUARTERLY, v. 8, no. 2, 1962, pp. 121-128.

Walcott, Derek. "Neo-realism Parallel Noted in West Indian Novels." SUNDAY GUARDIAN (Trinidad), April 24, 1960, p. 7.

Wickham, John. "West Indian Writing." BIM, v. 13, no. 50, January-June 1970, pp. 68-80.

Wyndham, Francis. "The New West Indian Writers." BIM, v. 7, no. 28, January-June 1959, pp. 188-190.

Wynter, Sylvia. "Strangers at the Gate, Caribbean Novelists in Search of Identity." SUNDAY GLEANER, January 18, 1959, p. 14.

Wynter, Sylvia. "We Must Learn to Sit Down Together and Talk About a Little Culture; Reflections on West Indian Writing and Criticism." JAMAICA JOURNAL, part 1, v. 2,

no. 4, December 1968, pp. 23-32; part 2, v. 3, no. 1,
March 1969, pp. 27-42.

Yarde, Gloria. "George Lamming--The Historical Imagination."
LITERARY HALF-YEARLY, v. 11, no. 2, 1970, pp. 35-45.

IN THE CASTLE OF MY SKIN (1953)

Anon. "Character and Customs." THE TIMES (london), March
21, 1953, p. 9.

Anon. "Youth In Barbados." TLS, March 27, 1953, p. 206.

Chandler, G. Lewis. "At the Edge of Two Worlds." PHYLON,
v. 14, 1953, pp. 437-439.

Charques, R. D. Review. SPECTATOR, v. 190, March 20, 1953,
p. 354.

Coddling, Eric. "West Indian Accent." PUBLIC OPINION, May
23, 1953, p. 5.

Escoffery, Gloria. Review. BIM, v. 5, no. 18, 1953, pp.
153-155.

Paul, David. Review. LSO, March 15, 1953, p. 9.

Prescott, Orville. Review. NYT, October 27, 1953, p. 25.

Pritchett, V. S. "A Barbados Village." NEW STATESMAN, v.
45, April 18, 1953.

Swan, Michael. Review. LONDON MAGAZINE, v. 1, no. 6, July
1954, pp. 92-98.

Sylvester, Harry. "Changing Landscape in Barbados." NYT,
Section 7, November 1, 1953, p. 4.

Thompson, Ivy. "Who's Who in the West Indian Novel."
CARIBBEAN CONTACT, v. 1, no. 5, April 1973, pp. 4, 18.

THE EMIGRANTS (1954)

Anon. "Not Enough Is Up to Standard." PUBLIC OPINION,
November 20, 1954, p. 6.

Anon. Review. BAJAN, v. 2, no. 9, May 1955, p. 28.

Lamming, George

Anon. Review. TLS, no. 2749, October 8, 1954, p. 637.

Coulthard, G. R. "The West Indian Novel of Immigration." PHYLON, v. 20, 1959, pp. 32-41.

Jennings, Elizabeth. "The Better Break." SPECTATOR, v. 193, October 1, 1954, pp. 411-412.

Muir, Edwin. "Indirections." LSO, September 19, 1954, p. 13.

Ramchand, Kenneth. "Decolonization in West Indian Literature." TRANSITION, v. 5, no. 22, pp. 48-49.

Rodman, Selden. "Fugitives from the Sun." NYT, Section 7, July 24, 1955, p. 16.

St. John, Bruce. Review. BIM, v. 6, no. 22, June 1955, pp. 130-132.

Stern, James. Review. LONDON MAGAZINE, v. 2, no. 5, May 1955, pp. 109-110.

OF AGE AND INNOCENCE (1958)

Anon. "Alas: There's No Story." SUNDAY GUARDIAN (Trinidad), January 11, 1959, p. 22.

Anon. Review. BAJAN, v. 7, no. 1, September 1959, pp. 16-17.

Anon. Review. THE TIMES (London), November 13, 1958, p. 15.

Anon. Review. TLS, no. 2960, November 21, 1958, p. 669.

Martin M. Combe. Review. BIM, v. 8, no. 29, June-December 1959, pp. 62-64.

Naipaul, V. S. Review. NEW STATESMAN, v. 56, December 6, 1958, pp. 826-827.

Nicholson, Geoffrey. Review. SPECTATOR. v. 201, November 14, 1958, p. 658.

Panton, George. "The New and Difficult Lamming." SUNDAY GLEANER, December 21, 1958, p. 14.

Lamming, George

Paul, David. "Two West Indians." PUBLIC OPINION, January 3, 1959, p. 7.

Red, Goronwy. Review. LISTENER, v. 60, December 18, 1958, p. 1046.

Seymour, A. J. Review. KYK-OVER-AL, v. 9, no. 26, December 1959, pp. 52-55.

THE PLEASURES OF EXILE (1960)

Anon. "A Place in the Sun." THE TIMES (London), July 28, 1960, p. 13.

Anon. Review. BAJAN, v. 8, no. 1, September 1960, p. 23.

Anon. Review. TLS, no. 3048, July 29, 1960, p. 475.

Carr, Bill. "Lamming to Little Purpose." PUBLIC OPINION, April 10, 1964, pp. 8-9.

Marshall, Harold. Review. BIM, v. 8, no. 32, January-June 1961, pp. 289-290.

Panton, George. "Angry Young West Indian." SUNDAY GLEANER, February 19, 1961, p. 14.

Pollins, Harold. Review. RACE, v. 2, no. 1, November 1960, pp. 78-79.

Pritchett, V. S. "The Heritage and Decline of Prospero." NEW STATESMAN, v. 60, July 30, 1960.

Walcott, Derek. "Author's Exile Bewilders." SUNDAY GUARDIAN, (Trinidad), September 4, 1960, p. 4.

Wilson, Angus. Review. LSO, August 28, 1960, p. 26.

Wyndham, Francis. "Emergent Novelists." SPECTATOR, v. 205, July 22, 1960.

SEASON OF ADVENTURE (1960)

Anon. Review. THE TIMES (London), October 27, 1960, p. 15.

Anon. Review. TLS, no. 3064, November 11, 1960, p. 721.

Lamming, George

Bermange, Barry. Review. JLW, v. 3, October 1960, p. 526.

Brathwaite, Edward. "The African Presence in Caribbean Literature." DAEDALUS, v. 103, no. 2, Spring 1974, pp. 73-109.

Grigson, Geoffrey. Review. SPECTATOR, v. 205, October 28, 1960, p. 664.

Lamming, George. "The West Indian People." NWQ, v. 2, no. 2, Croptime 1966, pp. 53-74.

Munroe, Ian. "George Lamming's SEASON OF ADVENTURE, The Failure of the Creative Imagination." SBL, v. 4, no. 1, Spring 1973. pp. 6-13.

Panton, George. "Social Problems of Independence." SUNDAY GLEANER, November 5, 1961, p. 14.

Ramchand, Kenneth. "The Artist in the Balm-Yard: SEASON OF ADVENTURE." NWQ, v. 5, nos. 1-2, Dead Season/Croptime, 1969, pp. 13-21.

Scott, Paul. Review. NEW STATESMAN, v. 60, October 29, 1960, pp. 664-666.

Wickham, John. "Lamming's Poetic Touch in His SEASON OF ADVENTURE." SUNDAY GUARDIAN (Trinidad), December 11, 1960, p. 36.

Wickham, John. Review. BIM, v. 9, no. 33, July-December 1961, pp. 69-72.

Wyndham, Francis. Review. LSO, October 23, 1960, p. 22.

WATER WITH BERRIES (1971)

Anon. "Another Lamming--Involuted and Mysterious." SUNDAY GLEANER, March 26, 1972, p. 37.

Anon. Review. THE TIMES (London), March 2, 1972, p. 12.

Anon. Review. TLS, no. 3650, February 11, 1972, p. 145.

Boxill, Anthony. "San Cristobal Unreached: George Lamming's Two Latest Novels." WLWE, v. 12, April 1973, pp. 111-116.

Index of Authors

LaRose, Anthony John

Clasp, Bertram. "Into the Realm of Fantasy." SUNDAY
GUARDIAN (Trinidad), March 26, 1972, p. 7.

Kent, George E. "Conversation with George Lamming." BLACK
WORLD, v. 22, no. 5, March 1973, pp. 4-15.

Questel, Victor. "Caliban's Circle of Death." TAPIA, v. 2,
no. 11, December 1972, p. 15.

St. Hill, Chalmer. Review. BIM, v. 14, no. 55, July-
December 1972, pp. 189-191.

NATIVES OF MY PERSON (1972)

Anon. "Lamming's Latest Book: Brooding and Mysterious."
SUNDAY GLEANER, February 20, 1972, p. 35.

Anon. "Symbols Ahoy." TLS, no. 3693, December 15, 1972,
p. 1521.

Craig, Susan. "A Ruthless/Rootless Enterprise; Notes and
Impressions on Reading George Lamming's NATIVES OF MY
PERSONS." KAIRI, 1976, pp. 8-9.

Edwards, Thomas R. Review. NYRB, v. 18, no. 4, 1972.

Hairston, Loyle. Review. FREEDOMWAYS, v. 12, 1st quarter
1972, pp. 68-70.

Johnson, B. S. Review. NEW STATESMAN, v. 84, December 1,
1972, p. 832.

Kent, George E. "Conversation with George Lamming." BLACK
WORLD, v. 22, no. 5, March 1973, pp. 4-15, 88-97.

Thwaite, Anthony. Review. LSO, October 8, 1972, p. 39.

CANNON SHOT AND GLASS BEADS (edited by George Lamming, 1975)

D'Costa, Jean. Review. JAMAICA JOURNAL, v. 9, no. 1, March
1975, pp. 38-39.

LA ROSE, ANTHONY JOHN. Trinidad, 1927-

FOUNDATIONS: A BOOK OF POEMS (1966)

Figueroa, Peter. Review. BIM, v. 12, no. 48, January-June

75

Lashley, Cliff

      1969, pp. 270-271.

    Foakes, R. A. "Caribbean Poetry." JCL, no. 6, January 1969, pp. 147-150.

    Walcott, Derek. "Fellowships." TGM, January 15, 1967, pp. 8-9.

LASHLEY, CLIFF. Jamaica, 1935-

  General

    Drayton, Arthur D. "Poetry of Cultural Precariousness, Introducing Cliff Lashley: A New Caribbean Voice." BLACK ORPHEUS, no. 22, August 1967, pp. 49-53.

LAUCHMONEN (pseud. PETER KEMPADOO). Guyana, 1926-

  General

    Seymour, A. J. "The Novel in Guyana." KAIE, no. 4, July 1967, pp. 59-63.

    Sparer, Joyce L. "Attitudes Towards 'Race' in Guyanese Literature." CARIBBEAN STUDIES, v. 8, no. 2, July 1968, pp. 46-47.

GUIANA BOY (1960)

    Altman, Wilfred. Review. JLW, v. 3, October 1960, p. 463.

    Dathorne, O. R. Review. BLACK ORPHEUS, no. 10, 1961, pp. 70-71.

    Ferguson, J. "Land of Sugar." LSO, January 8, 1961, p. 23.

    Panton, George. Review. SUNDAY GLEANER, December 4, 1960, p. 18.

    Scott, Paul. Review. NEW STATESMAN, v. 60, October 29, 1960, p. 666.

    Walcott, Derek. Review. SUNDAY GUARDIAN (Trinidad), October 2, 1960, p. 5.

OLD THOM'S HARVEST (1965)

Anon. Review. BAJAN, v. 13, no. 1, September 1965, p. 28.

Anon. Review. THE TIMES (London), July 1, 1965, p. 15.

McDonald, Ian. Review. NWF, v. 1, no. 21, August 20, 1965, pp. 25-27.

Walcott, Derek. "Rice Is Bitter." SUNDAY GUARDIAN (Trinidad), July 11, 1965, p. 8.

LAWRENCE, WALTER MACARTHUR. Guyana, 1896-

General

Cameron, Norman E. "Walter MacA. Lawrence." KYK-OVER-AL, v. 1, no. 2, June 1946, p. 17.

Daly, P. H. "Walter MacArthur Lawrence." KYK-OVER-AL, v. 1, no. 2, June 1946, pp. 18, 25.

Seymour, A. J. "The Literary Adventure of the West Indies." KYK-OVER-AL, v. 2, no. 10, April 1950, 40 pp.

Seymour, A. J. "The Poet of Guiana, Walter MacA. Lawrence." KYK-OVER-AL, v. 2, no. 9, December 1949, pp. 20-21.

Seymour, A. J. "The Poetry of Walter MacA. Lawrence." KYK-OVER-AL, v. 2, no. 6, June 1948, pp. 35-38.

LEE, ROBERT. St. Lucia,

FOUNDATION (1974)

Pantin, Raoul. "Writings of Two Young Poets." CARIBBEAN CONTACT, v. 3, no. 3, June 1975, p. 3.

Questel, Victor. "New Writings in the Caribbean." TAPIA, v. 6, no. 36, September 5, 1976, pp. 5-7.

LINDO, ARCHIE. Jamaica, 1905-

General

Mais, Roger. "Contemporary Jamaican Verse." PUBLIC OPINION, November 4, 1939, p. 10.

LOVELACE, EARL. Trinidad, 1935-

Lovelace, Earl

Brathwaite, Edward. "Jazz and the West Indian Novel." BIM,
part 1, v. 11, no. 44, January-June 1967, pp. 275-284;
part 2, v. 12, no. 45, July-December 1967, pp. 39-51; part
3, v. 12, no. 46, January-June 1968, pp. 115-126.

Brown, Wayne. "On Art, Artists and the People." SUNDAY
GUARDIAN (Trinidad), August 9, 1970, p. 10.

James, C. L. R. "Discovering Literature in Trinidad: The
Nineteen Thirties." JCL, no. 7, July 1969, pp. 73-80.
Also appears in SAVACOU, no. 2, September 1970, pp. 54-
60.

Pyne-Timothy, Helen. "Earl Lovelace: His View of Trinidad
Society in WHILE GODS ARE FALLING and THE SCHOOLMASTER.
NWQ, v. 4, no. 4, Cropover 1968, pp. 60-65.

Questel, Victor. "Views of West Indian Writer, Earl Lovelace". (interview). CARIBBEAN CONTACT, v. 5, no. 3, June
1977, pp. 15-16.

WHILE GODS ARE FALLING (1964)

Anon. Review. BAJAN, no 154, June 1966, p. 31.

Panton, George. "West Indies from Within and Without."
SUNDAY GLEANER, September 5, 1965, p. 4.

Roach, Eric. "Shy, Young and Unknown." SUNDAY GUARDIAN
(Trinidad), July 26, 1964, p. 6.

THE SCHOOLMASTER (1968)

Anon. Review. LSO, January 14, 1968, p. 31.

Anon. "School for Scandal." TLS, no. 3436, January 4, 1968,
p. 29.

Brathwaite, Edward. "Priest and Peasant." JCL, no. 7,
July 1969, pp. 117-122.

Brathwaite, Edward. Review. BIM, v. 12, no. 48, January-
June 1969, pp. 273-277.

Byatt, A. S. Review. NEW STATESMAN, v. 75, January 5, 1968,
p. 15.

Index of Authors

Lucie-Smith, Edward

Igoe, W. I. "Revelations." THE TIMES (London), February 3,
1968, p. 20.

Panton, George. "Slice of Trinidadian Rural Life." SUNDAY
GLEANER, April 14, 1967, p. 4.

LUCIE-SMITH, EDWARD. Jamaica, 1933-

General

Chapman, Esther. "The Poems of Edward Lucie-Smith." WIR,
v. 2, no. 3, Autumn 1964, p. 31.

Ewart, Gavin. Review of Poetry. LONDON MAGAZINE, New
Series, v. 8, no. 11, 1968, p. 85.

Hamilton, Ian. "Poetry." LONDON MAGAZINE, New Series, v. 4,
no. 9, December 1964, pp. 80-81.

Lucie-Smith, Edward. "A West Indian Childhood." WIR, v. 3,
no. 5, May 1958, pp. 38-40.

A TROPICAL CHILDHOOD (1961)

Anon. Review. NEW STATESMAN, v. 62, September 29, 1961,
p. 435.

Macbeth, George. Review. LONDON MAGAZINE, New Series, v. 1,
no. 9, December 1961, pp. 93-94.

Panton, George. "Modern Jamaican Poetry." SUNDAY GLEANER,
February 3, 1963, p. 14.

Skelton, Robin. Review. CRITICAL QUARTERLY, v. 3, Winter
1961, pp. 376-377.

Thwaite, Anthony. Review. SPECTATOR, v. 207, November 3,
1961, p. 634.

CONFESSIONS AND HISTORIES (1964)

Alvarez, A. Review. LSO, November 8, 1964, p. 27.

Anon. Review. THE TIMES (London), November 19, 1964, p. 17.

Anon. Review. TLS, no. 3271, November 5, 1964, p. 1000.

McDermot, T. H.

    Horder, John. Review. SPECTATOR, v. 213, October 30, 1964,
       p. 480.

    Panton, George. "A Jamaican Childhood." SUNDAY GLEANER,
       November 15, 1964, p. 4.

   TOWARDS SILENCE (1968)

    Anon. Review. SPECTATOR, v. 221, no. 7317, 1968, p. 397.

    Anon. Review. TLS, no. 3484, December 5, 1968.

    Brownjohn, Alan. Review. NEW STATESMAN, v. 76, September
       20, 1968, p. 363.

    Hamilton, Ian. Review. LSO, November 17, 1968, p. 28.

  Other Works

  BORROWED EMBLEMS (1967)

  THE LIVERPOOL SCENE (1968)

  SNOW POEM (1968)

  EGYPTIAN ODE (1969)

MACDERMOT, T. H. See REDCAM, TOM

MCDONALD, IAN. Trinidad, 1933-

  THE HUMMING-BIRD TREE (1969)

    Anon. "Mixed Company." TLS, no. 3497, March 6, 1969, p.
       225.

    Clasp, Bertrand. "With Fresh Light on Nature of Our Society
       Society." TGM, May 25, 1969, p. 3.

    Panton, George. Review. SUNDAY GLEANER, February 23, 1969,
       p. 4.

    Rohlehr, F. Gordon. "In Search of Innocence; An Introduction
       to Ian McDonald's THE HUMMING-BIRD TREE. TAPIA, part 1,
       v. 4, no. 49, December 1974, pp. 5, 8; part 2, v. 4,
       no. 50, January 1975, pp. 6-7; part 3, v. 4, no. 51,
       February 1975, pp. 4, 9.

McFarlane, John Ebenezer Clare

Wickham, John. Review. BIM, v. 13, no. 49, July-December
1969, pp. 61-63.

MCFARLANE, BASIL, Jamaica, 1922-

General

Anon. "The Miniature Poets." KYK-OVER-AL, v. 5, no. 15,
Year-end 1952, pp. 84-86.

Carew, Jan. "British West Indian Poets and Their Culture."
PHYLON, v. 14, 1953, pp. 71-73.

Oakley, Leo. "Ideas of Patriotism and National Dignity in
Some Jamaican Writings." JAMAICA JOURNAL, v. 4, no. 3,
September 1970, pp. 16-21. Also appears in SUNDAY
GLEANER (Jamaica), part 1, March 28, 1970, pp. 31, 34;
part 2, April 4, 1970, p. 27; part 3, April 11, 1970,
p. 25 as "Patriotism, National Dignity in Jamaican
Writings."

Walcott, Derek. "A New Poet, Jamaican." SUNDAY GUARDIAN
(Trinidad), June 20, 1965, p. 6.

Walcott, Derek. "Some Jamaican Poets." PUBLIC OPINION,
part 1, August 3, 1957, p. 7; part 2, August 10, 1957,
p. 7.

JACOB AND THE ANGEL (1952)

Mais, Roger. "The Poetry of McFarlane." PUBLIC OPINION,
June 28, 1952, p. 5.

SEVEN JAMAICAN POETS (edited by Mervyn Morris, 1971)

C. L. [Cedric Lindo]. "Worthy Examples of Our Poetry."
SUNDAY GLEANER, May 23, 1971, p. 29.

MCFARLANE, JOHN EBENEZER CLARE. Jamaica, 1894-1962

General

Bennett, Wycliffe. "The Jamaican Poets." LL, v. 57, no.
128, April 1948, pp. 58-61.

Brown, Wayne. "West Indian Poetry of the 1940's; Part
1. . . ." SUNDAY GUARDIAN (Trinidad), September 13, 1970,
p. 9.

McFarlane, John Ebenezer Clare

    Craig, Tom. "John Ebenezer Clare McFarlane." PUBLIC OPINION, June 21, 1940, p. 9.

    Jacobs, H. P. "The Literary Movement." PUBLIC OPINION, March 4, 1939, p. 3.

    James, Louis. "Caribbean Poetry in English--Some Problems." SAVACOU, no. 2, September 1970, pp. 78-86.

    Oakley, Leo. "Ideas of Patriotism and National Dignity in Some Jamaican Writings." JAMAICA JOURNAL, v. 4, no. 3, September 1970, pp. 16-21. Also appears in SUNDAY GLEANER, part 1, March 28, 1970, pp. 31, 34; part 2, April 4, 1970, p. 27; part 3, April 11, 1970, p. 25 as "Patriotism, National Dignity in Jamaican Writings."

    Owens, R. J. "West Indian Poetry." CARIBBEAN QUARTERLY, v. 7, no. 3, December 1961, pp. 120-127.

    Sen, Dilip Kumar. "An Indian Looks at West Indian Poetry: A Footnote to Caribbean Poetry Written in English." SUNDAY GLEANER, January 12, 1964, p. 4.

    Seymour, A. J. "The Literary Adventure of the West Indies." KYK-OVER-AL, v. 2, no. 10, April 1950, entire issue, 40 pp.

    Walcott, Derek. "Some Jamaican Poets." PUBLIC OPINION, part 1, August 3, 1957, p. 7; part 2, August 10, 1957, p. 7.

THE CHALLENGE OF OUR TIME (essays, 1945)

    Seymour, A. J. Review. KYK-OVER-AL, v. 1, no. 1, December 1945, p. 41.

THE MAGDALEN (1958)

    Collymore, Frank. Review. BIM, v. 7, no. 26, January-June 1958, pp. 120-121.

<u>Other Works</u>

DAPHNE: A TALE OF THE HILLS OF ST. ANDREW, JAMAICA (1931)

MACFARLANE, R. L. C. Jamaica, 1925-

McKay, Claude

General

Oakley, Leo. "Ideas of Patriotism and National Dignity in
Some Jamaican Writings." JAMAICA JOURNAL, v. 4, no. 3.
September 1970, pp. 16-21. Also appears in SUNDAY
GLEANER (Jamaica), part 1, March 28, 1970, pp. 31, 34;
part 2, April 4, 1970, p. 27; part 3, April 11, 1970, p.
25 as "Patriotism, National Dignity in Jamaican Writings."

Owens, R. J. "West Indian Poetry." CARIBBEAN QUARTERLY,
v. 7, no. 3, December 1961, pp. 120-127.

MCKAY, CLAUDE. Jamaica, 1889-1948

General

Anon. "Claude McKay--An Appreciation." PUBLIC OPINION, June
5, 1948, p. 3.

Anon. "Claude McKay in Paperback." SUNDAY GLEANER, July 20,
1975, p. 23.

Anon. "Claude McKay: Pioneer, Poet, Novelist et al."
SUNDAY GLEANER, June 28, 1974, p. 28.

Anon. "The First Classic of West Indian Prose." SUNDAY
GLEANER, July 18, 1971, p. 28.

Anon. "Lecture on Claude McKay." SUNDAY GLEANER, October
12, 1969, p. 4.

Asein, S. O. "The 'Protest' Tradition in West Indian
Poetry, from George Campbell to Martin Carter." JAMAICA
JOURNAL, v. 6, no. 2, March 1972, pp. 40-45.

Baugh, Edward. "The Poetry of Claude McKay." PUBLIC OPINION
OPINION, part 1, November 30, 1957, p. 9; part 2,
December 21, 1957, p. 6; part 3, January 18, 1958, p. 7.

Bennett, Wycliffe. "The Jamaican Poets." LL, v. 57, no.
128, April 1948, pp. 58-61.

Brathwaite, Edward. "The African Presence in Caribbean
Literature." DAEDALUS, v. 103, no. 2, Spring 1974, pp.
78-109.

Bronx, Stephen H. ROOTS OF NEGRO RACIAL CONSCIOUSNESS: THE

McKay, Claude

1920's; THREE HARLEM RENAISSANCE AUTHORS. New York:
Libra, 1964.

Brown, Lloyd W. "The American Image in British West Indian
Literature." CARIBBEAN STUDIES, v. 11, no. 1, April
1971, pp. 30-45.

Brown, Wayne. "Poetry of the Forties, Part 3, The Dilemma."
SUNDAY GUARDIAN (Trinidad), October 4, 1970, p. 11.

Cooper, Wayne. "Claude McKay and the New Negro of the 1920's
1920's." PHYLON, v. 25, Fall 1964, pp. 296-306.

Cooper, Wayne F., ed. THE PASSION OF CLAUDE MCKAY: SELECTED
POETRY AND PROSE, 1912-1948. New York: Schocken, 1973.

Cooper, Wayne, and Robert C. Reinders. "A Black Briton
Comes 'Home': Claude McKay in England, 1920." RACE, v.
9, no. 1, July 1967, pp. 67-81.

Cooper, Wayne, and Robert C. Reinders. "Claude McKay in
England, 1920." NEW BEACON REVIEWS, COLLECTION ONE.
London: New Beacon Books, 1968, pp. 3-21.

Coulthard, G. R. "Rejection of European Culture as a Theme
in Caribbean Literature." CARIBBEAN QUARTERLY, v. 5, no.
4, 1959, pp. 231-244.

Daniels, Alan. "Who Is Claude McKay?" PUBLIC OPINION,
January 12, 1963, p. 9.

Dathorne, O. R. "Africa in the Literature of the West
Indies." JCL, no. 1, September 1965, pp. 95-116.

Dathorne, O. R. "Africa in West Indian Literature." BLACK
ORPHEUS, no. 16, October 1964, pp. 42-53. Also appears
as "The Theme of Africa in West Indian Literature."
PHYLON, v. 26, Fall 1965, pp. 255-276.

Derrick, Anthony. "An Introduction to Caribbean Literature."
CARIBBEAN QUARTERLY, v. 5, nos. 1 and 3, June-September
1969, pp. 65-78.

Drayton, Arthur D. "The European Factor in West Indian
Literature." LITERARY HALF-YEARLY, v. 11, no. 1, 1970,
pp. 71-94.

McKay, Claude

Drayton, Arthur D. "McKay's Human Pity: A Note on His
Protest Poetry." BLACK ORPHEUS, no. 17, June 1965, pp.
39-48.

Gayle, Addison, Jr. CLAUDE MCKAY: THE BLACK POET AT WAR.
New York: Broadside Press, n. d.

Jacobs, H. P. "The Literary Movement." PUBLIC OPINION,
March 4, 1939, p. 3.

Kemoli, Arthur. "The Theme of 'The Past' in Caribbean
Literature." WLWE, v. 12, November 1973, pp. 304-325.

Kent, George E. "The Soulful Way of Claude McKay." BLACK
WORLD, v. 20, no. 1, November 1970, pp. 37-51.

Lacovia, R. M. "Caribbean Literature in English." BAR, v.
2, nos. 1 and 2, February 1971, pp. 109-125.

Lacovia, R. M. "English Caribbean Literature: A Brave New
World." BLACK IMAGES, v. 1, no. 1, January 1972, pp.
15-22.

Larson, Charles R. "African-Afro American Literary Relations: Basic Parallels." NEGRO DIGEST, v. 19.

Larson, Charles R. "Three Harlem Novels of the Jazz Age."
CRITIQUE, v. 11, no. 3, 1969, pp. 66-78.

Lindo, Archie. "Claude McKay." SUNDAY GLEANER, part 1,
July 18, 1948, p. 8; part 2, August 1, 1948, p. 8, part
3, August 29, 1948, p. 9.

McFarlane, J. E. G. "His Work Will Live; An Appreciation
of Claude McKay." SUNDAY GLEANER, June 6, 1948, p. 6.

Meikle, Rupert Errington. "Claude McKay--The Forgotten
Jamaican." SUNDAY GLEANER, June 18, 1972, p. 39.

Morris, Mervyn. "Contending Values; The Prose Fiction of
Claude McKay." JAMAICA JOURNAL, v. 9, nos. 2 and 3, 1975,
pp. 36-42, 52.

Priebe, Richard. "The Search for Community in the Novels of
Claude McKay." SBL, v. 3, no. 2, Summer 1972, pp. 22-30.

Roberts, W. Adolphe. "Caribbean Literature: The British

McKay, Claude

      Possessions." WIR, v. 4, no. 42, April 25, 1953, pp. 16-17.

    Sen, Dilip Kumar. "An Indian Looks at West Indian Poetry; A Footnote to Caribbean Poetry Written in English." SUNDAY GLEANER, January 12, 1964, p. 4.

    Smith, Robert A. "Claude McKay: An Essay in Criticism." PHYLON, v. 9, 1948, pp. 270-273.

    Walcott, Derek. "Fellowships." TGM, February 12, 1967, pp. 8-9.

    Wall, Cheryl A. "Paris and Harlem: Two Culture Capitals." PHYLON, v. 35, March 1974, pp. 64-73.

BANJO (1929)

    Kaye, Jacqueline. "Claude McKay's BANJO." PRESENCE AFRICAINE, no. 73, 1970, pp. 165-169.

BANANA BOTTOM (1933)

    Gomes, Albert. "Back to Banana Bottom." BEACON, v. 3, no. 3, October 1933, pp. 58-59.

    Ramchand, Kenneth. "Claude McKay and BANANA BOTTOM." SOUTHERN REVIEW, v. 4, no. 1, 1970, pp. 53-66.

    Ramchand, Kenneth. "Decolonization in West Indian Literature." TRANSITIONS, v. 5, no. 22, 1965, pp. 48-49.

A LONG WAY FROM HOME (1937)

    Chapman, Esther. "Claude McKay's New Book." WIR, v. 3, no. 9, May 1937, p. 23.

SELECTED POEMS OF CLAUDE MCKAY (1953)

    Jackson, Blyden. "The Essential McKay." PHYLON, v. 13, 1953, pp. 216-217.

Other Works

CONSTAB BALLADS (1912)

SONGS OF JAMAICA (1912)

McNeill, Anthony

SPRING IN NEW HAMPSHIRE AND OTHER POEMS (1920)

HARLEM SHADOWS (1922)

HOME TO HARLEM (1928)

GINGERTOWN (1932)

MCNEILL, ANTHONY. Jamaica, 1941-

General

> Mordecai, Martin. "Interview by Martin Mordecai with Anthony McNeill." JAMAICA JOURNAL, v. 4, no. 4, December 1970, pp. 40-43.

> Pennant, Dorothy. "Anthony McNeill, He Writes Poetry of the Mindscape." SUNDAY GLEANER, January 12, 1975, p. 22.

> Questel, Victor. "Their Tragic Destiny." TAPIA, v. 6, no. 20, May 16, 1976, pp. 4, 11.

> Rohlehr, F. Gordon. "Afterthoughts." TAPIA, no. 23, December 26, 1971, pp. 8, 13. Also appears in BIM, v. 14, no. 56, January-June 1973, pp. 227-230.

> Rohlehr, F. Gordon. "A Carrion Time." TAPIA, v. 4, no. 24, June 1974, pp. 5-8, 11. Also appears in BIM, v. 15, no. 58, June 1975, pp. 92-109.

> Rohlehr, F. Gordon. "West Indian Poetry: Some Problems of Assessment." TAPIA, no. 20, August 1971, pp. 11-14. Also appears in BIM, part 1, v. 14, no. 54, January-June 1972, pp. 80-88; part 2, v. 14, no. 55, July-December 1972, pp. 134-144. And under title "Some Problems of Assessment: A Look at New Expressions in the Arts of the Contemporary Caribbean." CARIBBEAN QUARTERLY, v. 17, nos. 3 and 4, 1971, pp. 92-113.

SEVEN JAMAICAN POETS (edited by Mervyn Morris, 1971)

> Forde, A. N. Review. BIM, v. 14, no. 54, January-June 1972, p. 117.

> C. L. [Cedric Lindo]. "Worthy Examples of Our Poetry." SUNDAY GLEANER, May 23, 1971, p. 29.

McTair, Roger

  HELLO UNGOD (1972)

    M. M. [Mervyn Morris]. "An Extreme Vision." SUNDAY
      GLEANER, January 28, 1973, p. 34.

  REEL FROM "THE LIFE MOVIE" (1972, 1975)

    Anon. "Highly Acclaimed Poetry." SUNDAY GLEANER, May 4,
      1975, p. 23.

    Brown, Stewart. "New Poetry from Jamaica." NEW VOICES,
      v. 3, no. 6, 1975, pp. 48-50.

    Brown, Stewart. Review. NOW, v. 1, Spring 1973, pp. 13-18.

    Brown, Wayne. "Lyricism and the Anguish of the Clown."
      TAPIA, v. 3, no. 13, April 1973, pp. 6-7.

    Brown, Wayne. Review. JAMAICA JOURNAL, v. 7, nos. 1-2
      March-June 1973, pp. 80-81.

MCTAIR, ROGER. Trinidad,

  General

    Anon. "The Pamphleteers. Natural Reformers in Our Society."
      SUNDAY GUARDIAN (Trinidad), April 25, 1965, pp. 4-5.

    Rohlehr, F. Gordon. "Afterthoughts." TAPIA, no. 23,
      December 26, 1971, pp. 8, 13. Also appears in BIM, v. 14,
      no. 56, January-June 1973, pp. 227-230.

    Rohlehr, F. Gordon. "West Indian Poetry: Some Problems of
      Assessment." TAPIA, no. 20, August 1971, pp. 11-14. Also
      appears in BIM, part 1, v. 14, no. 54, January-June 1972,
      pp. 80-82; part 2, v. 14, no. 55, July-December 1972,
      pp. 134-144; and under title "Some Problems of Assessment:
      A Look at New Expressions in the Arts of the Contemporary
      Caribbean." CARIBBEAN QUARTERLY, v. 17, nos. 3 and 4,
      1971, pp. 92-113.

    Walcott, Derek. "Young Trinidadian Poets." SUNDAY GUARDIAN
      (Trinidad), June 19, 1966, p. 5.

MAHABIR, DENNIS. Trinidad,

  THE CUTLASS IS NOT FOR KILLING (1971)

Mais, Roger

Jagessar, Ramdath. Review. MOKO, no. 66, August 6, 1971,
    p. 8.

Panton, George. "Another Self-Published West Indian Book."
    SUNDAY GLEANER, March 7, 1971, p. 27.

MAIS, ROGER. Jamaica, 1901-1955

General

Akanji, Sangodare. "Roger Mais." BLACK ORPHEUS, no. 5,
    May 1959, pp. 33-37.

Allsopp, Joy. "Thinking About Roger Mais." KYK-OVER-AL, v.
    8, no. 24, December 1958, pp. 75-77.

Allsopp, Joy; Dawes, Neville; Linton, N. O.; McFarlane,
    Basil; Mittelholzer, Edgar; Seymour, A. J.; and Fred
    Wilmot. "Memorial to Roger Mais: A Green Blade in
    Triumph." KYK-OVER-AL, v. 6, no. 20, Mid-year 1955, pp.
    147-170.

Anon. "FOCUS . . . The Short Stories." PUBLIC OPINION,
    December 18, 1948, pp. 10-11.

Anon. "Roger Mais, the Real Meaning of His Work." SUNDAY
    GLEANER, July 31, 1966, p. 4.

Brathwaite, Edward. "Brother Mais." TAPIA, v. 4, no. 43,
    October 1974, pp. 6-8.

Brathwaite, Edward. "Jazz and the West Indian Novel, Part
    3." BIM, v. 12, no. 46, January-June 1968, pp. 115-124.

Brathwaite, Edward. "Sir Galahad and the Islands." BIM,
    v. 7, no. 25, July-December 1957, pp. 8-16. Also appears
    in IOUANALOA, RECENT WRITING FROM ST. LUCIA. Castries,
    St. Lucia: Department of Extra-Mural Studies, 1963, pp.
    50-59.

Brown, Lloyd W. "The American Image in British West Indian
    Literature." CARIBBEAN STUDIES, v. 11, no. 1, April
    1971, pp. 30-45.

Brown, Lloyd W. "The Crisis of Black Identity in the West
    Indian Novel." CRITIQUE, v. 11, no. 3, 1969, pp. 97-112.

Mais, Roger

Brown, Wayne. "On Art, Artists and the People." SUNDAY GUARDIAN (Trinidad), August 9, 1970, p. 10.

Carew, Jan. "Language and Literature in Developing Countries." NWF, part 1, v. 1, no. 22, September 1965, pp. 25-29; part 2, v. 1, no. 23, September 1965, pp. 23-27.

Carr, Bill. "The Novels of Roger Mais." PUBLIC OPINION, Roger Mais Supplement, June 10, 1966, p. 4.

Carr, Bill. "Reflections on the Novel in the British Caribbean." QUEENS QUARTERLY, v. 70, Winter 1963, pp. 585-597.

Carr, Bill. "Roger Mais: Design from a Legend." CARIBBEAN QUARTERLY, v. 13, no. 1, March 1967, pp. 3-28.

Chapman, Esther. "Roger Mais." WIR, v. 7, no. 12, June 1955, p. 7.

Creary, Jean. "A Prophet Armed. The Novels of Roger Mais." THE ISLANDS IN BETWEEN. London: Oxford University Press, 1968, pp. 50-63.

Dathorne, Oscar R. "Roger Mais: The Man on the Cross." SIN, v. 1, no. 1, Summer 1972, pp. 275-83.

Fraser, F. E. F. "Roger Mais: A New Judgement." PUBLIC OPINION, June 15, 1957, p. 7.

Grandison, Winnifred B. "The Prose Style of Roger Mais." JAMAICA JOURNAL, v. 8, no. 1, March 1974, pp. 48-54.

Hall, Stuart M. "Lamming, Selvon, and Some Trends in the West Indian Novel." BIM, v. 6, no. 23, December 1955, pp. 172-178.

Hearne, John. "Barren Treasure." PUBLIC OPINION, November 11, 1950, pp. 6, 8.

Hearne, John. "New Landscapes--Paintings by Roger Mais." PUBLIC OPINION, June 23, 1951, p. 5.

Hearne, John. "Roger Mais, A Personal Memoir." PUBLIC OPINION, Roger Mais Supplement, June 10, 1966, p. 2.

Hearne, John. "Roger Mais: A Personal Memoir." BIM, v. 6, no. 23, 1955, pp. 146-150.

James, Louis. "Islands of Man, Reflections on the Emergence of a West Indian Literature." SOUTHERN REVIEW, v. 2, 1966, pp. 150-163.

Lacovia, R. M. "Roger Mais and the Problem of Freedom." BAR, v. 1, no. 3, Fall 1970, pp. 45-54. Also appears as "Roger Mais: An Approach to Suffering and Freedom." BLACK IMAGES, v. 1, no. 2, Summer 1972, pp. 7-11.

Lamming, George. "Tribute to a Tragic Jamaican." SUNDAY GLEANER, December 25, 1955, p. 10. Also appears in BIM, v. 6, no. 24, 1956, pp. 242-244, and in PUBLIC OPINION, Roger Mais Supplement, June 10, 1966, p. 3.

Lewis, Rupert. "Roger Mais' Work as Social Protest and Comment." SUNDAY GLEANER, March 26, 1967, pp. 4, 24.

McFarlane, Basil. "Roger Mais, Novelist and Painter, Poet and Patriot." PUBLIC OPINION, July 2, 1955, p. 4.

McFarlane, Basil. "Roger Mais--The Painter." PUBLIC OPINION, Roger Mais Supplement, June 10, 1966, p. 8.

Marr, N. J. "Roger Mais in Jamaica 300." SUNDAY GLEANER, May 22, 1955, p. 5.

Marr, N. J. "West Indian Literary Giants." SUNDAY GLEANER, January 23, 1955, p. 6.

Moore, Gerald. "Use Men Language." BIM, v. 15, no. 57, March 1974, pp. 69-76.

Oakley, Leo. "Ideas of Patriotism and National Dignity in Some Jamaican Writings." JAMAICA JOURNAL, v. 4, no. 3, September 1970, pp. 16-21. Also appears as "Patriotism, National Dignity in Jamaican Writings." SUNDAY GLEANER, part 1, March 28, 1970, pp. 31, 34; part 2, April 4, 1970, p. 27; part 3, April 11, 1970, p. 25.

Panton, George. "Roger Mais--Portrayer of an Inner Vision." SUNDAY GLEANER, March 16, 1975, p. 23.

Ramchand, Kenneth. "Literature and Society: The Case of Roger Mais." CARIBBEAN QUARTERLY, v. 15, no. 4, December

Mais, Roger

1969, pp. 23-30.

Ramchand, Kenneth. "Obeah and the Supernatural in West Indian Literature." JAMAICA JOURNAL, v. 3, no. 2, June 1969, pp. 52-54.

Rawlins, Randolph. ."Migrants with Manuscripts, Social Background of the West Indian Novel." BLACK ORPHEUS, no. 4, 1958, pp. 46-50.

Rickards, Colin. "A Most Original Talent." SUNDAY GLEANER, March 26, 1967, p. 4.

Roberts, W. Adolphe. "The Art of Roger Mais." PUBLIC OPINION, July 14, 1951, p. 5.

Rohlehr, F. Gordon. "Afterthoughts." TAPIA, no. 23, December 26, 1971, pp. 8, 13. Also appears in BIM, v. 14, no. 56, January-June 1973, pp. 227-230.

Rohlehr, F. Gordon. "The Folk in Caribbean Literature, Part 1." TAPIA, v. 2, no. 11, December 1972, pp. 7-8, 13-15.

Rohlehr, F. Gordon. "West Indian Poetry: Some Problems of Assessment." TAPIA, no. 20, August 1971, pp. 11-14. Also appears in BIM, part 1, v. 14, no. 54, January-June 1972, pp. 80-88; part 2, v. 14, no. 55, July-December 1972, pp. 134-144; and under title "Some Problems of Assessment: A Look at New Expressions in the Arts of the Contemporary Caribbean." CARIBBEAN QUARTERLY, v. 17, nos. 3 and 4, 1971, pp. 92-113.

Seymour, A. J. "The Literary Adventure of the West Indies." KYK-OVER-AL, v. 2, no. 10, April 1950, entire issue, 40 pp.

Seymour, A. J. "The Novel in the British Caribbean." BIM, part 1, v. 11, no. 42, January-June 1966, pp. 83-85; part 2, v. 11, no. 43, July-December 1966, pp. 176-180; part 3, v. 11, no. 44, January-June 1967, pp. 238-242; part 4, v. 12, no. 46, January-June 1968, pp. 75-80.

Wickham, John. "West Indian Writing." BIM, v. 13, no. 50, January-June 1970, pp. 68-80.

Williamson, Karina. "Roger Mais: West Indian Novelist." JCL, no. 2, December 1966, pp. 138-147.

Mais, Roger

Wilmot, Cynthia. "Two Shows--Two Artists." PUBLIC OPINION, July 26, 1952, p. 5.

Wright, Winston G. Series of Articles on Mais. SUNDAY GLEANER, part 1, "Roger Mais--The Novelist." September 10, 1967, p. 4; part 2, "Roger Mais, His Way of Life," September 17, 1967, p. 4; part 3, "Songs and Music in the Work of Roger Mais," September 24, 1967, p. 4; part 4, "Roger Mais, Racy and Dramatic Style," October 8, 1967, p. 4; part 5, "Major Elements of Roger Mais' Work," October 15, 1967, pp. 4, 10.

Wynter, Sylvia. "Strangers at the Gate, Caribbean Novelists in Search of Identity." SUNDAY GLEANER, January 18, 1959, p. 14.

Wynter, Sylvia. "We Must Learn to Sit Down Together and Talk About a Little Culture: Reflections on West Indian Writing and Criticism. JAMAICA JOURNAL, part 1, v. 2, no. 4, December 1968, pp. 23-32; part 2, v. 3, no. 1, March 1969, pp. 27-42.

AND MOST OF ALL MAN   (Short Stories, 1942)

Bruton, Jack. Review. PUBLIC OPINION, December 5, 1942, p. 3.

ATALANTA AT CALYDON   (1950)

Anon. "A New Venture In Play Making." PUBLIC OPINION, September 23, 1950, p. 6.

Hearne, John. Review. PUBLIC OPINION, September 30, 1950, p. 6.

THE HILLS WERE JOYFUL TOGETHER   (1953)

Allen, Walter. Review. NEW STATESMAN, April 25, 1953, v. 45, April 1953, p. 497.

Charques, R. D. Review. SPECTATOR, v. 190, April 1953, p. 494.

Coddling, Eric. "Sordid, Squalid--But Telling." PUBLIC OPINION, May 9, 1953, p. 5.

Escoffery, Gloria. Review. BIM, v. 5, no. 19, December

Mais, Roger

    1953, pp. 237-239.

    Escoffery, Gloria. Review. PUBLIC OPINION, July 4, 1953, p. 5.

    Goldsworthy, F. M. Review. SUNDAY GLEANER, October 4, 1953, p. 5.

    Marr, N. J. Review. SUNDAY GLEANER, June 14, 1953, p. 4.

    Mills, K. I. "Slum Clearance." SUNDAY GUARDIAN (Trinidad), July 12, 1953, p. 7a.

    Milner, Harry. "Two Artistic Events." SUNDAY GLEANER, September 13, 1953, p. 4.

    Paul, David. Review. LSO, April 26, 1953, p. 9.

    Wilson, Una. "Let the Hills Be Joyful Together." SUNDAY GLEANER, August 2, 1953, p. 7.

BROTHER MAN (1954)

    Anon. Review. THE TIMES (London), July 7, 1954, p. 10.

    Anon. Review. TLS, no. 2736, July 9, 1954, p. 437.

BLACK LIGHTNING (1955)

    Ramchand, Kenneth. "BLACK LIGHTNING." PUBLIC OPINION, Roger Mais Supplement, June 10, 1966, p. 5.

THE THREE NOVELS OF ROGER MAIS (1966)

    Panton, George. "Vivid Pictures." SUNDAY GLEANER, May 8, 1966, p. 4.

MALIK, ABDUL (pseud. of Delano de Coteau). Grenada/Trinidad, 1940-

General

    Anon. "A Poet of the Streets." CARIBBEAN CONTACT, v. 5, no. 4, July 1977, p. 24.

    Rohlehr, F. Gordon. "Afterthoughts." TAPIA, no. 23, December 26, 1971, pp. 8, 13. Also appears in BIM, v. 14, no. 56, January-June 1973, pp. 227-230.

Rohlehr, F. Gordon. "West Indian Poetry: Some Problems of
Assessment." TAPIA, no. 20, August 1971, pp. 11-14. Also
appears in BIM, part 1, v. 14, no. 54, January-June 1972,
pp. 80-88; part 2, v. 14, no. 55, July-December 1972,
pp. 134-144; and under title "Some Problems of Assessment:
A Look at New Expressions in the Arts of the Contemporary
Caribbean." CARIBBEAN QUARTERLY, v. 17, nos. 3 and 4,
1971, pp. 92-113.

BLACK UP   (1972)

Questel, Victor. "Drama of the Streets." TAPIA, v. 2, no.
13, December 31, 1972, pp. 8-10.

Other Works

REVO   (1975)

MARAJ, JAGDIP. Trinidad, 1942-

THE FLAMING CIRCLE   (1966)

Walcott, Derek. "Young Trinidadian Poets." SUNDAY
GUARDIAN (Trinidad), June 19, 1966, p. 5.

MARSON, UNA. Jamaica, 1905-1965

General

Aarons, R. L. C. "Una Marson--A True Trail-Blazer." SUNDAY
GLEANER, December 22, 1974, p. 32.

Anon. "Three Evenings with Six Poets." KYK-OVER-AL, v. 3,
no. 13, Year-end 1951, pp. 214-220.

Seymour, Arthur J. "Nature Poetry in the West Indies."
KYK-OVER-AL, v. 3, no. 11, October 1950, pp. 39-47.

Webster, Aimee. "What Una Had to Say." SUNDAY GLEANER,
May 9, 1965, p. 4.

Works

TOWARDS THE STARS: POEMS   (1945)

MENDES, ALFRED H. Trinidad, 1905-

Mendes, Alfred H.

General

    Brathwaite, Edward. "West Indian Prose Fiction in the Sixties, A Survey." CRITICAL SURVEY, v. 3, Winter, pp. 169-174. Also appears in BIM, v. 12, no. 47, July-December 1968, pp. 157-165 and in SUNDAY GLEANER, part 1, March 8, 1970, p. 27; part 2, March 15, 1970, p. 27; part 3, March 22, 1970, p. 27; part 4, March 29, 1970, p. 27.

    Pearse, Andrew. "West Indian Themes." CARIBBEAN QUARTERLY, v. 2, no. 2, September 1951, pp. 12-23.

    Ramchand, Kenneth. "Dialect in West Indian Fiction." CARIBBEAN QUARTERLY, v. 14, nos. 1 and 2, March-June 1968, pp. 27-42. Also appears in his THE WEST INDIAN NOVEL AND ITS BACKGROUND, London: Faber and Faber, 1970, pp. 96-116.

    Roberts, W. Adolphe. "Caribbean Literature: The British Possessions." WIR, v. 4, no. 42, April 1953, pp. 16-17.

    Seymour, Arthur J. "The Literary Adventure of the West Indies." KYK-OVER-AL, v. 2, no. 10, April 1950, entire issue, 40 pp.

    Wickham, John. "West Indian Writing." BIM, v. 13, no. 50, January-June 1970, pp. 68-80.

PITCH LAKE (1934)

    Anon. Review. TLS, no. 1711, November 15, 1935.

    Hyman, Esther. Review. WIR, v. 1, no. 5, January 1935, p. 23.

BLACK FAUNS (1935)

    Anon. "Women of Trinidad." TLS, no. 1762, November 9, 1935.

    Hyman, Esther. Review. WIR, v. 2, no. 6, February 1936, p. 5.

MILES, JUDY. Trinidad,

General

Index of Authors

Mittelholzer, Edgar Austin

Walcott, Derek. "Young Trinidadian Poets." SUNDAY
GUARDIAN (Trinidad), June 19, 1966, p. 5.

MITTELHOLZER, EDGAR AUSTIN. Guyana, 1909-1965

General

Agard, John. "World of Caribbean Artists: The Shame of
It All." CARIBBEAN CONTACT, v. 3, no. 2, May 1975, p. 9.

Anon. "The Caribbean Mixture, Variations and Fusions In
Race and Style." TLS, no. 3154, August 10, 1962, pp. 578.

Anon. "Caribbean Voices." TLS, no. 2788, August 5, 1955,
pp. 16-17.

Anon. "In England Now." WIR, v. 3, no. 8, August 1958, p.
69.

Birbalsingh, F. M. "Edgar Mittelholzer: Moralist or
Pornographer." JCL, no. 7, July 1969, pp. 88-103.

Brassington, F. D. "Mittelholzer as I Knew Him." SUNDAY
GUARDIAN (Trinidad), May 16, 1965, p. 6.

Brathwaite, Edward. "The Controversial Tree of Time." BIM,
v. 8, no. 30, January-June 1960, pp. 104-114.

Brathwaite, Edward. "Jazz and the West Indian Novel." BIM,
part 1, v. 11, no. 44, January-June 1967, pp. 275-284;
part 2, v. 12, no. 45, July-December 1967, pp. 39-51;
part 3, v. 12, no. 46, January-June 1968, pp. 115-126.

Brathwaite, Edward. "The New West Indian Novelists: Part
1." BIM, v. 8, no. 31, July-December 1960, pp. 199-210.

Brathwaite, Edward. "Sir Galahad and the Islands." BIM,
v. 7, no. 25, July-December 1957, pp. 8-16. Also appears
in IOUANALOU, RECENT WRITING FROM ST. LUCIA. Castries,
St. Lucia: Department of Extra-Mural Studies, 1963.

Carew, Jan. "An Artist in Exile--From the West Indies."
NWF, v. 1, nos. 27 and 28, 1965, pp. 23-30.

Carr, W. I. "Reflections on the Novel in the British
Caribbean." QUEENS QUARTERLY, v. 70, Winter 1963, pp.
585-597.

Mittelholzer, Edgar Austin

Cartey, Wilfred. "The Rhythm of Society and Landscape."
NWQ, Guyana Independence Issue, v. 2, no. 3, 1966, pp.
97-104.

Collymore, Frank A. "A Biographical Sketch." BIM, v. 10,
no. 41, June-December 1965, pp. 23-26.

Derrick, A. "An Introduction to Caribbean Literature."
CARIBBEAN QUARTERLY, v. 15, nos. 2 and 3, June-September
1969, pp. 65-78.

Drayton, Arthur D. "The European Factor in West Indian
Literature." LITERARY HALF-YEARLY, v. 11, no. 1, 1970,
pp. 71-94.

Guckian, Patrick. "The Balance of Colour, A Re-assessment of
the Work of Edgar Mittelholzer." JAMAICA JOURNAL, v. 4,
no. 1, March 1970, pp. 38-45.

Hall, Stuart M. "Lamming, Selvon, and Some Trends in the
West Indian Novel." BIM, v. 6, no. 23, December 1955,
pp. 172-173.

Howard, William J. "Edgar Mittelholzer's Tragic Vision."
CARIBBEAN QUARTERLY, v. 16, no. 4, December 1970, pp. 19-
28.

James, Louis. "Islands of Man, Reflections on the Emergence
of a West Indian Literature." SOUTHERN REVIEW, v. 2, 1966,
pp. 150-163.'

Lacovia, R. M. "Caribbean Literature in English." BAR, v.
2, nos. 1 and 2, 1971, pp. 109-125.

Lacovia, R. M. "English Caribbean Literature: A Brave
New World." BLACK IMAGES, v. 1, no. 1, January 1972,
pp. 15-22.

Lamming, George. "But Alas Edgar." NWQ, Guyana Independence
Issue, v. 2, no. 3, 1966, pp. 18-19.

Lewis, Gordon. "The New West Indies: Nationality and
Literature." SUNDAY GLEANER, December 8, 1957, p. 8.

Marr, N. J. "About Books." SUNDAY GLEANER, June 28, 1953,
p. 5.

Mittelholzer, Edgar Austin

Mittelholzer, Edgar. "Literary Criticism and the Creative Writer." KYK-OVER-AL, v. 5, no. 15, Year-end 1952, pp. 19-22.

Questel, Victor. "Their Tragic Destiny." TAPIA, v. 6, no. 20, May 16, 1976, pp. 4, 11.

Ramchand, Kenneth. "Dialect in West Indian Fiction." CARIBBEAN QUARTERLY, v. 14, nos. 1 and 2, March-June 1968, pp. 27-42. Also appears in his THE WEST INDIAN NOVEL AND ITS BACKGROUND. London: Faber and Faber, 1970, pp. 96-114.

Ramsaran, J. A. "The Social Groundwork of Politics in Some West Indian Novels." NEGRO DIGEST, v. 18, no. 10, 1969, pp. 71-77.

Rickards, Colin. "A Tribute to Edgar Mittelholzer." SUNDAY GLEANER, May 16, 1965, pp. 4, 8. Also appears in BIM v. 11, no. 42, January-June 1966, pp. 98-105.

Roberts, W. Adolphe. "Caribbean Literature: The British Possessions." WIR, v. 4, no. 42, April 1953, pp. 16-17.

Seymour, Arthur J. EDGAR MITTELHOLZER, THE MAN AND HIS WORK. THE 1967 EDGAR MITTELHOLZER LECTURES, Georgetown (Guyana), 1968.

Seymour, Arthur J. "Edgar Mittelholzer the Preacher." KAIE, no. 1, October 1965, pp. 31-33.

Seymour, Arthur J. "An Introduction to the Novels of Edgar Mittelholzer." KYK-OVER-AL, v. 8, no. 24, December 1958, pp. 60-74.

Seymour, Arthur J. "The Literary Adventure of the West Indies." KYK-OVER-AL, v. 2, no. 10, April 1950, entire issue, 40 pp.

Seymour, Arthur J. "The Novel in Guyana." KAIE, no. 4, July 1967, pp. 59-63.

Seymour, Arthur J. "The Novel in the British Caribbean, Part 3." BIM, v. 11, no. 44, January-June 1967, pp. 238-242.

Seymour, Arthur J. "West Indian Pen Portrait, Edgar

Mittelholzer, Edgar Austin

    Mittelholzer." KYK-OVER-AL, v. 5, no. 15, Year-end 1952, pp. 15-17.

    Sparer, Joyce L. "Attitudes towards 'Race' in Guyanese Literature." CARIBBEAN STUDIES, v. 8, no. 2, July 1968, pp. 23-63.

    Wagner, Geoffrey. "Edgar Mittelholzer: Symptoms and Shadows." BIM, v. 9, no. 33, July-December 1961, pp. 29-34.

    Walcott, Derek. "Neo-realism Parallel Noted in West Indian Novels." SUNDAY GUARDIAN (Trinidad), April 24, 1960, p. 7.

    Wyndham, Francis. "The New West Indian Writers." BIM, v. 7, no. 28, January-June 1959, pp. 188-190.

    Wynter, Sylvia. Strangers at the Gate, Caribbean Novelists in Search of Identity." SUNDAY GLEANER, January 18, 1959, p. 14.

A MORNING AT THE OFFICE (1950; also published as A MORNING IN TRINIDAD)

    Anon. Review. KYK-OVER-AL, v. 3, no. 11, October 1950, p. 72.

    Chapman, Esther. Review. WIR, v. 2, no. 5, June 3, 1950, p. 28.

    Collymore, Frank A. Review. BIM, v. 3, no. 12, 1949, pp. 354-356.

    Escoffery, Gloria. Review. PUBLIC OPINION, May 20, 1950, p. 6.

    Foster-Davis, Margery. Review. CARIBBEAN QUARTERLY, v. 1, no. 4, 1950, pp. 43-44.

    Gilkes, Michael. "The Spirit in the Bottle--A Reading of Mittelholzer's A MORNING AT THE OFFICE." WLWE, v. 14, April 1975, pp. 237-252.

    Herring, Robert. Review. LL, v. 65, no. 154, 1950, pp. 263-264.

Mittelholzer, Edgar Austin

Martin, Lane. Review. NYT, May 14, 1950, Section 7, p. 20.

Owens, R. J. "Back to the Office." SUNDAY GLEANER,
    September 3, 1961, p. 14.

Walcott, Derek. "Vintage Mittelholzer." SUNDAY GUARDIAN
    (Trinidad), June 21, 1964, p. 15.

White, Anthony. Review. NEW STATESMAN, May 1950, p. 552.

Wyndham, Francis. Review. LSO, May 7, 1950, p. 7.

SHADOWS MOVE AMONG THEM (1951)

Anon. Review. NEGRO DIGEST, v. 10, no. 1, 1951, p. 36.

Anon. Review. TLS, no. 2565, March 30, 1951, p. 193.

Charques, R. D. Review. SPECTATOR, v. 186, April 20, 1951,
    p. 534.

Harrison, John. Review. BIM, v. 4, no. 14, June 1951,
    pp. 147-148.

Laski, Marghanita. Review. LSO, March 25, 1951, p. 7.

Lord, Cecily. Review. KYK-OVER-AL, v. 3, no. 12, Mid-year
    1951, pp. 179-180.

Morris, Alice S. Review. NYT, September 9, 1951, Section 7,
    p. 5.

Paul, David. Review. LISTENER, v. 45, 1951, p. 633.

Prescott, Orville. Review. NYT, September 14, 1951, p. 23.

Raymond, John. Review. NEW STATESMAN, v. 41, May 19, 1951,
    pp. 573-574.

CHILDREN OF KAYWANA (1952)

Chrichlow Matthews, A. F. Review. BIM, v. 4, no. 16, June
    1952, p. 300.

Prescott, Orville. Review. NYT, August 25, 1952, p. 23.

Warren, Virginia Lee. "Dynasty of Death." NYT, September 2,

Mittelholzer, Edgar Austin

    1952, Section 7, p. 29.

  THE WEATHER IN MIDDENSHOT (1953)

    Anon. Review. BIM, v. 5, no. 18, 1953, pp. 155-156.

    Anon. Review. TLS, no. 2649, November 7, 1952, p. 721.

    Barker, J. S. "Is Mittelholzer Slipping?" SUNDAY GUARDIAN
      (Trinidad), May 17, 1953, p. 7.

    Coddling, Eric. "Facile and Trivial." PUBLIC OPINION,
      January 3, 1953, p. 5.

    Matthews, Nancy. "Lunatic at Large." NYT, May 31, 1953,
      Section 7, p. 10.

  THE LIFE AND DEATH OF SYLVIA (1953)

    Anon. Review. THE TIMES (London), May 9, 1953, p. 8.

    Anon. Review. TLS, no. 2676, May 15, 1953, p. 13.

    Anon. "Torn between Two Worlds." PUBLIC OPINION, January
      7, 1956, p. 6.

    Black, Clinton V. "Agonizing Pictures." PUBLIC OPINION,
      June 20, 1953, p. 5.

    Escoffery, Gloria. Review. BIM, v. 5, no. 19, December
      1953, pp. 237-239.

    Laski, Marghanita. Review. SPECTATOR, v. 190, May 15,
      1953, p. 652.

    Matthews, Nancy. "Cliques and Sub-cliques." NYT, January
      10, 1954, Section 7, p. 28.

    Mills, K. I. "The Decline and Fall." SUNDAY GUARDIAN
      (Trinidad), June 14, 1953, p. 7a.

    O'Toole, Al. "Life, Death of an Unequipped Virgin." PUBLIC
      OPINION, November 13, 1954, p. 6.

    Paul, David. Review. LSO, May 10, 1953, p. 11.

    Scott, J. D. Review. NEW STATESMAN, v. 45, May 30, 1953,

Mittelholzer, Edgar Austin

p. 651.

THE HARROWING OF HUBERTUS   (1954)

Allsopp, Joy. Review. KYK-OVER-AL, v. 6, no. 20, Mid-year
   1955, pp. 203-205.

Anon. "Engaging Dutchman." NYT, January 16, 1955, Section
   7, p. 27.

Anon. Review. TLS, no. 2718, March 5, 1954, p. 149.

Escoffery, Gloria. Review. PUBLIC OPINION, April 3, 1954,
   p. 5. Also appears in BIM, v. 5, no. 20, June 1954, pp.
   323-324.

Metcalf, John. Review. SPECTATOR, v. 192, February 19,
   1954, p. 216.

Smith, Stevie. Review. LSO, February 21, 1954, p. 9.

MY BONES AND MY FLUTE   (1955)

Anon. Review. BAJAN, v. 4, no. 1, September 1954, p. 35.

Anon. Review. NEW STATESMAN, v. 50, October 22, 1955, p.
   517.

Anon. Review. TLS, 2802, November 11, 1955, p. 669.

Barnes, W. Therold. Review. BIM, v. 6, no. 23, 1966, p.
   205.

Smith, Stevie. Review. LSO, October 23, 1955, p. 12.

OF TREES AND THE SEA   (1956)

Anon. "Mittelholzer's Bimshire." PUBLIC OPINION, December
   1, 1956, p. 7.

Anon. Review. THE TIMES (London), August 2, 1956, p. 11.

Anon. Review. TLS, no. 2842, August 17, 1956, p. 485.

Collymore, Frank A. Review. BIM, v. 6, no. 24, 1956,
   pp. 272-273.

103

Mittelholzer, Edgar Austin

Wain, John. Review. LSO, May 6, 1956, p. 9.

A TALE OF THREE PLACES   (1957)

Anon. Review. TLS, March 29, 1957, p. 189.

George, Daniel. Review. SPECTATOR, v. 198, March 22, 1957,
    p. 383.

Hopkinson, Tom. Review. LSO, March 10, 1957, p. 17.

St. Hill, Chalmer. Review. BIM, v. 7, no. 25, July-
    December 1957, pp. 58-59.

Simmons, Harold. Review. PUBLIC OPINION, May 4, 1957,
    p. 7.

WITH A CARIB EYE   (essays, 1958)

Anon. "Caribbean Sketchbook." TLS, no 2932, May 9, 1958,
    p. 257.

Anon. Review. BAJAN, v. 5, no. 12, August 1958, p. 17.

Collymore, Frank. Review. BIM, v. 7, no. 27, July-
    December 1958, p. 186.

Panton, George. "Through a Glass Darkly. . . ." SUNDAY
    GLEANER, May 11, 1958, p. 11.

KAYWANA BLOOD   (1958)

Allsopp, Joy. Review. KYK-OVER-AL, v. 8, no. 23, May
    1958, p. 46.

Anon. Review. TLS, no. 2919, February 7, 1958, p. 73.

Anon. "Sex and Race Prove a Surefire Formula." SUNDAY
    GUARDIAN (Trinidad), March 16, 1958, p. 18.

Collymore, Frank. Review. BIM, v. 7, no. 27, July-December
    1958, p. 186.

Hansford Johnson, Pamela. Review, NEW STATESMAN, v. 55,
    February 8, 1958, p. 176.

Matthews, Nancy. "Passion Was the Dominant Chord." NYT,

Mittelholzer, Edgar Austin

May 18, 1958, Section 7, p. 33.

Panton, George. "Too Rich for Hollywood." SUNDAY GLEANER, March 30, 1958, p. 11.

THE WEATHER FAMILY (1958)

Anon. Review. KYK-OVER-AL, v. 9, no. 26, December 1959, pp. 58-59.

Anon. Review. TLS, no. 2956, October 24, 1958, p. 614.

Nicholson, Geoffrey. Review. SPECTATOR, v. 201, October 17, 1958, p. 527.

St. Hill, Chalmer. Review. BIM, v. 8, no. 29, June-December 1959, p. 68.

A TINKLING IN THE TWILIGHT (1959)

Akanji, Sangodare. Review. BLACK ORPHEUS, no. 7, June 1960, p. 62.

Anon. Review. BAJAN, v. 7, no. 4, December 1959, p. 19.

Anon. Review. KYK-OVER-AL, v. 9, no. 26, December 1959, pp. 58-59.

Anon. Review. THE TIMES (London), July 30, 1959, p. 9.

Anon. Review. TLS, no. 2996, July 31, 1959, p. 445.

Coleman, John. Review. SPECTATOR, v. 203, July 31, 1959, p. 146.

Davenport, John. Review. LSO, July 26, 1959, p. 16.

St. Hill, Chalmer. Review. BIM, v. 8, no. 30, January-June 1960, pp. 136-137.

THE MAD MACMULLOCHS (1959)

Taubman, Robert. Review. NEW STATESMAN, v. 62, November 10, 1961, p. 714.

LATTICED ECHOES (1960)

Mittelholzer, Edgar Austin

    Anon. Review. BAJAN, v. 7, no. 9, May 1960, p. 23.

    Anon. Review. THE TIMES (London), January 28, 1960, p. 15.

    Anon. Review. TLS, no. 3023, February 5, 1960, p. 77.

    Bryden, Ronald. Review. SPECTATOR, v. 204, January 22,
        1960, p. 117.

    Marshall, Harold. Review. BIM, v. 8, no. 31, July–December
        1960, pp. 217-218.

    Seymour, Arthur J. Review. KYK-OVER-AL, v. 9, no. 27,
        December 1960, pp. 134-137.

ELTONSBRODY (1960)

    Anon. Review. TLS, no. 3061, October 21, 1960, p. 681.

    Collymore, Frank. Review. BIM, v. 8, no. 32, January–June
        1961, p. 291.

    Panton, George. Review. SUNDAY GLEANER, May 6, 1961, p. 14.

THUNDER RETURNING (1961)

    Anon. Review. BIM, v. 9, no. 33, July–December 1961, p. 76.

    Anon. Review. TLS, no. 3080, March 10, 1961, p. 149.

    Panton, George. "Tension . . . Tragedy." SUNDAY GLEANER,
        April 15, 1962, p. 14.

    Rickards, Colin. Review. SUNDAY GUARDIAN (Trinidad), April
        23, 1961, p. 4.

THE PILING OF CLOUDS (1961)

    Anon. Review. TLS, no. 3117, November 24, 1961, p. 851.

    Marshall, Harold. Review. BIM, v. 9, no. 35, July–December
        1962, pp. 228-229.

    Rickards, Colin. "Mittelholzer on the Attack." SUNDAY
        GUARDIAN (Trinidad), December 17, 1961, p. 22.

    Taubman, Robert. Review. NEW STATESMAN, v. 62, November 10,

Mittelholzer, Edgar Austin

1961, p. 714.

THE WOUNDED AND THE WORRIED (1962)

    Scannell, Vernon. Review. LISTENER, v. 68, July 12, 1962, p. 73.

    Sealy, Karl. Review. BIM, v. 9, no. 36, January–June 1963, p. 293.

    Taubman, Robert. Review. NEW STATESMAN, v. 64, July 13, 1963, p. 53.

A SWARTHY BOY (autobiography, 1963)

    Anon. "Alignment." TLS, no. 3182, February 22, 1963, p. 120.

    Anon. "Child of Guiana." THE TIMES (London), February 28, 1963, p. 15.

    Panton, George. "Two West Indian Writers." SGM, May 26, 1963, p. 13.

    Phelps, Gilbert. Review. NEW STATESMAN, v. 65, March 1, 1963, p. 309.

    Rees, David. Review. SPECTATOR, v. 210, March 29, 1963.

    Seymour, Arthur J. Review. BIM, v. 10, no. 38, January–June 1964, pp. 143–144.

    Vansittart, Peter. Review. LSO, February 24, 1963, p. 22.

UNCLE PAUL (1963)

    Bergonzi, Bernard. Review. NEW STATESMAN, v. 66, September 20, 1963, p. 363.

    Ewart, Gavin. Review. LONDON MAGAZINE, v. 4, no. 4, New Series, July 1964, pp. 94–95.

THE ALONENESS OF MRS. CHATHAM (1965)

    Morgan, Edwin. Review. NEW STATESMAN, v. 69, May 14, 1965, p. 772.

Morris, John

THE JILKINGTON DRAMA   (1965)

Wardle, Irving. Review. LSO, June 13, 1965, p. 21.

Other Works

CORENTYNE THUNDER (1941)

THE ADDING MACHINE   (1954)

MORRIS, JOHN   (pseudonym for John Hearne and Morris Cargill)

FEVER GRASS   (1969)

Anon. "Ingeniously Constructed Jamaican Thriller." SUNDAY
GLEANER, February 14, 1971, p. 23.

Anon. "New Jamaican Thriller." PUBLIC OPINION, July 25,
1969, p. 8.

Anon. Review. TLS, no. 3512, June 19, 1969, p. 666.

Panton, George. "Exciting Jamaican Thriller." SUNDAY
GLEANER, April 20, 1969, p. 4.

CANDYWINE FEVER   (1970)

Brown, Wayne. "West Indian Literature of the Past Year."
SUNDAY GUARDIAN (Trinidad), August 30, 1970, p. 5.

G. P. [George Panton]. "Jamaica Becomes Involved with the
Mafia and H-Bombs." SUNDAY GLEANER, April 26, 1970,
p. 27.

MORRIS, MERVYN. Jamaica, 1937-

General

Drayton, Arthur. "The European Factor in West Indian
Literature." LITERARY HALF-YEARLY, v. 11, no. 1, 1971,
pp. 71-94.

Moore, Gerald. "Use Men Language." BIM, v. 15, no. 57,
March 1974, pp. 69-76.

Panton, George. "The Tennis-Playing Poet." SUNDAY GLEANER,
May 25, 1975, pp. 23, 31.

Naipaul, Shiva

Questel, Victor. "Their Tragic Destiny." TAPIA, v. 6, no. 20, May 16, 1976, pp. 4, 11.

Rohlehr, F. Gordon. "Afterthoughts." TAPIA, no. 23, D December 26, 1971, pp. 8, 13. Also appears in BIM, v. 14, no. 56, January–June 1973, pp. 227–230.

Rohlehr, F. Gordon. "West Indian Poetry: Some Problems of Assessment." TAPIA, no. 20, August 1971, pp. 11–14. Also appears in BIM, part 1, v. 14, no. 54, January–June 1972, pp. 30–88; part 2, v. 14, no. 55, July–December 1972, pp. 134–144; and under title "Some Problems of Assessment: A Look at New Expression in the Arts of the Contemporary Caribbean." CARIBBEAN QUARTERLY, v. 17, nos. 3 and 4, 1971, pp. 92–113.

SEVEN JAMAICAN POETS (edited by Mervyn Morris, 1971)

Forde, A. N. Review. BIM, v. 14, no. 54, January–June 1972, p. 117.

C. L. [Cedric Lindo]. "Worthy Examples of Our Poetry." SUNDAY GLEANER, May 23, 1971, p. 29.

THE POND (1973)

Brown, Stewart. "New Poetry from Jamaica." NEW VOICES, v. 3, no. 6, 1973, pp. 48–50.

C. L. [Cedric Lindo]. "Modern Poetry for Many Moods." SUNDAY GLEANER, February 10, 1974.

Morris, Mervyn. "The Prints of Darkness." (reply to Questel review). TAPIA, v. 5, no. 15, April 1975, p. 3.

Questel, Victor. "Creole Poet in a Classical Castle." TAPIA, v. 5, no. 11, March 1975, pp. 6–7.

NAIPAUL, SHIVA. Trinidad, 1945–

General

Brown, Wayne. "New West Indian Writers of the Past Year." SUNDAY GUARDIAN (Trinidad), September 6, 1970, p. 8.

Naipaul, Shiva. "Living in London." LONDON MAGAZINE, New Series, v. 13, no. 3, August/September 1973, pp. 56–66.

Naipaul, Shiva

FIREFLIES (1970)

Anon. Review. ANTIOCH REVIEW, v. 31, no. 1, Spring 1971,
p. 132.

Anon. "Shades of Black and White." TLS, no. 3589, December
11, 1970, p. 1437.

Gathorne-Hardy, J. "Snow, Flak and Sunshine." LONDON
MAGAZINE, New Series, v. 10, no. 11, February 1971, pp.
98-100.

Grant, Annette. "Hindus Coming Apart in Trinidad." NYT,
February 7, 1971, Section 7, p. 6.

C. L. [Cedric Lindo]. "Detailed Look at Indians in
Trinidad." SUNDAY GLEANER, December 30, 1970, p. 39.

McDowell, Frederick. Review. CONTEMPORARY LITERATURE, v.
13, Summer 1972, p. 374.

Mahon, Derek. Review. LISTENER, v. 84, October 22, 1970,
p. 555.

Moss, John G. Review. WLWE, v. 12, April 1973, pp. 117-119.

Naipaul, Shiva. "Shiva Tells Story of a Woman." SUNDAY
GUARDIAN (Trinidad), July 4, 1971, p. 10.

Niven, Alastair. "A Sophisticated Talent." JCL, v. 8, no.
1, June 1973, pp. 131-133.

Ragunath, N. S. Review. LITERARY CRITERION, v. 11, no. 2,
Summer 1974, pp. 88-90.

Ramchand, Kenneth. "Before the People Became Popular. . . ."
CARIBBEAN QUARTERLY, v. 18, no. 4, 1972, pp. 70-73.

Wall, Stephen. Review. LSO, November 15, 1970, p. 31.

Waugh, Auberon. "The Old Order Changeth Not." SPECTATOR,
v. 225, October 31, 1970, p. 526.

Wickham, John. Review. BAJAN, no. 209, February 1971, p 12.

THE CHIP-CHIP GATHERERS (1973)

Naipaul, Vidia Surajprasad

Amis, Martin. "Educated Monsters." NEW STATESMAN, v. 85,
    April 20, 1973, p. 586.

Anon. "More Trinidadian Indian Life." SUNDAY GLEANER,
    February 11, 1973, p. 39.

Anon. Review. LISTENER, v. 89, April 12, 1973, p. 489.

Anon. "Wasting Away." TLS, no. 3710, April 13, 1973, p.
    409.

Davies, Russell. Review. LSO, April 15, 1973, p. 39.

Mellors, John. Review. LONDON MAGAZINE, New Series, v. 13,
    no. 3, August/September 1973, p. 151.

Symons, Julian. "Triumphant Portrait." SUNDAY GUARDIAN
    (Trinidad), April 22, 1973, p. 7.

Questel, Victor. "Literary Jackals on the Make." TAPIA,
    v. 3, no. 51, December 16, 1973, pp. 6-7.

Waugh, Auberon. Review. SPECTATOR, v. 230, April 21, 1973,
    p. 494.

NAIPAUL, VIDIA SURAJPRASAD. Trinidad, 1932-

General

    Anon. "An Area of Brilliance." SUNDAY GUARDIAN (Trinidad),
        December 5, 1971, p. 5.

    Anon. "Another Kind of Sentimentality." TGM, February 12,
        1967, pp. 8-9.

    Anon. "The Caribbean Mixture, Variations and Fusions in
        Race and Style." TLS, no. 3154, August 10, 1962, p. 578.

    Anon. "An Exile Returns." SUNDAY GUARDIAN (Trinidad),
        September 25, 1960, p. 7.

    Anon. "Naipauls's Article on Black Power Criticized." MOKO,
        no. 43, October 1970, p. 3.

    Boxill, Anthony. "V. S. Naipaul's Starting Point." JCL,
        v. 10, no. 1, August 1975, pp. 1-9.

Naipaul, Vidia Surajprasad

Brathwaite, Edward. "Jazz and the West Indian Novel." BIM, part 1, v. 11, no. 44, January–June 1967, pp. 275–284, part 2, v. 12, no. 45, July–December 1967, pp. 39–51; part 3, v. 12, no. 46, January–June 1968, pp. 115–126.

Brathwaite, Edward. "The New West Indian Novelists." BIM, part 1, v. 8, no. 31, July–December 1960, pp. 199–210; part 2, v. 8, no. 32, January–June 1961, pp. 271–280.

Brathwaite, Edward. "Roots." BIM, v. 10, no. 37, July–December 1963, pp. 10–21.

Brathwaite, Edward. "Timehri." SAVACOU, no. 2, September 1970, pp. 35–44. Also appears in IS MASSA DAY DEAD? New York: Doubleday, 1974, pp. 29–44.

Brathwaite, Edward. "West Indian Prose Fiction in the Sixties, A Survey." CRITICAL SURVEY, v. 3, Winter, pp. 169–174. Also appears in BIM, v. 12, no. 47, July–December 1968, pp. 157–165 and SUNDAY GLEANER, part 1, March 8, 1970, p. 27; part 2, March 15, 1970, p. 27; part 3, March 22, 1970, p. 27; part 4, March 29, 1970, p. 27.

Brown, Wayne. "The First Generation of West Indian Writers." SUNDAY GUARDIAN (Trinidad), June 7, 1970, pp. 6, 11.

Brown, Wayne. "On Art, Artists and the People." SUNDAY GUARDIAN (Trinidad), August 9, 1970, p. 10.

Brown, Wayne. "On Exile and the Dialect of the Tribe." SUNDAY GUARDIAN (Trinidad), November 8, 1970, p. 19.

Brown, Wayne. "The Possibilities for West Indian Writing." SUNDAY GUARDIAN (Trinidad), November 22, 1970, p. 21.

Bryden, Ronald. "The Hurricane" (reviews Naipaul's journalism). LISTENER, v. 88, November 9, 1972, p. 641.

Carr, Bill. "Reflections on the Novel in the British Caribbean." QUEENS QUARTERLY, v. 70, Winter 1963, pp. 585–597.

Carr, Bill. "The West Indian Novelist: Prelude and Context." CARIBBEAN QUARTERLY, v. 11, nos. 1 and 2, March and June 1965, pp. 71–84.

Naipaul, Vidia Surajprasad

Cartey, Wilfred. "The Knights Companion--Ganesh, Biswas, and Stone; Novels by Vidia Naipaul." NWQ, v. 2, no. 1, Dead Season 1965, pp. 93-98.

Clarke, Austin. "Some Speculations as to the Absence of Racialistic Vindictiveness in West Indian Literature." THE BLACK WRITER IN AFRICA AND THE AMERICAS. Los Angeles: Hennessey and Ingalls, 1973.

Davies, Barrie. "The Personal Sense of a Society--Minority View: Aspects of the 'East Indian'Novel in the West Indies." SIN, v. 4, no. 2, Summer 1972, pp. 284-295.

Derrick, Anthony. "An Introduction to Caribbean Literature." CARIBBEAN QUARTERLY, v. 15, nos. 2 and 3, June-September 1969, pp. 65-78.

Derrick, Anthony. "Naipaul's Technique as a Novelist." JCL, no. 7, July 1969, pp. 32-44.

Drayton, Arthur D. "The European Factor in West Indian Literature." LITERARY HALF-YEARLY, v. 11, no. 1, 1970, pp. 71-94.

Fraser, Fitzroy. "A Talk with Vidia Naipaul." SUNDAY GLEANER, December 25, 1960, pp. 14, 19.

Garebian, Keith. "V. S. Naipaul's Negative Sense of Place." JCL, v. 1, no. 1, August 1975, pp. 23-35.

Gowda, H. H. Anniah. "India in Naipaul's Artistic Consciousness." LITERARY HALF-YEARLY, v. 16, no. 1, January 1975, pp. 27-39.

Grant, Lennox. "Naipaul Joins the Chorus, an Interview with Gordon Rohlehr." TAPIA, part 1, v. 5, no. 27, July 1975, pp. 6-7; part 2, v. 5, no. 28, July 1975, pp. 6-7.

Gurr, A. J. "Third-World Novels: Naipaul and After." JCL, v. 7, no. 1, June 1972, pp. 6-13.

Hamilton, Ian. "Without a Place, V. S. Naipaul in Con-versation with Ian Hamilton." TLS, no. 3622, July 30, 1971, pp. 897-898.

Hamner, Robert Daniel. V. S. Naipaul. New York: Twayne, 1973.

Naipaul, Vidia Surajprasad

Hamner, Robert Daniel. "V. S. Naipaul: A selected Bibliography." JCL, v. 10, no. 1, August 1975.

Harris, Michael. "Naipaul on Campus: Sending Out a Plea for Rationality." TAPIA, v. 5, no. 26, June 1975, p. 2.

Harrison, John. "From the West Indies." BIM, v. 10, no. 37, July–December 1963, pp. 60–63.

James, C. L. R. "The Disorder of Vidia Naipaul." TGM, February 21, 1965, p. 6.

James, C. L. R. "Home Is Where They Want to Be." TGM, February 14, 1965, pp. 4–5.

James, Louis. "Islands of Man, Reflections on the Emergence of a West Indian Literature." SOUTHERN REVIEW, v. 2, 1966, pp. 150–163.

Kemoli, Arthur. "The Theme of 'The Past' in Caribbean Literature." WLWE, v. 12, November 1973, pp. 304–325.

King, Lloyd. "The Trauma of Naipaulana." SUNDAY GUARDIAN (Trinidad), September 24, 1967, pp. 16–19.

Lacovia, R. M. "Caribbean Literature in English: 1949–1970." BAR, v. 2, nos. 1 and 2, 1971, pp. 109–125.

Lacovia, R. M. "The Medium Is the Divide; An Examination of V. S. Naipaul's Early Works." BLACK IMAGES, v. 1, no. 2, Summer 1972, pp. 3–6.

Lewis, Gordon. "The New West Indies: Nationality and Literature." SUNDAY GLEANER, December 8, 1957, p. 8.

MacDonald, Bruce F. "Symbolic Action in Three of V. S. Naipaul's Novels." JCL, v. 9, no. 3, April 1975, pp. 41–52.

McSweeney, Kerry. "V. S. Naipaul: Sensibility and Schemata." CRITICAL QUARTERLY, v. 18, Autumn 1976, pp. 73–79.

Maes-Jelinek, Hena. "The Myth of El Dorado in the Caribbean Novel." JCL, v. 6, no. 1, June 1971, pp. 113–127.

Mohr, Eugene V. "West Indian Fiction Is Alive and Well."

Naipaul, Vidia Surajprasad

CARIBBEAN REVIEW, v. 5, no. 4, 1973, pp. 23-29.

Moore, Gerald. "East Indians and West, The Novels of V. S. Naipaul." BLACK ORPHEUS, no. 7, June 1960, pp. 11-15.

Nettleford, Rex. "Caribbean Perspectives--The Creative Potential and the Quality of Life." CARIBBEAN QUARTERLY, v. 17, nos. 3 and 4, September-December 1971, pp. 118-119.

Ormerod, David. "In a Derelict Land: The Novels of V. S. Naipaul." CONTEMPORARY LITERATURE, v. 9, Winter 1968, pp. 74-90.

Page, Malcolm. "West Indian Writers." NOVEL, v. 3, no. 2, Winter 1970, pp. 167-172.

Pantin, Raoul. "Portrait of an Artist: What Makes Naipaul Run" (interview). CARIBBEAN CONTACT, v. 1, no. 6, May 1973, pp. 15, 18-19.

Panton, George. "V. S. Naipaul, the Most Famous West Indian Writer." SUNDAY GLEANER, June 22, 1975, pp. 23, 31.

Ramchand, Kenneth. "History and the Novel: A Literary Critic's Approach." SAVACOU, v. 1, no. 5, June 1971, pp. 103-113.

Ramchand, Kenneth. "Obeah and the Supernatural in West Indian Literature." JAMAICA JOURNAL, v. 3, no. 2, June 1969, pp. 52-54.

Ramsaran, J. A. "The Social Groundwork of Politics in Some West Indian Novels." NEGRO DIGEST, v. 18, no. 10, August 1969, pp. 71-77.

Ramsingh, Ashook. "A Question of Creative Writing vs. Paul Theroux and V. S. Naipaul's Autobiographers, Ganesh Ramsumair and Ralph Singh." CORLIT, part 1, v. 1, no. 2, April 1974, pp. 22, 42-45, 49, 54; part 2, v. 1, no. 3, July 1974, pp. 49-50.

Rohlehr, F. Gordon. "The Creative Writer and West Indian Society." KAIE, no. 11, August 1973, pp. 48-77.

Rohlehr, F. Gordon. "The Ironic Approach; The Novels of V. S. Naipaul." THE ISLANDS IN BETWEEN (edited by Louis James). London: Oxford University Press, 1968.

NaiPaul, Vidia Surajprasad

Rowe-Evans, Adrian. "V. S. Naipaul." TRANSITION, v. 8, no. 40, 1971, pp. 56-62.

Seymour, Arthur J. "The Novel in the British Caribbean, Part 3." BIM, v. 11, no. 44, January-June 1967, pp. 238-242.

Theroux, Paul. V. S. NAIPAUL, AN INTRODUCTION TO HIS WORK. London: Heinemann, 1972.

Thieme, John. "V. S. Naipaul's Third World: A Not So Free State." JCL, v. 10, no. 1, August 1975, pp. 10-22.

Walcott, Derek. "The Gift of Comedy." TGM, October 22, 19 1967, pp. 2-3.

Walcott, Derek. "Neo-realism Parallel Noted in West Indian Novels." SUNDAY GUARDIAN (Trinidad), April 24, 1960, p. 7.

Walsh, William. V. S. NAIPAUL. Edinburgh: Oliver and Boyd, 1973.

Walsh, William. "V. S. Naipaul: Mr. Biswas." LITERARY CRITERION, v. 10, no. 2, Summer 1972, pp. 27-37.

Wickham, John. "West Indian Writing." BIM, v. 13, no. 50, January-June 1970, pp. 68-80.

Wyndham, Francis. "The New West Indian Writers." BIM, v. 7, no. 28, January-June 1959, pp. 188-190.

Wynter, Sylvia. "Novel and History, Plot and Plantation." SAVACOU, v. 1, no. 5, June 1971, pp. 95-102.

Wynter, Sylvia. "Strangers at the Gate, Caribbean Novelists in Search of Identity." SUNDAY GLEANER, January 18, 1959, p. 14.

Wynter, Sylvia. "We Must Learn to Sit Down Together and Talk About a Little Culture; Reflections on West Indian Writing and Criticism." JAMAICA JOURNAL, part 1, v. 2, no. 4, December 1968, pp. 23-32; part 2, v. 3, no. 1, March 1969, pp. 27-42.

THE MYSTIC MASSEUR (1957)

Naipaul, Vidia Surajprasad

Anon. "Ganesh in the Years of Guilt." SUNDAY GUARDIAN
(Trinidad), June 16, 1957, pp. 23, 27.

Anon. Review. PUBLIC OPINION, April 27, 1957, p. 7.

Anon. Review. SUNDAY GLEANER, May 19, 1957, p. 12.

Anon. Review. THE TIMES (London), May 23, 1957, p. 15.

Anon. Review. TLS, May 31, 1957, p. 333.

Bagley, John. Review. SPECTATOR, v. 198, May 1957, p. 688.

Bryden, Ronald. Review. LISTENER, v. 57, 1957, p. 890.

Collymore, Frank. Review. BIM, v. 7, no. 26, January-June
1958, pp. 119-120.

Levin, Martin. "How the Ball Bounces Down Trinidad Way."
NYT, April 12, 1959, Section 7, p. 5.

Quinton, Anthony. Review. NEW STATESMAN, v. 53, May 18,
1957, p. 649.

Ross, Angus. "A Shaggy Mystic." PUBLIC OPINION, August 24,
1957, p. 7.

Seymour, Arthur J. Review. KYK-OVER-AL, v. 8, no. 24,
December 1958, pp. 84-85.

THE SUFFRAGE OF ELVIRA (1958)

Anon. Review. THE TIMES (London), April 24, 1958, p. 13.

Anon. Review. TLS, no. 2931, May 2, 1958, p. 237.

Davenport, John. Review. LSO, April 20, 1958, p. 17.

Newby, P. H. Review. LONDON MAGAZINE, v. 5, no. 11,
November 1958, pp. 82-84.

Panton, George. "Satire on Trinidad." SUNDAY GLEANER, June
22, 1958, p. 11.

MIGUEL STREET (1959)

Anon. "Naipaul Does It Again." SUNDAY GUARDIAN (Trinidad),

Naipaul, Vidia Surajprasad

    May 17, 1959, p. 22.

  Anon. Review. THE TIMES (London), April 23, 1959, p. 15.

  Anon. "Street Scene." TLS, no. 2982, April 24, 1959, p. 237.

  Coleman, John. Review. SPECTATOR, v. 202, April 24, 1959, p. 595.

  Collymore, Frank. Review. BIM, v. 8, no. 29, June-December 1959, p. 67.

  Davenport, John. Review. LSO, April 19, 1959, p. 22.

  James, Louis. "The Sad Initiation of Lamming's 'G.' . . ." COMMON WEALTH: PAPERS DELIVERED AT THE CONFERENCE OF COMMONWEALTH LITERATURE, AARHUS UNIVERSITY, APRIL 26-30, 1971. Aarhus, Denmark: Aarhus University, 1971, pp. 138-139.

  Moore, Gerald. Review. BLACK ORPHEUS, no. 9, June 1961, pp. 66-67.

  Panton, George. Review. SUNDAY GLEANER, November 1, 1959, p. 14.

  Richardson, Maurice. Review. NEW STATESMAN, v. 57, May 1959, p. 618.

  Rodman, Selden. "Catfish Row, Trinidad." NYT, May 15, 1960, Section 7, p. 43.

  Wyndham, Francis. LONDON MAGAZINE, v. 6, no. 9, September 1959, pp. 80-81.

A HOUSE FOR MR. BISWAS (1961)

  Anon. Review. THE TIMES (London), October 5, 1961, p. 16.

  Anon. Review. TLS, no. 3109, September 29, 1961, p. 641.

  Argyle, Barry. "V. S. Naipaul's A HOUSE FOR MR. BISWAS." LITERARY HALF-YEARLY, v. 14, no. 2, July 1973, pp. 81-95.

  Argyle, Barry. "A West Indian Epic." CARIBBEAN QUARTERLY,

Index of Authors

Naipaul, Vidia Surajprasad

v. 16, no. 4, December 1970, pp. 61-69.

Bagai, Leona Bell. Review. BOOKS ABROAD, v. 36, Autumn 1962, p. 453.

Butler, Rupert. Review. JLW, v. 5, October 1961, p. 419.

Carr, Bill. "A House for Mr. Naipaul." PUBLIC OPINION, March 20, 1964, pp. 8-10.

Fido, Martin. "Mr. Biswas and Mr. Polly." ARIEL, v. 5, no. 4, October 1974, pp. 30-37.

Fuller, John. Review. LISTENER, v. 66, October 19, 1961, p. 621.

Gilbert, Morris. "Hapless Defiance." NYT, June 24, 1962, Section 7, p. 30.

Jacobson, Dan. "Self-help in Hot Places." NEW STATESMAN, v. 62, September 29, 1961, p. 440.

Krikler, Bernard. Review. LISTENER, v. 71, February 13, 1964, pp. 270-271.

Ligny, Michel. Review (French). PRESENCE AFRICAINE, no. 52, 1964, pp. 233-235.

MacInnes, Colin. "Caribbean Masterpiece." LSO, October 1, 1961, p. 31. Also appears in PUBLIC OPINION, October 7, 1961, p. 3; and in BIM, v. 9, no. 35, July-December 1962, pp. 221-223.

Mitchell, Julian. Review. SPECTATOR, v. 207, October 6, 1961, p. 472.

Ormerod, David. "Theme and Image in V. S. Naipaul's A HOUSE FOR MR. BISWAS." TSL, v. 8, no. 4, Winter 1967, pp. 589-602.

Owens, R. J. Review. CARIBBEAN QUARTERLY, v. 7, no. 4, April 1962, pp. 217-219.

Panton, George. "West Indian Writing Comes of Age." SUNDAY GLEANER, December 3, 1961, p. 14.

Ramchand, Kenneth. "The World of A HOUSE FOR MR. BISWAS."

Naipaul, Vidia Surajprasad

> CARIBBEAN QUARTERLY, v. 15, no. 1, March 1969, pp. 60-72.
> Also appears in his THE WEST INDIAN NOVEL AND ITS BACK-
> GROUND. London: Faber and Faber, 1970.

> Rohlehr, F. Gordon. "Character and Rebellion in A HOUSE FOR
> MR. BISWAS." NEW WORLD QUARTERLY, v. 4, no. 4, Cropover
> 1968, pp. 66-72.

> Rohlehr, F. Gordon. "Predestination, Frustration and Sym-
> bolic Darkness in Naipaul's A HOUSE FOR MR. BISWAS."
> CARIBBEAN QUARTERLY, v. 10, no. 1, 1964, pp. 3-11.

> Warner, Maureen. "Cultural Confrontation, Disintegration
> and Syncretism in A HOUSE FOR MR. BISWAS." CARIBBEAN
> QUARTERLY, v. 16, no. 4, December 1970, pp. 70-79.

> Wyndham, Francis. Review. LONDON MAGAZINE, v. 1, no. 7,
> New Series, October 1971, pp. 90-93.

THE MIDDLE PASSAGE (1962)

> Allen, Walter. "Fear of Trinidad." NEW STATESMAN, v. 64,
> August 3, 1962, pp. 149-150.

> Anon. "The Case for Naipaul." SUNDAY GUARDIAN (Trinidad),
> February 17, 1963, p. 3.

> Anon. "On and Off Miguel Street." THE TIMES (London),
> August 2, 1962, p. 13.

> Anon. Review. BAJAN, v. 10, no. 10, June 1963, p. 24.

> Anon. "The Re-Engagement of Mr. Naipaul." TLS, no. 3154,
> August 10, 1962, p. 578.

> Bedford, Sybille. "Stoic Traveler." NYRB, v. 1, no. 6,
> 1963, pp. 4-5.

> Brathwaite, Doris. Review. IOUNALOA, RECENT WRITING FROM
> ST. LUCIA. Castries, St. Lucia: Department of Extra-
> Mural Studies, 1963, pp. 72-73.

> Bryden, Ronald. "New Map of Hell." SPECTATOR, v. 209,
> August 3, 1962, p. 161.

> Carr, Bill. "The Annoying Ironist." PUBLIC OPINION, March
> 26, 1964, pp. 8-9.

Index of Authors

Naipaul, Vidia Surajprasad

Carr, Bill. "The Irony of West Indian Society." SUNDAY
    GLEANER, January 27, 1963, pp. 14, 24.

Chapman, Esther. Review. WIR, January 1963, p. 7.

Hearne, John. Review. CARIBBEAN QUARTERLY, v. 8, no. 4,
    December 1962, pp. 65-66. Also appears in SUNDAY GLEANER,
    February 3, 1963, p. 14; and under the title "John Hearne
    Hearne's Unsentimental Journey with V. S. Naipaul." in
    SUNDAY GUARDIAN (Trinidad), February 3, 1963, pp. 3, 4.

Jabavu, Noni. "Return of an Insider." NYT, September 22,
    1963, Section 7, p. 14.

Marshall, Harold. Review. BIM, v. 9, no. 36, January-June
    1963, p. 290.

Panton, George. "Slavery's Greatest Damage." SUNDAY
    GLEANER, September 9, 1962, p. 14.

Poore, Charles. "A Native's Return to the Caribbean World."
    NYT, September 7, 1963, p. 17.

Pope-Hennessy. "Return to the Caribbean." LSO, July 29,
    1962, p. 18.

Walcott, Derek. "History and Picong." SUNDAY GUARDIAN
    (Trinidad), September 30, 1962, p. 9.

MR. STONE AND THE KNIGHTS COMPANION (1963)

Allen, Walter. "London Again." NYRB, v. 2, no. 3, 1964,
    p. 21.

Anon. Review. THE TIMES (London), May 30, 1963, p. 16.

Anon. "Sunk in Suburbia." TLS, 3196, May 31, 1963, p. 385.

Boxill, Anthony. "The Concept of Spring in V. S. Naipaul's
    MR. STONE AND THE KNIGHTS COMPANION. ARIEL, v. 5, no. 4,
    October 1974, pp. 21-28.

Brooke, Jocelyn. Review. LISTENER, v. 69, May 30, 1963,
    p. 934.

Carr, Bill. "A Prison of One's Own." PUBLIC OPINION,
    September 7, 1963, p. 11.

Naipaul, Vidia Surajprasad

Dathorne, O. R. Review. BLACK ORPHEUS, no. 14, February 1964, pp. 59-60.

Mitchell, Adrian. Review. SPECTATOR, v. 210, June 21, 1963.

Panton, George. "The Absence of an Old Age Cure." SGM, August 25, 1963, p. 10.

Pritchett, V. S. "Climacteric." NEW STATESMAN, v. 65, May 31, 1963, pp. 831-832.

Raphael, Frederick. "The Latter Spring of Mr. Stone." SUNDAY GUARDIAN (Trinidad), June 9, 1963, p. 15.

Raven, Simon. Review. LSO, May 26, 1963, p. 21.

Ross, Alan. Review. LONDON MAGAZINE, v. 3, no. 5, New Series, August 1963, p. 88.

Willis, David. "A Compassionate Spectator." SUNDAY GUARDIAN (Trinidad), January 10, 1971, p. 9.

AN AREA OF DARKNESS (1964)

Anon. "Mr. Naipaul's Passage to India." TLS, no. 3265, September 24, 1964, p. 881.

Anon. Review. BAJAN, v. 12, no. 6, February 1965, p. 29.

Anon. Review. THE TIMES (London), November 16, 1968, p. 25.

Anon. "West Indian Writer Visits Home of His Ancestors." THE TIMES (London), September 17, 1964, p. 17.

Biswas, Robin. "Exhaustion and Persistence." TAMARACK REVIEW, no. 35, Spring 1965, pp. 75-80.

Dathorne, O. R. Review. BLACK ORPHEUS, no. 18, October 1965, pp. 60-61.

Delany, Austin. "Mother India as Bitch." TRANSITION, v. 6, no. 26, 1966, pp. 50-51.

Gowda, H. H. Anniah. "Naipaul in India." LITERARY HALF-YEARLY, v. 11, no. 2, 1970, pp. 163-170.

Naim, C. M. Review. BOOKS ABROAD, v. 40, no. 2, Spring

Naipaul, Vidia Surajprasad

1966, p. 230.

Narasimhaiah, C. D. "Somewhere Something Has Snapped; A Close Look at V. S. Naipaul's AN AREA OF DARKNESS. LITERARY CRITERION, v. 6, no. 4, Summer 1964, pp. 83-96.

Panton, George. "More Seeking by West Indians." SUNDAY GLEANER, October 4, 1964, p. 4.

Prescott, Orville. "The Land of His Ancestors." NYT, April 16, 1965, p. 17.

Pritchett, V. S. "Back to India." NEW STATESMAN, v. 68, September 11, 1964, pp. 361-362.

Reed, Henry. "Passage to India." SPECTATOR, v. 213, October 2, 1964, p. 452.

Singh, K. Natwar. "Unhappy Pilgrim." NYT, July 11, 1965, Section 7, p. 35.

Wain, John. "Mother India." LSO, September 13, 1964, p. 24.

Walcott, Derek. "Mr. Naipaul's Passage to India." SUNDAY GUARDIAN (Trinidad), September 20, 1964, p. 4.

Walsh, William. "Meeting Extremes." JCL, no. 1, September 1965, pp. 169-172.

THE MIMIC MEN (1967)

Anon. Review. BAJAN, no. 168, August 1967, p. 26.

Anon. Review. THE TIMES (London), April 27, 1967, p. 16.

Anon. "Suburbia in the Sun." TLS, no. 3400, April 27, 1967, p. 349.

Corke, Hilary. Review. LISTENER, v. 77, May 25, 1967, p. 693.

Gray, Simon. Review. NEW STATESMAN, v. 73, May 5, 1967, pp. 622-623.

Moore, Gerald. Review. BIM, v. 12, no. 46, January-June 1968, pp. 134-136.

Naipaul, Vidia Surajprasad

Panton, George. "The West Indian Scene." SUNDAY GLEANER,
June 18, 1967, p. 4.

Pritchett, V. S. "Crack-up." NYRB, v. 10, no. 7, 1968.

Pryce-Jones, David. Review. LONDON MAGAZINE, New Series,
v. 7, no. 2, May 1967, pp. 82-84.

Ramraj, Victor. "The All Embracing Christlike Vision: Tone
and Attitude in THE MIMIC MEN." COMMON WEALTH, PAPERS
DELIVERED AT THE CONFERENCE OF COMMONWEALTH LITERATURE,
AARHUS UNIVERSITY, APRIL 26-30, 1971. Aarhus, Denmark:
Aarhus University, 1971, pp. 125-134.

Rao, K. S. Narayana. Review. BOOKS ABROAD, v. 42, no. 1,
Winter 1968, p. 167.

Seymour-Smith, Martin. Review. SPECTATOR, v. 218, May 5,
1967, p. 528.

Thorpe, Marjorie. "The Mimic Men; A Study of Isolation."
NWQ, v. 4, no. 4, Cropover 1968, pp. 55-59.

Wain, John. Review. NYRB, v. 9, no. 7, 1967, pp. 33-35.

Walcott, Derek. "Is V. A. Naipaul an Angry Young Man." TGM,
August 6, 1967, pp. 8-9.

Wilson, Angus. "Between Two Islands." LSO, April 30, 1967,
p. 27.

A FLAG ON THE ISLAND   (1967)

Anon. "Movietone." TLS, no. 3420, September 14, 1967, p.
813.

Anon. "Mr. Naipaul's Other Island." LSO, September 10,
1967, p. 22.

Anon. Review. THE TIMES (London), September 14, 1967, p.
p. 11.

Buchan, William. Review. SPECTATOR, v. 219, September 22,
1967, p. 328.

Crosskill, D. Review. PUBLIC OPINION, July 11, 1969, p. 3.

Naipaul, Vidia Surajprasad

MacNamara, Desmond. Review. NEW STATESMAN, v. 74,
September 15, 1967, p. 325.

Panton, George. "West Indian Satirist." SUNDAY GLEANER,
December 3, 1967, p. 4.

Pritchett, V. S. "Crack-up." NYRB, v. 10, no. 7, 1968.

Wain, John. "Characters in the Sun." NYT, April 7, 1968,
Section 7, p. 4.

THE LOSS OF ELDORADO (1969)

Anon. Review. BAJAN, no. 203, July 1970, p. 22.

Anon. Review. TLS, no. 3539, December 25, 1969, p. 1471.

Bryden, Ronald. "Between the Epics." NEW STATESMAN, v. 78,
November 7, 1969, pp. 661-662.

Carnegie, J. A. "Rediscovery from Outside." SAVACOU, v. 1,
no. 5, June 1971, pp. 125-128.

Clasp, Bertram. "Another View of THE LOSS OF ELDORADO."
SUNDAY GUARDIAN (Trinidad), December 21, 1969, p. 4.

Elliot, J. H. "Triste Trinidad." NYRB, v. 14, no. 10, 1970.

Greene, Graham. "Terror in Trinidad." LSO, October 26,
1969, p. 34.

Hosein, Clyde. "Naipaul's Latest Called a Novel About
History." SUNDAY GUARDIAN (Trinidad), December 14, 1969,
p. 20.

Innes, Hammond. Review. SPECTATOR, v. 223, November 8,
1969, p. 647.

Lask, Thomas. "Brave New World." NYT, June 20, 1970, p. 27.

Noel, Jesse A. "Historicity and Homelessness in Naipaul."
CARIBBEAN STUDIES, v. 11, no. 3, October 1971, pp. 83-87.

Paterson, James Hamilton. "Hot Little Off-Shore Island."
SUNDAY GUARDIAN (Trinidad), November 16, 1969, p. 5.

Rabassa, Gregory. Review. NYT, May 24, 1970, Section 7,

Naipaul, Vidia Surajprasad

p. 7.

Wade, C. Alan. "The Novelist as Historian." LITERARY HALF-
YEARLY, v. 11, no. 2, 1970, pp. 179-184.

IN A FREE STATE (1971)

Anon. "Nowhere to Go." TLS, no. 3631, August 10, 1971,
p. 1199.

Anon. "Trinidadian Literature Today and Yesterday." SUNDAY
GLEANER, October 17, 1971, p. 31

Calder, Angus. "Darkest Naipaul." NEW STATESMAN, v. 82,
October 8, 1971.

Dopson, Andrew. "I'll Stop Writing for Less. . . ." SUNDAY
GUARDIAN (Trinidad), December 12, 1971, p. 18.

Gordimer, Nadine. "White Expatriates and Black Mimics."
NYT, October 17, 1971, Section 7, p. 5.

Hamilton, Ian. Interview. SAVACOU, no. 9/10, 1974, pp. 120-
126.

Hope, Francis. "Displaced Persons." LSO, October 3, 1971,
p. 37.

Kazin, Alfred. "Displaced Persons." NYRB, v. 17, no. 11,
1971, pp. 3-4.

Lane, M. Travis. "The Casualties of Freedom: V. S.
Naipaul's IN A FREE STATE." WLWE, v. 12, April 1973,
pp. 106-110.

Lask, Thomas. "Where Is the Enemy?" NYT, December 25, 1971,
p. 15.

McDowell, Frederick. Review. CONTEMPORARY LITERATURE, v.
13, Summer 1972, pp. 379-380.

McGuiness, Frank. "A Rough Game." LONDON MAGAZINE, v. 11,
no. 4, New Series, October/November 1971, pp. 156-158.

Potter, Dennis. "A Long Way from Home." THE TIMES (London),
October 4, 1971, p. 15.

Nicholas, Arthur

Waugh, Auberon. Review. SPECTATOR, v. 227, October 9, 1971,
p. 511.

Whitely, John. "Naipaul's New Book." SUNDAY GUARDIAN
(Trinidad), October 10, 1971, p. 7.

THE OVERCROWDED BARRACOON (1972)

Anon. "In Search of Another Country." TLS, no. 3689,
November 17, 1972, p. 1391.

Anon. Review. NYT, September 16, 1973, Section 7, p. 18.

Harrison, Tony. Review. LONDON MAGAZINE, v. 12, no. 5,
New Series, December 1972/January 1973, pp. 135-140.

Hope, Francis. "Areas of Darkness." LSO, October 29, 1972,
p. 38.

C. L. Lindo, Cedric . Review. SUNDAY GLEANER, November 5,
1972, p. 39.

McSweeney, Kerry. Review. QUEENS QUARTERLY, v. 80, Autumn
1973, pp. 495-497.

Pantin, Raoul. "The Ultimate Transient." CARIBBEAN CONTACT,
v. 1, no. 2, January 1973, pp. 4, 23.

Potter, Dennis. "The Writer and His Myth." THE TIMES
(London), December 4, 1972, p. 6.

GUERILLAS (1975)

Anon. "West Indian GUERILLAS." SUNDAY GLEANER, November 23,
1975, p. 23.

Broyard, Anatole. "The Author vs. His Characters." NYT,
November 20, 1975, p. 39.

Jones, D. A. N. Review. TLS, no. 3835, September 12, 1975,
p. 1013.

Theroux, Paul. "An Intelligence from the Third World." NYT,
November 16, 1975, Section 7, pp. 1-2.

NICHOLAS, ARTHUR. Jamaica, 1875-1934

Nicholas, Arthur

General

Oakley, Leo. "Ideas of Patriotism and National Dignity in Some Jamaican Writings." JAMAICA JOURNAL, v. 4, no. 3, September 1970, pp. 16-21. Also appears in SUNDAY G GLEANER, part 1, March 28, 1970, pp. 31, 34; part 2, April 4, 1970, p. 27; part 3, April 11, 1970, p. 25, as "Patriotism, National Dignity in Jamaican Writings."

Other Works

ARCADIA: POEMS   (1949)

NICOLE, CHRISTOPHER. Guyana, 1930-   (some novels under pseudonyms Andrew York and Peter Grange)

General

Rickards, Colin. "Christopher Nicole, Mystery Man among West Indian Writers." SUNDAY GLEANER, March 16, 1969, pp. 4, 11.

Seymour, Arthur J. "The Novel in Guyana." KAIE, no. 4, July 1967, pp. 59-63.

Sparer, Joyce L. "Attitudes Towards 'Race' in Guyanese Literature." CARIBBEAN STUDIES, v. 8, no. 2, July 1968, pp. 23-63.

SHADOWS IN THE JUNGLE   (1961)

Rickards, Colin. "Bumper Year for West Indian Books." SUNDAY GLEANER, January 7, 1962, p. 14.

Walcott, Derek. "A Story of the B. G. Bush." SUNDAY GUARDIAN (Trinidad), October 29, 1961, p. 4.

DARK NOON   (1963)

Panton, George. "Sex in the Tropics." SUNDAY GLEANER, February 17, 1963, p. 14.

BLOOD AMYOT   (1964)

Panton, George. Review. SUNDAY GLEANER, September 27, 1964, p. 4.

Ogilvie, William G.

THE AMYOT CRIME (1965)

    Panton, George. Review. SUNDAY GLEAMER, January 9, 1966,
       p. 4.

WHITE BOY (1966)

    Anon. Review. BAJAN, no. 155, July 1966, p. 31.

    Panton, George. Review. SUNDAY GLEANER, June 12, 1966, p.
       4.

KING CREOLE (1966)

    Panton, George. "Happy Goes the Lucky." SUNDAY GLEANER,
       December 11, 1966, p. 4.

THE SELF-LOVERS (1967)

    Panton, George. Review. SUNDAY GLEANER, August 18, 1967,
       p. 4.

THE ELIMINATOR (1966)

    Rickards, Colin. "Caribbean Bookshelf." SUNDAY GLEANER,
       May 18, 1969, p. 4.

THE DEVIATOR (1969)

    Panton, George. Review. SUNDAY GLEANER, July 26, 1970,
       p. 32.

    Rickards, Colin. "Caribbean Bookshelf." SUNDAY GLEANER,
       May 18, 1969, p. 4.

Other Works

OFF-WHITE (1959)

RATOON (1962)

AMYOT'S CAY (1964)

THE CO-ORDINATOR (1967)

OGILVIE, WILLIAM G. Jamaica,

Palmer, C. Everard

CACTUS VILLAGE   (1953)

Wilmot, Cynthia. Review. PUBLIC OPINION, November 7, 1953,
p. 5.

THE GHOST BANK   (1953)

Anon. Review. SUNDAY GLEANER, November 3, 1974, p. 25.

Wilmot, Cynthia. Review. PUBLIC OPINION, February 6, 1954,
p. 5.

PALMER, C. EVERARD.   Jamaica, 1941-

General

Panton, George. "C. Everard Palmer, the Boy's Ideal Story-
Teller." SUNDAY GLEANER, November 3, 1974, p. 25.

A BROKEN VESSEL   (1960)

Panton, George. Review. SUNDAY GLEANER, June 26, 1960, p.
14.

THE CLOUD WITH THE SILVER LINING   (1966)

Panton, George. Review. SUNDAY GLEANER, September 11,
1966, p. 4.

Panton, George. Review. SUNDAY GLEANER, December 25, 1966,
p. 4.

BIG DOC BITTERFOOT   (1967)

Panton, George. "Jamaican Country Life--For Children."
SUNDAY GLEANER, August 4, 1967, p. 4.

THE SUN SALUTES YOU   (1970)

M. M. [Mervyn Morris]. Review. SUNDAY GLEANER, May 3,
1970, p. 29.

THE HUMMINGBIRD PEOPLE   (1971)

Panton, George. Review. SUNDAY GLEANER, June 6, 1971,
p. 29.

Salkey, Andrew. Review. MOKO, no. 65, July 24, 1971, p. 9.

THE WOOING OF BEPPO TATE (1972)

G. P. [George Panton]. "Life in a Vanishing Rural Jamaica."
SUNDAY GLEANER, March 26, 1972, p. 37.

A COW CALLED BOY (1973)

Anon. "Delightful Jamaican Story for Boys." SUNDAY
GLEANER, February 17, 1974, p. 14.

MY FATHER, SUN-SUN JOHNSON (1973)

Anon. "Delightful Jamaican Story for Boys." SUNDAY
GLEANER, February 17, 1974, p. 14.

BABA AND MR. BIG (1974)

Anon. Review. SUNDAY GLEANER, November 10, 1974, p. 27.

Other Works

THE ADVENTURES OF JIMMY MAXWELL (1962)

A TASTE OF DANGER (1963)

PANTIN, RAOUL. Trinidad,

JOURNEY (1976)

Guerin, Verne. "Voice That Speaks for a Private 'I.'"
TAPIA, v. 6, no. 32, August 1976, p. 6.

Questel, Victor. "New Writing in the Caribbean." TAPIA,
v. 6, no. 36, September 5, 1976, pp. 5-7.

PATTERSON, ORLANDO. Jamaica, 1940-

General

Brathwaite, Edward. "Jazz and the West Indian Novel." BIM,
part 1, v. 11, no. 44, January-June 1967, pp. 275-284;
part 2, v. 12, no. 45, July-December 1967, pp. 39-51;
part 3, v. 12, no. 45, January-June 1968, pp. 115-126.

Brathwaite, Edward. "Timehri." SAVACOU, no. 2, September

Patterson, Orlando

      1970, pp. 35-44. Also appears in IS MASSA DAY DEAD.
      New York: Doubleday, 1974, pp. 29-44.

    Brathwaite, Edward. "West Indian Prose Fiction in the
      Sixties, A Survey." CRITICAL SURVEY, v. 3, Winter 1967,
      pp. 169-174. Also appears in BIM, v. 12, no. 47, July-
      December 1968, pp. 157-165 and SUNDAY GLEANER, part 1,
      March 8, 1970, p. 27; part 2, March 15, 1970, p. 27;
      part 3, March 22, 1970, p. 27; part 4, March 29, 1970,
      p. 27.

    Brown, Lloyd W. "The American Image in British West Indian
      Literature." CARIBBEAN STUDIES, v. 11, no. 1, April 1971,
      pp. 30-45.

    Carew, Jan. "Language and Literature in Developing
      Countries." NWF, part 1, v. 1, no. 22, September 3, 1965,
      pp. 25-29; part 2, v. 1, no. 23, September 17, 1965,
      pp. 23-27.

    James, Louis. "Islands of Man, Reflections on the Emergence
      of a West Indian Literature." SOUTHERN REVIEW, v. 2,
      1966, pp. 150-163.

    Jones, Bridget. "Some French Influences in the Fiction of
      Orlando Patterson. SAVACOU, no. 11/12, September 1975,
      pp. 27-38.

    Ramchand, Kenneth. "Obeah and the Supernatural in West
      Indian Literature." JAMAICA JOURNAL, v. 3, no. 2, June
      1969, pp. 52-54.

THE CHILDREN OF SISYPHUS (1964)

    Anon. "Delusions." TLS, no. 3240, April 2, 1964, p. 269.

    Anon. Review. LSO, March 15, 1964, p. 27.

    Coulthard, G. R. Review. CARIBBEAN QUARTERLY, v. 10, no.
      1, March 1964, pp. 69-71.

    Hogg, Donald W. Review. CARIBBEAN STUDIES, v. 5, no. 4,
      January 1966, pp. 59-60.

    Morris, Mervyn. "The Dungle Observed." PUBLIC OPINION,
      April 24, 1964, pp. 7, 13.

Index of Authors

Panton, George. "Not for the Squemish." SUNDAY GLEANER, March 29, 1964, p. 4.

Rickards, Colin. "Brilliant First Novel." SUNDAY GLEANER, April 5, 1964, p. 4.

Vernon, Kay. Review. FLAMBEAU, no. 1, June 1965, p. 30.

Walcott, Derek. "A New Jamaican Novelist." SUNDAY GUARDIAN (Trinidad), May 17, 1964, p. 15.

AN ABSENCE OF RUINS (1967)

Anon. Review. THE TIMES (London), April 6, 1967, p. 9.

Drayton, Arthur D. "Awkward Questions for Jamaicans." JCL, no. 7, July 1969, pp. 125-127.

Moore, Gerald. Review. BIM, v. 12, no. 46, January-June 1968, pp. 134-136.

Morris, Mervyn. Review. PUBLIC OPINION, May 19, 1967, p. 5.

Panton, George. "Jamaican Successor to Albert Camus." SUNDAY GLEANER, June 4, 1967, p. 4.

Ramsaran, J. A. "The Social Groundwork of Politics in Some West Indian Novels." NEGRO DIGEST, v. 18, no. 10, August 1969, pp. 71-77.

Rhode, Eric. Review. NEW STATESMAN, v. 73, April 7, 1967, pp. 477-478.

DIE THE LONG DAY (1972)

Anon. "Interesting Picture of Jamaica's Past." SUNDAY GLEANER, September 22, 1974, p. 32.

Gant, Liz. Review. BLACK WORLD, v. 22, no. 4, February 1973, pp. 78-79.

Hearne, John. "The Novel as Sociology as Bore." CARIBBEAN QUARTERLY, v. 18, no. 4, 1972, pp. 78-81.

C. L. [Cedric Lindo]. "Jamaica in the Days of Slavery." SUNDAY GLEANER, August 27, 1972, p. 45.

Quayle, Ada

QUAYLE, ADA. Jamaica,

   THE MISTRESS (1957)

      Anon. "West Indian Novelist Paints Sorry Picture of Old
        Jamaica." SUNDAY GUARDIAN (Trinidad), March 30, 1958,
        p. 18.

      Collymore, Frank. Review. BIM, v. 7, no. 27, July–December
        1958, pp. 185–186.

QUESTEL, VICTOR D. Trinidad,

   General

      Fraser, Alfred. "The Experience of the 70's." NEW VOICES,
        no. 2, 1973, pp. 33–35.

      Rohlehr, F. Gordon. "Afterthoughts." TAPIA, no. 23,
        December 26, 1971, pp. 8, 13. Also appears in BIM, v.
        14, no. 56, January–June 1973, pp. 227–230.

      Rohlehr, F. Gordon. "West Indian Poetry: Some Problems of
        Assessment, Part 1." BIM, v. 14, no. 54, pp. 80–88.

   SCORE (with Anson Gonzalez, 1973)

      Brown, Stewart. Review. NOW, no. 2, Summer 1973, pp. 9–12.

      Hackett, Winston. "Survival." TAPIA, v. 5, no. 34, August
        1975, pp. 4–5, 9; part 2, no. 36, September 1975, pp. 6–7.

   RAMKEESOON, PETER. Trinidad,

   SUNDAY MORNING COMING DOWN (1976)

      Massy, Alvin. "Seized Novel a Sexy Meet-the-People Jaunt."
        TAPIA, v. 6, no. 30, July 25, 1976, p. 5.

REDCAM, TOM (pseudonym of Thomas Henry McDermot). Jamaica,
   1870–1933

   General

      R. L. C. A. [R. L. C. Aarons]. "Jamaica's First Poet
        Laureate." SUNDAY GLEANER, June 30, 1974, p. 32.

Anon. "T. H. McDermot, Pioneer of Modern Jamaica." SUNDAY
GLEANER, June 21, 1970, p. 33.

Bennett, Wycliffe. "The Jamaican Poets." LL, v. 57, no.
128, April 1948, pp. 58-61.

Bennett, Wycliffe. "Tom Redcam, Father of Jamaican Poetry."
SUNDAY GLEANER, July 6, 1947, p. 6.

Bennett, Wycliffe. "Tom Redcam, Poet-Prophet." SUNDAY
GLEANER, August 18, 1946, pp. 8, 9.

Brown, Wayne. "West Indian Poetry of the 1940's: Part 1."
SUNDAY GUARDIAN (Trinidad), September 13, 1970, p. 9.

Chapman, Esther. "Some Books of West Indian Interest; More
Pioneer Press Books." WIR, v. 3, no. 6, June 9, 1951,
p. 16.

Jacobs, H. P. "The Literary Movement." PUBLIC OPINION,
March 4, 1939, p. 3.

Jacobs, H. P. "Tom Redcam Re-assessed." PUBLIC OPINION,
March 30, 1957, p. 7.

McFarlane, Basil. "On Jamaican Poetry." KYK-OVER-AL, v. 3,
no. 13, Year-end 1951, pp. 207-209.

Morris, Mervyn. "The All-Jamaica Library." JAMAICA JOURNAL,
v. 6, no. 1, March 1972, pp. 47-49.

Oakley, Leo. "Ideas of Patriotism and National Dignity in
Some Jamaican Writing." JAMAICA JOURNAL, v. 4, no. 3,
September 1970, pp. 16-21. Also appears in SUNDAY
GLEANER, part 1, March 28, 1970, pp. 31, 34; part 2,
April 4, 1970, p. 27; part 3, April 11, 1970, p. 25.

Roberts, W. Adolphe. "Caribbean Literature: The British
Possessions." WIR, v. 4, no. 42, April 25, 1953, pp.
16-17.

Roberts, W. Adolphe. "That Jamaica May Remember--Tom
Redcam, Founder of Our Literature." SUNDAY GLEANER,
March 1, 1959, p. 8.

Sen, Dilip Kumar. "An Indian Looks at West Indian Poetry;
A Footnote to Caribbean Poetry Written in English."

Redcam, Tom

   SUNDAY GLEANER, January 12, 1964, p. 4.

   Seymour, Arthur J. "The Literary Adventures of the West
      Indies." KYK-OVER-AL, v. 2, no. 10, April 1950, entire
      issue. 40 pp.

Other Works

BECKA'S BUCKRA BABY (1903)

ONE BROWN GIRL AND-- (1909)

REID, VICTOR STAFFORD. Jamaica, 1913-

General

   Amis, Kingsley. "Fresh Winds from the West." SPECTATOR,
      v. 200, May 1958, pp. 565-566.

   Anon. "FOCUS. . . The Short Stories." PUBLIC OPINION,
      December 18, 1948, pp. 10-11.

   Anon. "Victor Reid's Vivid Prose." SUNDAY GLEANER, December
      12, 1948, p. 8.

   Brathwaite, Edward. "Jazz and the West Indian Novel." BIM,
      part 1, v. 11, no. 44, January-June 1967, pp. 275-284;
      part 2, v. 12, no. 45, July-December 1967, pp. 39-51;
      part 3, v. 12, no. 46, January-June 1968, pp. 115-126.

   Brathwaite, Edward. "The New West Indian Novelists: Part
      One." BIM, v. 8, no. 31, July-December 1960, pp. 207-
      208.

   Brown, Lloyd W. "The Crisis of Black Identity in the West
      Indian Novel." CRITIQUE, v. 11, no. 3, 1969, pp. 97-112.

   Carew, Jan. "Language and Literature in Developing
      Countries." NWF, part 1, v. 1, no. 22, September 3, 1965,
      pp. 25-29; part 2, v. 1, no. 23, September 17, 1965,
      pp. 23-27.

   Carr, Bill. "Reflections on the Novel in the British
      Caribbean." QUEENS QUARTERLY, v. 7, Winter 1963,
      pp. 585-597.

   Dewar, Lilian. "Jamaica in the Novel." KYK-OVER-AL, v. 3,

Index of Authors

Reid, Victor Stafford

no. 12, Mid-year 1951, pp. 108-113.

Hall, Stuart M. "Lamming, Selvon, and Some Trends in the
West Indian Novel." BIM, v. 6, no. 23, December 1955,
pp. 172-178.

James, Louis. "Islands of Man, Reflections on the Emergence
of a West Indian Literature." SOUTHERN REVIEW, v. 2,
1966, pp. 150-163.

James, Louis. "Of Redcoats and Leopards, Two Novels by V. S.
Reid." THE ISLANDS IN BETWEEN. London: Oxford University Press, 1968, pp. 64-72.

Lacovia, R. M. "Caribbean Literature in English: 1949-
1970." BAR, v. 2, nos. 1 and 2, 1971, pp. 109-125.

Maxwell, Marina. "Towards a Revolution in the Arts."
SAVACOU, no. 2, September 1970, pp. 19-32.

Moore, Gerald. "Use Men Language." BIM, v. 15, no. 57,
March 1974, pp. 69-76.

Oakley, Leo. "Ideas of Patriotism and National Dignity in
Some Jamaican Writings." JAMAICA JOURNAL, v. 4, no. 3,
September 1970, pp. 16-21. Also appears in SUNDAY
GLEANER (Jamaica), part 1, March 28, 1970, pp. 31-34;
part 2, April 4, 1970, p. 27; part 3, April 11, 1970, p.
25 as "Patriotism, National Dignity in Jamaican Writings."

Panton, George. "NEW DAY Man--A Trail Blazer." SUNDAY
GLEANER, September 29, 1974, p. 27.

Ramchand, Kenneth. "Dialect in West Indian Fiction."
CARIBBEAN QUARTERLY, v. 14, nos. 1 and 2, March-June
1968, pp. 27-42. Also appears in his THE WEST INDIAN
NOVEL AND ITS BACKGROUND. London: Faber and Faber, 1970,
pp. 96-116.

Ramchand, Kenneth. "History and the Novel: A Literary
Critics Approach." SAVACOU, v. 1, no. 5, June 1971,
pp. 103-113.

Rawlins, Randolph. "Migrants with Manuscripts, Social
Background of the West Indian Novel." BLACK ORPHEUS,
no. 4, 1958, pp. 46-50.

Reid, Victor Stafford

> Roberts, W. Adolphe. "Caribbean Literature: The British
> Possessions." WIR, v. 4, no. 42, April 25, 1953, pp.
> 16-17.
>
> Seymour, Arthur J. "The Literary Adventure of the West
> Indies." KYK-OVER-AL, v. 2, no. 10, April 1950, entire
> issue, 40 pp.
>
> Seymour, Arthur J. "The Novel in the British Caribbean."
> BIM, part 1, v. 11, no. 42, January-June 1966, pp. 83-
> 85; part 2, v. 11, no. 43, July-December 1966, pp. 176·
> 180; part 3, v. 11, no. 44, January-June 1967, pp. 328-
> 242; part 4, v. 12, no. 46, January-June 1968, pp. 75-80.
>
> Wyndham, Francis. "The New West Indian Writers." BIM, v.
> 7, no. 28, January-June 1959, pp. 188-190.
>
> Wynter, Sylvia. "Novel and History, Plot and Plantation."
> SAVACOU, v. 1, no. 5, June 1971, pp. 95-102.

NEW DAY (1949)

> Anon. Review. NEGRO DIGEST, v. 7, no. 8, June 1949, p. 80.
>
> Anon. Review. NEW STATESMAN, v. 39, April 1, 1950, p. 378.
>
> Anon. Review. SUNDAY GLEANER, January 17, 1971, p. 27.
>
> Archibald, Charles. Review. BIM, v. 3, no. 12, 1949.
>
> Beck, Ervin. Review. BOOKS ABROAD, v. 48, no. 3, Summer
> 1974.
>
> Carter, Martin. "A Note on Vic Reid's NEW DAY." KYK-OVER-
> AL, v. 8, no. 24, December 1958, pp. 81-82.
>
> Escoffery, Gloria. Review. PUBLIC OPINION, April 9, 1949,
> p. 6.
>
> Goodman, Anne L. Review. NYT, March 27, 1949, Section 7,
> p. 31.
>
> Hale, Lionel. Review. LSO, February 19, 1950, p. 7.
>
> Holman, M. Carl. "Rebellion in Retrospect." PHYLON, v. 10,
> 1949, pp. 187-188.

Reid, Victor Stafford

Iremonger, Lucille. Review. LL, v. 64, no. 151, 1950,
pp. 233-235.

Jacobs, H. P. "The Dialect of Victor Reid." WIR, v. 1,
no. 1, May 1949, pp. 12-15.

Jacobs, H. P. "The Historic Foundation of NEW DAY." WIR,
part 1, v. 1, no. 2, May 14, 1949, pp. 21-22; part 2, v.
1, no. 3, May 21, 1949, pp. 10-11; part 3, v. 1, no. 4,
May 28, 1949, pp. 18-19.

James, Louis. "The Sad Initiation of Lamming's 'G.' . . ."
COMMON WEALTH, PAPERS DELIVERED AT THE CONFERENCE OF
COMMONWEALTH LITERATURE, AARHUS UNIVERSITY, APRIL 26-30,
1971. Aarhus, Denmark: Aarhus University, 1971, pp. 135-
143.

Sherlock, Phillip M. Review. CARIBBEAN QUARTERLY, v. 1,
no. 1, 1949, pp. 31-32.

THE LEOPARD (1958)

Anon. "A Monument of Tragedy is Reid's Second Novel."
SUNDAY GUARDIAN (Trinidad), April 13, 1958, p. 18.

Anon. Review. TLS, no. 2925, March 28, 1958, p. 165.

Barkham, John. "The Enemy Was Bwana." NYT, April 13, 1956,
Section 7, p. 40.

Beier, Ulli. Review. BLACK ORPHEUS, no. 5, May 1959,
pp. 52-54.

Coddling, Eric. "Truly an Impressive Work." PUBLIC OPINION,
April 19, 1958, p. 7.

Dathorne, O. R. "Africa in the Literature of the West
Indies." JCL, no. 1, September 1965, pp. 95-116.

Dathorne, O. R. "Africa in West Indian Literature." BLACK
ORPHEUS, no. 16, October 1964, pp. 42-53. Also appears
as THE THEME OF AFRICA IN WEST INDIAN LITERATURE IN
PHYLON, v. 26, Fall 1965, pp. 255-276.

Panton, George. Review. SUNDAY GLEANER, February 27, 1971,
p. 47.

Panton, George. "Vic Reid Makes Triumphant Return." SUNDAY GLEANER, April 6, 1958, p. 11.

Seymour, A. J. Review. KYK-OVER-AL, v. 8, no. 24, December 1958, pp. 83-84.

SIXTY-FIVE (1960)

Anon. "The Romance of Jamaican History." SUNDAY GLEANER, December 25, 1960, p. 14.

THE YOUNG WARRIORS (1967)

Panton, George. "For Young Jamaicans." SUNDAY GLEANER, May 7, 1967, p. 4.

RHYS, JEAN. Dominica, 1898-1979

General

Braybrooke, Neville. "Between Dog and Wolf." SPECTATOR, v. 219, July 21, 1967, pp. 77-78.

Braybrooke, Neville. "The Return of Jean Rhys." CARIBBEAN QUARTERLY, v. 16, no. 4, December 1970, pp. 43-46.

Casey, Nancy. "The 'Liberated' Woman in Jean Rhys' Later Short Fiction." RRI, v. 4, no. 2, Summer 1974, pp. 264-272.

Lane, Margaret. "Life and Hard Times." SPECTATOR, v. 222, May 16, 1969, pp. 649-650.

Mellown, Elgin W. "Character and Themes in the Novels of Jean Rhys." CONTEMPORARY LITERATURE, v. 13, Autumn 1972, pp. 458-475.

Panton, George. "Excellent Writer from Dominica." SUNDAY November 17, 1968, p. 4.

Questel, Victor. "Their Tragic Destiny." TAPIA, v. 4, no. 20, May 16, 1976, pp. 4, 11.

Ramchand, Kenneth. "Terrified Consciousness." JCL, no. 7, July 1969, pp. 8-19. Also appears in his THE WEST INDIAN NOVEL AND ITS BACKGROUND. London: Faber and Faber, 1970, pp. 223-236.

Index of Authors

Rhys, Jean

Wyndham, Francis. "Introduction to Jean Rhys." LONDON
MAGAZINE, New Series, v. 7, no. 1, April 1967, pp. 15-18.

VOYAGE IN THE DARK (1934)

Anon. Review. TLS, no. 3412, July 20, 1967, p. 644.

Casey, Nancy. "Study in the Alienation of a Creole Woman."
CARIBBEAN QUARTERLY, v. 19, no. 3, September 1973, pp. 95-
102.

QUARTET (1929, original title, POSTURES, 1928)

Anon. Review. NYT, October 13, 1974, Section 7, p. 44.

Bailey, Paul. "Bedrooms in Hell." LSO, May 18, 1969, p. 30.

Hazzard, Shirley. Review. NYT, April 11, 1971, p. 6.

AFTER LEAVING MR. MACKENZIE (1931)

Bailey, Paul. "Bedrooms in Hell." LSO, May 18, 1969, p. 30.

Naipaul, V. S. "Without a Dog's Chance." NYRB, v. 18, no.
9, 1972.

GOOD MORNING MIDNIGHT (1939)

Anon. Review. TLS, 3412, July 20, 1967, p. 644.

Broyard, Anatole. "A Difficult Year for Hats." NYT, March
26, 1974, p. 39.

Ricks, Christopher. Review. NYRB, v. 15, no. 2, 1970.

WIDE SARGASSO SEA (1966)

Anon. Review. NEW STATESMAN, v. 72, October 28, 1966, p.
638.

Anon. Review. BAJAN, no. 184, December 1968, p. 28.

Braybrooke, Neville. "Shadow and the Substance." SPECTATOR,
v. 217, October 28, 1966, pp. 561-562.

Casey Fulton, Nancy J. "Jean Rhys's WIDE SARGASSO SEA:
Exterminating the White Cockroach." RRI, v. 4, no. 3,
Fall 1974, pp. 340-349.

West Indian Literature

Rhys, Jean

Corke, Hilary. Review. LISTENER, v. 77, January 19, 1967, p. 103.

Look Lai, Wally. "The Road to Thornfield Hall." NWQ, v. 4, no. 2, Croptime 1968, pp. 17-27. Also appears in NEW BEACON REVIEWS: COLLECTION ONE. London: New Beacon Books, 1968.

Luengo, Anthony E. "WIDE SARGASSO SEA and the Gothic Mode." WLWE, v. 15, April 1976, pp. 229-245.

MacInnes, Colin. "Nightmare in Paradise." LSO, October 30, 1966, p. 28.

Panton, George. "Our Country--Past and Future." SUNDAY GLEANER, October 23, 1966, p. 4.

Ross, Alan. Review. LONDON MAGAZINE, New Series, v. 6, no. 8, November 1966, pp. 99-101.

TIGERS ARE BETTER LOOKING (1968)

Anon. "Losing Battles." TLS, no. 3453, May 2, 1968.

Bailey, Paul. Review. LONDON MAGAZINE, New Series, v. 8, no. 3, June 1968, pp. 110-111.

Byatt, A. S. Review. NEW STATESMAN, v. 75, March 29, 1968, pp. 422.

Heppenstall, Rayner. Review. SPECTATOR, v. 220, April 5, 1968, pp. 446-447.

Hope, Francis. "Did You Once See Paris Plain?" LSO, March 31, 1968, p. 29.

Stade, George. Review. NYT, October 20, 1974, Section 7, p. 5.

Sullivan, Mary. Review. LISTENER, v. 79, April 25, 1968, p. 549.

SLEEP IT OFF LADY (1976)

Macauley, Robie. Review. NYT, November 21, 1976, Section 7, p. 7.

ROACH, ERIC. Tobago, 1915-1974

General

    Anon. "Purest Poet of Them All, A Profile of Eric Roach."
      SUNDAY GUARDIAN (Trinidad), January 8, 1961, p. 7.

    Brathwaite, Edward. "The African Presence in Caribbean
      Literature." DAEDALUS, v. 103, no. 2, Spring 1974, pp.
      78-109.

    Brathwaite, Edward. "Sir Galahad and the Islands." BIM,
      v. 7, no. 25, July-December 1957, pp. 8-16. Also appears
      in IOUANALOA, RECENT WRITING FROM ST. LUCIA. Castries,
      St. Lucia: Department of Extra-Mural Studies, 1963, pp.
      50-59.

    Brown, Wayne. "Poetry of the Forties, Part 3: 'The
      Dilemma.'" SUNDAY GUARDIAN (Trinidad), October 4, 1970,
      p. 11.

    Brown, Wayne. "Poetry of the Forties, Part 5: The Mulatto
      Question." SUNDAY GUARDIAN (Trinidad), October 11, 1970,
      p. 11.

    Dathorne, O. R. "Africa in the Literature of the West
      Indies." JCL, no. 1, September 1965, pp. 95-116.

    Dathorne, O. R. "Africa in West Indian Literature." BLACK
      ORPHEUS, no. 16, October 1964, pp. 42-53. Also appears as
      "The Theme of Africa in West Indian Literature." in
      PHYLON, v. 26, Fall 1965, pp. 255-276.

    Forde, A. N. "Eric Roach--Poet with Soul." BAJAN, no. 247,
      June 1974, p. 16.

    Fraser, Fitzroy. "A Talk with Eric Roach." SUNDAY GLEANER,
      January 29, 1961, pp. 14, 20.

    Owens, R. J. "West Indian Poetry." CARIBBEAN QUARTERLY,
      v. 7, no. 3, December 1961, pp. 120-127.

    Rohlehr, F. Gordon. "Blues for Eric Roach." TAPIA, v. 4,
      no. 17, April 1974, p. 2.

    Rohlehr, F. Gordon. "A Carrion Time." BIM, v. 15, no. 58,
      June 1975, pp. 92-109. Also appears in TAPIA, v. 4, no.

Roach, Eric

24, June 1974, pp. 5-8, 11.

Rohlehr, F. Gordon. "West Indian Poetry: Some Problems
of Assessment." TAPIA, no. 21, August 1971, pp. 11-14.
Also appears in BIM, part 1, v. 14, no. 54, January-June
1972, pp. 80-88; part 2, v. 14, no. 55, July-December
1972, pp. 134-144 and under title "Some Problems of
Assessment: A Look at New Expressions in the Arts of the
Contemporary Caribbean." CARIBBEAN QUARTERLY, v. 17, nos.
3 and 4, September-December 1971, pp. 92-113.

Walcott, Derek. "In Praise of Peasantry; The Poetry of E.
M. Roach." SUNDAY GUARDIAN (Trinidad), July 18, 1965,
p. 9.

Williams, Cheryl. "Eric Roach's Poetry." TAPIA, part 1,
v. 4, no. 17, April 1974, pp. 3-4, 9; part 2, v. 4, no.
18, May 1974, pp. 5-8.

BELLE FANTO (play, 1966)

Anon. "Poetic Simplicity." SUNDAY GUARDIAN (Trinidad),
April 3, 1966, p. 6.

ROBERTS, WALTER ADOLPHE. Jamaica, 1886-1962.

General

R. L. C. A. [R. L. C. Aarons]. "W. Adolphe Roberts--The
Poet as Nationalist." SUNDAY GLEANER, July 21, 1974,
p. 24.

Anon. "Three Evenings with Six Poets." KYK-OVER-AL, v. 3,
no. 13, Year-end 1951, pp. 214-220.

Anon. "W. Adolphe Roberts, Novelist and Editor Was Leader
in Jamaica." SUNDAY GLEANER (reprint from NYT, September
17, 1962, p. 31), October 14, 1962, p. 14.

Bennett, Wycliffe. "The Jamaican Poets." LL, v. 57, no.
128, April 1948, pp. 58-61.

Bennett, Wycliffe. "W. Adolphe Roberts, the Man and the
Poet." SUNDAY GLEANER, September 30, 1962, p. 14.

Birbalsingh, Frank. "W. Adolphe Roberts: Creole Romantic."
CARIBBEAN QUARTERLY, v. 19, no. 2, June 1973, pp. 100-107.

Coulthard, G. R. "The Coloured Woman in Caribbean Poetry
(1800-1960)." RACE, v. 2, May 1961, pp. 53-61.

Hearne, John. "Barren Treasury." PUBLIC OPINION, November
11, 1950, pp. 6, 8.

Jacobs, H. P. "Adolphe Roberts: The Meaning of His Life."
PUBLIC OPINION, December 1, 1962, p. 2.

Milner, Harry. "W. Adolphe Roberts." SUNDAY GLEANER,
September 23, 1962, p. 14.

Seymour, Arthur J. "The Literary Adventure of the West
Indies." KYK-OVER-AL, v. 2, no. 10, April 1950, entire
issue, 40 pp.

THE POMEGRANATE (1941)

Manley, Edna. Review. PUBLIC OPINION, May 17, 1941, p. 7.

Sherlock, Phillip M. Review. PUBLIC OPINION, March 22,
1941, pp. 8-9.

THE SINGLE STAR (1949)

Cumper, George. "New World Liberalism." PUBLIC OPINION,
July 20, 1957, p. 7.

Other Works

PIERROT WOUNDED AND OTHER POEMS (1919)

THE HAUNTING HAND (1926)

PAN AND PEACOCKS (POEMS) (1928)

THE MIND READER (1929)

THE MORALIST (1931)

THE TOP FLOOR KILLER (1935)

ROYAL STREET, A NOVEL OF OLD NEW ORLEANS (1944)

BRAVE MARDI GRAS, A NEW ORLEANS NOVEL OF THE 60's (1946)

CREOLE DUSK, A NEW ORLEANS NOVEL OF THE 80's (1948)

Roy, Namba

ROY, NAMBA.   Jamaica, 1910-1961

General

> Anon. "Namba Roy--His Life--And His Work." SUNDAY GLEANER, December 31, 1961, p. 13.

> Brathwaite, Edward. "The African Presence in Caribbean Literature." DAEDALUS, v. 103, no. 2, 1974, pp. 78-109.

> Dathorne, O. R. "Africa in the Literature of the West Indies." JCL, no. 1, September 1965, pp. 95-116.

> Dathorne, O. R. "Africa in West Indian Literature." BLACK ORPHEUS, no. 16, October 1964, pp. 42-53. Also appears as "The Theme of Africa in West Indian Literature." in PHYLON, v. 26, Fall 1965, pp. 255-276.

BLACK ALBINO   (1961)

> Panton, George. "A Real History of Jamaica." SUNDAY GLEANER, April 16, 1961, p. 14.

SADEEK, SHEIK M.   Guyana,

General

> McDowell, Robert E. "Interview with Sheik Sadeek--A Guyanese Popular Writer." WLWE, v. 14, November 1975, pp. 525-535.

> Poynting, Jeremy. "A Small Indian Voice in Guyana." JCL, v. 5, no. 2, December 1971, pp. 152-154.

Works

WINDSWEPT AND OTHER STORIES   (1969)

DREAMS AND REFLECTIONS   (1969)

REFLECTIONS AND DREAMS AND MORE POEMS   (1974)

THE PORK KNOCKERS AND 4 OTHER STORIES   (1974)

THE DIAMOND THIEVES AND 4 MORE STORIES   (1974)

ACROSS THE GREEN FIELDS AND FIVE OTHER STORIES   (1974)

St. Omer, Garth

BUNDARIE BOY (1974)

NO GREATER DAY AND 4 MORE ADULT STORIES (1974)

SONG OF THE SUGAR CANES (1975)

ST. JOHN, BRUCE. Barbados,

General

>   Brathwaite, Edward. "The African Presence in Caribbean
>   Literature." DAEDALUS, v. 103, no. 2, Spring 1974, pp.
>   78-109.
>
>   Fido, Elaine. "Sex and Class in the Poetry of Bruce St.
>   John." TAPIA, v. 5, no. 34, August 1975, pp. 6-8.
>
>   Gilkes, Michael. "The Poetry of Bruce St. John." TAPIA,
>   v. 5, no. 24, June 1975, pp. 6-8.
>
>   Laird, Christopher. "Bruce St. John at Kairi House, an
>   Introduction." KAIRI, no. 4/5, 1974, 10 pp.
>
>   Moore, Gerald. "Use Men Language." BIM, v. 15, no. 57,
>   March 1974, pp. 69-76.

ST. OMER, GARTH. St. Lucia, 1931-

General

>   Brathwaite, Edward. "West Indian Prose Fiction in the
>   Sixties." BLACK WORLD, v. 20, no. 11, September 1971,
>   pp. 15-29.
>
>   Brown, Wayne. "On Art, Artists and the People." SUNDAY
>   GUARDIAN (Trinidad), August 9, 1970, p. 10.
>
>   Clasp, Bertram. "Three Novels by New St. Lucian Writer."
>   SUNDAY GUARDIAN (Trinidad), November 30, 1969, p. 9.
>
>   Kaye, Jacqueline. "Anonymity and Subjectivism in the Novels
>   of Garth St. Omer." JCL, v. 10, no. 1, August 1975,
>   pp. 45-52.
>
>   Rohlehr, F. Gordon. "Small Island Blues, A Short Review
>   of the Novels of Garth St. Omer." VOICES, v. 2, no. 1,
>   September-December 1969, pp. 22-28.

St. Omer, Garth

SYROP   (1964)

Brathwaite, Edward. Review. CARIBBEAN QUARTERLY, v. 10,
no. 1, March 1964, pp. 68-69. Also appears in BIM, v.
10, no. 40, January-June 1965, pp. 290-291.

Panton, George. "Tragedy in the West Indies." SUNDAY
GLEANER, February 2, 1964, p. 4.

A ROOM ON THE HILL   (1968)

Anon. Review. BAJAN, no. 181, September 1968, p. 11.

Anon. Review. LSO, March 10, 1968, p. 28.

Anon. "Uneventful." TLS, no. 3445, March 7, 1968, p. 221.

Graham, Bernard. Review. BIM, v. 12, no. 47, July-December
1968, pp. 208-209.

Lashley, Cliff. Review. CARIBBEAN QUARTERLY, v. 17, no. 1,
March 1971, pp. 58-59.

Panton, George. Review. SUNDAY GLEANER, March 3, 1967,
p. 4.

SHADES OF GREY   (1968)

Anon. "Growth and Sloth." TLS, no. 3487, December 21, 1968,
p. 1449.

Capitanchik, Maurice. Review. SPECTATOR, v. 221, December
20, 1968, pp. 881-882.

Nott, Kathleen. Review. LSO, December 15, 1968, p. 28.

Panton, George. Review. SUNDAY GLEANER, January 19, 1969,
p. 4.

Rickards, Colin. "Caribbean Bookshelf." SUNDAY GLEANER,
May 18, 1969, p. 4.

Wickham, John. Review. BAJAN, no. 200, April 1970, pp. 24-
25.

Wickham, John. Review. BIM, v. 13, no. 49, July-December
1969, pp. 63-64.

Salkey, Andrew

NOR ANY COUNTRY (1969)

Anon. Review. TLS, no. 3509, May 29, 1969, p. 589.

Baugh, Edward. "A Graceful Wisdom." SUNDAY GLEANER, July 13, 1969, p. 4.

Baugh, Edward. Review. BIM, v. 13, no. 50, January–June 1970, pp. 128-130.

Capitanchik, Maurice. Review. SPECTATOR, v. 222, May 9, 1969, p. 620.

Hemmings, John. Review. LISTENER, v. 81, May 8, 1969.

Jordon, Clive. Review. NEW STATESMAN, v. 77, May 9, 1969, p. 666.

Panton, George. "A Man and His Country." SUNDAY GLEANER, June 8, 1969, p. 4.

Star, Leonie. Review. WLWE, no. 19, April 1971, p. 92.

Tomalin, Claire. Review. LSO, May 4, 1969, p. 30.

J--BLACK BAM AND THE MASQUERADERS (1972)

Anon. "Brothers In Inaction." TLS, no. 3678, August 25, 1972, p. 985.

Coleman, John. Review. LSO,   June 25, 1972, p. 30.

Cunningham, Valentine. Review. LISTENER, v. 88, July 20, 1972, p. 89.

Lee, Robert. "Peter Plays for Paul." TAPIA, v. 4, no. 10, March 1974, pp. 6-7.

Panton, George. Review. SUNDAY GLEANER, August 20, 1972, p. 33.

SALKEY, ANDREW. Jamaica, 1928–

General

Brathwaite, Edward. "Jazz and the West Indian Novel." BIM, v. 11, no. 44, January–June 1967, pp. 275-284; v. 12,

Salkey, Andrew

no. 45, July–December 1967, pp. 39–51; v. 12, no. 46, January–June 1968, pp. 115–126.

Brathwaite, Edward. "The New West Indian Novelists." BIM, part one, v. 8, no. 31, July–December 1960, pp. 199–210; part two, v. 8, no. 32, January–June 1961, pp. 271–280.

Brown, Lloyd W. "The American Image in British West Indian Literature." CARIBBEAN STUDIES, v. 11, no. 1, April 1971, pp. 30–45.

Brown, Lloyd W. "The Crisis of Black Identity in the West Indian Novel." CRITIQUE, v. 11, no. 3, 1969, pp. 97–112.

Brown, Wayne. "The First Generation of West Indian Novelists." SUNDAY GUARDIAN (Trinidad), June 7, 1970, pp. 6, 11.

Carr, Bill. "A Complex Fate; The Novels of Andrew Salkey." THE ISLANDS IN BETWEEN. London: Oxford University Press, 1968, pp. 100–108.

Carr, Bill. "Reflections on the Novel in the British Caribbean." QUEENS QUARTERLY, v. 70, Winter 1963, pp. 585–597.

Dathorne, O. R. "Africa in the Literature of the West Indies." JCL, no. 1, September 1965, pp. 95–116.

Dathorne, O. R. "Africa in West Indian Literature." BLACK ORPHEUS, no. 16, October 1964, pp. 42–53. Also appears as "The Theme of Africa in West Indian Literature," in PHYLON, v. 26, Fall 1965, pp. 255–276.

Gray, C. R. "Mr. Salkey's Truth and Illusion." JAMAICA JOURNAL, v. 2, no. 2, June 1968, pp. 46–54.

Kemoli, Arthur. "The Theme of 'The Past' in Caribbean Literature." WLWE, v. 12, November 1973, pp. 304–325.

Panton, George. "Andrew Salkey: Versatile and Prolific." SUNDAY GLEANER, part 1, April 20, 1975, p. 23; part 2, April 27, 1975, p. 23.

Page, Malcolm. "West Indian Writers." NOVEL, v. 3, no. 2, Winter 1970, pp. 167–172.

Salkey, Andrew

Ramchand, Kenneth. "Obeah and the Supernatural in West Indian Literature." JAMAICA JOURNAL, v. 3, no. 2, June 1969, pp. 52-54.

A QUALITY OF VIOLENCE (1959)

Anon. "Distance Lends to Distortion." SUNDAY GUARDIAN (Trinidad), February 21, 1960, p. 19.

Anon. Review. THE TIMES (London), October 8, 1959, p. 15.

Anon. Review. TLS, no. 3006, October 9, 1959, p. 573.

Brathwaite, Edward. "The African Presence in Caribbean Literature." DAEDALUS, v. 103, no. 2, Spring 1974, pp. 73-109.

Brathwaite, Edward. Review. BIM, v. 8, no. 31, July-December 1960, pp. 219-220.

Hough, Graham. Review. LISTENER, v. 62, October 22, 1959, p. 698.

Richardson, Maurice. Review. NEW STATESMAN, v. 58, October 10, 1959, p. 487.

ESCAPE TO AN AUTUMN PAVEMENT (1960)

Anon. Review. THE TIMES (London), July 7, 1960, p. 15.

Anon. Review. TLS, no. 3046, July 15, 1960, p. 445.

Boxill, Anthony. "The Emasculated Colonial." PRESENCE AFRICAINE, no. 75, 1970, pp. 146-149.

Coleman, John. Review. SPECTATOR, v. 205, July 8, 1960, p. 73.

Panton, George. "The Middle-Class Miasma." SUNDAY GLEANER, August 21, 1960, p. 14.

Ramchand, Kenneth. "Decolonization in West Indian Literature." TRANSITION, v. 5, no. 22, 1965, pp. 48-49.

Waterhouse, Keith. Review. NEW STATESMAN, v. 60, July 9, 1960, p. 63.

Salkey, Andrew

HURRICANE (1964)

Anon. Review. TLS, no. 3254, July 9, 1964, p. 610.

Panton, George. "Hurricane in Jamaica." SUNDAY GLEANER, May 31, 1964, p. 4.

Richards, Colin. "Now Salkey Tries Children's Fiction." SUNDAY GLEANER, July 5, 1964, p. 4.

Walcott, Derek. "Writing for Children." TGM, January 23, 1966, p. 2.

EARTHQUAKE (1965)

Panton, George. Review. SUNDAY GLEANER, October 31, 1965, p. 4.

DROUGHT (1966)

Anon. "Drought in Jamaica." SUNDAY GLEANER, July 3, 1966, p. 4.

RIOT (1967)

Anon. Review. TLS, no. 3404, May 25, 1967, p. 455.

Panton, George. "The W.I. Scene." SUNDAY GLEANER, June 18, 1967, p. 4.

THE LATE EMANCIPATION OF JERRY STOVER (1968)

Anon. "Post-Colonial Despair." TLS, no. 3442, February 15, 1968.

Anon. Review. LSO, February 18, 1968, p. 27.

Arnason, David. Review. WLWE, no. 19, April 1971, pp. 90-92.

Byatt, A. S. Review. NEW STATESMAN, v. 75, February 16, 1968, p. 209.

Drayton, Arthur D. "Awkward Questions for Jamaicans." JCL, no. 7, July 1969, pp. 125-127.

Moore, Gerald. Review. BIM, v. 12, no. 48, January-June

Salkey, Andrew

1969, pp. 268-269.

Nightingale, Benedict. "Too Late." THE TIMES (London),
February 17, 1968, p. 20.

Ramsaran, J. A. "The Social Groundwork of Politics in some
West Indian Novels." NEGRO DIGEST, v. 18, no. 10, 1969,
pp. 71-77.

THE ADVENTURES OF CATULLUS KELLY (1968)

Anon. "Another Novel by Andrew Salkey." SUNDAY GLEANER,
July 17, 1968, p. 4.

Anon. Review. TLS, no. 3495, February 20, 1969, p. 192.

Arnason, David. Review. WLWE, no. 19, April 1971, pp. 90-
92.

Brown, Wayne. "Black Beautiful and--." SUNDAY GUARDIAN
(Trinidad), July 19, 1970, p. 6.

Cole, Barry. Review. SPECTATOR, v. 222, February 14, 1969,
p. 213.

Graham, Kenneth. Review. LISTENER, v. 81, February 20,
1969, p. 247.

Haworth, David. Review. NEW STATESMAN, v. 77, February 14,
1969, p. 230.

Panton, George. "Love and the West Indian Migrant in London
London." SUNDAY GLEANER, May 18, 1969, p. 4.

Rickards, Colin. "Caribbean Bookshelf." SUNDAY GLEANER,
May 18, 1969, p. 4.

Wall, Stephen. Review. LSO, February 9, 1969, p. 30.

JONAH SIMPSON (1969)

Poyser, John. Review. THE TIMES (London), September 20,
1969, p. 20.

HAVANA JOURNAL (1971)

Levy, Oscar. Review. CARIBBEAN CONTACT, v. 1, no. 3,

Salkey, Andrew

February 1973, pp. 4, 14.

Lewis, Rupert. "HAVANA JOURNAL: A Major Document." SUNDAY
GLEANER, July 11, 1971, p. 29.

GEORGETOWN JOURNAL (1972)

Levy, Oscar. Review. CARIBBEAN CONTACT, v. 1, no. 3,
February 1973, pp. 4, 14.

Lindo, Cedric. "Salkey's Latest Journal." SUNDAY GLEANER,
December 3, 1972, p. 43.

ANANCY'S SCORE (1973)

Anon. Review. CORLIT, v. 1. no. 3, July 1974, pp. 51-52.

Knight, Mary McAnally. Review. NEW LETTERS, v. 41, no. 2,
December 1974, pp. 121-123.

Questel, Victor. "Towards Anancy Becoming One Total Person."
KAIRI, no. 2, 1974, p. 9.

JAMAICA (1974)

Anon. "Jamaica's Past Set in Verse." SUNDAY GLEANER, July
21, 1974, p. 24.

JOEY TYSON (1974)

Drayton, Kathleen. "Now a Novel on the Politics of Banning."
CARIBBEAN CONTACT, v. 2, no. 12, 1975, p. 3.

Gosine, Vishnu. Review. CORLIT, v. 2, nos. 1 and 2, April-
July 1975, p. 46.

SCOTT, DENNIS. Jamaica, 1939-

General

Anon. "International Poetry Forum Award Winner." SUNDAY
GLEANER, December 30, 1973, p. 16.

James, Louis. "Islands of Man, Reflections on the Emergence
of a West Indian Literature." SOUTHERN REVIEW, v. 2,
1966, pp. 150-163.

Selvon, Samuel

McNeill, Anthony. "Dennis Scott, Maker. Part 1, Journeys."
JAMAICA JOURNAL, v. 5, no. 4, December 1971, pp. 49-52.

Moore, Gerald. "Use Men Language." BIM, v. 15, no. 57,
March 1974, pp. 69-76.

Panton, George. "Dennis Scott--Prize-Winning Poet." SUNDAY
GLEANER, October 13, 1974, p. 27.

Questel, Victor. "Their Tragic Destiny." TAPIA, v. 6, no.
20, May 16, 1976, pp. 4, 11.

SEVEN JAMAICAN POETS (1971)

Forde, A. N. Review. BIM, v. 14, no. 54, January-June 1972,
p. 117.

Lindo, Cedric. "Worthy Examples of Our Poetry." SUNDAY
GLEANER, May 23, 1971, p. 29.

UNCLE TIME (1973)

Brown, Stewart. "New Poetry From Jamaica." NEW VOICES, v.
3, no. 6, 1975, pp. 48-50.

Panton, George. "Acclaim of a Poet." SUNDAY GLEANER,
January 6, 1974, p. 23.

Questel, Victor. "UNCLE TIME: A Pointer to the Shape of
Things to Come." TAPIA, v. 6, no. 26, June 1976, pp.
6-7, 8.

SEALEY, CLIFFORD. Trinidad, 1927-

Pearse, Andrew. "West Indian Themes." CARIBBEAN QUARTERLY,
v. 2, no. 2, 1952, pp. 12-23.

SEALEY, KARL. Barbados,

Pearse, Andrew. "West Indian Themes." CARIBBEAN QUARTERLY,
v. 2, no. 2, 1952, pp. 12-23.

SELVON, SAMUEL. Trinidad, 1923-

General

Anon. "Caribbean Voices." TLS, no. 2788, August 5, 1955,

Selvon, Samuel

pp. 16-17.

Brathwaite, Edward. "Jazz and the West Indian Novel." BIM,
v. 11, no. 44, January-June 1967, pp. 275-284; v. 12, no.
45, July-December 1967, pp. 39-51; v. 12, no. 46, January-
June 1968, pp. 115-126.

Brathwaite, Edward. "The New West Indian Novelists: Part
One." BIM, v. 8, no. 31, July-December 1960, pp. 208-
210.

Brathwaite, Edward. "Roots." BIM, v. 10, no. 37, July-
December 1963, pp. 10-21.

Brathwaite, Edward. "Sir Galahad and the Islands." BIM,
v. 7, no. 25, July-December 1957, pp. 8-16. Also appears
in IOUANALOA: RECENT WRITING FROM ST. LUCIA. Castries,
St. Lucia: Department of Extra-Mural Studies, 1963,
pp. 50-59.

Brathwaite, Edward. "Timehri." SAVACOU, no. 2, September
1970, pp. 35-44. Also appears in IS MASSA DAY DEAD? New
York: Doubleday, 1974, pp. 29-44.

Brown, Lloyd W. "The Calypso Tradition in West Indian
Literature." BAR, v. 2, nos. 1 and 2, 1971, pp. 127-143.

Brown, Wayne. "The First Generation of West Indian
Novelists." SUNDAY GUARDIAN (Trinidad), June 7, 1970,
pp. 6, 11.

Davies, Barrie. "The Personal Sense of a Society--Minority
View: Aspects of the 'East Indian' Novel in the West
Indies." SIN, v. 4, no. 2, Summer 1972, pp. 275-283.

Douglas, Karl. "Angry! Not Me, Says Selvon," (interview).
SUNDAY GUARDIAN (Trinidad), December 30, 1962, p. 12.

Drayton, Arthur D. "The European Factor in West Indian
Literature." LITERARY HALF-YEARLY, v. 11, no. 1, 1970,
pp. 71-94.

Fuller, Roy. "Caribbean Poetry." SUNDAY GLEANER, June 13,
1948, p. 9.

Hall, Stuart M. "Lamming, Selvon and Some Trends in the West
Indian Novel." BIM, v. 6, no. 23, December 1955, pp. 172-

Index of Authors

Selvon, Samuel

Lewis, Gordon. "The New West Indies: Nationality and
Literature." SUNDAY GLEANER, December 8, 1957, p. 8.

Lucie-Smith, Mary. "In England Now." WIR, v. 3, no. 2,
February 1958, pp. 55-57.

Mohr, Eugene V. "West Indian Fiction is Alive and Well."
CARIBBEAN REVIEW, v. 5, no. 4, 1973, pp. 23-29.

Page Malcolm. "West Indian Writers." NOVEL, v. 3, no. 2,
Winter, 1970, pp. 167-172.

Pearse, Andrew. "West Indian Themes." CARIBBEAN QUARTERLY,
v. 2, no. 2, September 1952, pp. 12-23.

Ramchand, Kenneth. "Dialect in West Indian Fiction."
CARIBBEAN QUARTERLY, v. 14, nos. 1 and 2, March-June 1968,
pp. 27-42. Also appears in his THE WEST INDIAN NOVEL AND
ITS BACKGROUND. London: Faber and Faber, 1970.

Rawlins, Randolph. "Migrants with Manuscripts, Social Background of the West Indian Novel." BLACK ORPHEUS, no. 4,
October 1958, pp. 46-50.

Roberts, W. Adolphe. "Caribbean Literature: The British
Possessions." WIR, v. 4, no. 42, April 25, 1953, pp.
16-17.

Rohlehr, F. Gordon. "The Folk in Caribbean Literature, Part
One." TAPIA, v. 2, no. 11, December 17, 1972, pp. 7-8,
13-15.

Walcott, Derek. "Neo-Realism Parallel Noted in W.I. Novels."
SUNDAY GUARDIAN (Trinidad), April 24, 1960, p. 7.

Wickham, John. "West Indian Writing." BIM, v. 13, no. 50,
January-June 1970, pp. 68-80.

Wyndham, Francis. "The New West Indian Writer." BIM, v. 7,
no. 28, January-June 1959, pp. 188-190.

Wynter, Sylvia. "Strangers At the Gate, Caribbean Novelists
in Search of Identity." SUNDAY GLEANER, January 18, 1959,
p. 14.

A BRIGHTER SUN (1952)

Selvon, Samuel

    Anon. Review. TLS, no. 3650, February 11, 1972, p. 145.

    Efron, Edith. "Dreamer At the Edge of a Swamp." NYT, September 2, 1952, Section 7, p. 5.

    Hale, Lionel. Review. LSO, February 3, 1952, p. 7.

    Holder, G. A. Review. BIM, v. 4, no. 16, June 1952, pp. 295-296.

    Ibberson, Dora. Review. CARIBBEAN QUARTERLY, v. 3, no. 1, April 1953, p. 61.

    Manley, Michael. "The New Trinidad." PUBLIC OPINION, March 22, 1952, p. 5.

    Seymour, Arthur J. Review. KYK-OVER-AL, v. 5, no. 15, Year-End 1952, pp. 82-83.

AN ISLAND IS A WORLD (1955)

    Anon. "New Novel Filled with the Complexity of Trinidad Life." SUNDAY GUARDIAN (Trinidad), July 10, 1955, p. 76.

    Anon. Review. BAJAN, v. 3, no. 4, December 1955, pp. 35, 38.

    Anon. Review. TLS, no. 2778, May 27, 1955, p. 281.

    Holder, G. A. Review. BIM, v. 6, no. 23, 1955, p. 202.

    Quigly, Isabel. Review. Spectator, v. 194, April 15, 1955, p. 480.

    Richardson, Maurice. Review. NEW STATESMAN, v. 49, April 23, 1955, p. 586.

THE LONELY LONDONERS (1956)

    Anon. Review. BAJAN, v. 4, no. 8, April 1957, pp. 32-33.

    Anon. Review. THE TIMES (London), December 6, 1956, p. 13.

    Anon. Review. TLS, no. 2860, December 21, 1956, p. 761.

    Baugh, Edward. "Selvon the Humorist." PUBLIC OPINION, August 24, 1957, p. 7.

Selvon, Samuel

Coulthard, G. R. "The West Indian Novel of Immigration."
PHYLON, v. 20, 1959, pp. 32-41.

Hamilton, Bruce. Review. BIM, v. 7, no. 25, July-December
1957, pp. 61-62.

Hopkinson, Tom. Review. LSO, December 16, 1956, p. 11.

Richardson, Maurice. Review. NEW STATESMAN, v. 52, December
29, 1956, p. 846.

WAYS OF SUNLIGHT (1957)

Anon. Review. BAJAN, v. 5, no. 10, June 1958, p. 25.

Anon. Review. THE TIMES (London), February 6, 1958, p. 11.

Anon. Review. TLS, no. 2917, January 31, 1958, p. 57.

Cockburn, Claud. Review. NEW STATESMAN, v. 55, March 15,
1958, p. 354.

Collymore, Frank. Review. BIM, v. 7, no. 27, July-December
1958, p. 185.

Hernandez, Richardo. "Sam Selvon Scores in Short Sharp
Bursts." SUNDAY GUARDIAN (Trinidad), March 9, 1958, p.
18.

Newby, P. H. Review. LONDON MAGAZINE, v. 5, no. 11, November
1958, pp. 82-84.

Ramchand, Kenneth. "Decolonization in West Indian
Literature." TRANSITION, v. 5, no. 22, 1965, pp. 48-49.

Toynbee, Phillip. "Two Languages." LSO, January 19, 1958,
p. 16. Reprinted in PUBLIC OPINION, February 8, 1958,
p. 7.

TURN AGAIN TIGER (1958)

Anon. "Now Tiger Turns Away from Books." SUNDAY GUARDIAN
(Trinidad), December 21, 1958, p. 22.

Anon. Review. THE TIMES (London), November 27, 1958, p. 13.

Anon. Review. TLS, no. 2964, December 19, 1958, p. 733.

Selvon, Samuel

    Lucie-Smith, Mary. Review. WIR, v. 4, no. 3, March 1959, p. 50.

    Naipaul, V. S. Review. NEW STATESMAN, v. 56, December 6, 1958, pp. 826-827.

    Nicholson, Geoffrey. Review. SPECTATOR, v. 201, November 28, 1958, p. 787.

    Panton, George. "Surface Description of Trinidad Village Life." SUNDAY GLEANER, December 28, 1958, p. 14.

    Paul, David. "Two West Indians." PUBLIC OPINION, January 3, 1959, p. 7.

    Rodman, Seldon. "Time of Decisions." NYT, May 3, 1959, Section 7, p. 28.

    Wyndham, Francis. Review. LONDON MAGAZINE, v. 6, no. 3, March 1959, pp. 74-75.

I HEAR THUNDER   (1963)

    Anon. Review. BAJAN, v. 10, no. 11, July 1963, p. 32.

    Anon. Review. THE TIMES (London), April 11, 1963, p. 15.

    Anon. Review. TLS, no. 3191, April 26, 1963, p. 292.

    Burgess, Anthony. Review. LSO, April 7, 1963, p. 22.

    Carr, Bill. "An Exhausted Talent?" PUBLIC OPINION, September 14, 1963, p. 11.

    Forde, A. N. Review. BIM, v. 8, no. 29, June-December 1959, pp. 60-61.

    Walcott, Derek. "The Action Is Panicky." SUNDAY GUARDIAN (Trinidad), May 5, 1963, p. 4.

THE HOUSING LARK   (1965)

    Anon. Review. BAJAN, v. 12, no. 11, July 1965, p. 29.

    Anon. Review. THE TIMES (London), March 25, 1965, p. 15.

    Panton, George. "W.I. Novels--And a Lecture on Them."

Selvon, Samuel

SUNDAY GLEANER, August 8, 1965, p. 4.

Vansittart, Peter. Review. SPECTATOR, v. 214, March 26, 1965, p. 410.

Walcott, Derek. "Selvon Has Returned to the Old Form." SUNDAY GUARDIAN (Trinidad), June 27, 1965, p. 7.

THE PLAINS OF CARONI (1970)

Lindo, Cedric. Review. SUNDAY GLEANER, February 7, 1971, p. 23.

Ramchand, Kenneth. "Before the People Became Popular. . ." CARIBBEAN QUARTERLY, v. 18, no. 4, 1972, pp. 70-73.

Salkey, Andrew. Review. MOKO, no. 45, November 6, 1970, p. 3.

Scott, Andrew P. Review. WLWE, no. 19, April 1971, pp. 92-93.

Wickham, John. Review. BIM, v. 13, no. 51, July-December 1970, pp. 191-192.

THOSE WHO EAT THE CASCASURA (1972)

Anon. Review. TLS, no. 3650, February 11, 1972, p. 145.

Feinstein, Elaine. Review. LONDON MAGAZINE, New Series, v. 12, no. 1, April/May 1972, p. 144.

James, Louis. "Fragmentation of Experience." LITERARY HALF-YEARLY, v. 13, no. 1, January 1972, pp. 173-176.

Lindo, Cedric. "The New Selvon--Set in Rural Trinidad." SUNDAY GLEANER, February 20, 1972, p. 35.

Muir, Edwin. Review. LISTENER, v. 87, January 27, 1972, p. 120.

St. Hill, Chalmer. Review. BIM, v. 14, no. 55, July-December 1972, p. 188.

MOSES ASCENDING (1975)

Anon. Review. SUNDAY GLEANER, March 7, 1976, p. 8.

Selvon, Samuel

Wickham, John. Review. BAJAN, no. 263, October 1975, p. 26.

SEYMOUR, ARTHUR JAMES. Guyana, 1914-

General

Brathwaite, Edward. "KYK-OVER-AL and the Radicals." NWQ, Guyana Independence Issue, v. 2, no. 3, 1966, pp. 55-57.

Brown, Lloyd W. "The Guyanese Voice in West Indian Poetry: A Review of Arthur J. Seymour." WLWE, v. 15, April 1976, pp. 246-252.

Dolphin, Celeste. "The Poetry of A. J. Seymour." NWF, v. 1, no. 13, April 1965, pp. 31-39.

James, Louis. "The Necessity of Poetry." NWQ, Guyana Independence Issue, v. 2, no. 3, 1966, pp. 111-115.

Keane, E. McG. "Some Religious Attitudes in West Indian Poetry." BIM, part one, v. 4, no. 15, December 1951, pp. 169-174; part two, v. 4, no. 16, June 1952, pp. 266-271.

Sparer, Joyce L. "Attitudes Towards 'Race' in Guyanese Literature." CARIBBEAN STUDIES, v. 8, no. 2, July 1968, pp. 23-63.

Swanzy, Henry. "Caribbean Prolegomena to West Indian Culture." CARIBBEAN QUARTERLY, v. 1, no. 2, September 1949, pp. 21-28. Reprinted in CARIBBEAN QUARTERLY, v. 8, no. 2, 1962, pp. 121-128.

THE GUIANA BOOK (1948)

Bell, Gordon O. Review. BIM, v. 3, no. 10, June 1949, pp. 176-178.

Harris, Wilson. Review. KYK-OVER-AL, v. 2, no. 7, December 1948, pp. 37-40.

SELECTED POEMS (1965)

Collymore, Frank. Review. BIM, v. 11, no. 42, January-June 1966, pp. 143-144.

Other Works

Sherlock, Sir Philip M.

VERSE   (1937)

MORE POEMS   (1940)

MONOLOGUE   (1940)

OVER GUIANA CLOUDS   (1944)

SUNS IN MY BLOOD   (1944)

POETRY IN THESE SUNNY LANDS   (1945)

SIX SONGS   (1946)

LEAVES FROM THE TREE (1951)

THEMES OF SONG   (1961)

BLACK SONG   (1971)

I, ANANCY   (1971)

SONG TO MAN   (1973)

ITALIC   (1974)

SHERLOCK, SIR PHILIP M. Jamaica, 1902-

General

>   Anon. "Three Evenings with Six Poets." KYK-OVER-AL, v. 3,
>   no. 13, Year-End 1951, pp. 214-220.
>
>   Brathwaite, Edward. "The African Presence in Caribbean
>   Literature." DAEDALUS, v. 103, no. 2, Spring 1974, pp.
>   73-109.
>
>   Brown, Wayne. "Poetry of the Forties, Part Three: The
>   Dilemma." SUNDAY GUARDIAN (Trinidad), October 4, 1970,
>   p. 11.
>
>   Dathorne, O. R. "Africa in the Literature of the West
>   Indies." JCL, no. 1, September 1965, pp. 95-116.
>
>   Dathorne, O. R. "Africa in West Indian Literature." BLACK
>   ORPHEUS, no. 16, October 1964, pp. 42-53. Also appears
>   as "The Theme of Africa in West Indian Literature."

Sherlock, Sir Philip M.

PHYLON, v. 26, Fall 1965, pp. 255-276.

Derrick, Anthony. "An Introduction to Caribbean Literature." CARIBBEAN QUARTERLY, v. 15, nos. 1 and 2, June-
September 1969, pp. 65-78.

Drayton, Arthur D. "The European Factor in West Indian
Literature." LITERARY HALF-YEARLY, v. 11, no. 1, 1970,
pp. 71-94.

Fuller, Roy. "Caribbean Poetry." SUNDAY GLEANER, June 13,
1948, p. 9.

Hearne, John. "Barren Treasury." PUBLIC OPINION, November
11, 1950, pp. 6, 8.

James, Louis. "Caribbean Poetry in English--Some Problems."
SAVACOU, no. 2, September 1970, pp. 78-86.

Owens, R. J. "West Indian Poetry." CARIBBEAN QUARTERLY,
v. 7, no. 3, December 1961, pp. 120-127.

Panton, George. "A Prolific Writer, Historian, Poet."
SUNDAY GLEANER, July 28, 1974, p. 27.

Seymour, Arthur J. "Nature Poetry in the West Indies."
KYK-OVER-AL, v. 3, no. 11, October 1950, pp. 39-47.

Walcott, Derek. "Some Jamaican Poets." PUBLIC OPINION,
part one, August 3, 1957, p. 7; part two, August 10,
1957, p. 7.

ANANSI AND THE ALLIGATOR EGGS (1975)

Aarons, R. L. C. "Anansi Story Now Children's Book."
SUNDAY GLEANER, December 14, 1975, p. 16.

Other Works

ANANSI, THE SPIDER MAN (1954)

THREE FINGER JACK'S TREASURE (1961)

WEST INDIAN FOLK TALES (1966)

THE IGUANA'S TALE, CRICK CRACK STORIES FROM THE CARIBBEAN (1969)

Smith, M. G.

EARS AND TAILS AND COMMON SENSE, MORE STORIES FROM THE
    CARIBBEAN (1974, with Hilary Sherlock)

SIMPSON, LOUIS. Jamaica, 1923-

    THE ARRIVISTES: POEMS 1940-49 (1949)

        Escoffery, Gloria. Review. PUBLIC OPINION, September 24,
            1949, p. 6.

        Harrison, John. Review. BIM, v. 4, no. 14, June 1951,
            pp. 145-147.

    Other Works

    A DREAM OF GOVERNORS: POEMS (1959)

    RIVERSIDE DRIVE (1962)

    AT THE END OF THE OPEN ROAD (1963)

    SELECTED POEMS (1965)

SMITH, M. G. Jamaica, 1921-

    General

        Brown, Wayne. "Poetry of the Forties, Part 3. The Dilemma."
            SUNDAY GUARDIAN (Trinidad), October 4, 1970, p. 11.

        Dawes, Neville. "Thoughts on West Indian Poetry." PUBLIC
            OPINION, January 3, 1953, p. 5.

        Keane, E. McG. "Some Religious Attitudes in West Indian
            Poetry." BIM, part 1, v. 4, no. 15, December 1951,
            pp. 169-174; part 2, v. 4, no. 16, June 1952, pp. 266-271.

        Oakley, Leo. "Ideas of Patriotism and National Dignity in
            some Jamaican Writings." JAMAICA JOURNAL, v. 4, no. 3,
            1970, pp. 16-21. Also appears in SUNDAY GLEANER, part 1,
            March 28, 1970, p. 31, 34; part 2, April 4, 1970, p. 27;
            part 3, April 11, 1970, p. 25 as "Patriotism, National
            Dignity in Jamaican Writings."

        Owens, R. J. "West Indian Poetry." CARIBBEAN QUARTERLY, v.

Smith, M. G.

       7, no. 3, December 1961, pp. 120-127.

    Seymour, A. J. "Native Poetry in the West Indies." KYK-OVER-AL, v. 3, no. 11, October 1950, pp. 39-47.

    Swanzy, Henry. "Caribbean Voices, Prolegomena to a West Indian Culture." CARIBBEAN QUARTERLY, v. 1, no. 2, September 1949, pp. 21-28. Reprinted in CARIBBEAN QUARTERLY, v. 8, no. 2, 1962, pp. 121-128.

    Walcott, Derek. "A New Poet, Jamaican." SUNDAY GUARDIAN (Trinidad), June 20, 1965, p. 6.

    Walcott, Derek. "The Poetry of M. G. Smith." PUBLIC OPINION, July 27, 1957, p. 7.

    Walcott, Derek. "West Indian Writing." PUBLIC OPINION, January 26, 1957, p. 7.

  TESTAMENT (1957)

    Doherty, Joseph J. "The Life of Contemplation in M. G. Smith's TESTAMENT." BIM, v. 7, no. 25, July-December 1957, pp. 36-42.

STEWART, JOHN. Trinidad, 1933-

  General

  LAST COOL DAYS (1971)

    Hodge, Merle. "Towards a Caribbean-Afro-American Consciousness." TAPIA, no. 21, October 3, 1971, p. 9.

  CURVING ROAD (1975)

    Joseph, Barbara. Review. CORLIT, v. 2, nos. 1-2, April-July 1975, pp. 44-45.

TELEMAQUE, HAROLD M. Trinidad, 1910-

  General

    Dathorne, O. R. "Africa in the Literature of the West Indies." JCL, no. 1, September 1965, pp. 95-116.

    Dathorne, O. R. "Africa in West Indian Literature." BLACK

Thomas, G. C.

ORPHEUS, no. 16, October 1964, pp. 42-53. Also appears as "The Theme of Africa in West Indian Literature." PHYLON, v. 26, Fall 1965, pp. 255-276.

Drayton, Arthur D. "The European Factor in West Indian Literature." LITERARY HALF-YEARLY, v. 11, no. 1, 1970 pp. 71-94.

Fuller, Roy. "Caribbean Poetry." SUNDAY GLEANER, June 13, 1948, p. 9.

Keane, E. McG. "Some Religious Attitudes in West Indian Poetry." BIM, part 1, v. 4, no. 15, December 1951, pp. 169-174; part 2, v. 4, no. 16, June 1952, pp. 266-271.

Lindo, Archie. "Harold Telemaque, Poet of Trinidad." SUNDAY GLEANER, June 13, 1948, p. 9.

Seymour, Arthur J. "The Literary Adventure of the West Indies." KYK-OVER-AL, v. 2, no. 10, April 1950, entire issue, 40 pp.

Swanzy, Henry. "Caribbean Voices, Prolegomena to a West Indian Culture." CARIBBEAN QUARTERLY, v. 1, no. 2, September 1949, pp. 21-28. Reprinted in CARIBBEAN QUARTERLY, v. 8, no. 2, 1962, pp. 121-128.

BURNT BUSH (1948, with A. M. Clarke)

Bell, G. O. Review. BIM, v. 3, no. 9, 1948, pp. 74-77.

THOMAS, G. C. Barbados,

RULER IN HIROONA (1973)

Anon. "Past Imperfect, Present Continuous, Future Perfect?" CARIBBEAN CONTACT, v. 2, no. 1, March 1974, p. 2.

Levy, Oscar. "The Politics of Corruption--And Failure." CARIBBEAN CONTACT, v. 1, no. 6, May 1973, pp. 4, 16.

Lindo, Cedric. "West Indian Politics in a First Novel." SUNDAY GLEANER, December 24, 1972, p. 21.

Nicholas, Hollis. "Political Banditry." NEW VOICES, v. 2, no. 4, June 1974, p. 51.

Thomas, Odette

Odum. Review. BAJAN, no. 243, February 1974, p. 23.

Roach, Eric. "Politics on a Tiny Island." SUNDAY GUARDIAN (Trinidad), May 13, 1973, p. 6.

Solomon, Denis. "A House of Pitch Pine in a Land of Arrowroot." TAPIA, v. 2, no. 8, November 26, 1972, p. 10.

THOMAS, ODETTE. Jamaica,

RAIN FALLING SUN SHINING (1975)

Anon. Review. SUNDAY GLEANER, January 18, 1976, p. 8.

Anon. "Focus . . . The Short Stories." PUBLIC OPINION, December 18, 1948, pp. 10-11.

UNDERHILL, EVELYN. Jamaica,

General

Mais, Roger. "Contemporary Jamaican Verse." PUBLIC OPINION, November 4, 1939, p. 10.

VAUGHN, H. A. Barbados,

General

Anon. "Three Evenings with Six Poets." KYK-OVER-AL, v. 3, no. 13, Year-end 1951, pp. 214-220.

Drayton, Arthur D. "The European Factor in West Indian Literature." LITERARY HALF-YEARLY, v. 11, no. 1, pp. 71-94.

Seymour, Arthur J. "The Literary Adventure of the West Indies." KYK-OVER-AL, v. 2, no. 10, April 1950, entire issue, 40 pp.

Seymour, Arthur J. "Nature Poetry in the West Indies." KYK-OVER-AL, v. 3, no. 11, October 1950, pp. 39-47.

VIRTUE, VIVIAN. Jamaica, 1911-

Walcott, Derek

General

Bennett, Wycliffe. "The Jamaican Poets." LL, v. 57, no.
128, April 1948, pp. 58-61.

Mais, Roger. "Contemporary Jamaican Verse." PUBLIC OPINION,
November 4, 1939, p. 10.

Oakley, Leo. "Ideas of Patriotism and National Dignity in
Some Jamaican Writings." JAMAICA JOURNAL, v. 4, no. 3,
September 1970, pp. 16-21.
Also appears in SUNDAY GLEANER, part 1, March 28, 1971,
pp. 31, 34; part 2, April 4, 1971, p. 27; part 3, April
11, 1971, p. 25, as "Patriotism, National Dignity in
Jamaican Writings."

Owens, R. J. "West Indian Poetry." CARIBBEAN QUARTERLY,
v. 7, no. 3, December 1961, pp. 120-127.

Walcott, Derek. "Some Jamaican Poets." PUBLIC OPINION,
part 1, August 3, 1957, p. 7; part 2, August 10, 1957,
p. 7.

WALCOTT, DEREK. St. Lucia, 1930-

General

Anon. "Honour for to Derek in His Prime." SUNDAY GUARDIAN
(Trinidad), January 28, 1973, p. 15.

Anon. "Special Week to Honour Caribbean Writer." SUNDAY
GLEANER, March 17, 1967, p. 11.

Anon. "Three Evenings with Six Poets." KYK-OVER-AL, v. 3,
no. 13, Year-end 1951, pp. 214-220.

Baugh, Edward. "Metaphor and Plainess in the Poetry of
Derek Walcott." LITERARY HALF-YEARLY, v. 11, no. 2,
1970, pp. 47-58.

Brathwaite, Edward. "The African Presence in Caribbean
Literature." DAEDALUS, v. 103, no. 2, Spring 1974,
pp. 78-109.

Brathwaite, Edward. "Sir Galahad and the Islands." BIM,
v. 7, no. 25, July-December 1957, pp. 8-16.
Also appears in IOUANALOA, RECENT WRITING FROM ST. LUCIA

Walcott, Derek

    Castries, St. Lucia: Department of Extra-Mural Studies, 1963, pp. 50-59.

    Brathwaite, Edward. "Timehri." SAVACOU, no. 2, September 1970, pp. 35-44. Also appears in IS MASSA DAY DEAD? New York: Doubleday, 1974, pp. 29-44.

    Brown, Lloyd W. "The Calypso Tradition in West Indian Literature." BAR, v. 2, nos. 1 and 2, pp. 127-143.

    Brown, Wayne. "On Art, Artists and the People." SUNDAY GUARDIAN (Trinidad), August 9, 1970, p. 10.

    Brown, Wayne. "The Possibilities for West Indian Writing." SUNDAY GUARDIAN (Trinidad), November 22, 1970, p. 21.

    Carr, Bill. "The Significance of Derek Walcott." PUBLIC OPINION, February 28, 1964, pp. 8-9, 14.

    Clarke, Austin. "Some Speculations as to the Absence of Racialistic Vindictiveness in West Indian Literature." THE BLACK WRITER IN AFRICA AND THE AMERICAS. Los Angeles: Hennesey and Ingalls, 1973, pp. 165-194.

    Collymore, Frank A. "An Introduction to the Poetry of Derek Walcott." BIM, v. 3, no. 10, June 1949, pp. 125-132.

    Colson, Theodore. "Derek Walcott's Plays: Outrage and Compassion." WLWE, v. 12, April 1973, pp. 80-96.

    Dawes, Neville. "Thoughts on W.I. Poetry." PUBLIC OPINION, January 3, 1953, p. 5.

    Dathorne, O. R. "Africa in the Literature of West Indies." JCL, no. 1, September 1965, pp. 95-116.

    Dathorne, O. R. "Africa in West Indian Literature." BLACK ORPHEUS, no. 16, October 1964, pp. 42-53. Also appears as "The Theme of Africa in West Indian Literature." PHYLON, v. 26, Fall 1965, pp. 42-53.

    Derrick, Anthony. "An Introduction to Caribbean Literature." CARIBBEAN QUARTERLY, v. 15, nos. 2 and 3, June-September 1969, pp. 65-78.

    Drayton, Arthur D. "The European Factor in West Indian

Walcott, Derek

Literature." LITERARY HALF-YEARLY, v. 11, no. 1, 1970, pp. 71-94.

Hackett, Winston. "Identity in the Poetry of Derek Walcott." MOKO, no. 8, February 14, 1969, p. 2.

Ismond, Patricia. "Walcott vs. Brathwaite." CARIBBEAN QUARTERLY, v. 17, nos. 3 and 4, 1971, pp. 54-70.

Jacobs, Carl. "At 35 Walcott Is Something of a Phenomenon." SUNDAY GUARDIAN (Trinidad), May 15, 1966, p. 9.

Jacobs, Carl. "There's No Bitterness in Our Literature" (interview). SUNDAY GUARDIAN (Trinidad), May 22, 1966, p. 9.

James, Louis. "Caribbean Poetry in English--Some Problems." SAVACOU, no. 2, September 1970, pp. 78-86.

James, Louis. "Islands of Man, Reflections on the Emergence of a West Indian Literature." SOUTHERN REVIEW, v. 2, 1966, pp. 150-163.

Keane, E. McG. "Some Religious Attitudes in West Indian Poetry." BIM, part one, v. 4, no. 15, December 1951, pp. 169-174; part two, v. 4, no. 16, June 1952, pp. 266-271.

Kemoli, Arthur. "The Theme of 'The Past' in Caribbean Literature." WLWE, v. 12, November 1973, pp. 304-325.

King, Cameron. "The Poems of Derek Walcott." CARIBBEAN QUARTERLY, v. 10, no. 3, September 1964, pp. 3-30.

King, Cameron, and Louis James. "In Solitude for Company. The Poetry of Derek Walcott." THE ISLANDS IN BETWEEN. London: Oxford University Press, 1968, pp. 86-99.

King, Lloyd. "Derek Walcott: The Literary Humanist in the Caribbean." CARIBBEAN QUARTERLY, v. 16, no. 4, December 1970, pp. 36-42.

King, Lloyd. "Bard in the Rubbish Heap; The Problem of Walcott's Poetry." TAPIA, no. 5, February 1, 1970, pp. 7-8.

Lacovia, R. M. "Caribbean Literature in English: 1949-1970." BAR, v. 2, nos. 1 and 2, 1971, pp. 109-125.

Walcott, Derek

Lane, M. Travis. "At Home in Homelessness; The Poetry of
Derek Walcott." DALHOUSIE REVIEW, v. 53, no. 2, Summer
1973, pp. 325-338.

Lewis, Gordon. "The New West Indies: Nationality and
Literature." SUNDAY GLEANER, December 8, 1957, p. 8.

Mills, Therese. "Conversation with Derek Walcott" (interview). SUNDAY GUARDIAN (Trinidad), June 20, 1971, pp.
10-17.

Moore, Gerald. "Use Men Language." BIM, v. 15, no. 57,
March 1974, pp. 69-76.

Morris, Mervyn. "Walcott and the Audience for Poetry."
CARIBBEAN QUARTERLY, v. 14, nos. 1 and 2, March-June
1968, pp. 7-24.

Owens, R. J. "West Indian Poetry." CARIBBEAN QUARTERLY,
v. 7, no. 3, December 1961, pp. 120-127.

Pantin, Raoul. "We are Still Being Betrayed" (interview).
CARIBBEAN CONTACT, part one, v. 1, no. 7, 1973, pp. 14,
16; part two, v. 1, no. 8, 1973, pp. 14-16.

Questel, Victor. "The Horns of Derek's Dilemma." TAPIA,
v. 3, no. 12, March 25, 1973, pp. 4-5.

Questel, Victor. "Their Tragic Destiny." TAPIA, v. 6, no.
20, May 16, 1976, pp. 4, 11.

Ramchand, Kenneth. "Before the People Became Popular. . . ."
CARIBBEAN QUARTERLY, v. 18, no. 4, December 1972, pp. 70-
73.

Ramsaran, J. A. "The 'Twice-Born' Artist's Silent Revolution." BLACK WORLD, v. 20, no. 7, 1971, pp. 58-67.

Rohlehr, F. Gordon. "Afterthoughts." TAPIA, no. 23,
December 26, 1971, pp. 8, 13. Also appears in BIM, v. 14,
no. 56, January-June 1973, pp. 227-230.

Rohlehr, F. Gordon. "A Carrion Time." BIM, v. 15, no. 58,
June 1975, pp. 92-109.

Rohlehr, F. Gordon. "The Creative Writer and West Indian
Society." KAIE, no. 11, August 1973, pp. 48-77.

Walcott, Derek

Also appears in TAPIA, part one, v. 4, no. 31, August 1973, pp. 5-9; part two, v. 4, no. 32, August 1973, pp. 6-7; part three, v. 4, no. 33, August 1973, pp. 4-6; part four, v. 4, no. 35, August 1973, pp. 4-5, no. 7 (Literary Supplement).

Rohlehr, F. Gordon. "The Folk in Caribbean Literature." TAPIA, part one, v. 2, no. 11, December 17, 1972, pp. 7-8, 13-15.

Rohlehr, F. Gordon. "West Indian Poetry: Some Problems of Assessment." TAPIA, no. 20, August 1971, pp. 11-14. Also appears in BIM, part 1, v. 14, no. 54, January-June 1972, pp. 80-88; part 2, v. 14, no. 55, July-December 1972, pp. 134-144, and under title "Some Problems of Assessment: A Look at New Expressions in the Arts of the Contemporary Caribbean." CARIBBEAN QUARTERLY, v. 17, nos. 3 and 4, September-December 1971, pp. 92-113.

Scott, Dennis. "Walcott on Walcott" (interview). CARIBBEAN QUARTERLY, v. 14, nos. 1 and 2, March-June 1968, pp. 77-82.

Seymour, Arthur J. "The Literary Adventure of the West Indies." KYK-OVER-AL, v. 2, no. 10, April 1950, entire issue, 40 pp.

Swanzy, Henry. "Caribbean Voices, Prolegomena to a West Indian Culture." CARIBBEAN QUARTERLY, v. 1, no. 2, September 1949, pp. 21-28. Reprinted in CARIBBEAN QUARTERLY, v. 8, no. 2, 1962, pp. 121-128.

Wade, Henling. "Derek Walcott to Us." SUNDAY GLEANER, November 1, 1970, p. 29.

Walcott, Derek. "Derek Walcott, A Self-Interview Raises Questions of Identity." SUNDAY GUARDIAN (Trinidad), October 16, 1966, p. 7.

Walcott, Derek. "Meanings." SAVACOU, no. 2, September 1970, pp. 45-51.

Walmsley, Anne. "Dimensions of Song, A Comment on the Poetry of Derek Walcott and Edward Brathwaite." BIM, v. 13, no. 51, July-December 1970, pp. 152-167.

Wickham, John. "Derek Walcott Poet and Dramatist." BAJAN,

Walcott, Derek

no. 197, January 1970, pp. 4, 6.

POETRY

25 POEMS (1949)

Simmons, Harold. "A West Indian Poet Fulfills his Promise."
SUNDAY GLEANER, February 27, 1949, p. 7.

EPITAPH FOR THE YOUNG (1949)

Alleyne, Keith. Review. BIM, v. 3, no. 11, December 1949,
pp. 267-272.

Hendriks, A. L. Review. PUBLIC OPINION, December 31, 1949,
p. 6.

POEMS (1951)

Anon. Review. PUBLIC OPINION, October 6, 1951, pp. 5,6.

Collymore, Frank. Review. BIM, v. 4, no. 15, December 1951,
pp. 224-227.

Milner, Harry. "Poet at the Crossroads." SUNDAY GLEANER,
October 14, 1951, p. 4.

IN A GREEN NIGHT (1962)

Carr, Bill. "The Clear-Eyed Muse." SUNDAY GLEANER,
January 20, 1963, pp. 14, 20, 23.

Figueroa, John J. Review. CARIBBEAN QUARTERLY, v. 8, no. 4,
December 1962, pp. 67-69.

Figueroa, John J. "Some Subtleties of the Isle: A Commentary on Certain Aspects of Derek Walcott's Sonnet
Sequence, TALES OF THE ISLANDS." WLWE, v. 15, April 1976,
pp. 190-224.

Forde, A. N. Review. BIM, v. 9, no. 36, January-June 1963,
pp. 288-290.

James, C. L. R. "Here's a Poet Who Sees the REAL West
Indies." SUNDAY GUARDIAN (Trinidad), May 6, 1962, p. 5.

Montague, John. Review. SPECTATOR, v. 208, June 29, 1962,

p. 864.

Panton, George. "The Magic of Words." SUNDAY GLEANER, May 13, 1962, p. 4.

Williams, Hugo. Review. LONDON MAGAZINE, New Series, v. 2, no. 4, July 1962, pp. 77-79.

SELECTED POEMS (1964)

Dickey, James. Review. NYT, September 13, 1964, Section 7, p. 44.

Mazzocco, Robert. Review. NYRB, v. 3, no. 10, 1964, pp. 18-19.

Panton, George. "Major Poet." SUNDAY GLEANER, October 18, 1964, p. 4.

Randall, Dudley. Review. NEGRO DIGEST, v. 14, no. 11, 1965, pp. 52, 86.

THE CASTAWAY (1965)

Alvarez, A. Review. LSO, October 24, 1965, p. 27.

Anon. Review. NWF, v. 1, no. 37, April 1, 1966, pp. 23-25.

Anon. Review. SUNDAY GLEANER, December 26, 1965, p. 4.

Anon. Review. TLS, no. 3337, February 10, 1966, p. 104.

Brathwaite, Edward. Review. BIM, v. 11, no. 42. January-June 1966, pp. 139-141.

Ireland, Kevin. "Place and Poetic Identity." JCL, no. 2, December 1966, pp. 157-158.

Martin, Graham. Review. LISTENER, v. 75, March 10, 1966, p. 359.

Ramchand, Kenneth. "Readings of 'Laventille.'" TAPIA, v. 5, no. 50, December 1975, pp. 6-7.

Ross, Allan. Review. LONDON MAGAZINE, New Series, v. 5, no. 10, January 1966, pp. 88-89.

Walcott, Derek

THE GULF   (1969)

Anon.   Review.   BAJAN, no. 197, January 1970, p. 18.

Anon.   Review.   TLS, no. 3539, December 25, 1969, p. 1467.

Brown, Wayne.   "W.I. Literature of the Past Year."   SUNDAY
   GUARDIAN (Trinidad), August 30, 1970, p. 5.

Donoghue, Denis.   Review.   NYRB, v. 16, no. 8, 1971.

Fuller, Roy.   Review.   LONDON MAGAZINE, New Series, v. 9,
   no. 8, November 1969, pp. 89-90.

Lawton, David.   Review.   RRI, v. 2, no. 2, Summer 1972,
   pp. 242-247.

Morris, Mervyn.   "New Poetry by Brathwaite and Walcott."
   SUNDAY GLEANER, November 30, 1969, p. 4.

Rodman, Seldon.   Review.   NYT, October 11, 1970, Section 7,
   p. 24.

ANOTHER LIFE   (1973)

Anon.   "A Crystal of Ambiguities."   SUNDAY GLEANER,
   September 30, 1973, p. 23.

Baugh, Edward.   Review.   QUEENS QUARTERLY, v. 18, Summer
   1974, pp. 317-318.

Edwards, Thomas R.   Review.   NYRB, v. 21, no. 10, 1974, pp.
   38-39.

Fabre, Michel.   "'Adam's Task of Giving Things Their Name,'
   The Poetry of Derek Walcott."   NEW LETTERS, v. 41, no. 1,
   Fall 1974, pp. 91-107.

Figueroa, John J.   Review.   BIM, v. 15, no. 58, June 1975,
   pp. 160-170.

Garfitt, Roger.   Review.   LONDON MAGAZINE, New Series, v. 13,
   no. 5, December 1973-January 1974, pp. 124-127.

Lamming, George.   Review.   NYT, May 6, 1973, Section 7, p.
   36.

Porter, Peter. Review. LSO, August 5, 1973, p. 28.

Questel, Victor. "Walcott's Major Triumph." TAPIA, part 1, v. 3, no. 51, December 23, 1973, pp. 6-7; part 2, v. 3, no. 52, December 30, 1973, pp. 6-7.

Tomalin, Claire. Review. NEW STATESMAN, v. 88, December 20, 1974, pp. 908.

SEA GRAPES (1976)

Hamner, Robert D. "New World Burden: Derek Walcott's SEA GRAPES." WLWE, v. 16, April 1977, pp. 212-214.

Hirsch, Edward. Review. NYT, October 31, 1976, Section 7, p. 38.

DRAMA

HENRI CHRISTOPHE (1949)

Anon. Review. KYK-OVER-AL, v. 3, no. 11, October 1950, pp. 73-74.

Douglas-Smith. Review. BIM, v. 3, no. 12, 1949, pp. 349-353.

Holder, G. A. Review. BIM, v. 4, no. 14, June 1951, pp. 141-142.

Swanzy, Henry. Review. BIM, v. 5, no. 17, 1952, pp. 75-76.

HARRY DERNIER (1952)

Anon. Review. BIM, v. 5, no. 17, 1952, pp. 79-80.

THE DYING GODS (unpublished, 1953)

Milner, Harry. Review. SUNDAY GLEANER, February 15, 1953, p. 4.

THE SEA AT DAUPHIN (1954)

Wickham, John. "A Look at Ourselves." BIM, v. 6, no. 22, June 1955, pp. 128-130.

THE WINE OF THE COUNTRY (1956)

Walcott, Derek

    Anon. "Violent Walcott Verse Play." PUBLIC OPINION, August
    18, 1956, p. 8.

    St. John, Orford. "A New West Indian Play." WIR, v. 1, no.
    9, September 1956, p. 32.

  IONE (1957)

    St. John, Orford. Review. WIR, v. 2, no. 3, March 1957,
    pp. 47-48.

  DRUMS AND COLOURS (1958)

    Jenkin, Veronica. Review. BIM, v. 7, no. 27, July–December
    1958, pp. 183-184.

    Swann, Tony. "DRUMS AND COLOURS--Guts at Least." PUBLIC
    OPINION, May 10, 1958, p. 7.

  TI-JEAN AND HIS BROTHERS (1958)

    Ashaolo, Albert Olu. "Allegory in TI-JEAN AND HIS BROTHERS."
    WLWE, v. 16, April 1977, pp. 203-211.

    Coke, Lloyd. "Walcott's Mad Innocents." SAVACOU, v. 1,
    no. 5, June 1971, pp. 121-124.

    Lowhar, Syl. "A Struggle for Freedom; Derek Walcott's
    TI-JEAN." TAPIA, no. 8, August 9, 1970, p. 6.

    Reid, Stanley. "A Moving Interpretation of Local Tradition."
    LINK, v. 2, nos. 2 and 3, April-September 1970, p. 13.

    Roach, Eric. "This Musical Fuses Both Traditions of Folk
    Legend." SUNDAY GUARDIAN (Trinidad), June 28, 1970, p.
    11.

    St. John, Orford. Review. WIR, v. 4, no. 4, April 1959,
    p. 57.

    Walcott, Derek. "Derek's Most West Indian Play." TGM,
    June 21, 1970, p. 7.

    Wickham, John. Review. BAJAN, no. 204, September 1970, pp.
    22, 24-25.

  DREAM ON MONKEY MOUNTAIN (1967)

Walcott, Derek

Brown, Lloyd W. "Dreamers and Slaves; The Ethos of Revolution in Walcott and Leroi Jones." CARIBBEAN QUARTERLY, v. 17, nos. 3 and 4, September-December 1971, pp. 36-41.

Coke, Lloyd. "Walcott's Mad Innocents." SAVACOU, v. 1, no. 5, June 1971, pp. 121-124.

Morsberger, Robert E. and Katherine M. Review. BOOKS ABROAD, v. 46, no. 1, Winter 1972, p. 172.

Questel, Victor. "DREAM ON MONKEY MOUNTAIN IN PERSPECTIVE." TAPIA, part 1, v. 4, no. 35, September 1974, pp. 2-3; part 2, v. 4, no. 36, September 1974, pp. 6-7, 11; part 3, v. 4, no. 37, September 1974, pp. 6-7; part 4, v. 4, no. 39, September 1974, pp. 6, 8.

Rodman, Selden. Review. RRI, v. 1, no. 2, Winter 1972, pp. 158-160.

Solomon, Denis. "Ape and Essence." TAPIA, no. 7, April 19, 1970, p. 6.

Wickham, John. Review. BIM, v. 12, no. 48, January-June 1969, pp. 267-268.

IN A FINE CASTLE (1970)

Lowhar, Syl. "Another Station of the Cross." TAPIA, De December 26, 1971, p. 19.

Nunez, Philip. Review. MOKO, no. 73, October 29, 1971, pp. 12-13.

FRANKLIN, A TALE OF THE ISLANDS (1973)

Solomon, Denis. "Beginning of the End?" TAPIA, v. 3, no. 16, April 22, 1973, pp. 2-3.

THE CHARLATAN (1973)

Solomon, Denis. "Divided by Class, United by Bacchanal." TAPIA, v. 3, no. 27, July 8, 1973, p. 6.

THE JOKER OF SEVILLE (1974)

Ismond, Patricia. "Breaking Myths and Maidenheads." TAPIA, part 1, v. 5, no. 20, May 1975, pp. 4-5, 9; part 2, v. 5,

Wallace, George B.

     no. 22, May 1975, pp. 6-8.

     Mills, Therese. "Don Juan Was a Stickman" (interview). SUNDAY GUARDIAN (Trinidad), November 18, 1973, p. 4.

     Solomon, Denis. "Liberation and Libido." TAPIA, v. 4, no. 49. December 1974, p. 3.

Other Works

O BABYLON (drama, 1975)

REMEMBRANCES (drama, 1976)

WALLACE, GEORGE B. Jamaica, 1905-

    INEFFABLE MOMENTS (poetry, 1954)

     Anon. "Few Good Moments in the Sixth." PUBLIC OPINION, November 20, 1954, p. 6.

WALROND, ERIC. Guyana,

    TROPIC DEATH (1926)

     Panton, George. Review. SUNDAY GLEANER, July 2, 1972, p. 15.

     Ramchand, Kenneth. "The Writer Who Ran Away: Eric Walrond and TROPIC DEATH." SAVACOU, no. 2, September 1970, pp. 67-75

WICKHAM, JOHN. Barbados,

    CASUARINA ROW (1975)

     Anon. "West Indian Stories and Sketches." SUNDAY GLEANER, October 5, 1975, p. 24.

     Odum. Review. BAJAN, no. 255, March 1975, p. 22.

WILLIAMS, DANIEL. St. Vincent,

     Keane, E. McG. "Some Religious Attitudes in West Indian Poetry." BIM, part 1, v. 4, no. 15, December 1951, pp. 169-174; part 2, v. 4, no. 16, June 1952, pp. 266-271.

WILLIAMS, DENIS. Guyana, 1923-

General

> Brown, Wayne. "On Art, Artists and the People." SUNDAY
> GUARDIAN (Trinidad), August 9, 1970, p. 10.

> Carty, Wilfred. "The Rhythm of Society and Landscape." NWQ,
> Guyana Independence Issue, v. 2, no. 3, 1966, pp. 97-104.

> Dathorne, O. R. "Africa in the Literature of the West
> Indies," JCL, no. 1, September 1965, pp. 95-116.

> Dathorne, O. R. "Africa in West Indian Literature." BLACK
> ORPHEUS, no. 16, October 1964, pp. 42-53. Also appears
> as "The Theme of Africa in West Indian Literature."
> PHYLON, v. 26, no. 3, Fall 1965, pp. 255-276.

> Derrick, Anthony. "An Introduction to Caribbean Literature."
> CARIBBEAN QUARTERLY, v. 15, nos. 2 and 3, June-September
> 1969, pp. 65-78.

> Drayton, Arthur D. "The European Factor in West Indian
> Literature." LITERARY HALF-YEARLY, v. 11, no. 1, 1970,
> pp. 71-94.

> James, Louis. "Islands of Man, Reflections on the Emergence
> of a West Indian Literature." SOUTHERN REVIEW, v. 2,
> 1966, pp. 150-163.

> Seymour, Arthur J. "The Novel in Guyana." KAIE, no. 4,
> July 1967, pp. 59-63.

> Sparer, Joyce L. "Attitudes towards 'Race' in Guyanese
> Literature." CARIBBEAN STUDIES, v. 8, no. 2, July 1968,
> pp. 23-63.

OTHER LEOPARDS (1963)

> Akanji. Review. BLACK ORPHEUS, no. 13, November 1963, pp.
> 59-60.

> Anon. Review. TLS, no. 3203, July 19, 1963, p. 521.

> James, Louis. "Or the Hopeful Dawn." PUBLIC OPINION, June
> 18, 1965, pp. 14-15.

Williams, Denis

> Panton, George. "New Caribbean Voices." SUNDAY GLEANER, December 15, 1963, p. 14.
>
> Rowe-Evans, Adrian. "Other Freedoms." TRANSITION, v. 3, no. 10, 1963, pp. 57-58.
>
> Walcott, Derek. "His Is the Pivotal One About Race." SUNDAY GUARDIAN (Trinidad), December 1, 1963, p. 23.

THE THIRD TEMPTATION (1968)

> Anon. Review. TLS, no. 3482, November 21, 1968, p. 1321.
>
> Owen, A. L. Review. WLWE, no. 19, April 1971, pp. 93-94.

WYNTER, SYLVIA. Jamaica,

General

> Brown, Wayne. "On Art, Artists and the People." SUNDAY GUARDIAN (Trinidad), August 9, 1970, p. 10.
>
> Carew, Jan. "Language and Literature in Developing Countries." NWF, part 1, v. 1, no. 22, September 1965, pp. 25-29; part 2, v. 2, no. 23, September 1965, pp. 23-27.
>
> Dathorne, O. R. "Africa in the Literature of the West Indies." JCL, no. 1, September 1965, pp. 95-116.
>
> Dathorne, O. R. "Africa in West Indian Literature." BLACK ORPHEUS, no. 16, October 1964, pp. 42-53. Also appears as "The Theme of Africa in West Indian Literature" in PHYLON, v. 26, Fall 1965, pp. 255-276.
>
> Ramchand, Kenneth. "Obeah and the Supernatural in West Indian Literature." JAMAICA JOURNAL, v. 3, no. 2, June 1969, pp. 52-54.

THE HILLS OF HEBRON (1962)

> Anon. Review. THE TIMES (London), September 13, 1962, p. 11 11.
>
> Anon. Review. TLS, no. 3161, September 28, 1962, p. 765.
>
> Baird, Keith E. Review. FREEDOMWAYS, v. 3, Winter 1963,

pp. 111-112.

Charles, Pat. Review. IOUANALOA, RECENT WRITING FROM ST. LUCIA. Castries, St. Lucia: Department of Extra-Mural Studies, 1963, pp. 66-68.

Gilbert, Morris. "The Rise and Fall of Prophet Moses." NYT, July 15, 1962, Section 7, p. 24.

Panton, George. "Bedward--In New Guise." SUNDAY GLEANER, July 22, 1962, p. 14.

Sealy, Karl. Review. BIM, v. 9, no. 36, January-June 1963, p. 292.

Sherratt, Ann. Review. JLW, v. 7, October 1962, p. 324.

SHH . . . IT'S A WEDDING (drama, 1963)

McFarlane, Basil. "Views of a Slum Yard." PUBLIC OPINION, January 26, 1963, p. 13.

WORREL, PATRICIA. Trinidad

Pantin, Raoul. "Writings of Two Young Poets." CARIBBEAN CONTACT, v. 3, no. 3, 1975, p. 3.

Part II
Index of Critics and Reviewers

AARONS, R. L. C.

"Remembering H. G. de Lisser." SUNDAY GLEANER, June 9, 1974, p. 22.

"Jamaica's First Poet Laureate" (Redcam). SUNDAY GLEANER, June 30, 1974, p. 32.

"W. Adolphe Roberts--The Poet as Nationalist." SUNDAY GLEANER, July 21, 1974, p. 24.

"Una Marson--A True Trail-blazer." SUNDAY GLEANER, December 22, 1974, p. 32.

"Anansi Story Now Children's Book" (Sherlock, P. M. ANANSI AND THE ALLIGATOR EGGS). SUNDAY GLEANER, December 14, 1975, p. 16.

"George Lamming--Novelist as Exile." SUNDAY GLEANER, part 1, February 8, 1976, pp. 23, 31; part 2, February 15, 1976, p. 8.

ADAMS, ROLSTON

"Two Critics On BLACK MARSDEN, A Pursuit of Archetypes of Culture. . . ." (Harris). CARIBBEAN QUARTERLY, v. 19, no. 4, December 1973, pp. 53-55.

ADLER, JOYCE SPARER; See Also SPARER, JOYCE

"Wilson Harris and the Twentieth Century Man." NEW LETTERS, v. 40, no. 1, Fall 1973, pp. 49-61.

"TUMATUMARI and the Imagination of Wilson Harris." JCL, no. 7, July 1969, pp. 20-31.

AGARD, JOHN

Akanji, Sangodare

   [Review of] THE THIRD GIFT, by Jan Carew. CARIBBEAN CONTACT,
     v. 2, no. 10, January 1975, p. 3.

   "World of Caribbean Artists; The Shame of It All" (interview
     with Michael Gilkes). CARIBBEAN CONTACT, v. 3, no. 2, May
     1975, p. 9.

AKANJI, SANGODARE

   "Roger Mais," BLACK ORPHEUS, no. 5, May 1959, pp. 33-37.

   [Review of] TO SIR WITH LOVE, by E. R. Braithwaite. BLACK
     ORPHEUS, no. 6, November 1959, pp. 51-52.

   [Review of] A TINKLING IN THE TWILIGHT, by Edgar Mittelholzer.
     BLACK ORPHEUS, no. 7, June, 1960, p. 62.

   [Review of] AUTUMN EQUINOX, by John Hearne. BLACK ORPHEUS, v.
     8, 1960, pp. 53-54.

   [Review of] OTHER LEOPARDS, by Denis Williams. BLACK ORPHEUS,
     no. 13, November 1963, pp. 59-60.

ALLAN, GREIG

   [Review of] STRANGER AT THE GATE, by John Hearne, BIM, v. 6,
     no. 24, 1956, pp. 271-272.

ALLEN, WALTER

   [Review of] THE HILLS WERE JOYFUL TOGETHER, by Roger Mais. NEW
     STATESMAN, v. 45, April 25, 1953, p. 497.

   "Fear of Trinidad" (Naipaul, V. S., THE MIDDLE PASSAGE). NEW
     STATESMAN, v. 64, August 3, 1962, pp. 149-150.

   "London Again" (Naipaul, V. S., MR STONE AND THE KNIGHTS
     COMPANION). NYRB, v. 2, no. 3, 1964, p. 21.

ALLEYNE, KEITH

   [Review of] EPITAPH FOR THE YOUNG, by Derek Walcott. BIM, v. 3,
     no. 11, December 1949, pp. 267-272.

ALLSOPP, JOY

   "Memorial to Roger Mais: A Green Blade in Triumph--BROTHER

MAN." KYK-OVER-AL, v. 6, no. 20, Mid-year 1955, pp. 159-160.

[Review of] THE HARROWING OF HUBERTUS, by Edgar Mittelholzer. KYK-OVER-AL, v. 6, no. 20, Mid-year 1955, pp. 203-205.

"Thinking about Roger Mais." KYK-OVER-AL, v. 8, no. 24, December 1958, pp. 75-77.

[Review of] TO SIR WITH LOVE, by E. R. Braithwaite. KYK-OVER-AL, v. 9, no. 26, December 1959, pp. 56-57.

ALTMAN, WILFRED

[Review of] GUIANA BOY, by Lauchmonen. JLW, v. 3, October 1960, p. 463.

ALVAREZ, A.

[Review of] CONFESSIONS AND HISTORIES, by Edward Lucie-Smith. LSO, November 8, 1964, p. 27.

[Review of] THE CASTAWAY, by Derek Walcott. LSO, October 24, 1965, p. 27.

AMIS, KINGSLEY

"Fresh Winds from the West." SPECTATOR, v. 200, May 2, 1958, pp. 565-566.

AMIS, MARTIN

"Educated Monsters" (Naipaul, Shiva, THE CHIP-CHIP GATHERERS). NEW STATESMAN, v. 85, April 20, 1973, p. 586.

ANTHONY, MICHAEL

"Growing Up with Writing: A Particular Experience." JCL, no. 7, July 1969, pp. 80-87. Also appears in SAVACOU, no. 2, September 1970, pp. 61-66.

ARAGBABULU, OMIDJI

[Review of] THE WILD COAST, by Jan Carew. BLACK ORPHEUS, no. 7, June 1960, pp. 63-64.

[Review of] THE SCHOLAR-MAN, by O. R. Dathorne. BLACK ORPHEUS, no. 18, October 1965, pp. 62-63.

Archbold-Rousseau, Daphne

ARCHBOLD-ROUSSEAU, DAPHNE

"West Indian Writers: Future of Individual." SUNDAY GUARDIAN
(Trinidad), April 20, 1969, p. 10.

ARCHIBALD, CHARLES H.

"West Indian Writing in the Infant Days." TAPIA, v. 7, no. 5,
January 30, 1977. Reprint of article in THE ROYALIAN, v. 2,
no. 1, September 1933.

[Review of] NEW DAY, by V. S. Reid. BIM, v. 3, no. 12, 1949,
pp. 348-349.

ARGYLE, BARRY

"A West Indian Epic" (Naipaul, V. S., A HOUSE FOR MR. BISWAS).
CARIBBEAN QUARTERLY, v. 16, no. 4, December 1970, pp. 61-69.

"V. S. Naipaul's A HOUSE FOR MR. BISWAS." LITERARY HALF-YEARLY,
v. 14, no. 2, July 1973, pp. 81-95.

ARNASON, DAVID

[Review of] THE LATE EMANCIPATION OF JERRY STOVER, THE ADVEN-
TURES OF CATULLUS KELLY, by Andrew Salkey. WLWE, no. 19
April 1971, pp. 90, 92.

ARTHUR, KEVYN ALAN

[Review of] SURVIVORS OF THE CROSSING, by Austin Clarke. BIM,
v. 10, no. 40, January-June 1965, pp. 291-292.

[Review of] THE YEAR IN SAN FERNANDO, by Michael Anthony. BIM,
v. 10, no. 41, June-December 1965, pp. 70-71.

ASEIN, SAMUEL OMO

"The Concept of Form: A Study of Some Ancestral Elements in
Braithwaite's Trilogy." ASAWI, no. 4, December 1971, pp.
9-38.

"West Indian Poetry in English, 1900-1970: A Selected
Bibliography." BLACK IMAGES, v. 1, no. 2, Summer 1972,
pp. 12-15.

"Bastien's ANANCY STORY: A Critique." BLACK IMAGES, v. 1, no.

2, Summer 1972, pp. 25-27.

"The 'Protest' Tradition in West Indian Poetry, from George
   Campbell to Martin Carter." JAMAICA JOURNAL, v. 6, no. 2
   June 1972, pp. 40-45

BAGAI, LEONA BELL

[Review of] A HOUSE FOR MR. BISWAS, by V. S. Naipaul. BOOKS
   ABROAD, v. 36, no. 4, Autumn 1962, p. 453.

BAILEY, PAUL

[Review of] TIGERS ARE BETTER-LOOKING, by Jean Rhys. LONDON
   MAGAZINE, New Series, v. 8, no. 3, June 1968, pp. 110-11.

"Bedrooms in Hell" (Rhys, QUARTET, AFTER LEAVING MR. MACKENZIE).
   LSO, May 18, 1969, p. 30.

[Review of] BLACK MARSDEN, by Wilson Harris. LONDON MAGAZINE,
   New Series, v. 12, no. 6, February/March 1973, p. 160.

BAIRD, KEITH E.

[Review of] THE HILLS OF HEBRON, by Sylvia Wynter. FREEDOMWAYS,
   v. 3, Winter 1963, pp. 111-112.

BAKER, PETA-ANNE

"Louise Bennett-Coverly: A Poet of Utterance." CARIBBEAN
   CONTACT, v. 1, no. 8, August 1973, p. 6.

BANHAM, MARTIN

[Review of] DUMPLINGS IN THE SOUP, by O. R. Dathorne. BOOKS
   ABROAD, v. 39, no. 1, Winter 1965, pp. 111-112.

BARKER, J. S.

"Is Mittelholzer Slipping?" (THE WEATHER IN MIDDENSHOT).
   SUNDAY GUARDIAN (Trinidad), May 17, 1953, p. 7.

BARKHAM, JOHN

"The Enemy Was Bwana." (Reid, THE LEOPARD). NYT, April 13,
   1956, Section 7, p. 40.

Barnes, W. T.

BARNES, W. T.

[Review of] MY BONES AND MY FLUTE, by Edgar Mittelholzer, BIM,
v. 6, no. 23, 1955, p. 205.

BAUGH, EDWARD

"Selvon the Humorist" (THE LONELY LONDONERS). PUBLIC OPINION,
August 24, 1957, p. 7.

"The Poetry of Claude McKay." PUBLIC OPINION, part 1, November
30, 1957, p. 9; part 2, December 21, 1957, p. 6; part 3,
January 18, 1958, p. 7.

"Frank Collymore and the Miracle of BIM." NWQ, Barbados
Independence Issue, v. 3, nos. 1 and 2, Dead Season 1966/
Croptime 1967, pp. 129-133.

[Review of] THIS ISLAND NOW, by Peter Abrahams. BIM, v. 11, no.
44, January-June 1967, pp. 298-299.

[Review of] RIGHTS OF PASSAGE, by E. R. Braithwaite. BIM, v.
12, no. 45, July-December 1967, pp. 66-68.

[Review of] SONG FOR MUMU, by Lindsay Barrett. CARIBBEAN
QUARTERLY, v. 13, no. 4, December 1967, pp. 53-54.

"Towards a West Indian Criticism." CARIBBEAN QUARTERLY, v. 14,
nos. 1 and 2, March-June 1968, pp. 140-144.

[Review of] MASKS, by Edward Brathwaite. BIM, v. 12, no. 47,
July-December 1968, pp. 209-211.

"A Graceful Wisdom" (St. Omer, NOR ANY COUNTY). SUNDAY
GLEANER, July 13, 1969, p. 4.

"Metaphor and Plainess in the Poetry of Derek Walcott."
LITERARY HALF-YEARLY, v. 11, no. 2, 1970, pp. 47-58.

[Review of] NOR ANY COUNTRY, by Garth St. Omen. BIM, v. 13,
no. 50, January-June 1970, pp. 128-130.

[Review of] SELECTED POEMS, by Frank Collymore. BIM, v. 13,
no. 53, July-December 1971, pp. 58-60.

"Questions and Imperatives for a Young Literature." HAR, v. 24,
no. 1, Winter 1973, pp. 13-24.

Bell, Gordon O.

[Review of] ANOTHER LIFE, by Derek Walcott. QUEENS QUARTERLY,
   v. 81, Summer 1974, pp. 317-318.

BRAYBROOKE, NEVILLE

"Shadow and the Substance" (Rhys, WIDE SARGASSO SEA).
   SPECTATOR, v. 217, October 28, 1966, pp. 561-562.

"Between Dog and Wolf" (Rhys). SPECTATOR, v. 219, July 21,
   1967, pp. 77-78.

"The Return of Jean Rhys." CARIBBEAN QUARTERLY, v. 16, no. 4,
   December 1970, pp. 43-46.

BAYLEY, JOHN

[Review of] THE FACES OF LOVE, by John Hearne. SPECTATOR, v.
   198, April 26, 1957, p. 401.

[Review of] THE MYSTIC MASSEUR, by V. S. Naipaul. SPECTATOR,
   v. 198, May 1957, p. 688.

BEASLEY, W. CONGER, JR.

[Review of] COMPANIONS OF THE DAY AND NIGHT, by Wilson Harris.
   NEW LETTERS, v. 42, no. 1, Fall 1975, pp. 114-115.

BECK, ERVIN

[Review of] NEW DAY, by V. S. Reid. BOOKS ABROAD, v. 48, no.
   3, Summer 1974, p. 322.

BEDFORD, SYBILLE

"Stoic Traveler" (Naipaul, V. S., THE MIDDLE PASSAGE). NYRB,
   v. 1, no. 6, 1963, pp. 4-5.

BEEBE, DEAN

"Writing and Publishing in the West Indies; An Interview with
   George Lamming." WLWE, no. 19, April 1971, pp. 17-22.

BEIER, ULLI

[Review of] THE LEOPARD, by V. S. Reid. BLACK ORPHEUS, no. 5,
   May 1959, pp. 52-54.

BELL, GORDON O.

[Review of] BURNT BUSH, by Harold Telemaque. BIM, v. 3, no. 9,

Bell, Vera

1948, pp. 74-77.

[Review of] GUIANA BOOK, by A. J. Seymour. BIM, v. 3, no. 10, June 1969, pp. 176-178.

BELL, VERA

[Review of] A PLAY WITHOUT SCENERY, by George Campbell. PUBLIC OPINION, March 29, 1940, p. 7.

BENNETT, WYCLIFFE

"Tom Redcam, Poet-Prophet." SUNDAY GLEANER, August 18, 1946, pp. 8, 9.

"Tom Redcam, Father of Jamaican Poetry." SUNDAY GLEANER, July 6, 1947, p. 6.

"The Jamaican Poets." LL, v. 57, no. 128, April 1948, pp. 58-61.

"Poets Play Part in Jamaica's Life." SUNDAY GLEANER, October 17, 1948, p. 6.

"W. Adolphe Roberts, the Man and the Poet." SUNDAY GLEANER, September 30, 1962, p. 14.

BERGONZI, BERNARD

[Review of] UNCLE PAUL, by Edgar Mittelholzer. NEW STATESMAN, v. 66, September 20, 1963, p. 363.

BERMANGE, BARRY

[Review of] SEASON OF ADVENTURE, by George Lamming. JLW, v. 3, October 1960, p. 526.

BILDER, J. RABAN

"London Knows, Do You?" (Figueroa, ed., CARIBBEAN VOICES), CARIBBEAN REVIEW, v. 4, nos. 1/2, 1972, pp. 24-27.

BIRAM, BRENDA M.

[Review of] PAID SERVANT, by E. R. Braithwaite. NEGRO DIGEST, v. 18, no. 6, 1969, pp. 92-93.

BIRBALSINGH, FRANK M.

"To John Bull with Hate" (Braithwaite). CARIBBEAN QUARTERLY,
v. 14, no. 4, September 1968, pp. 74-81.

"Edgar Mittelholzer: Moralist or Pornographer?" JCL, no. 7,
July 1969, pp. 88-103.

"Escapism in the Novels of John Hearne." CARIBBEAN QUARTERLY,
v. 16, no. 1, March 1970, pp. 28-38.

"The Novels of Ralph de Boissiere." JCL, no. 9, July 1970, pp.
104-108.

"W. Adolphe Roberts: Creole Romantic." CARIBBEAN QUARTERLY,
v. 19, no. 2, June 1973, pp. 100-107.

BISWAS, ROBIN

"Exhaustion and Persistence" (Naipaul, V. S., AN AREA OF DARK-
NESS). TAMARACK REVIEW, no. 35, Spring 1965, pp. 75-80.

BLACK, ANNA

"We Die Alone" (Hearne, VOICES UNDER THE WINDOW). PUBLIC
OPINION, October 15, 1955, p. 5.

BLACK, CLINTON

"Daylight for New Writings." PUBLIC OPINION, September 23,
1950, p. 6.

"Agonizing Pictures" (Mittelholzer, THE LIFE AND DEATH OF
SYLVIA). PUBLIC OPINION, June 20, 1953, p. 5.

"Buccaneer Blood" (de Lisser, MORGAN'S DAUGHTER). PUBLIC
OPINION August 15, 1953, p. 5.

BLACKMAN, PETER

"Is There a West Indian Literature?" LL, v. 59, no. 135, 1948,
pp. 96-102.
Also Appears in SUNDAY GLEANER, January 28, 1949, p. 7.

"Some Thoughts on West Indian Writing." PRESENCE AFRICAINE,
no. 14-15, 1957, pp. 296-300.

Blundell, Margaret S.

BLUNDELL, MARGARET S.

    Review (Khan, THE OBEAH MAN). CARIBBEAN QUARTERLY, v. 11, nos. 1 and 2, March-June 1965, pp. 95-97.

    "Caribbean Readers and Writers." BIM, v. 11, no. 43, July-December 1966, pp. 163-167.

BOXILL, ANTHONY

    "The Emasculated Colonial" (Salkey, ESCAPE TO AN AUTUMN PAVE-MENT). PRESENCE AFRICAINE, no. 75, 1970, pp. 146-149.

    [Review of] THE SLEEPERS OF RORAIMA, by Wilson Harris. WLWE, no. 19, April 1971, pp. 86-87.

    "San Christobal Unreached: George Lamming's Two Latest Novels" (WATER WITH BERRIES; NATIVES OF MY PERSON). WLWE, v. 12, April 1973, pp. 111-116.

    "The Concept of Spring in V. S. Naipaul's MR. STONE AND THE KNIGHTS COMPANION." ARIEL, v. 5, October 1974, pp. 21-28.

    "V. S. Naipauls's Starting Point." JCL, v. 10, no. 1, August 1975, pp. 1-9.

BRAHMS, F.

    "A Reading of Wilson Harris' PALACE OF THE PEACOCK." NEW LETTERS, v. 40, no. 1, Fall 1973.

BRASSINGTON, F. E.

    "Mittelholzer as I Knew Him." SUNDAY GUARDIAN (Trinidad), May 16, 1965, p. 6.

    "Analyzing West Indian Writers." SUNDAY GUARDIAN (Trinidad), July 26, 1970, p. 6.

BRATHWAITE, DORIS

    [Review of] THE MIDDLE PASSAGE, by V. S. Naipaul. IOUANALOA, RECENT WRITING FROM ST. LUCIA (edited by Edward Brathwaite). Castries, St. Lucia: Department of Extra-Mural Studies, 1963, pp. 72-73.

BRATHWAITE, EDWARD

Index of Critics and Reviewers

Brathwaite, Edward

[Review of] THE FACES OF LOVE, by John Hearne. BIM, v. 7, no. 25, July-December 1957, pp. 63-64.

"Sir Galahad and the Islands." BIM, v. 7, no. 25, July-December 1957, pp. 8-16.
Also appears in IOUANALOA, RECENT WRITING FROM ST. LUCIA (edited by Edward Brathwaite). Castries, St. Lucia: Department of Extra-Mural Studies, 1963, pp. 50-59.

"The Controversial Tree of Time." BIM, v. 8, no. 30, January-June 1960, pp. 104-114.

[Review of] A QUALITY OF VIOLENCE, by Andrew Salkey. BIM, v. 8, no. 31, July-December 1960, pp. 219-220.

[Review of] THE AUTUMN EQUINOX, by John Hearne. BIM, v. 8, no. 31, July-December 1960, pp. 215-217.

"The New West Indian Novelists." BIM, part 1, v. 8, no. 31, July-December 1960, pp. 199-210; part 2, v. 8, no. 32, January-June 1961, pp. 271-280.

[Review of] THE LAST ENCHANTMENT, by Neville Dawes. BIM, v. 9, no. 33, July-December 1961, pp. 74-75.

"Roots." BIM, v. 10, no. 37, July-December 1963, pp. 10-21.

[Review of] "Syrop" in INTRODUCTION 2: STORIES BY NEW WRITERS. CARIBBEAN QUARTERLY, v. 10, no. 1, March 1964, pp. 68-69. Also appears in BIM, v. 10, no. 40, January-June 1965, pp. 290-291.

[Review of] THE SCHOLAR-MAN, by O. A. Dathorne. BIM, v. 10, no. 41, July-December 1965, pp. 68-69.

[Review of] THE CASTAWAY, by Derek Walcott. BIM, v. 11, no. 42, January-June 1966, pp. 139-141.

"KYK-OVER-AL and the Radicals." NWQ, Guyana Independence Issue, v. 2, no. 3, High Season 1966, pp. 55-57.

"Jazz and the West Indian Novel." BIM, part 1, v. 11, no. 44, January-June 1967, pp. 275-284; part 2, v. 12, no. 45, July-December 1967, pp. 39-51; part 3, v. 12, no. 46, January-June 1968, pp. 115-126.

"West Indian Prose Fiction in the Sixties, A Survey." CRITICAL SURVEY, v. 3, Winter 1967, pp. 169-174. Also appears in

Brathwaite, Edward

BIM, v. 12, no. 47, July-December 1968, pp. 157-165, and in
SUNDAY GLEANER, part 1, March 8, 1970, p. 27; part 2, March 15,
1970, p. 27; part 3, March 22, 1970, p. 27; part 4, March
29, 1970, p. 27.
Appears with additional material in BLACK WORLD, v. 20, no.
11, September 1971, pp. 14-29.

"CAM Comment: Gordon Rohlehr's 'Sparrow and the Language of
the Calypso.'" CARIBBEAN QUARTERLY, v. 14, nos. 1 and 2,
March-June 1968, pp. 91-96.

"The Caribbean Artists Movement." CARIBBEAN QUARTERLY, v. 14,
nos. 1 and 2, March-June 1968, pp. 57-59.

"Caribbean Critics." NWQ, v. 5, nos. 1-2, Dead Season/Croptime
1969, pp. 5-11.
Also appears in CRITICAL QUARTERLY, v. 11, Autumn 1969, pp.
268-276, and under title "Reflections on West Indian Literature," in SOUTHERN REVIEW, v. 3, 1969, pp. 264-272.

[Review of] THE SCHOOLMASTER, by Earl Lovelace. BIM, v. 12,
no. 48, January-June 1969, pp. 273-277.
Also appears in JCL, no. 7, July 1969, pp. 117-122.

"Creative Literature of the British West Indies during the
Period of Slavery." SAVACOU, v. 1, no. 1, June 1970, pp. 46-
73.

[Review of] THE EXPATRIATE--POEMS 1963-68, by Faustin Charles.
CARIBBEAN QUARTERLY, v. 16, no. 2, June 1970, pp. 65-69.
Also appears in BIM, v. 13, no. 52, January-June 1971, pp.
252-255.

"Timehri." SAVACOU, no. 2, September 1970, pp. 35-44.
Also appears in IS MASSA DAY DEAD? (edited by Orde Coombs).
New York: Doubleday, 1974, pp. 29-44.

"West Indian History and Society in the Art of Paule Marshall's
Novel." JBS, v. 1, no. 2, December 1970, pp. 255-238.

"Foreword." SAVACOU, nos. 3/4, March 1971, pp. 5-9.

"The African Presence in Caribbean Literature." DAEDALUS, v.
103, no. 2, Spring 1974, pp. 73-109.

"Brother Mais." TAPIA, v. 4, no. 43, October 1974, pp. 6-8.

BROOKE, JOCELYN

Brown, Stewart

[Review of] MR. STONE AND THE KNIGHTS COMPANION, by V. S.
Naipaul. LISTENER, v. 69, May 30, 1963, p. 934.

BROOKE-ROSE, CHRISTINE

[Review of] ZOHARA, by Geoffrey Drayton. LSO, August 13, 1961,
p. 20.

[Review of] LAND OF THE LIVING, by John Hearne. LSO, November
5, 1961, p. 29.

BROPHY, BRIGID

[Review of] DUMPLINGS IN THE SOUP, by O. R. Dathorne. NEW
STATESMAN, v. 65, April 5, 1963, p. 497.

[Review of] MOSCOW IS NOT MY MECCA, by Jan Carew. NEW STATES-
MAN, v. 68, November 6, 1964, p. 763.

BROWN, LLOYD W.

"The Crisis of Black Identity in the West Indian Novel."
CRITIQUE, v. 11, no. 3, 1969, pp. 97-112.

"The West Indian Novel in North America: A Study of Austin
Clarke." JCL, no. 9, July 1970, pp. 89-103.

"Beneath the North Star: The Canadian Image in Black Literature." DALHOUSIE REVIEW, v. 50, no. 3, Autumn 1970, pp. 317-
329.

"The Calypso Tradition in West Indian Literature." BAR, v. 2,
nos. 1 and 2, 1971, pp. 127-143.

"The American Image in British West Indian Literature."
CARIBBEAN STUDIES, v. 11, no. 1, April 1971, pp. 30-45.

"Dreamers and Slaves: The Ethos of Revolution in Walcott and
Leroi Jones." CARIBBEAN QUARTERLY, v. 17, nos. 3 and 4,
September-December 1971, pp. 36-41.

"The Guyanese Voice in West Indian Poetry: A Review of Arthur
J. Seymour." WLWE, v. 15, April 1976, pp. 246-252.

BROWN, STEWART

[Review of] MUEY, by A. L. Henriks. NOW, v.1, Spring 1973,

Brown, Stewart

pp. 25-27.

[Review of] REEL FROM "THE LIFE MOVIE," by Anthony McNeill.
NOW, v. 1, Spring 1973, pp. 13-18.

[Review of] SCORE, by Anson Gonzalez and Victor Questel. NOW,
no. 2, Summer 1973, pp. 9-12.

"New Poetry from Jamaica." NEW VOICES, v. 3, no. 6, 1975, pp.
48-50.

BROWN, WAYNE

"West Indian Writings." SUNDAY GUARDIAN (Trinidad), May 31,
1970, p. 17.

"The First Generation of West Indian Novelists." SUNDAY
GUARDIAN (Trinidad), June 7, 1970, pp. 6, 11.

"The Politics of the Educators." SUNDAY GUARDIAN (Trinidad),
June 14, 1970, p. 6.

"Trinidadian English." SUNDAY GUARDIAN (Trinidad), June 21,
1970, p. 6.

"Growing Up in Colonial T'dad" (Hodge, CRICK-CRACK MONKEY).
SUNDAY GUARDIAN (Trinidad), June 28, 1970, pp. 6, 17.

"Teaching Poetry in West Indian Schools." SUNDAY GUARDIAN
(Trinidad), July 12, 1970, p. 6.

"Black Beautiful and _____" (Salkey, THE ADVENTURE OF
CATULLUS KELLY). SUNDAY GUARDIAN (Trinidad), July 19, 1970,
p. 6.

"An Exciting Trinidad Poet" (Charles, THE EXPATRIATE). SUNDAY
GUARDIAN (Trinidad), August 2, 1970, p. 15.

"On Art Artists, and the People." SUNDAY GUARDIAN (Trinidad),
August 9, 1970, p. 10.

"The Little Magazines in the West Indies." SUNDAY GUARDIAN
(Trinidad), August 16, 1970, p. 9.

"On West Indian Critics and Historians." SUNDAY GUARDIAN
(Trinidad), August 23, 1970, p. 17.

Index of Critics and Reviewers

Broyard, Anatole

"Art in Its Widest Sense and Reconstruction." TGM, August 30, 1970, pp. 12-13, 17.

"W. I. Literature of the Past Year." SUNDAY GUARDIAN (Trinidad), August 30, 1970, p. 5.

"New W.I. Writers of the Past Year." SUNDAY GUARDIAN (Trinidad), September 6, 1970, p. 8.

"West Indian Poetry of the 1940's." SUNDAY GUARDIAN (Trinidad), part 1, September 13, 1970, p. 9; part 2, September 20, 1970, p. 11; part 3, October 4, 1970, p. 11; part 5, October 11, 1970, p. 11; part 6, October 18, 1970, p. 6; part 7, October 25, 1970, p. 16.

"On Exile and the Dialect of the Tribe." SUNDAY GUARDIAN (Trinidad), November 8, 1970, p. 19.

"Talking About Aesthetics Seriously!" SUNDAY GUARDIAN (Trinidad), November 15, 1970, p. 15.

"The Possibilities of West Indian Writing." SUNDAY GUARDIAN (Trinidad), November 29, 1970, p. 15.

"Little Magazine from St. Lucia." SUNDAY GUARDIAN (Trinidad), November 29, 1970, p. 15.

"The New Battleground." SUNDAY GUARDIAN (Trinidad), part 1, December 6, 1970, pp. 9, 20; part 2, December 13, 1970, pp. 15, 20.

"Thinking about Commonwealth Literature." SUNDAY GUARDIAN (Trinidad), December 20, 1970, p. 10.

"For the Reviewer, A Time to Change." SUNDAY GUARDIAN (Trinidad), December 25, 1970, p. 13.

"Review of Anthony McNeill's REEL FROM 'THE LIFE MOVIE.'" JAMAICA JOURNAL, v. 7, nos. 1-2, March-June 1973, pp. 80-81.

BROWNJOHN, ALAN

[Review of] TOWARDS SILENCE, by Edward Lucie-Smith. NEW STATESMAN, v. 76, September 20, 1968, p. 363.

BROYARD, ANATOLE

199

Brucker, Milton

"A Difficult Year for Hats" (Rhys, GOOD MORNING MIDNIGHT). NYT, March 26, 1974, p. 39.

"The Author vs. His Characters" (Naipaul, V. S., GUERILLAS). NYT, November 20, 1975, p. 39.

BRUCKER, MILTON

"A Mixed Bag of Impressions" (Braithwaite: A KIND OF HOME-COMING). NYT, August 5, 1962, Section 7, p. 3.

BRUTON, JACK

[Review of] AND MOST OF ALL MAN, by Roger Mais. PUBLIC OPINION, December 5, 1942, p. 3.

BRYDEN, RONALD

[Review of] THE FACES OF LOVE, by John Hearne. LISTENER, v. 57, 1957, p. 726.

[Review of] THE MYSTIC MASSEUR, by V. S. Naipaul. LISTENER, v. 57, 1957, p. 890.

[Review of] LATTICED ECHOES, by Edgar Mittelholzer. SPECTATOR, v. 204, January 22, 1960, p. 117.

[Review of] PALACE OF THE PEACOCK, by Wilson Harris. SPECTATOR, v. 205, September 23, 1960, p. 454.

"New Map of Hell" (Naipaul, V. S., THE MIDDLE PASSAGE). SPECTATOR, v. 209, August 3, 1962, p. 161.

"Between the Epics" (Naipaul, V. S., THE LOSS OF ELDORADO). NEW STATESMAN, v. 78, November 7, 1969, pp. 661-662.

"The Hurricane" (V. S. Naipaul's journalism). LISTENER, v. 88, November 9, 1972, p. 641.

[Review of] THE CHIP-CHIP GATHERERS, by V. S. Naipaul. LISTENER, v. 89, April 12, 1973, p. 489.

BUCHAN, WILLIAM

[Review of] A FLAG ON THE ISLAND, by V. S. Naipaul. SPECTATOR, v. 219, September 22, 1967, p. 328.

BURGESS, ANTHONY

[Review of] THE SECRET LADDER, by Wilson Harris. LSO, February 10, 1963, p. 18.

[Review of] I HEAR THUNDER, by Samuel Selvon. LSO, April 7, 1963, p. 22.

[Review of] EYE OF THE SCARECROW, by Wilson Harris. SPECTATOR, v. 215, December 3, 1965.

BUTLER, RUPERT

[Review of] A HOUSE FOR MR. BISWAS, by V. S. Naipaul. JLW, v. 5, October 1961, p. 419.

[Review of] WOUNDS IN THE FLESH, by Fitzroy Fraser. JLW, v. 6, April 1962, p. 384.

BYATT, A. S.

[Review of] THE SCHOOL MASTER, by Earl Lovelace. NEW STATESMAN, v. 75, January 5, 1968, p. 15.

[Review of] THE LATE EMANCIPATION OF JERRY STOVER, by Andrew Salkey. NEW STATESMAN, v. 75, February 16, 1968, p. 209.

[Review of] TIGERS ARE BETTER-LOOKING, by Jean Rhys. NEW STATESMAN, v. 75, March 29, 1968, p. 422.

CALDER, ANGUS

"Darkest Naipaul" (IN A FREE STATE). NEW STATESMAN, v. 82, October 8, 1971, p. 530.

CAMERON, NORMAN E.

"Walter Mac A. Lawrence." KYK-OVER-AL, v. 1, no. 2, June 1946, p. 17.

CAPITANCHIK, MAURICE

[Review of] SHADES OF GREY, by Garth St. Omer. SPECTATOR, v. 221, December 20, 1968, pp. 881-882.

[Review of] NOR ANY COUNTRY, by Garth St. Omer. SPECTATOR, v. 222, May 9, 1969, p. 620.

Carew, Jan

CAREW, JAN

"The West Indian Artist in the Contemporary World." PHYLON, v. 13, 1952, pp. 136-140.

"British West Indian Poets and Their Culture." PHYLON, v. 14, 1953, pp. 71-73.

"Language and Literature in Developing Countries." NWF, part 1, v. 1, no. 22, September 23, 1965, pp. 25-29; part 2, v. 1 no. 23, September 17, 1965, pp. 23-27.

"An Artist in Exile--From the West Indies." NWF, v. 1, nos. 27 and 28, November 12, 1965, pp. 23-30.

"African Literature--From the Breath of Gods" (Abrahams, WILD CONQUEST). NYT, April 2, 1972, Section 7, p. 7.

CAREY, JOHN

[Review of] ON THE COAST, by Wayne Brown. LONDON MAGAZINE New Series, v. 13, no. 2, June/July 1973, pp. 120-121.

CARNEGIE, J. A.

[Review of] FEVER GRASS, by John Morris. PUBLIC OPINION, July 25, 1969, p. 8.

"Rediscovery from Outside" (Naipaul, V. S., THE LOSS OF ELDORADO). SAVACOU, v. 1, no. 5, June 1971, pp. 125-128.

CARR, W. I. (Bill)

"The West Indian Novelist ... A Footnote." SUNDAY GLEANER, April 23, 1961, pp. 14, 20.

"The Unreal World of Mr. Hearne." SUNDAY GLEANER, August 27, 1961, p. 14. n

[Review of] LAND OF THE LIVING, by John Hearne. CARIBBEAN QUARTERLY, v. 8, no. 1, June 1962, pp. 54-55.

[Review of] JAMAICAN INDEPENDENCE ANTHOLOGY. SUNDAY GLEANER, August 5, 1962, p. 18.

[Review of] IN A GREEN NIGHT, by Derek Walcott. SUNDAY GLEANER, January 20, 1963, pp. 14, 20, 23.

Index of Critics and Reviewers

Carr, W. I. (Bill)

"The Irony of W.I. Society" (Naipaul, V. S., THE MIDDLE
PASSAGE). SUNDAY GLEANER, January 27, 1963, pp. 14, 24.

"A Prison of One's Own" (Naipaul, V. S., MR. STONE AND THE
KNIGHTS COMPANION). PUBLIC OPINION, September 7, 1963,
p. 11.

"An Exhausted Talent?" (Selvon, I HEAR THUNDER). PUBLIC
OPINION, September 14, 1963, p. 11.

"Reflections on the Novel in the British Caribbean." QUEENS
QUARTERLY, v. 70, Winter 1963, pp. 585-597.

"C. L. R. James' New Book" (BEYOND A BOUNDARY). PUBLIC OPINION,
November 16, 1963, p. 16.

"The Significance of Derek Walcott." PUBLIC OPINION, February
28, 1964, pp. 8-9, 14.

"A View of John Hearne" (LAND OF THE LIVING). PUBLIC OPINION,
March 6, 1964, pp. 8-9.

"A House for Mr. Naipaul" (A HOUSE FOR MR. BISWAS). PUBLIC
OPINION, March 20, 1964, pp. 8-10.

"The Annoying Ironist" (Naipaul, V. S., THE MIDDLE PASSAGE).
PUBLIC OPINION, March 26, 1964, pp. 8-9.

[Review of] BEYOND A BOUNDARY, by C. L. R. James. PUBLIC
OPINION, April 3, 1964, pp. 8-9.

"Lamming to Little Purpose" (PLEASURES OF EXILE). PUBLIC
OPINION, April 10, 1964, pp. 8-9.

"The West Indian Novelist: Prelude and Context." CARIBBEAN
QUARTERLY, v. 11, nos. 1 and 2, March-June 1965, pp. 71-84.

"The Novels of Roger Mais." PUBLIC OPINION, Roger Mais
Supplement, June 10, 1966, p. 4.

"Roger Mais: Design from a Legend." CARIBBEAN QUARTERLY, v. 13
13, no. 1, March 1967, pp. 3-28.

"A Complex Fate. The Novels of Andrew Salkey." THE ISLANDS
IN BETWEEN. London: Oxford University Press, 1968, pp.
100-108.

Carter, Martin

[Review of] FROM THE GREEN ANTILLES; CARIBBEAN LITERATURE, AN
    ANTHOLOGY. CARIBBEAN STUDIES, v. 8, no. 3, October 1968,
    pp. 59-61.

CARTER, MARTIN

"A Note on Vic Reid's NEW DAY." KYK-OVER-AL, v. 8, no. 24,
    December 1958, pp. 81-82.

CARTEY, WILFRED

"The Knights Companion--Ganesh, Biswas and Stone: Novels by
    Vidia Naipaul." NWQ, v. 2, no. 1, Dead Season 1965, pp. 93-
    98.

"The Rhythm of Society and Landscape." NWQ, Guyana Independence
    Issue, 1966, pp. 97-104.

"Lamming and the Search for Freedom." NWQ, Barbados Indepen-
    dence Issue, v. 3, nos. 1 and 2, Dead Season 1966/Croptime
    1967, pp. 121-128.

"The Novels of John Hearne." JCL, no. 7, July 1969, pp. 45-58.

CASEY, NANCY J.; SEE ALSO FULTON, NANCY J. CASEY

"Study in the Alienation of a Creole Woman" (Rhys, A VOYAGE
    IN THE DARK). CARIBBEAN QUARTERLY, v. 19, no. 3, September
    1973, pp. 95-102.

"The 'Liberated' Woman in Jean Rhys' Later Short Fiction." RRI,
    v. 4, no. 2, Summer 1974, pp. 264-272.

CAWLEY, JOHN ALPHA

"Jamaican Novelist with Fire in His Heart" (Hearne, STRANGER
    AT THE GATE). PUBLIC OPINION, May 26, 1956, p. 6.

CHANDLER, G. LEWIS

"At the Edge of Two Worlds" (Lamming, IN THE CASTLE OF MY
    SKIN). PHYLON, v. 14, 1953, pp. 437-439.

CHAPMAN, ESTHER HYMAN

[Review of] PITCH LAKE, by Alfred Mendes, WIR, v. 1, no. 5,
    January 1935, p. 23.

Charles, Pat

[Review of] BLACK FAUNS, by Alfred Mendes, WIR, v. 2, no. 6,
February 1936, p. 5.

"Claude McKay's New Book" (A LONG WAY FROM HOME). WIR, v. 3,
no. 9, May 1937, p. 23.

[Review of] A MORNING AT THE OFFICE by Edgar Mittelholzer. WIR,
v. 2, no. 5, New Series, June 3, 1950, p. 28.

"Pioneer Books--A Literary Event." WIR, v. 2, no. 20, New
Series, September 16, 1950, p. 19.

"Some Books of West Indian Interest: More Pioneer Press Books."
WIR, v. 3, no. 6, New Series, June 9, 1951, p. 16.

[Review of] PSYCHE, by H. G. de Lisser. WIR, v. 4, no. 20,
New Series, September 13, 1952, p. 12.

"Roger Mais." WIR, v. 7, no. 12, New Series, June 25, 1955,
p. 7.

"John Hearne's Second Novel." WIR, v. 1, no. 7, New Series,
July 1956, p. 9.

[Review of] THE FACES OF LOVE by John Hearne. WIR, v. 2, no.
6, New Series, June 1957, p. 68.

"West Indian Writers." WIR, v. 3, no. 9, New Series, September
1958, p. 15.

[Review of] THE COMING OF THE HARVEST, by Fitzroy Fraser. WIR,
v. 4, no. 3, New Series, March 1959, p. 61.

[Review of] THE MIDDLE PASSAGE, by V. S. Naipaul. WIR, January
1963, p. 7.

"The Poems of Edward Lucie-Smith." WIR, v. 2, no. 3, Autumn
1964, p. 31.

CHARLES, PAT

[Reviews of] VILLAGE OF LOVE, by Merrill Ferguson; LAND OF THE
LIVING, by John Hearne; THE HILLS OF HEBRON, by Sylvia
Wynter. IOUANALOA, RECENT WRITING FROM ST. LUCIA (edited by
Edward Brathwaite). Castries, St. Lucia: Department of
Extra-Mural Studies, 1963, pp. 66-68.

Charques, R. D.

[Review of] RIGHTS OF PASSAGE, by Edward Brathwaite. LINK, v. 1, no. 1, July-September 1968, pp. 32-34.

CHARQUES, R. D.

[Review of] SHADOWS MOVE AMONG THEM, by Edgar Mittelholzer. SPECTATOR, v. 186, April 20, 1951, p. 534.

[Review of] IN THE CASTLE OF MY SKIN, by George Lamming. SPECTATOR, v. 190, March 20, 1953, p. 354.

[Review of] THE HILLS WERE JOYFUL TOGETHER, by Roger Mais. SPECTATOR, v. 190, April 17, 1953, p. 494.

CLARK, EDWARD

[Review of] VOICES UNDER THE WINDOW, by John Hearne. PHYLON, v. 18, 1957, pp. 97-98.

[Review of] A WREATH FOR UDOMO, by Peter Abrahams. PHYLON, v. 18, 1957, pp. 97-98.

CLARKE, AUSTIN

"Some Speculations as to the Absence of Racialistic Vindictiveness in West Indian Literature." THE BLACK WRITER IN AFRICA AND THE AMERICAS (edited by Lloyd Brown). Los Angeles: Hennessey and Ingalls, 1973, pp. 165-194.

CLASP, BERTRAND

"With Fresh Light on Nature of Our Society" (McDonald, THE HUMMING-BIRD TREE). TGM, May 25, 1965, p. 3.

"Three Novels by New St. Lucian Writer" (St. Omer). SUNDAY GUARDIAN (Trinidad), November 30, 1969, p. 9.

"Another View of THE LOSS OF EL DORADO" SUNDAY GUARDIAN (Trinidad), December 21, 1969, p. 4.

"Into the Realm of Fantasy" (Lamming, WATER WITH BERRIES). SUNDAY GUARDIAN (Trinidad), March 26, 1972, p. 7.

COCKBURN, CLAUD

[Review of] WAYS OF SUNLIGHT, by Samuel Selvon. NEW STATESMAN, v. 55, March 15, 1958, p. 354.

CODDLING, ERIC

"Facile and Trivial" (Mittelholzer, THE WEATHER IN MIDDENSHOT).
PUBLIC OPINION, January 3, 1953, p. 5.

"Sordid, Squalid--But Telling" (Mais, THE HILLS WERE JOYFUL
TOGETHER). PUBLIC OPINION, May 9, 1953, p. 5.

"West Indian Accent" (Lamming, IN THE CASTLE OF MY SKIN).
PUBLIC OPINION, May 23, 1953, p. 5.

"Truly an Impressive Work" (Reid, THE LEOPARD). PUBLIC
OPINION, April 19, 1958, p. 7.

COKE, LLOYD

"Walcott's Mad Innocents" (TI-JEAN AND HIS BROTHERS, DREAM ON
MONKEY MOUNTAIN). SAVACOU, v. 1, no. 5, June 1971, pp.
121-124.

COLE, BARRY

[Review of] THE ADVENTURES OF CATULLUS KELLY, by Andrew Salkey.
SPECTATOR v. 222, February 14, 1969, p. 213.

[Review of] ASCENT TO OMAI, by Wilson Harris. SPECTATOR, v.
224, February 21, 1970, p. 246

COLEMAN, JOHN

[Review of] MIGUEL STREET, by V. S. Naipaul. SPECTATOR, v. 202,
April 24, 1959, p. 595.

[Review of] A TINKLING IN THE TWILIGHT, by Edgar Mittelholzer,
SPECTATOR, v. 203, July 31, 1959, p. 146.

[Review of] THE AUTUMN EQUINOX, by John Hearne. SPECTATOR, v.
203, November 6, 1959, p. 641.

[Review of] ESCAPE TO AN AUTUMN PAVEMENT, by Andrew Salkey.
SPECTATOR, v. 205, July 8, 1960, p. 73.

[Review of] THE WAITING ROOM, by Wilson Harris. LSO, May 21,
1967, p. 27.

"Mr. Naipaul's Other Island." (A FLAG ON THE ISLAND). LSO,
September 10, 1967, p. 22.

Coleman, John

[Review of] J--BLACK BAM AND THE MASQUERADERS, by Garth St. Omer. LSO, June 25, p. 30.

COLLYMORE, FRANK A.

"An Introduction to the Poetry of Derek Walcott." BIM, v. 3, no. 10, June 1949, pp. 125-132.

[Review of] MORNING AT THE OFFICE, by Edgar Mittelholzer. BIM, v. 3, no. 12, 1949, pp. 354-356.

[Review of] POEMS, by Derek Walcott. BIM, v. 4, no. 15, December 1951, pp. 224-227.

[Review of] OF TREES AND THE SEA, by Edgar Mittelholzer. BIM, v. 6, no. 24, 1956, pp. 272-273.

[Review of] THE MYSTIC MASSEUR, by V. S. Naipaul. BIM v. 7, no. 26, January-June 1958, pp. 119-120.

[Review of] THE MAGDALEN, by J. E. C. McFarlane. BIM, v. 7, no. 26, January-June 1958, pp. 120-121.

[Review of] WAYS OF SUNLIGHT, by Samuel Selvon: BIM, v. 7, no. 27, July-December 1958, p. 185.

[Review of] KAYWANA BLOOD, by Edgar Mittelholzer. BIM, v. 7, no. 27, July-December 1958, p. 186.

[Review of] WITH A CARIB EYE, by Edgar Mittelholzer. BIM, v. 7, no. 27, July-December 1958, p. 186.

"The West Indian Novelists." BAJAN, v. 6, no. 7, March 1959, pp. 20-21.

[Review of] MIGUEL STREET, by V. S. Naipaul. BIM, v. 8, no. 29, June-December 1959, p. 67.

"Writing in the West Indies; A Survey." TAMARACK REVIEW, no. 14, 1960, pp. 111-124.

[Review of] ELTONSBRODY, by Edgar Mittelholzer. BIM, v. 8, no. 32, January-June 1961, p. 291.

[Review of] THE LAST BARBARIAN, by Jan Carew. BIM, v. 9, no. 34, January-June 1962, pp. 149-150.

Coulthard, G. R.

"Edgar Mittelholzer, A Biographical Sketch." BIM, v. 10, no. 41, June-December 1965, pp. 23-26.

[Review of] SELECTED POEMS, by A. J. Seymour. BIM, v. 11, no. 42, January-June 1966, pp. 143-144.

COLSON, THEODORE

"Derek Walcott's Plays; Outrage and Compassion." WLWE, v. 12, April 1973, pp. 80-96.

COMFORT, ALEX

[Review of] THE FACES OF LOVE, by John Hearne. NEW STATESMAN, v. 53, no. 1363, April 7, 1957, p. 548.

COOKE, MICHAEL G.

"West Indian Picaresque" (De Lisser, JANE'S CAREER). NOVEL. v. 7, no. 1, Fall 1973, pp. 93-96.

COOMBS, ORDE

[Review of] RELUCTANT NEIGHBORS, by E. R. Braithwaite, NYT, September 19, 1972, Section 7, p. 4.

COOPER, WAYNE

THE PASSION OF CLAUDE McKAY: SELECTED POETRY AND PROSE, 1912-1948 (edited by Wayne Cooper). New York: Schocken, 1963.

"Claude McKay and the New Negro of the 1920's. PHYLON, v. 25, Fall 1964, pp. 296-306.

"A Black Briton Comes 'Home:' Claude McKay in England, 1920" (with Robert C. Reinders). RACE, v. 9, no. 1, July 1967, pp. 67-81.
Also appears in NEW BEACON REVIEWS, COLLECTION ONE (edited by John LaRose). London: New Beacon Books, 1968, pp. 3-21.

CORKE, HILARY

[Review of] THE MIMIC MEN, by V. S. Naipaul. LISTENER, v. 77, May 25, 1967, p. 693.

[Review of] WIDE SARGASSO SEA, by Jean Rhys. LISTENER, v. 77, January 19, 1967, p. 103.

COULTHARD, G. R.

Cox, C. B.

"The West Indian Novel of Immigration." PHYLON, v. 20, 1959, pp. 32-41.

"Rejection of European Culture as a Theme in Caribbean Literature." CARIBBEAN QUARTERLY, v. 5, no. 4, June 1959, pp. 231-234.

"The Coloured Woman in Caribbean Poetry (1800-1960)." RACE, v. 2, no. 2, May 1961, pp. 53-61.

[Review of] THE CHILDREN OF SISYPHUS, by Orlando Patterson. CARIBBEAN QUARTERLY, v. 10, no. 1, March 1964, pp. 69-71.

"Literature of Latin America and the Caribbean." CARIBBEAN QUARTERLY, v. 10, no. 4, December 1964, pp. 46-54.

COX, C. B.

[Review of] RIGHTS OF PASSAGE, by Edward Brathwaite. SPECTATOR, v. 218, March 24, 1967, p. 343.
Also appears in CRITICAL SURVEY, v. 3, Summer 1967, p. 107.

CRAIG, SUSAN

"A Ruthless/Rootless Enterprise, Notes and Impressions on Reading George Lamming's NATIVES OF MY PERSON." KAIRI, 1976, pp. 8-9.

CRAIG, TOM

"John Ebenezer Clare McFarlane." PUBLIC OPINION, June 21, 1940, p. 9.

CROFT, MICHAEL

"Classroom War" (Braithwaite, TO SIR WITH LOVE). LSO, March 29, 1959, p. 15.

CROSSKILL, D.

[Review of] A FLAG ON THE ISLAND, by V. S. Naipaul. PUBLIC OPINION, July 11, 1969, p. 3.

CUMPER, GEORGE

"Literary Period Piece" (McFarlane, J. E. C., A LITERATURE IN THE MAKING). PUBLIC OPINION, January 26, 1957, p. 7.

Dathorne, Oscar Ronald

"New World Liberalism" (Roberts, A SINGLE STAR). PUBLIC
OPINION, July 20, 1957, p. 7.

CUNNINGHAM, VALENTINE

[Review of] J--BLACK BAM AND THE MASQUERADERS, by Garth St.
Omer. LISTENER, v. 88, July 20, 1972, p. 89.

DALT, GARY MICHAEL

[Review of] THE MEETING POINT, by Austin Clarke. TAMARACK
REVIEW, no. 45, Autumn 1967, pp. 117, 120.

DALY, P. H.

"Walter MacArthur Lawrence." KYK-OVER-AL, v. 1, no. 2, June
1946, pp. 18-25.

DANIELS, ALAN

"Who Is Claude McKay?" PUBLIC OPINION, January 12, 1963, p. 9.

DATHORNE, OSCAR RONALD

[Review of] GUIANA BOY, by Lauchmonen. BLACK ORPHEUS, no. 10,
1961, pp. 70-71.

[Review of] MR. STONE AND THE KNIGHTS COMPANION, by V. S.
Naipaul. BLACK ORPHEUS, no. 14, February 1964, pp. 59-60.

[Review of] THE WHOLE ARMOUR: THE SECRET LADDER, by Wilson
BLACK ORPHEUS, no. 14, February 1964, pp. 61-62.

"Africa in West Indian Literature." BLACK ORPHEUS, no. 16,
October 1964, pp. 42-54.
Also appears under title "The Theme of Africa in West
Indian Literature." PHYLON, v. 26, Fall 1965, pp. 255-276,
and as "Africa in the Literature of the West Indies," JCL,
no. 1, September 1965, pp. 95-116.

[Review of] HEARTLAND, by Wilson Harris. BLACK ORPHEUS, no. 17,
June 1965, pp. 59-60.

[Review of] AN AREA OF DARKNESS, by V. S. Naipaul. BLACK
ORPHEUS, no. 18, October 1965, pp. 60-61.

"Roger Mais: The Man on the Cross." SIN, v. 1, no. 1, Summer,
1972, pp. 275-283.

Davenport, John

DAVENPORT, JOHN

[Review of] THE FACES OF LOVE, by John Hearne. LSO, April 28, 1957, p. 13.

[Review of] THE SUFFRAGE OF ELVIRA, by V. S. Naipaul. LSO, April 20, 1958, p. 17.

[Review of] MIGUEL STREET, by V. S. Naipaul. LSO, April 19, 1959, p. 22.

[Review of] A TINKLING IN THE TWILIGHT, by Edgar Mittelholzer. LSO, July 26, 1959, p. 16.

[Review of] WEST INDIAN STORIES. LSO, December 11, 1960, p. 29.

DAVIDSON, BASIL

[Review of] A KIND OF HOMECOMING, by E. R. Braithwaite. NEW STATESMAN, v. 65, no. 1684, June 21, 1963, p. 940.

DAVIES, BARRIE

"The Seekers. The Novels of John Hearne." THE ISLANDS IN BETWEEN (edited by Louis James). London: Oxford University Press, 1968, pp. 109-120.

"The Personal Sense of a Society--Minority View: Aspects of the 'East Indian' Novel in the West Indies." SIN, v. 4, no. 2, Summer 1972, pp. 284-295.

[Review of] CHRISTOPHER, by Geoffrey Drayton. WLWE, v. 12, no. 1, April 1973, pp. 119-121.

DAVIES, RUSSELL

Review of THE CHIP-CHIP GATHERERS, by Shiva Naipaul. LSO, April 15, 1973, p. 39.

DAWES, NEVILLE

"Thoughts on W.I. Poetry." PUBLIC OPINION (Jamaica), January 3, 1953, p. 5.

"Memorial to Roger Mais: A Green Blade in Triumph--BLACK LIGHTENING." KYK-OVER-AL, v. 6, no. 20, Mid-year 1955, pp. 147-170.

Doherty, Joseph J.

D'COSTA, JEAN CREARY

"A Prophet Armed. The Novels of Roger Mais." THE ISLANDS IN
BETWEEN (edited by Louis James). London: Oxford University
Press, 1968, pp. 50-63.

"Poetry Review; The Poetry of Edward Brathwaite." JAMAICA
JOURNAL, v. 2, no. 3, September 1968, pp. 24-28.

[Review of] CANNON SHOT AND GLASS BEADS (edited by George
Lamming). JAMAICA JOURNAL, v. 9, no. 1, March 1975, pp. 38-
39.

[Review of] A MAN COME HOME, by Roy Heath. JAMAICA JOURNAL, v.
9, nos. 2 and 3, 1975, pp. 53-58.

DELANY, AUSTIN

"Mother India as Bitch" (Naipaul, V. S., AN AREA OF DARKNESS).
TRANSITION, v. 6, no. 26, 1966, pp. 50-51.

DERRICK, ANTHONY C.

"Naipaul's Technique as a Novelist." JCL, no. 7, July 1969,
pp. 32-44.

"An Introduction to Caribbean Literature." CARIBBEAN QUARTERLY,
v. 15, nos. 2 and 3, June-September 1969, pp. 65-78.

DEWAR, LILLIAN

"Jamaica in the Novel." KYK-OVER-AL, v. 3, no. 12, Mid-year
1951, pp. 108-113.

DICKEY, JAMES

[Review of] SELECTED POEMS, by Derek Walcott. NYT, September
13, 1964, Section 7, p. 44.

DIAZ, ARTURO MALDONALDO

"Place and Nature in George Lamming's Poetry." RRI, v. 4, no.
3, Fall 1974, pp. 402-410.

DOHERTY, JOSEPH J.

"The Life of Contemplation in M. G. Smith's TESTAMENT." BIM,

Dolphin, Celeste

    v. 7, no. 25, July-December 1957, pp. 36-42.

DOLPHIN, CELESTE

    "The Poetry of A. J. Seymour." NWF, v. 1, no. 13, April 30, 1965, pp. 31-39.

DONDY, FARRUKH

    "Little Ventured, Little Gained" (Braithwaite, HONORARY WHITE). TAPIA, v. 5, no. 41, October 1975, p. 8.

DONOGHUE, DENIS

    [Review of] THE GULF, by Derek Walcott. NYRB, v. 16, no. 8, 1971.

DOPSON, ANDREW

    "I'll Stop Writing for Less" (Naipaul, V. S., IN A FREE STATE). SUNDAY GUARDIAN (Trinidad), December 12, 1971, p. 18.

DOUGLAS, KARL

    "Angry! Not Me, Says Selvon" (interview). SUNDAY GUARDIAN (Trinidad), December 30, 1962, p. 12.

DOUGLAS-SMITH, AUBREY

    [Review of] HENRI-CHRISTOPHE, by Derek Walcott. BIM, v. 3, no. 12, 1949, pp. 349-353.

DRAYTON, ARTHUR

    [Review of] THE GAMES WERE COMING, by Michael Anthony. BLACK ORPHEUS, no. 15, August 1964, p. 61.

    "McKay's Human Pity: A Note on His Protest Poetry." BLACK ORPHEUS, no. 17, June 1965, pp. 39-48.

    "Poetry of Cultural Precariousness. Introducing Cliff Lashley: A New Caribbean Voice." BLACK ORPHEUS, no. 22, August 1967, pp. 49-53.

    "Awkward Questions for Jamaicans" (Patterson, AN ABSENCE OF RUINS; Salkey, THE LATE EMANCIPATION OF JERRY STOVER). JCL, no. 7, July 1969, pp. 125-127.

El Mukrane, Hadj

"The European Factor in West Indian Literature." LITERARY HALF-
    YEARLY, v. 11, no. 1, 1970, pp. 71-94.

"West Indian Consciousness in West Indian Verse." JCL, no. 9,
    July 1970, pp. 66-88.

DRAYTON, GEOFFREY

"The Recitation of Poetry." BIM, v. 4, no. 15, December 1951,
    pp. 179-180.

DRAYTON, KATHLEEN

[Review of] THE ISLANDS IN BETWEEN (edited by Louis James).
    CARIBBEAN STUDIES, v. 9, no. 2, July 1969, pp. 84-91.

"Now a Novel on the Politics of Banning" (Salkey, JOEY TYSON).
    CARIBBEAN CONTACT, v. 2, no. 12, March 1975, p. 3.

EARLY, L. R.

"The Two Novels of Harold Ladoo." WLWE, v. 15, April 1976, pp.
    174-184.

EDWARDS, PAUL

"Caribbean Anthologies." JCL, no. 3, July 1967, pp. 120-122.

"The Art of Memory: Michael Anthony's THE YEAR IN SAN FERNANDO"
    (with Kenneth Ramchand). JCL, no. 7, July 1969, pp. 59-72.

EDWARDS, THOMAS R.

[Review of] NATIVES OF MY PERSON, by George Lamming. NYRB, v.
    18, no. 4, 1972.

[Review of] ANOTHER LIFE, by Derek Walcott. NYRB, v. 21, no.
    10, 1975, pp. 38-39

EFRON, EDITH

"Dreamer At the Edge of a Swamp" (Selvon, A BRIGHTER SUN), NYT,
    September 2, 1952, Section 7, p. 5.

EL MUKRANE, HADJ

[Review of] UNE COURONNE POUR UDOMO, by Peter Abrahams (in

Elliot, J. H.

French). PRESENCE AFRICAINE, no. 17-18, 1958, pp. 238-239.

ELLIOT, J. H.

"Triste Trinidad" (Naipaul, V. S., THE LOSS OF EL DORADO).
NYRB, v. 14, no. 10, 1970.

ESCOFFERY, GLORIA

[Review of] NEW DAY, by V. S. Reid. PUBLIC OPINION, April 9,
1949, p. 6.

[Review of] THE ARRIVISTES, by Louis Simpson. PUBLIC OPINION,
September 24, 1949, p. 6.

[Review of] A MORNING AT THE OFFICE, by Edgar Mittelholzer.
PUBLIC OPINION, May 20, 1950, p. 6.

[Review of] IN THE CASTLE OF MY SKIN, by George Lamming. BIM,
v. 5, no. 18, June 1953, pp. 153-155.

"Gloria Escoffery Comments on ... Roger Mais Novel" (THE HILLS
WERE JOYFUL TOGETHER). PUBLIC OPINION, July 4, 1953, p. 5.

[Reviews of] THE HILLS WERE JOYFUL TOGETHER, by Roger Mais;
THE LIFE AND DEATH OF SYLVIA, by Edgar Mittelholzer. BIM,
v. 5, no. 19, December 1953, pp. 235-239.

[Review of] THE HARROWING OF HUBERTUS, by Edgar Mittelholzer.
PUBLIC OPINION, April 3, 1954, p. 5.
Also appears in BIM, v. 5, no. 20, June 1954, pp. 323-324.

ESPINET, EMILE

[Review of] NO PAIN LIKE THIS BODY, by Harold Ladoo. BLACK
IMAGES, v. 2, no. 1, Spring 1973, pp. 60-62.

EWART, GAVIN

[Review of] UNCLE PAUL, by Edgar Mittelholzer. LONDON
MAGAZINE, New Series, v. 4, no. 4, July 1964, pp. 94-95.

Review (Lucie-Smith). LONDON MAGAZINE, New Series, v. 8, no.
11, February 1969, p. 85.

FABRE, MICHEL

Figueroa, John J.

"Adam's Task of Giving Things Their Name; The Poetry of Derek
   Walcott" (ANOTHER LIFE). NEW LETTERS, v. 41, no. 1, Fall
   1974, pp. 91-107.

FEINSTEIN, ELAINE

   [Review of] THOSE WHO EAT THE CASCADURA, by Samuel Selvon.
   LONDON MAGAZINE, New Series, v. 12, no. 1, April/May 1972,
   p. 144.

FELD, MICHAEL

   [Review of] CRICK-CRACK MONKEY, by Merle Hodge. LONDON MAGAZINE
   MAGAZINE, New Series, v. 10, no. 2, May 1970, p. 104.

FERGUSON, J. HALCO

   [Review of] JAMAICA, by Peter Abrahams. LSO, March 9, 1958,
   p. 17.

   "Land of Sugar" (Lauchmonen, GUIANA BOY). LSO, January 8, 1961,
   p. 23.

FIDO, ELAINE

   "Sex and Class in the Poetry of Bruce St. John." TAPIA, v. 5,
   no. 34, August 1975, pp. 6-8.

FIDO, MARTIN

   "Mr. Biswas and Mr. Polly," ARIEL, v. 5, no. 4, October 1974,
   pp. 30-37.

FIGUEROA, JOHN J.

   [Review of] LA LITERATURA DE LAS ANTILLAS ANGLESAS (edited by
   G. R. Coulthard, in English). BIM, v. 6, no. 23, 1955,
   pp. 203-204.

   [Review of] IN A GREEN NIGHT, by Derek Walcott. CARIBBEAN
   QUARTERLY, v. 8, no. 4, December 1962, pp. 67-69.

   "John Hearne, West Indian Writer." RRI, v. 2, Spring 1972,
   pp. 72-79

   "JANE'S CAREER." WLWE, v. 12, April 1973, pp. 97-105.

Figueroa, Peter

[Review of] ANOTHER LIFE, by Derek Walcott. BIM, v. 15, no. 58, June 1975, pp. 160-170.

"Some Subtleties of the Isle: A Commentary on Certain Aspects of Derek Walcott's Sonnet Sequence TALES OF THE ISLANDS." WLWE, v. 15, April 1976, pp. 190-224.

FIGUEROA, PETER

[Review of] FOUNDATIONS, by John LaRose. BIM, v. 12, no. 48, January--June 1969, pp. 270-271.

FOAKES, R. A.

"Caribbean Poetry." JCL, no. 6, January 1969, pp. 147-150.

FORDE, A. N.

[Review of] TURN AGAIN TIGER, by Samuel Selvon. BIM, v. 8, no. 29, June-December 1959, pp. 60-61.

[Review of] CHRISTOPHER, by Geoffrey Drayton. BIM, v. 8, no. 29, June-December 1959, p. 67.

[Review of] IN A GREEN NIGHT, by Derek Walcott. BIM, v. 9, no. 36, January-June 1963, pp. 288-290.

[Review of] LOVE LEAPS HERE, by John Figueroa. BIM, v. 10, no. 37, July-December 1963, pp. 63-65.

[Review of] SEVEN JAMAICAN POETS (edited by Mervyn Morris). BIM, v. 14, no. 54, January--June 1972, pp. 116-117.

Review of THESE GREEN ISLANDS; MUET, by A. L. Hendriks. BIM, v. 14, no. 55, July-December 1972, pp. 186-188.

"Eric Roach--Poet with Soul." BAJAN, no. 247, June 1974, p. 16.

FOSTER-DAVIS, MARGARET

[Review of] A MORNING AT THE OFFICE, by Edgar Mittelholzer. CARIBBEAN QUARTERLY, v. 1, no. 4, 1950, pp. 43-44.

FRASER, ALFRED

"The Experience of the 70's." NEW VOICES, no. 2, 1973, pp. 33-35.

FRASER, FITZROY

"Roger Mais; A New Judgment." PUBLIC OPINION, June 15, 1957,
p. 7.

"A Talk with Vidia Naipaul." SUNDAY GLEANER, January 25, 1960,
pp. 14, 19.

"Jamaica Government Moves to Aid Artists" (with Derek Walcott).
SUNDAY GUARDIAN (Trinidad), September 18, 1960, p. 7.

"A Talk with Eric Roach." SUNDAY GLEANER, January 1961, pp. 14,
19.

FULLER, JOHN

"Caribbean Poetry." SUNDAY GLEANER, June 13, 1948, p. 9.

[Review of] A HOUSE FOR MR. BISWAS, by V. S. Naipaul. LISTENER,
v. 66, October 19, 1961, p. 621.

[Review of] THE GULF AND OTHER POEMS, by Derek Walcott. LONDON
MAGAZINE, v. 9, no. 8, November 1969, pp. 89-90.

FULTON, NANCY J. CASEY; SEE ALSO CASEY, NANCY J.

"Jean Rhys' WIDE SARGASSO SEA: Exterminating the White Cockroach." RRI, v. 4, no. 3, Fall 1974, pp. 340-349.

FYFIELD, C. W.

"A New Venture in Play Making" (Mais, ATALANTA AT CALYDON).
PUBLIC OPINION, September 23, 1950, p. 6.

GANT, LIZ

[Review of] BREAKLIGHT: THE POETRY OF THE CARIBBEAN (edited by
Andrew Salkey). BLACK WORLD, v. 22, no. 3, January 1973,
pp. 81-85.

[Review of] DIE THE LONG DAY, by Orlando Patterson. BLACK
WORLD, v. 22, no. 4, February 1973, pp. 78-79.

GAREBIAN, KEITH

"V. S. Naipaul's Negative Sense of Place." JCL, v. 10, no. 1,
August 1975, pp. 23-35.

Garfitt, Roger

GARFITT, ROGER

    [Review of] ANOTHER LIFE, by Derek Walcott. LONDON MAGAZINE,
    New Series, v. 13, no. 5, December 1973/January 1974, pp.
    124-127.

GARIOCH, ROBERT

    [Review of] THE SLEEPERS OF RORAIMA, by Wilson Harris.
    LISTENER, v. 84, September 17, 1970, p. 383.

GATHORNE-HARDY, J.

    "Snow, Flak and Sunshine" (Naipaul, Shiva, FIREFLIES). LONDON
    MAGAZINE, New Series, v. 10, no. 11, February 1971, pp. 98-
    100.

GEORGE, DANIEL

    [Review of] A TALE OF THREE PLACES, by Edgar Mittelholzer.
    SPECTATOR, v. 198, March 22, 1957, p. 383.

GILBERT, MORRIS

    "Three Faces of Love on the Island of Cayuna" (Hearne, AUTUMN
    EQUINOX). NYT, November 19, 1961, Section 7, p. 58.

    "Hapless Defiance" (Naipaul, V. S., A HOUSE FOR MR. BISWAS).
    NYT, June 24, 1962, Section 7, p. 24.

    "The Rise and Fall of Prophet Moses" (Wynter, THE HILLS OF
    HEBRON). NYT, July 15, 1962, Section 7, p. 24.

GILKES, MICHAEL

    "The Art of Extremity: A Reading of Wilson Harris' ASCENT TO
    OMAI." CARIBBEAN QUARTERLY, v. 17, nos. 3 and 4, September-
    December 1971, pp. 83-90.
    Also appears in LITERARY HALF-YEARLY, v. 15, no. 1, January
    1974, pp. 120-133.

    "Two Critics on BLACK MARSDEN: A Double Vision--A Tabula Rasa
    Comedy...." CARIBBEAN QUARTERLY, v. 19, no. 4, December
    1973, pp. 57-58.

    "Magical Reality" (Harris, BLACK MARSDEN). JCL, v. 9, no. 3,
    August 1974, pp. 77-79.

Goodman, Anne L.

WILSON HARRIS AND THE CARIBBEAN NOVEL. London: Longman
    Caribbean, 1975.

RACIAL IDENTITY AND INDIVIDUAL CONSCIOUSNESS IN THE CARIBBEAN
    NOVEL. Georgetown, Guyana: Ministry of Information and
    Culture, National History and Arts Council, 1975.

"The Spirit in the Bottle--A Reading of Mittelholzer's A
    MORNING AT THE OFFICE." WLWE, v. 14, April 1975, pp. 237-
    252.

"World of Caribbean Artists: The Shame of It All" (interview
    by John Agard). CARIBBEAN CONTACT, v. 3, no. 2, May 1975,
    p. 9.

"The Poetry of Bruce St. John." TAPIA, v. 5, no. 24, June 1975,
    p. 9.

"An Infinite Canvas: Wilson Harris' COMPANIONS OF THE DAY AND
    NIGHT." WLWE, v. 15, April 1976, pp. 161-173.

GOCKING, C. V.

"The Early Case for a West Indian Literature." TAPIA, v. 6,
    no. 52, December 26, 1976, pp. 6-7 (reprint of 1932 article
    in THE ROYALIAN).

GOLDSWORTHY, F. M.

[Review of] THE HILLS WERE JOYFUL TOGETHER, by Roger Mais.
    SUNDAY GLEANER, October 4, 1953, p. 5.

GOMES, ALBERT

"Back to Banana Bottom." BEACON, v. 3, no. 3, October 1933,
    pp. 58-59.

GONZALEZ, ANSON

"Our Theatre Is Looking Homeward." TGM, August 27, 1972, pp.
    28-29.

TRINIDAD AND TOBAGO LITERATURE ON AIR. Trinidad: National
    Cultural Council, 1973.

"Possibility in W.I. Creative Writing." NEW VOICES, no. 4,
    June 1974, pp. 3-10; 43-50.

GOODMAN, ANNE L.

Gool, Reshard

  [Review of] NEW DAY, by V. S. Reid. NYT, March 27, 1949, Sec-
    tion 7, p. 31.

GOOL, RESHARD

  "To Harris with Love" (THE EYE OF THE SCARECROW). NWQ, v. 3,
    no. 4, Cropover 1967, pp. 73-74.

GORDIMER, NADINE

  "White Expatriates and Black Mimics" (Naipaul, V. S., IN A FREE
    STATE). NYT, October 17, 1971, Section 7, p. 5.

GOSINE, VISHNU

  [Review of] JOEY TYSON, by Andrew Salkey. CORLIT, v. 2, nos.
    1-2, April-July 1975, p. 46.

  [Review of] THE BIGGER LIGHT, by Austin Clarke. CORLIT, v. 2,
    nos. 1-2, April-July 1975, p. 47.

GOWDA, H. H. ANNIAH

  "Wilson Harris' TUMATUMARI." LITERARY HALF-YEARLY, v. 11, no.
    1, 1970, pp. 31-38.

  "Naipaul in India" (AN AREA OF DARKNESS). LITERARY HALF-YEARLY,
    v. 11, no. 2, 1970, pp. 163-170.

  "Civilization through Fables" (Harris, THE SLEEPERS OF RORAIMA,
    THE AGE OF THE RAINMAKERS). LITERARY HALF-YEARLY, v. 14,
    no. 1, pp. 169-174.

  "India in Naipaul's Artistic Consciousness." LITERARY HALF-
    YEARLY, v. 16, no. 1, January 1975, pp. 27-39.

GOYEN, WILLIAM

  "Splendor Was the Spoiler" (Carew, A TOUCH OF MIDAS). NYT,
    September 17, 1958, Section 7, p. 39.

GRADUSSOV, ALEX

  [Review of] MOSCOW IS NOT MY MECCA, by Jan Carew. BIM, v. 11,
    no. 43, July-December 1966, pp. 224-255.

  [Review of] THE ISLANDS IN BETWEEN (edited by Louis James).

Gray, Simon

PUBLIC OPINION, June 28, 1968, p. 6.

GRAHAM, BERNARD

[Review of] A ROOM ON THE HILL, by Garth St. Omer. BIM, v. 12, no. 47, July-December 1968, pp. 208-209.

GRAHAM, KENNETH

[Review of] THE ADVENTURES OF CATULLUS KELLY, by Andrew Salkey. LISTENER, v. 81, February 20, 1969, p. 247.

GRANDISON, WINIFRED B.

"The Prose Style of Roger Mais." JAMAICA JOURNAL, v. 8, no. 1, March 1974, pp. 48-54.

GRANT, ANNETTE

"Hindus Coming Apart in Trinidad" (Naipaul, Shiva, FIREFLIES). NYT, February 7, 1971, Section 7, p. 6.

GRANT, DAMIAN

"Emerging Images: The Poetry of Edward Brathwaite." CRITICAL QUARTERLY, v. 12, Summer 1970, pp. 186-193.

GRAY, CECIL

"'Folk' Themes in West Indian Drama: An Analysis." CARIBBEAN QUARTERLY, v. 14, nos. 1 and 2, March-June 1968, pp. 102-109.

"Mr. Salkey's Truth and Illusion." JAMAICA JOURNAL, v. 2, no. 2, June 1968, pp. 46-54.

"A Way of Teaching--A Review of a Literary Series." CARIBBEAN QUARTERLY, v. 17, nos. 3 and 4, September-December 1971, pp. 139-143.

[Review of] CARIBBEAN VOICES (edited by John Figueroa). BIM, v. 14, no. 55, July-December 1972, pp. 182-185.

GRAY, SIMON

[Review of] THE MIMIC MEN, by V. S. Naipaul. NEW STATESMAN, v. 73, May 5, 1967, pp. 622-623.

Greene, Graham

GREENE, GRAHAM

"Terror in Trinidad" (Naipaul, V. S., THE LOSS OF ELDORADO).
LSO, October 26, 1969, p. 34.

GRIFFITHS, GARETH

"The Language of Disillusion in the African Novel."
COMMON WEALTH: PAPERS DELIVERED AT THE CONFERENCE OF
COMMONWEALTH LITERATURE, AARHUS UNIVERSITY, APRIL 26-30,
1971. Aarhus, Denmark: Aarhus University, 1971, pp. 62-65.

GRIGSON, GEOFFREY

[Review of] SEASON OF ADVENTURE, by George Lamming. SPECTATOR,
v. 205, October 28, 1960, p. 664.

[Review of] THE LAST BARBARIAN, by Jan Carew. SPECTATOR, v.
206, March 31, 1971.

GUCKIAN, PATRICK

"The Balance of Color, A Re-Assessment of the Work of Edgar
Mittelholzer." JAMAICA JOURNAL, v. 4, no. 1, March 1970,
pp. 38-45.

GUERIN, VERNE

"Voice That Speaks for a Private 'I'" (Pantin, JOURNEYS),
TAPIA, v. 6, no. 32, August 8, 1976, p. 6.

GUNTER, HELMUT

"George Lamming." BLACK ORPHEUS, no. 6, November 1959, pp. 39-
43.

GURR, A. J.

"Third World Novels: Naipaul and After." JCL, v. 7, no. 1,
June 1972, pp. 6-13.

HACKETT, WINSTON

"Identity in the Poetry of Derek Walcott." MOKO, no. 8,
February 14, 1969, p. 2.

"Survival" (Questel, Gonzalez, SCORE). TAPIA, v. 5, no. 34,

August 1975, pp. 4-5, no. 36, August 1975, pp. 6-11.

HAIRSTON, LOYLE

[Review of] NATIVES OF MY PERSON, by George Lamming. FREEDOM-
WAYS, v. 12, First Quarter 1972, pp. 68-70.

HALE, LIONEL

[Review of] NEW DAY, by V. S. Reid. LSO, February 19, 1950, p.
7.

[Review of] WILD CONQUEST, by Peter Abrahams. LSO, June 24,
1951, p. 7.

[Review of] A BRIGHTER SUN, by Samuel Selvon. LSO, February 3,
1952, p. 7.

HALL, STUART

"Lamming, Selvon and Some Trends in the West Indian Novel."
BIM, v. 6, no. 23, December 1955, pp. 172-178.

HAMILTON, BRUCE

"New World of the Caribbean." BIM, v. 7, no. 25, July-
December 1957, pp. 53-55.

[Review of] THE LONELY LONDONERS, by Samuel Selvon. BIM, v.
7, no. 25, July-December 1957, pp. 61-62.

HAMILTON, IAN

"Poetry" (Lucie-Smith). LONDON MAGAZINE, New Series, v. 4,
no. 9, December 1964, pp. 80-81

[Review of] TOWARDS SILENCE, by Edward Lucie-Smith. LSO,
November 17, 1968, p. 28.

Interview (Naipaul, V. S.). SAVACOU, no. 9/10, 1974, pp. 120-126.

HAMNER, ROBERT D.

"V. S. Naipaul: A Selected Bibliography." JCL, v. 10, no. 1,
August 1975.

[Review of] A MAN COME HOME, by Roy Heath. WLWE, v. 15, April
1976, pp. 253-255.

Hansford Jones, Pamela

"New World Burden. Derek Walcott, SEA GRAPES." WLWE, v. 16,
April 1977, pp. 212-214.

HANSFORD JOHNSON, PAMELA

[Review of] KAYWANA BLOOD, by Edgar Mittelholzer. NEW STATES-
MAN, v. 55, February 8, 1958, p. 176.

HARRIS, MICHAEL

"Naipaul on Campus: Sending Out a Plea for Rationality."
TAPIA, v. 5, no. 26, 1975, p. 2.

HARRIS, WILSON

[Review of] THE GUIANA BOOK, by A. J. Seymour. KYK-OVER-AL,
v. 2, no. 7, December 1948, pp. 37-40.

"The Reality of Trespass." KYK-OVER-AL, v. 2, no. 9, December
1949, pp. 21-22.

"The Question of Form and Realism in the West Indian Artist."
KYK-OVER-AL, v. 5, no. 15, Year-end 1952, pp. 23-27.

[Review of] POEMS, by Leo Austin. KYK-OVER-AL, v. 6, no. 20,
Mid-year 1955, pp. 205-206.

"The Unresolved Constitution." CARIBBEAN QUARTERLY, v. 14, nos.
1 and 2, March-June 1968, pp. 43-47.

"Interior of the Novel: Amerindian/European/African Relations."
NATIONAL IDENTITY; PAPERS DELIVERED AT THE COMMONWEALTH
LITERATURE CONFERENCE, UNIVERSITY OF QUEENSLAND, BRISBANE,
9th-15th August 1968. London: Heineman, 1970, pp. 138-
147.

"History, Fable and Myth in the Caribbean and Guianas."
CARIBBEAN QUARTERLY, v. 16, no. 2, June 1970, pp. 1-32.

"The Phenomenal Legacy." LITERARY HALF-YEARLY, v. 11, no. 2,
1970, pp. 1-6.

"The Native Phenomenon." COMMON WEALTH, PAPERS DELIVERED AT THE
CONFERENCE OF COMMONWEALTH LITERATURE, AARHUS UNIVERSITY,
April 26-30, 1971 (edited by Anna Rutherford). Aarhus,
Denmark: Aarhus University, 1971, pp. 144-150.

Hearne, John

"The Enigma of Values." NEW LETTERS, v. 40, no. 1, Fall 1973, pp. 141-149.

"A Talk on the Subjective Imagination." NEW LETTERS, v. 40, no. 1, Fall 1973, pp. 37-48.

HARRISON, JOHN

[Review of] THREE MERIDIANS, by Geoffrey Drayton. BIM, v. 4, no. 14, June 1951, pp. 144-145.

[Review of] THE ARRIVISTES, by Louis Simpson. BIM, v. 4, no. 14, June 1951, pp. 145-147.

[Review of] SHADOWS MOVE AMONG THEM, by Edgar Mittelholzer. BIM BIM, v. 4, no. 14, June 1951, pp. 147-148.

"From the West Indies, A Radio Talk...." BIM, v. 10, no. 37, July-December 1963, pp. 60-63.

HARRISON, TONY

[Review of] THE OVERCROWDED BARRACOON, by V. S. Naipaul. LONDON MAGAZINE, New Series, v. 12, no. 5, December 1972/January 1973, pp. 135-140.

HARVEY, ELIZABETH

[Review of] CRICK-CRACK MONKEY, by Merle Hodge. WLWE, no. 19, April 1971, p. 87.

HAWORTH, DAVID

[Review of] THE ADVENTURES OF CATULLUS KELLY, by Andrew Salkey. NEW STATESMAN, v. 77, February 14, 1969, p. 230.

HAZZARD, SHIRLEY

[Review of] QUARTET, by Jean Rhys. NYT, April 11, 1971, p. 6.

HEARNE, JOHN

[Review of] ATALANTA AT CALYDON, by Roger Mais. PUBLIC OPINION, September 30, 1950, p. 6.

"Ideas on a West Indian Culture." PUBLIC OPINION, October 14, 1950, p. 6.

Hemmings, John

"Barren Treasury" (MacFarlane, ed., TREASURY OF JAMAICAN POETRY
POETRY). PUBLIC OPINION, November 11, 1950, pp. 6, 8.

"New Landscapes—Paintings by Roger Mais." PUBLIC OPINION, June
23, 1951, p. 5.

"Roger Mais: A Personal Memoir." BIM, v. 6, no. 23, December
1955, pp. 146-150.

[Review of] THE MIDDLE PASSAGE, by V. S. Naipaul. CARIBBEAN
QUARTERLY, v. 8, no. 4, December 1962, pp. 65-66. Also
appears as "John Hearne's Unsentimental Journey with V. S.
Naipaul." SUNDAY GUARDIAN (Trinidad), February 3, 1963,
pp. 3, 4, and in SUNDAY GLEANER, February 3, 1963, p. 14.

"El Dorado of the Soul" (Harris, GUIANA QUARTET). PUBLIC
OPINION, April 6, 1963, p. 12.

"Roger Mais, A Personal Memoir." PUBLIC OPINION, Roger Mais
Supplement, June 10, 1966, p. 2.

"The Naked Footprint: An Enquiry into Crusoe's Island." - REL,
v. 8, no. 4, October 1967, pp. 97-107.

"The Fugitive in the Forest: A Study of Four Novels by Wilson
Harris." JCL, no. 4, December 1967, pp. 99-112.
Also appears in THE ISLANDS IN BETWEEN (edited by Louis
James). London: Oxford University Press, 1968, pp. 140-153.

"Home from the Wars ... An Epitaph." JAMAICA JOURNAL, v. 1,
no. 1, December 1967, pp. 82-84.

"The Novel as Sociology as Bore" (Patterson, DIE THE LONG DAY).
CARIBBEAN QUARTERLY, v. 18, no. 4, 1972, pp. 78-81.

HEMMINGS, JOHN

[Review of] A NIGHT OF THEIR OWN, by Peter Abrahams. NEW
STATESMAN, v. 69, March 26, 1965.

[Review of] NOR ANY COUNTRY, by Garth St. Omer. LISTENER, v.
81, May 8, 1969.

HENCH, MICHAEL M.

"The Fearful Symmetry of THE WHOLE ARMOUR" (Harris). RRI, v. 4,
no. 3, Fall 1974, pp. 446-451.

HENDRIKS, A. L.

[Review of] EPITAPH FOR THE YOUNG, by Derek Walcott. PUBLIC OPINION, December 31, 1949, p. 6.

HEPPENSTALL, RAYNER

[Review of] TIGERS ARE BETTER-LOOKING, by Jean Rhys. SPECTATOR, v. 220, April 5, 1968, pp. 446-447.

HERNANDEZ, RICHARDO

"Sam Selvon Scores in Short Sharp Bursts" (WAYS OF SUNLIGHT). SUNDAY GUARDIAN (Trinidad), March 9, 1958, p. 18.

HERRING, ROBERT

[Review of] A MORNING AT THE OFFICE, by Edgar Mittelholzer. LL, v. 65, no. 154, 1950, pp. 263-264.

HILL, ERROL

"The West Indian Artist." WIR, v. 4, no. 15, August 9, 1952, pp. 13-14.

"West Indian Culture in England." WIR, v. 2, no. 9, September 1957, pp. 9-10.

HILL, FRANK A.

[Review of] UNDER THE SUN, by H. G. de Lisser. PUBLIC OPINION, October 30, 1937, p. 9.

HIRSCH, EDWARD

[Review of] SEA GRAPES, by Derek Walcott. NYT, October 31, 1976, Section 7, p. 38.

HODGE, MERLE

"W.I. Culture Still Being Defined." SUNDAY GUARDIAN (Trinidad), April 4, 1971, p. 12.

"Towards a Caribbean-Afro-American Consciousness" (Stewart, LAST COOL DAYS). TAPIA, no. 21, October 3, 1971, p. 9.

"Peeping Tom in the Nigger Yard" (James, MINTY ALLEY). TAPIA, no. 25, April 2, 1972, pp. 11-12.

Hogg, Donald W.

HOGG, DONALD W.

    [Review of] CHILDREN OF SISYPHUS, by Orlando Patterson.
    CARIBBEAN STUDIES, v. 5, no. 4, January 1966, pp. 59-60.

HOLDER, GEOFFREY A.

    [Review of] HENRI CHRISTOPHE, by Derek Walcott. BIM, v. 4, no.
    14, June 1951, pp. 141-142.

    [Review of] A BRIGHTER SUN, by Samuel Selvon. BIM, v. 4, no.
    16, June 1952, pp. 295-296.

    [Review of] AN ISLAND IS A WORLD, by Samuel Selvon. BIM, v. 6,
    no. 23, December 1955, p. 202.

HOLMAN, CARL M.

    "Rebellion in Retrospect" (Reid, NEW DAY). PHYLON, v. 10, 1949,
    pp. 187-188.

HOOD, STUART

    [Review of] CRICK-CRACK MONKEY, by Merle Hodge. LISTENER, v.
    83, March 19, 1970.

HOPE, FRANCIS

    [Review of] PAID SERVANT, by E. R. Braithwaite. LSO, October
    28, 1962, p. 27.

    "Did You Once See Paris Plain?" (Rhys, TIGERS ARE BETTER-LOOK-
    ING). LSO, March 31, 1968, p. 29.

    "Displaced Persons" (Naipaul, V. S., IN A FREE STATE). LSO,
    October 3, 1971, p. 37.

    "Areas of Darkness" (Naipaul, V. S., THE OVERCROWDED BARRACOON).
    LSO, October 29, 1972, p. 38.

HOPKINSON, TOM

    "Dark Beginnings" (Abrahams, TELL FREEDOM). LSO, June 20, 1954,
    p. 9.

    [Review of] THE LONELY LONDONERS, by Samuel Selvon. LSO,
    December 16, 1956, p. 11.

[Review of] A TALE OF THREE PLACES, by Edgar Mittelholzer. LSO, March 10, 1957, p. 17.

HORDER, JOHN

[Review of] CONFESSIONS AND HISTORIES, by Edward Lucie-Smith. SPECTATOR, v. 213, October 30, 1964, p. 480.

HOSEIN, CLYDE

"Naipaul's Latest Called a Novel About History" (THE LOSS OF EL DORADO). SUNDAY GUARDIAN (Trinidad), December 14, 1969, p. 20.

HOUGH, GRAHAM

[Review of] A QUALITY OF VIOLENCE, by Andrew Salkey. LISTENER, v. 62, October 22, 1959, p. 698.

HOWARD, WILLIAM J.

"Wilson Harris and the 'Alchemical Imagination.'" LITERARY HALF-YEARLY, v. 11, no. 2, 1970, pp. 17-26.

"Wilson Harris' 'Guiana Quartet'; From Personal Myth to National Identity." ARIEL, v. 1, no. 1, January 1970, pp. 46-60.

"Edgar Mittelholzer's Tragic Vision." CARIBBEAN QUARTERLY, v. 16, no. 4, December 1970, pp. 19-28.

HOYTE, CLYDE

"Yes, Hearne Has Arrived." PUBLIC OPINION, November 25, 1961, p. 4.

HUDSON, JO

[Review of] PAID SERVANT, by Edward Braithwaite. FREEDOMWAYS, v. 8, Third quarter 1968, pp. 275-276.

HUNTE, GEORGE H.

[Review of] ONE TOUCH OF NATURE, by Lionel Hutchinson. BAJAN, no. 209, p. 22.

IBBERSON, DORA

[Review of] A BRIGHTER SUN, by Samuel Selvon. CARIBBEAN QUARTERLY, v. 3, no. 1, June 1953, p. 61.

Igoe, W. J.

IGOE, W. J.

"Revelations" (Lovelace, THE SCHOOLMASTER). THE TIMES (London). February 3, 1968, p. 20.

INNES, HAMMOND

[Review of] THE LOSS OF EL DORADO, by V. S. Naipaul. SPECTATOR, v. 223, November 8, 1969, p. 647.

IRELAND, KEVIN

"Place and Poetic Identity" (Walcott, THE CASTAWAY). JCL, no. 2, December 1966, pp. 157-158.

IREMONGER, LUCILLE

[Review of] NEW DAY, by V. S. Reid. LL, v. 64, no. 151, 1950, pp. 233-235.

IRISH, J. A. GEORGE

"Magical Realism: A Search for Caribbean and Latin American Roots." RRI, v. 4, no. 3, Fall 1974, pp. 411-421.

ISMOND, PATRICIA

"Walcott vs. Brathwaite." CARIBBEAN QUARTERLY, v. 17, nos. 3 and 4, September-December 1971, pp. 54-70.

"Breaking Myths and Maidenheads" (Walcott, THE JOKER OF SEVILLE). TAPIA, part 1, v. 5, no. 20, May 1975, pp. 4-5, 9; part 2, v. 5, no. 22, May 1975, pp. 6-8.

JABAVU, NONI

"Return of an Insider" (Naipaul, V. S., THE MIDDLE PASSAGE). NYT, September 22, 1963, Section 7, p. 14.

JACKMAN, OLIVER

[Review of] THE WILD COAST, by Jan Carew. BIM, v. 8, no. 29, June-December 1959, pp. 64-67.

JACKSON, BLYDEN

[Review of] WILD CONQUEST, by Peter Abrahams. PHYLON, v. 11,

Jagessar, Ramdath

1950, pp. 290-291.

"The Essential McKay" (SELECTED POEMS OF CLAUDE MCKAY). PHYLON, v. 13, 1953, pp. 216-217.

Review (Abrahams, TELL FREEDOM). PHYLON, v. 14, 1954, pp. 410-411.

JACOBS, CARL

"At 35 Walcott Is Something of a Phenomenon." SUNDAY GUARDIAN (Trinidad), May 15, 1966, p. 9.

"There's No Bitterness in Our Literature" (interview with Derek Walcott). SUNDAY GUARDIAN (Trinidad), May 22, 1966, p. 9.

JACOBS, H. P.

"The Literary Movement." PUBLIC OPINION, March 4, 1939, p. 3.

"The Era of New Eras" (De Lisser). PUBLIC OPINION, March 11, 1939, p. 3.

"The Dialect of Victor Reid" (NEW DAY). WIR, New Series, v. 1, May 1949, pp. 12-15.

"The Historic Foundation of New Day." WIR, part 1, New Series, v. 1, no. 2, May 14, 1949, pp. 21-22; part 2, v. 1, no. 3, May 21, 1949, pp. 10-11, 25; part 3, v. 1, no. 4, May 28, 1949, pp. 18-19.

"Tom Redcam Reassessed." PUBLIC OPINION, March 30, 1957, p. 7.

"Adolphe Roberts: The Meaning of His Life." PUBLIC OPINION, December 1, 1962, p. 2.

JACOBSON, DAN

"Self-Help in Hot Places" (Naipaul, V. S. A HOUSE FOR MR. BISWAS). NEW STATESMAN, v. 62, September 29, 1961, p. 440.

[Review of] A NIGHT OF THEIR OWN, by Peter Abrahams. LSO, March 28, 1965, p. 26.

JAGESSAR, RAMDATH

[Review of] THE CUTLASS IS NOT FOR KILLING, by Dennis Mahabir. MOKO, no. 66, August 6, 1971, p. 8.

Jahn, Janheinz

JAHN, JANHEINZ

"The Contribution of the West Indies to Poetry." BIM, v. 6, no. 21, 1954, pp. 16-22.

"Anthology of 29 Poets a Success." SUNDAY GUARDIAN (Trinidad), September 9, 1962, p. 9.

JAMES, C. L. R.

"Here's A Poet Who Sees the REAL West Indies" (Walcott, IN A GREEN NIGHT). SUNDAY GUARDIAN (Trinidad), May 6, 1962, p. 5.

"Home Is Where They Want to Be." TGM, February 14, 1965, pp. 4-5.

"The Disorder of Vidia Naipaul." TGM, February 21, 1965, p. 6.

"Discovering Literature in Trinidad: The Nineteen-Thirties." JCL, no. 7, July 1969, pp. 73-80.
Also appears in SAVACOU, no. 2, September 1970, pp. 54-60.

JAMES, LOUIS

"Or the Hopeful Dawn" (Williams, OTHER LEOPARDS). PUBLIC OPINION, June 18, 1965, pp. 14-15.

"Islands of Man, Reflections on the Emergence of a West Indian Literature." SOUTHERN REVIEW, v. 2, 1966, pp. 150-163.

"The Necessity of Poetry." NWQ, Guyana Independence Issue, 1966, pp. 111-115.

[Review of] RIGHTS OF PASSAGE, by Edward Brathwaite. CARIBBEAN QUARTERLY, v. 13, no. 1, March 1967, pp. 38-41.

"Of Redcoats and Leopards. Two Novels by V. S. Reid." THE ISLANDS IN BETWEEN (edited by Louis James). London: Oxford University Press, 1968, pp. 64-72.

"In Solitude for Company. The Poetry of Derek Walcott." THE ISLANDS IN BETWEEN. London: Oxford University Press, 1968, pp. 86-99.

"Caribbean Poetry in English--Some Problems." SAVACOU, no. 2, September 1970, pp. 78-86.

"The Sad Initiation of Lammings 'G' and Other Caribbean Green
Tales." COMMON WEALTH: PAPERS DELIVERED AT THE CONFERENCE
OF COMMONWEALTH LITERATURE, AARHUS UNIVERSITY APRIL 26-30,
1971 (edited by Anna Rutherford). Aarhus, Denmark: Aarhus
University, 1971, pp. 135-143.

"Fragmentation of Experience" (Selvon, THOSE WHO EAT THE
CASCADURA). LITERARY HALF-YEARLY, v. 13, no. 1, January
1972, pp. 173-176.

JARDINE, MONICA

[Review of] UNIVERSITY OF HUNGER, by Jan Carew. NWF, v. 1, no.
48, September 19, 1966, pp. 23-25.

JEFFERS, KEITH

"Clarke: Promise and Insight with Flaws" (WHEN HE WAS FREE
AND YOUNG AND HE USED TO WEAR SILKS). BLACK IMAGES, v. 1,
no. 1, January 1972.

JEFFERSON, MILES M.

Review (Abrahams, THE PATH OF THUNDER). PHYLON, v. 11, 1948,
pp. 188-189.

JENKIN, VERONICA

[Review of] DRUMS AND COLOURS, by Derek Walcott. BIM, v. 7, no.
27, July-December 1958, pp. 183-184.

JENNINGS, ELIZABETH

"The Better Break" (Lamming, THE EMIGRANTS). SPECTATOR, v. 193,
October 1, 1954, pp. 411-412.

[Review of] TO SIR WITH LOVE, by E. R. Braithwaite. LONDON
MAGAZINE, v. 6, no. 10, October 1959, pp. 67-78.

JE'SMAN, CZESLAW

[Review of] A KIND OF HOMECOMING, by E. R. Braithwaite. RACE,
v. 5, no. 1, July 1963, pp. 95-96.

JOHNSON, B. S.

[Review of] BLACK MARSDEN, by Wilson Harris; NATIVES OF MY

Johnson, Lee S. B.

   PERSON, by George Lamming. NEW STATESMAN, v. 84, December 1,
   1972, p. 832.

JOHNSON, LEE S. B.

   [Review of] ON THE COAST, by Wayne Brown. CARIBBEAN QUARTERLY,
   v. 18, no. 4, 1972, pp. 84-86.

JONES, BRIDGET

   "Some French Influence in the Fiction of Orlando Patterson."
   SAVACOU, nos. 11/12, September 1975, pp. 27-38.

JORDAN, CLIVE

   [Review of] CRICK-CRACK MONKEY, by Merle Hodge. NEW STATESMAN,
   v. 79, March 6, 1969, p. 334.

   [Review of] NOR ANY COUNTRY, by Garth St. Omer. NEW STATESMAN,
   v. 77, May 9, 1969, p. 666.

JOSEPH, BARBARA

   [Review of] CURVING ROAD, by John Stewart. CORLIT, v. 2, nos.
   1-2, April-July 1975, pp. 44-45.

KAYE, JACQUELINE

   "Claude McKay's BANJO." PRESENCE AFRICAINE, no. 73, 1970, pp.
   165-169.

   "Anonymity and Subjectivism in the Novels of Garth St. Omer."
   JCL, v. 10, no. 1, August 1975, pp. 45-52.

KAZIN, ALFRED

   "Displaced Person" (Naipaul, V. S., IN A FREE STATE). NYRB,
   v. 17, no. 11, 1971, pp. 3-4.

KEANE, E. MC.

   "The Contribution of the West Indian to Literature." BIM, v. 4,
   no. 14, June 1951, pp. 102-106.

   "Some Religious Attitudes in West Indian Poetry." BIM, part 1,
   v. 4, no. 15, December 1951, pp. 169-174; part 2, v. 4, no.
   16, June 1952, pp. 266-271.

KEMOLI, ARTHUR

"The Theme of 'The Past' in Caribbean Literature." WLWE, v. 12, November 1973, pp. 304-325.

KENT, GEORGE

"The Soulful Way of Claude McKay." BLACK WORLD, v. 20, no. 1, November 1970, pp. 37-51.

"Conversation with George Lamming." BLACK WORLD, v. 22, no. 5, March 1973, pp. 4-15, 88-97.

KETTLE, ARNOLD

"Two West Indian Novelists" (Braithwaite, CHOICE OF STRAWS; Dathorne, THE SCHOLAR-MAN). JCL, no. 2, December 1966, pp. 173-175.

KHAN, ISMITH

"Dialect in West Indian Literature." THE BLACK WRITER IN AFRICA AND THE AMERICAS (edited by Lloyd W. Brown). Los Angeles: Hennessey and Ingalls, 1973, pp. 141-164.

KING, CAMERON

"Martin Carter--Voice of Resistance." SUNDAY GLEANER, August 9, 1964, p. 4.

"The Poems of Derek Walcott." CARIBBEAN QUARTERLY, v. 10, no. 3, September 1964, pp. 3-30.

"A. L. Hendriks, Poetic Journey." SUNDAY GLEANER, part 1, March 6, 1966, p. 4; part 2, April 24, 1966, p. 4.

"In Solitude for Company. The Poetry of Derek Walcott." THE ISLANDS IN BETWEEN (edited by Louis James). London: Oxford University Press, 1968, pp. 86-99.

KING, ERIC

[Review of] THE YEAR IN SAN FERNANDO, by Michael Anthony. CARIBBEAN QUARTERLY, v. 16, no. 4, December 1970, pp. 87-91.

KING, LLOYD

Knight, Mary McAnally

"The Trauma of Naipaulana." SUNDAY GUARDIAN (Trinidad),
September 24, 1967, pp. 16-19.

"Bard in the Rubbish Heap; The Problem of Walcott's Poetry."
TAPIA, no. 5, February 1, 1970, pp. 7-8.

"Derek Walcott: The Literary Humanist in the Caribbean."
CARIBBEAN QUARTERLY, v. 16, no. 4, December 1970, pp. 36-42.

"A Call to Two Different Worlds" (Jones, PAN BEAT). TAPIA,
v. 3, no. 20, May 20, 1973, p. 4.

KNIGHT, MARY MC ANALLY

[Review of] ANANCY'S SCORE, by Andrew Salkey. NEW LETTERS, v.
41, no. 2, December 1974, pp. 121-123.

KRIKLER, BERNARD

[Review of] A HOUSE FOR MR. BISWAS, by V. S. Naipaul. LISTENER,
v. 71, February 13, 1964, pp. 270-271

LACOVIA, R. M.

"Roger Mais and the Problem of Freedom." BAR, v. 1, no. 3,
Fall, 1970, pp. 45-54.

"Caribbean Literature in English: 1949-1970." BAR, v. 2, nos.
1 and 2, 1971, pp. 109-125.

"English Caribbean Literature: A Brave New World." BLACK
IMAGES, v. 1, no. 1, January 1972, pp. 15-22.

"Roger Mais: An Approach to Suffering and Freedom." BLACK
IMAGES, v. 1, no. 2, Summer 1972, pp. 7-11.

"The Medium Is the Divide: An Examination of V. S. Naipaul's
Early Works." BLACK IMAGES, v. 1, no. 2, Summer 1972, pp.
3-6.

"Ismith Khan and the Theory of Rasa." BLACK IMAGES, v. 1, nos.
3 and 4, Autumn and Winter 1972, pp. 23-27.

"Caribbean Aesthetics: A Prolegomenon" (Harris). BLACK IMAGES,
v. 2, no. 2, 1973, 47 pp. (Black Images Monograph no. 1).

LAIRD, CHRISTOPHER

Lane, M. Travis

"Hiding behind Language Bar, An Essay on Creole, The Writer and Society in the Caribbean." KAIRI, no. 3, 1974, 12 pp.

"Bruce St. John at Kairi House, An Introduction." KAIRI, no. 4/5, 1974, 10 pp.

"The Novel of Tomorrow, Today" (Ladoo, YESTERDAYS). KAIRI, no. 1, 1975, 12 pp.

LAMMING, GEORGE

[Reviews of] NO IDLE WINDS, by W. S. Arthur; POEMS, by Leo Austin. BIM, v. 6, no. 22, June 1955, pp. 132-133.

"The Negro Writer and His World." PRESENCE AFRICAINE, nos. 8-9-10, June-November 1956, pp. 318-325. Also appears in CARIBBEAN QUARTERLY, v. 5, no. 2, February 1958, pp. 109-115.

[Review of] THE LAST ENCHANTMENT, by Neville Dawes. RACE, v. 2, no. 2, May 1961, p. 92.

"The West Indian People." NWQ, v. 2, no. 2, Croptime 1966, pp. 63-74.

"But Alas Edgar." NWQ, Guyana Independence Issue, 1966, pp. 18-19.

"Tribute to a Tragic Jamaican." SUNDAY GLEANER, December 25, 1955, p. 10. Also appears in BIM, v. 6, no. 24, 1956, pp. 242-244; and in PUBLIC OPINION, Roger Mais Supplement, June 10, 1966, p. 3.

[Review of] ANOTHER LIFE, by Derek Walcott. NYT, May 6, 1973, Section 7, p. 36.

LANE, MARGARET

"Life and Hard Times" (Rhys). SPECTATOR, v. 222, May 16, 1969, pp. 649-650.

LANE, M. TRAVIS

"The Casualties of Freedom: V. S. Naipaul's IN A FREE STATE." WLWE, v. 12, April 1973, pp. 106-110.

"At Home in Homelessness; The Poetry of Derek Walcott."

Larson, Charles R.

    DALHOUSIE REVIEW, v. 53, no. 2, Summer 1973, pp. 325-338.

LARSON, CHARLES R.

    "Three Harlem Novels of the Jazz Age" (McKay). CRITIQUE, v. 11,
    no. 3, 1969.

    "African-Afro-American Literary Relations; Basic Parallels."
    NEGRO DIGEST, v. 19, no. 1, 1969, pp. 35-42.

LASH, JOHN S.

    [Review of] A WREATH FOR UDOMO, by Peter Abrahams. PHYLON, v.
    17, 1956, pp. 296-297.

LASHLEY, CLIFF

    [Review of] A ROOM ON THE HILL, by Garth St. Omer. CARIBBEAN
    QUARTERLY, v. 17, no. 1, March 1971, pp. 58-59.

LASK, THOMAS

    "Brave New World" (Naipaul, V. S., THE LOSS OF ELDORADO). NYT,
    June 20, 1970, p. 27.

    "Where Is the Enemy?" (Naipaul, V. S., IN A FREE STATE). NYT,
    December 25, 1971, p. 15.

LASKI, MARGHANITA

    [Review of] SHADOWS MOVE AMONG THEM, by Edgar Mittelholzer.
    LSO, March 25, 1951, p. 7.

    [Review of] THE PATH OF THUNDER, by Peter Abrahams. LSO, March
    9, 1952, p. 7.

    [Review of] THE LIFE AND DEATH OF SYLVIA, by Edgar Mittelholzer.
    SPECTATOR, v. 190, May 15, 1953, p. 652.

    [Review of] THE ORCHID HOUSE, by Phyllis Allfrey. LSO, July 19,
    1953, p. 8.

LAURENCE, S. M.

    "West Indian Writing in the Infant Days." Reprint from THE
    ROYALIAN, v. 1, no. 3, March 1933. TAPIA, v. 7, no. 4,
    January 23, 1977.

LAWTON, DAVID

> [Review of] THE GULF, by Derek Walcott. RRI, v. 2, no. 2, Summer 1972, pp. 242-247.

LE PAGE, R. B.

> [Review of] THREE MERIDIANS, by Geoffrey Drayton. CARIBBEAN QUARTERLY, v. 2, no. 1, April 1950, p. 45.

> [Review of] L'OUBLI, by E. McG. Keane. CARIBBEAN QUARTERLY, v. 2, no. 1, April 1950, p. 46.

> "Dialect in West Indian Literature." JCL, no. 7, July 1969, pp. 1-7.

LEE, ROBERT

> "Peter Plays for Paul" (St. Omer, J., BLACK BAM AND THE MASQUERADERS). TAPIA, v. 4, no. 5, February 1974, pp. 6-7.

> "THE JOKER OF SEVILLE, A Review of the St. Lucia Production" (Walcott). TAPIA, v. 5, no. 26, June 1975.

LEVIN, MARTIN

> "How the Ball Bounces Down Trinidad Way" (Naipaul, V. S., THE MYSTIC MASSEUR). NYT, April 12, 1959, Section 7, p. 5.

> [Review of] LAND OF THE LIVING, by John Hearne. NYT, August 12, 1962, Section 7, p. 24.

> [Review of] THE GAMES WERE COMING, by Michael Anthony. NYT, April 14, 1968, Section 7, p. 31.

> [Review of] THE BIGGER LIGHT, by Austin Clarke. NYT, February 16, 1975, Section 7, p. 12.

LEVY, OSCAR

> [Review of] HAVANA JOURNAL, GEORGETOWN JOURNAL, by Andrew Salkey. CARIBBEAN CONTACT, v. 1, no. 3, February 1973, pp. 4, 14.

> "The Politics of Corruption--And Failure" (Thomas, RULER IN HIROONA). CARIBBEAN CONTACT, v. 1, no. 6, May 1973, pp. 4, 16.

241

Lewis, Gordon

LEWIS, GORDON

"The New West Indies: Nationality and Literature." SUNDAY
GLEANER, December 8, 1957, p. 8.

LEWIS, MAUREEN WARNER; See Also WARNER, MAUREEN

"Odomankoma Kyerema Se..." (Brathwaite, THE ARRIVANTS).
CARIBBEAN QUARTERLY, v. 19, no. 2, June 1973, pp. 51-99

LEWIS, PRIMULA

"Politics and the Novel; An Appreciation of A WREATH FOR UDOMO
and THIS ISLAND NOW by Peter Abrahams." ZUKA, no. 2, May
1968, pp. 41-47.

LEWIS, RUPERT

"Roger Mais' Work as Social Protest and Comment." SUNDAY
GLEANER, March 26, 1967, pp. 4, 24.

"HAVANA JOURNAL: A Major Document" (Salkey). SUNDAY GLEANER,
July 11, 1971, p. 29.

LIGNY, MICHEL

[Review of] A HOUSE FOR MR. BISWAS, by V. S. Naipaul. PRESENCE
AFRICAINE, no. 52, 1964, pp. 233-235.

LINDO, ARCHIE

"Louise Bennett's New Book" (ANANCY STORIES). SUNDAY GLEANER,
January 7, 1945, p. 4.

"Caribbean Voices--A Challenge to Jamaica Writers." SUNDAY
GLEANER, January 25, 1948, p. 9.

"Harold Telemaque, Poet of Trinidad." SUNDAY GLEANER, June 13,
1948, p. 9.

"Claude McKay." SUNDAY GLEANER, part 1, July 18, 1948, p. 8;
part 2, August 1, 1948, p. 8; part 3, August 29, 1948, p. 9.

"The Poetry League." SUNDAY GLEANER, September 19, 1948, p. 11.

LINDO, CEDRIC

Index of Critics and Reviewers

Lindo, Cedric

"Brilliant Portrayal of West Indian Society" (Marshall, THE
CHOSEN PLACE, THE TIMELESS PEOPLE). SUNDAY GLEANER, October
11, 1970, p. 27.

[Review of] THE SLEEPERS OF RORAIMA, by Wilson Harris. SUNDAY
GLEANER, October 18, 1970, p. 27.

"Detailed Look at Indians in Trinidad" (Naipaul, S., FIREFLIES).
SUNDAY GLEANER, December 13, 1970, p. 39.

[Review of] ONE TOUCH OF NATURE, by Lionel Hutchinson. SUNDAY
GLEANER, February 7, 1971, p. 23.

[Review of] PLAINS OF CARONI, by Samuel Selvon. SUNDAY GLEANER,
February 7, 1971, p. 23.

"Worthy Examples of Our Poetry" (SEVEN JAMAICAN POETS). SUNDAY
GLEANER, May 23, 1971, p. 29.

"Enjoyable Collection by a Jamaican Poet" (Hendriks, THESE
GREEN ISLANDS). SUNDAY GLEANER, January 23, 1972, p. 25.

"The New Selvon--Set in Rural Trinidad" (THOSE WHO EAT THE
CASCADURA). SUNDAY GLEANER, February 20, 1972, p. 35.

[Review of] MUET, by A. L. Hendriks. SUNDAY GLEANER, March 5,
1972, p. 27.

"Jamaica in the Days of Slavery" (Patterson, DIE THE LONG DAY).
SUNDAY GLEANER (Jamaica), August 27, 1972, p. 45.

[Review of] THE OVERCROWDED BARRACOON, by V. S. Naipaul.
SUNDAY GLEANER, November 5, 1972, p. 39.

"Salkey's Latest Journal" (GEORGETOWN JOURNAL). SUNDAY GLEANER,
December 3, 1972, p. 43.

"A Scottish Wilson Harris Puzzle" (BLACK MARSDEN). SUNDAY
GLEANER, December 10, 1972, p. 47.

"West Indian Politics in a First Novel" (Thomas, RULER IN
HIROONA). SUNDAY GLEANER, December 24, 1972, p. 21.

"Readable Slice of Trinidadian Life" (Jones, PAN BEAT). SUNDAY
GLEANER, April 8, 1973, p. 35.

"Poetic Bridge to Africa" (Brathwaite, THE ARRIVANTS). SUNDAY

Linton, N. O.

GLEANER, January 30, 1974, p. 26.

"Modern Poetry for Many Moods" (Morris, THE POND). SUNDAY
GLEANER, February 10, 1974.

LINTON, N. O.

"Memorial to Roger Mais: A Green Blade in Triumph--THE HILLS
WERE JOYFUL TOGETHER." KYK-OVER-AL, v. 6, no. 20, Mid-year
1955, pp. 147-170.

LOOK LAI, WALLY

"The Road to Thornfield Hall; An Analysis of Jean Rhys' Novel
WIDE SARGASSO SEA." NEW BEACON REVIEWS (edited by John La
Rose). London: New Beacon Books, 1968, pp. 38-52.
Also appears in NWQ, v. 4, no. 2, Croptime 1968, pp. 17-27.

LORD, CECILY

[Review of] SHADOWS MOVE AMONG THEM, by Edgar Mittelholzer.
KYK-OVER-AL, v. 3, no. 12, Mid-year 1951, pp. 179-180.

LOWHAR, SYL

"A Struggle for Freedom; Derek Walcott's TI-JEAN." TAPIA, no.
8, August 9, 1970, p. 6.

"Another Station of the Cross" (Walcott, IN A FINE CASTLE).
TAPIA, no. 23, December 26, 1971, p. 19.

"Carter's 'Resistance' and 'Succession.'" CARIBBEAN CONTACT,
v. 5, no. 5, August 1977, p. 7.

LUCIE-SMITH, MARY

"In England Now." WIR, v. 3, no. 2, February 1958, pp. 55,57.

[Review of] TURN AGAIN TIGER, by Samuel Selvon. WIR, v. 4, no.
3, March 1959, p. 50.

LUENGO, ANTHONY

"Growing Up in San Fernando: Change and Growth in Michael
Anthony's THE YEAR IN SAN FERNANDO" ARIEL, v. 6, no. 2, April
1975, pp. 81-95.

McDowell, Frederick

"WIDE SARGASSO SEA and the Gothic Mode" (Rhys). WLWE, v. 15, April 1976, pp. 229-245.

MACBETH, GEORGE

[Review of] A TROPICAL CHILDHOOD, by Edward Lucie-Smith. LONDON MAGAZINE, New Series, v. 1, no. 9, December 1961, pp. 93-94.

MACAULEY, ROBIE

[Review of] SLEEP IT OFF LADY, by Jean Rhys. NYT, November 21, 1976, Section 7, p. 7.

MCCOLGAN, KATHLEEN

"Born Yesterday." WIR, v. 4, no. 45, May 16, 1953, p. 17.

MACCULLOCH, CLARE

"Look Homeward Bajan; A Look at the Work of Austin Clarke, A Barbadian Expatriate as Seen by an Outsider." BIM, v. 14, no. 55, July-December 1972, pp. 179-182.

MACDONALD, BRUCE F.

"Symbolic Action in Three of V. S. Naipaul's Novels." JCL, v. 9, no. 3, April 1975, pp. 41-52.

MCDONALD, IAN

"The Unsteady Flame: A Short Account of Guianese Poetry." NWF, part 1, v. 1, no. 17, June 25, 1965, pp. 20-22; part 2, v. 1, no. 18, July 9, 1965, pp. 24-25; part 3, v. 1, no. 19, July 23, 1965, pp. 19-20.

[Review of] OLD THOM'S HARVEST, by Lauchmonen. NWF, v. 1, no. 21, August 20, 1965, pp. 25-27.

"Introduction to 'Jail Me Quickly--Five Poems by Martin Carter.'" NWF, v. 1, no. 34, February 18, 1966, pp. 19-20.

"Poetry in Guyana." KAIE, no. 4, July 1967, pp. 64-66.

MCDOWELL, FREDERICK

[Reviews of] FIREFLIES, by Shiva Naipaul; IN A FREE STATE, by

245

McDowell, Robert E.

V. S. Naipaul. CONTEMPORARY LITERATURE, v. 13, Summer 1972, pp. 374-380.

MCDOWELL, ROBERT E.

"Interview with Sheik Sadeek--A Guyanese Popular Writer." WLWE, v. 14, no. 2, November 1975, pp. 525-535.

MCFARLANE, BASIL

"George Campbell: The Road We Travel" (FIRST POEMS). PUBLIC OPINION, March 22, 1947, p. 7.

"On Jamaican Poetry." KYK-OVER-AL, v. 3, no. 13, Year-end 1951, pp. 207-209.

"Memorial to Roger Mais: A Green Blade in Triumph." KYK-OVER-AL, v. 6, no. 20, Mid-year 1955, pp. 147-149.

"Roger Mais, Novelist and Painter, Poet and Patriot." PUBLIC OPINION, July 2, 1955, p. 4.

"Views of a Slum-Yard" (Wynter, SHH ... IT'S A WEDDING). PUBLIC OPINION, January 26, 1963, p. 13.

"Roger Mais--The Painter." PUBLIC OPINION, Roger Mais Supplement, June 10, 1966, p. 8.

"The Century of Exile, Basil McFarlane Speaks with Wayne Brown." JAMAICA JOURNAL, v. 7, no. 3, September 1973, pp. 38-44.

"Jamaican Novel. A Review, THE LAST ENCHANTMENT" (Dawes). JAMAICA JOURNAL, nos. 2 and 3, 1975, pp. 51-52.

"His Work will Live; An Appreciation of Claude McKay." SUNDAY GLEANER, June 6, 1948, p. 6.

MCGLASHAN, COLIN

[Review of] RELUCTANTANT NEIGHBORS, by E. R. Braithwaite. NEW STATESMAN, v. 84, October 20, 1971, p. 558

MCGUINNESS, FRANK

"West Indian Windfall" (Anthony, THE GAMES WERE COMING, GREEN DAYS BY THE RIVER). LONDON MAGAZINE, New Series, v. 7, no. 1 1, April 1967, pp. 117-120.

McSweeny, Kerry

"A Rough Game" (Naipaul, V. S., IN A FREE STATE). LONDON
MAGAZINE, New Series, v. 11, no. 4, October/November 1971,
pp. 156-158.

MACINNES, COLIN

"Caribbean Masterpiece (Naipaul, V. S., A HOUSE FOR MR. BISWAS).
LSO, October 1, 1961, p. 31.
Also reprinted in PUBLIC OPINION, October 7, 1961, p. 3, and
BIM, v. 9, no. 35, July-December 1962, pp. 221-223.

"Nightmare In Paradise" (Rhys, WIDE SARGASSO SEA). LSO,
October 30, 1966, p. 28.

MACKOON, LINDSAY

"A Poet with Rare Vision" (Hosein, TORTURE OF SUNSET). SUNDAY
GUARDIAN (Trinidad), February 17, 1963, p. 10.

MACLAREN-ROSS, J.

[Review of] VOICES UNDER THE WINDOW, by John Hearne, LISTENER,
v. 54, 1955, p. 391.

MACMILLAN, M.

"Language and Change" (Anthony, THE YEAR IN SAN FERNANDO). JCL,
no. 1, September 1965, p. 175.

MACNAMARA, DESMOND

[Review of] A FLAG ON THE ISLAND, by V. S. Naipaul. NEW
STATESMAN, v. 74, September 15, 1967, p. 325.

[Review of] WHEN HE WAS FREE AND YOUNG AND HE USED TO WEAR
SILKS, by Austin Clarke. QUEENS QUARTERLY, v. 79, Spring
1972, p. 120.

MCNEILL, ANTHONY

"Dennis Scott, Maker; 'Journeys.'" JAMAICA JOURNAL, v. 5, no.
4, December 1971, pp. 49-52.

MCSWEENY, KERRY

Review (Naipaul, V. S., THE OVERCROWDED BARRACOON). QUEENS
QUARTERLY, v. 80, Autumn 1973, pp. 495-497.

Maes-Jelinek, Hena

"V. S. Naipaul: Sensibility and Schemata." CRITICAL QUARTERLY, v. 18, Autumn 1976, pp. 73-79.

MAES-JELINEK, HENA

"The Myth of El Dorado in the Caribbean Novel." JCL, v. 6, no. 1, June 1971, pp. 113-127.

"The True Substance of Life: Wilson Harris's PALACE OF THE PEACOCK." COMMON WEALTH: PAPERS DELIVERED AT THE CONFERENCE OF COMMONWEALTH LITERATURE, AARHUS UNIVERSITY, APRIL 26-30, 1971 (edited by Anna Rutherford). Aarhus, Denmark: Aarhus University, 1971, pp. 151-159.

"Ascent to Omai" (Harris). LITERARY HALF-YEARLY, v. 13, no. 1, January 1972, pp. 1-8.

"Natural and Psychological Landscapes" (Harris, THE SLEEPERS OF RORAIMA: THE AGE OF THE RAINMAKERS). JCL, v. 7, no. 1, June 1972, pp. 117-120.

MAHON, DEREK

[Review of] FIREFLIES, by Shiva Naipaul. LISTENER, v. 84, October 22, 1970, p. 555.

MAIS, ROGER

"Contemporary Jamaican Verse." PUBLIC OPINION, November 4, 1939, p. 10.

"Let Us Paraphrase." PUBLIC OPINION, February 3, 1940, p. 6.

"Where the Roots Lie." PUBLIC OPINION, March 9, 1940, p. 12.

"The Critics Criticized." PUBLIC OPINION, part 1, May 3, 1952, p. 5; part 2, May 17, 1952, p. 5.

"The Poetry of McFarlane." PUBLIC OPINION, June 28, 1952, p. 5.

"W.I. Nationalism, Poetry Like--'Cold Embers of a Spent Passion'" (KYK-OVER-AL ANTHOLOGY OF WEST INDIAN POETRY). PUBLIC OPINION, July 12, 1952, p. 5.

MANLEY, EDNA

Marshall, Harold

[Review of] THE POMEGRANATE, by Adolphe Roberts. PUBLIC
OPINION, May 17, 1941, p. 7.

MANLEY, MICHAEL

"The New Trinidad" (Selvon, A BRIGHTER SUN). PUBLIC OPINION,
March 22, 1952, p. 5.

MARR, N. J.

[Review of] THE HILLS WERE JOYFUL TOGETHER, by Roger Mais.
SUNDAY GLEANER, June 14, 1953, p. 5.

"About Books" (Mittelholzer). SUNDAY GLEANER, June 28, 1953,
p. 5.

"West Indian Literary Giants" (Mais, Lamming). SUNDAY GLEANER,
January 23, 1955, p. 6.

"Roger Mais in Jamaica 300." SUNDAY GLEANER, May 22, 1955, p.
5.

MARSHALL, HAROLD

[Review of] LATTICED ECHOES, by Edgar Mittelholzer. BIM, v. 8,
no. 31, July-December 1960, pp. 217-218.

[Review of] THE PLEASURES OF EXILE, by George Lamming. BIM,
v. 8, no. 32, January-June 1961, pp. 289-290.

[Review of] ZOHARA, by Geoffrey Drayton. BIM, v. 9, no. 34,
January-June 1962, p. 152.

[Review of] THE PILING OF CLOUDS, by Edgar Mittelholzer. BIM,
v. 9, no. 35, July-December 1962, pp. 228-229.

[Review of] THE MIDDLE PASSAGE, by V. S. Naipaul.
v. 9, no. 36, January-June 1963, p. 290.

[Review of] THE GAMES WERE COMING, by Michael Anthony. BIM, v.
10, no. 38, January-June 1964, p. 145.

[Review of] DUMPLINGS IN THE SOUP, by O. R. Dathorne. BIM, v.
10, no. 39, July-December 1964, pp. 226-227.

[Review of] FOUR PLAYS FOR PRIMARY SCHOOLS, by Edward
Brathwaite. BIM, v. 11, no. 42, January-June 1966, pp. 71-72.

Marson, Una

> [Review of] WHEN HE WAS FREE AND YOUNG AND HE USED TO WEAR
> SILKS, by Austin Clarke. BIM, v. 14, no. 54, January-June
> 1972, pp. 113-116.

> [Review of] THE MEETING POINT, by Austin Clarke. BAJAN, no.
> 226, August 1972, pp. 33, 36.

MARSON, UNA

> "Wanted: Writers and Publishers." PUBLIC OPINION, June 12,
> 1937, p. 6.

> "We Want Books--But Do We Encourage Our Writers?" SUNDAY
> GLEANER, October 23, 1949, p. 7.

MARTIN, GRAHAM

> [Review of] THE CASTAWAY, by Derek Walcott. LISTENER, v. 75,
> March 10, 1966, p. 359.

MARTIN, JANE

> [Review of] A MORNING IN TRINIDAD, by Edgar Mittelholzer. NYT,
> May 14, 1950, Section 7, p. 20.

MARTIN, M. COMBE

> [Review of] OF AGE AND INNOCENCE, by George Lamming. BIM, v. 8,
> no. 29, June-December 1959, pp. 62-64.

MASSIAH, E. B. B.

> [Review of] THINGS, by Michael Foster. BIM, v. 11, no. 42,
> January-June 1966, pp. 141-143.

MASSY, ALVIN

> "Seized Novel a Sexy Meet-the-People Jaunt" (Ramkeesoon,
> SUNDAY MORNING COMING DOWN). TAPIA, v. 6, no. 30, July 25,
> 1976, p. 5.

MATTHEWS, A. F. CRICHLOW

> [Reviews of] KYK-OVER-AL ANTHOLOGY OF WEST INDIAN POETRY;
> CHILDREN OF KAYWANA, by Edgar Mittelholzer. BIM, v. 4, no.
> 16, June 1952, pp. 298-300.

MATTHEWS, NANCY

"Lunatic At Large" (Mittelholzer, THE WEATHER IN MIDDENSHOT).
NYT, May 31, 1953, Section 7, p. 10.

"Cliques and Sub-cliques" (Mittelholzer, THE LIFE AND DEATH OF
SYLVIA). NYT, January 10, 1954, Section 7, p. 28.

"Passion Was the Dominant Chord" (Mittelholzer, THE OLD BLOOD).
NYT, May 18, 1958, Section 7, p. 33.

MAXWELL, MARINA

"Towards a Revolution in the Arts." SAVACOU, no. 2, September
1970, pp. 19-32.

MAYNE, RICHARD

[Review of] LAND OF THE LIVING, by John Hearne. NEW STATESMAN,
v. 62, September 29, 1961, p. 440.

MAZZOCCO, ROBERT

[Review of] SELECTED POEMS, by Derek Walcott. NYRB, v. 3, no.
10, 1964, pp. 18-19.

MEIKLE, RUPERT ERRINGTON

"Claude McKay--The Forgotten Jamaican." SUNDAY GLEANER, June
18, 1972, p. 39.

MELLORS, JOHN

[Review of] THE CHIP-CHIP GATHERERS, by Shiva Naipaul. LONDON
MAGAZINE, New Series, v. 13, no. 3, August/September 1973,
p. 151.

MELLOWN, ELGIN W.

"The Character and Themes in the Novels of Jean Rhys."
CONTEMPORARY LITERATURE, v. 13, Autumn 1972, pp. 458-475.

METCALF, JOHN

[Review of] THE HARROWING OF HUBERTUS, by Edgar Mittelholzer.
SPECTATOR, v. 192, February 19, 1954, p. 216.

Miller, Karl

MILLER, KARL

[Review of] THE AUTUMN EQUINOX, by John Hearne. LSO, November
8, 1959, p. 23.

MILLS, K. I.

"The Decline and Fall" (Mittelholzer, THE LIFE AND DEATH OF
SYLVIA). SUNDAY GUARDIAN (Trinidad), June 14, 1953, p. 7a.

"Slum Clearance" (Mais, THE HILLS WERE JOYFUL TOGETHER). SUNDAY
GUARDIAN (Trinidad), July 12, 1953, p. 7a.

MILLS, THERESE

"This Is an Experiment in Courage" (Walcott and the Trinidad
Theatre Workshop). SUNDAY GUARDIAN (Trinidad), April 15,
1973, p. 8.

"BIM'S Grand Old Man Retires." SUNDAY GUARDIAN (Trinidad),
July 8, 1973, p. 7.

"Poet at the Crossroads" (Walcott, POEMS). SUNDAY GLEANER,
October 14, 1951, p. 4.

MILNER, HARRY

[Review of] THE DYING GODS, by Derek Walcott. SUNDAY GLEANER,
February 15, 1953, p. 4.

"Two Artistic Events" (Mais, THE HILLS ARE JOYFUL TOGETHER).
SUNDAY GLEANER, September 13, 1953, p. 4.

"W. Adolphe Roberts." SUNDAY GLEANER, September 23, 1962, p.
14.

MITCHELL, ADRIAN

[Review of] MR. STONE AND THE KNIGHTS COMPANION, by V. S.
Naipaul. SPECTATOR, v. 210, June 21, 1963.

MITCHELL, JULIAN

[Review of] A HOUSE FOR MR. BISWAS, by V. S. Naipaul.
SPECTATOR, v. 207, October 6, 1961, p. 472.

MITTELHOLZER, EDGAR

Moore, Gerald

"Literary Criticism and the Creative Writer." KYK-OVER-AL, v. 5, no. 15, Year-end 1952, pp. 19-22.

"Memorial to Roger Mais: A Green Blade in Triumph." KYK-OVER-AL, v. 6, no. 20, Mid-year 1955, pp. 164-165.

"Is There a West Indian Way of Life." KYK-OVER-AL, v. 6, no. 20, Mid-year 1955, pp. 200-201.

MOHR, EUGENE V.

"West Indian Fiction Is Alive and Well." CARIBBEAN REVIEW, v. 5, 5, no. 4, 1973, pp. 23-29.

MONTAGUE, JOHN

[Review of] IN A GREEN NIGHT, by Derek Walcott. SPECTATOR, v. 208, June 29, 1962, p. 864.

MOORE, GERALD

"East Indians and West, The Novels of V. S. Naipaul." BLACK ORPHEUS, no. 7, June 1960, pp. 11-15.

[Review of] MIGUEL STREET, by V. S. Naipaul. BLACK ORPHEUS, no. 9, June 1961, pp. 66-67.

"The Negro Poet and His Landscape." BLACK ORPHEUS, no. 22, August 1967, pp. 33-34.

"West Indian Poet" (Brathwaite, RIGHTS OF PASSAGE). TRANSITION, v. 7, no. 32, 1967, pp. 62-63.

[Reviews of] THE MIMIC MEN, by V. S. Naipaul; AN ABSENCE OF RUINS, by Orlando Patterson. BIM, v. 12, no. 46, January-June 1968, pp. 134-136.

"Confident Achievement" (Brathwaite, MASKS). JCL, no. 7, 1969, pp. 122-124.

[Review of] THE LATE EMANCIPATION OF JERRY STOVER, by Andrew Salkey. BIM, v. 12, no. 48, January-June 1969, pp. 268-269.

[Review of] TUMATUMARI, by Wilson Harris. BIM, v. 13, no. 51, July-December 1970, pp. 193-194.

[Review of] ISLANDS, by Edward Brathwaite. BIM, v. 13, no. 51,

Mordecai, Martin

    July-December 1970, pp. 186-189.

    "Use Men Language." BIM, v. 15, no. 57, March 1974, pp. 69-76.

MORDECAI, MARTIN

    Interview (Anthony McNeill). JAMAICA JOURNAL, v. 4, no. 4,
    December 1970, pp. 40-43.

MORGAN, EDWIN

    [Review of] THE ALONENESS OF MRS. CHATHAM, by Edgar Mittelholzer.
    NEW STATESMAN, v. 69, May 14, 1965, p. 772.

MORRIS, ALICE S.

    [Review of] SHADOWS MOVE AMONG THEM, by Edgar Mittelholzer.
    NYT, September 9, 1951, Section 7, p. 5.

MORRIS, MERVYN

    [Review of] LOVE LEAPS HERE, by John Figueroa. CARIBBEAN
    QUARTERLY, v. 9, nos. 1 and 2, 1963, pp. 91-95.

    "The Dungle Observed" (Patterson, THE CHILDREN OF SISYPHUS).
    PUBLIC OPINION, April 24, 1964, pp. 7, 13.

    [Review of] ON THIS MOUNTAIN, by A. L. Hendriks. BIM, v. 11,
    no. 43, July-December 1966, pp. 225-228.

    [Review of] THIS ISLAND NOW, by Peter Abrahams. PUBLIC OPINION,
    November 4, 1966, p. 3.

    [Review of] JAMAICA LABRISH, by Louise Bennett. PUBLIC
    OPINION, November 25, 1966, p. 5.

    "George Lamming, Author." PUBLIC OPINION, March 10, 1967, p. 7.

    [Review of] BROWN SUGAR, by J. B. Emtage. PUBLIC OPINION, May
    19, 1967, p. 5.

    [Review of] AN ABSENCE OF RUINS, by Orlando Patterson. PUBLIC
    OPINION, May 19, 1967, p. 5.

    "West Indian Literature: Some Cheap Anthologies." CARIBBEAN
    QUARTERLY, v. 13, no. 2, June 1967, pp. 36-39.

Index of Critics and Reviewers

Morris, Mervyn

"Niggers Everywhere" (Brathwaite, RIGHTS OF PASSAGE). NWQ,
   v. 3, no. 4, Cropover, 1967, pp. 61-65.

"On Reading Louise Bennett, Seriously." SUNDAY GLEANER, part 1,
   June 7, 1965, pp. 4, 23; part 2, June 14, p. 4; part 3, June
   21, p. 4; part 4, June 28, p. 4.
   Also appears in JAMAICA JOURNAL, v. 1, no. 1, December 1967,
   pp. 69-74.

"The Poet as Novelist. The Novels of George Lamming." THE
   ISLANDS IN BETWEEN (edited by Louis James). London: Oxford
   University Press, 1968, pp. 73-85.

"Walcott and the Audience for Poetry." CARIBBEAN QUARTERLY, v.
   14, nos. 1 and 2, March-June 1968, pp. 7-24.

[Review of] THE SUN'S EYE: WEST INDIAN WRITING FOR YOUNG
   READERS (edited by Anne Walmsley). CARIBBEAN QUARTERLY, v.
   15, no. 1, March 1969, pp. 57-59.

"New Poetry by Brathwaite and Walcott." SUNDAY GLEANER,
   November 30, 1969, p. 4.

"Tropical English Literature" (Moore, THE CHOSEN TONGUE).
   SUNDAY GLEANER, December 14, 1969, p. 4.

"This Broken Ground, Edward Brathwaite's Trilogy of Poems."
   NWQ, v. 5, no. 3, 1970, pp. 14-26.

[Review of] NEW BEACON REVIEW: COLLECTION ONE (edited by
   John La Rose). BIM, v. 13, no. 50, January-June 1970, pp.
   131-132.

[Review of] THE SUN SALUTES YOU, by C. Everard Palmer. SUNDAY
   GLEANER, May 3, 1970, p. 29.

"Pattern and Meaning in VOICES UNDER THE WINDOW" (Hearne).
   JAMAICA JOURNAL, v. 5, no. 1, March 1971, pp. 53-56.

"Some Views on CARRIBBEAN VOICES v. 2." CARIBBEAN QUARTERLY,
   v. 17, no. 1, March 1971, pp. 48-49.

"The All-Jamaica Library." JAMAICA JOURNAL, v. 6, no. 1, March
   1972, pp. 47-49.

"An Extreme Vision" (McNeill, HELLO UNGOD). SUNDAY GLEANER,
   January 28, 1973, p. 34.

255

Morsberger, Robert E.

"Below the Surface" (Brown, ON THE COAST). SUNDAY GLEANER,
    September 16, 1973, p. 31.

"Contending Values. The Prose Fiction of Claude McKay."
    JAMAICA JOURNAL, v. 9, nos. 2 and 3, 1975, pp. 36-42, 52.

MORSBERGER, ROBERT E.

[Review of] DREAM ON MONKEY MOUNTAIN AND OTHER PLAYS, by Derek
    Walcott. BOOKS ABROAD, v. 46, no. 1, Winter 1972, p. 172.

MOSS, JOHN G.

[Review of] ASCENT TO OMAI, by Wilson Harris. WLWE, no. 19,
    April 1971, pp. 84-85.

[Review of] FIREFLIES, by Shiva Naipaul. WLWE, v. 12, April
    1973, pp. 117-119.

"William Blake and Wilson Harris: The Objective Vision." JCL,
    v. 9, no. 3, April 1975, pp. 29-40.

MOYNAHAN, JULIAN

[Review of] THE GAMES WERE COMING, by Michael Anthony. LSO,
    November 17, 1963, p. 24.

MPHAHLELE, EZEKIEL

[Review of] HONORARY WHITE, by E. R. Braithwaite. NYT, July
    13, 1975, Section 7, p. 18.

MUIR, EDWIN

"Indirection" (Lamming, THE EMIGRANTS). LSO, September 19,
    1954, p. 13.

[Review of] THOSE WHO EAT THE CASCADURA, by Samuel Selvon.
    LISTENER, v. 87, January 27, 1972, p. 120.

MUNRO, IAN

"Writing and Publishing in the West Indies; An Interview with
    George Lamming" (with Reinhard Sander and Dean Beebe). WLWE,
    no. 19, April 1971, pp. 17-22.

"George Lamming's SEASON OF ADVENTURE. The Failure of the
    Creative Imagination." SBL, v. 4, no. 1, Spring 1973, pp. 6-13.

Narayana, Rao, K. S.

"The Manuscript of ASCENT TO OMAI" (Harris). NEW LETTERS, v.
40, no. 1, Fall 1973, pp. 37-48.

NAIM, C. M.

[Review of] AN AREA OF DARKNESS, by V. S. Naipaul. BOOKS
ABROAD, v. 40, no. 2, Spring 1966, p. 230.

NAIPAUL, SHIVA

"The Writer without a Society." COMMON WEALTH: PAPERS DELIVERED
AT THE CONFERENCE OF COMMONWEALTH LITERATURE, AARHUS UNI-
VERSITY. April 26-30, 1971 (edited by A. Rutherford).
Aarhus, Denmark: Aarhus University, 1971, pp. 114-123.

"Living in London." LONDON MAGAZINE, New Series, v. 13, no. 3,
August/September 1973, pp. 56-66.

NAIPAUL, V. S.

"Honesty Needed in West Indian Writing." SUNDAY GUARDIAN
(Trinidad), October 28, 1956, p. 29.

[Reviews of] TURN AGAIN TIGER, by Samuel Selvon; OF AGE AND
INNOCENCE, by George Lamming; THE WILD COAST, by Jan Carew.
NEW STATESMAN, v. 56, December 6, 1958, pp. 826-827.

"Critics and Criticism." BIM, v. 10, no. 38, January-June 1964,
pp. 74-77.

"Images" (COMMONWEALTH LITERATURE). NEW STATESMAN, v. 70,
September 24, 1965, p. 453.

"Without a Dog's Chance" (Rhys, AFTER LEAVING MR. MACKENZIE).
NYRB, v. 18, no. 9, 1972.

"V. S. Naipaul Tells How Writing Changes a Writer." TAPIA, v.
3, no. 48, December 2, 1973, p. 11.

NARASIMHAIAH, C. D.

"Somewhere Something Has Snapped, A Close Look at V. S.
Naipaul's AN AREA OF DARKNESS." LITERARY CRITERION, v. 6,
no. 4, Summer 1965, pp. 83-96.

NARAYANA, RAO, K. S.

Nettelford, Rex

[Review of] THE MIMIC MEN, by V. S. Naipaul. BOOKS ABROAD, v. 42, no. 1, Winter 1968, p. 167.

NETTELFORD, REX

"Caribbean Perspectives--The Creative Potential and the Quality of Life.' CARIBBEAN QUARTERLY, v. 17, nos. 3 and 4, 1971, pp. 114-127.

NEWBY, P. H.

[Reviews of] BLACK MIDAS, by Jan Carew; THE SUFFRAGE OF ELVIRA, by V. S. Naipaul; WAYS OF SUNLIGHT, by Samuel Selvon. LONDON MAGAZINE, v. 5, no. 11, November 1958, pp. 82-84.

NEWTON, DUFF

[Review of] THE AUTUMN EQUINOX, by John Hearne. JLW, v. 1, December 1959, p. 328.

NICHOLAS, HOLLIS

"Political Banditry" (Thomas, RULER IN HIROONA). NEW VOICES, v. 2, no. 4, June 1974, p. 51.

NICHOLSON, GEOFFREY

[Review of] THE WEATHER FAMILY, by Edgar Mittelholzer. SPECTATOR, v. 201, October 17, 1958, p. 527.

[Review of] OF AGE AND INNOCENCE, by George Lamming. SPECTATOR, v. 201, November 14, 1958, p. 658.

[Reviews of] TURN AGAIN TIGER, by Samuel Selvon; THE WILD COAST, by Jan Carew. SPECTATOR, v. 201, November 28, 1958, p. 787.

NIGHTINGALE, BENEDICT

"Too Late" (Salkey, THE LATE EMANCIPATION OF JERRY STOVER). THE TIMES (London). February 17, 1968, p. 20.

NIVEN, ALASTAIR

[Review of] FIREFLIES, by Shiva Naipaul. JCL, v. 8, no. 1, June 1973, pp. 131-133.

NOEL, JESSE A.

Olu Ashaolo, Albert

"Historicity and Homelessness in Naipaul" (THE LOSS OF EL DORADO). CARIBBEAN STUDIES, v. 11, no. 3, October 1971, pp. 83-87.

NOTT, KATHLEEN

[Review of] SHADES OF GRAY, by Garth St. Omer. LSO, December 15, 1968, p. 28.

NUNEZ PHILIP

[Review of] IN A FINE CASTLE, by Derek Walcott. MOKO, no. 73, October 29, 1971, pp. 12-13.

NYABONGO, VIRGINIA SIMMONS

[Review of] ON THE COAST, by Wayne Brown. BOOKS ABROAD, v. 48, no. 1, Winter 1974, p. 204.

OAKLEY, LEO

"Ideas of Patriotism and National Dignity in Some Jamaican Writings." JAMAICA JOURNAL, v. 4, no. 3, September 1970, pp. 16-21.
Also appears in Sunday Gleaner, part 1, March 28, 1971, pp. 31, 34; part 2, April 4, p. 27; part 3, April 11, p. 25.

ODUM

[Review of] RULER IN HIROONA, by G. C. Thomas. BAJAN, no. 243, February 1974, p. 23.

[Review of] CASUARINA ROW, by John Wickham. BAJAN, no. 256, March 1975, p. 29.

OGUNGBESON, KOLAWOLE

"The Political Novels of Peter Abrahams." PRESENCE AFRICAINE, no. 83, 1972, pp. 33-50.

"The Politics of THIS ISLAND NOW" (Abrahams), JCL, v. 8, no. 1, June 1973, pp. 33-41.

"The Political Novels of Peter Abrahams." PHYLON, v. 34, December 1973, pp. 419-432.

OLU ASHAOLO, ALBERT

Omerod, David

"Allegory in TI-JEAN AND HIS BROTHERS." WLWE, v. 16, April
1977, pp. 203-211.

ORMEROD, DAVID

"Theme and Image in V. S. Naipaul's A HOUSE FOR MR. BISWAS."
TSLL, v. 8, no. 4, Winter 1967, pp. 589-602.

"In a Derelict Land: The Novels of V. S. Naipaul." CONTEMPORARY
LITERATURE, v. 9, Winter 1968, pp. 74-90.

O'TOOLE, AL

"Life and Death of an Unequipped Virgin" (Mittelholzer, THE LIFE
AND DEATH OF SYLVIA). PUBLIC OPINION, November 13, 1954, p.
6.

OWEN, A. L.

[Review of] THE THIRD TEMPTATION, by Denis Williams. WLWE, no.
19, April 1971, pp. 93-94.

OWENS, J. V.

"Literature on the Rastafari" 1955-1974, A Review." SAVACOU,
no. 11/12, September 1975, pp. 86-105.

OWENS, R. J.

"Derek Walcott's Verse." SUNDAY GLEANER, February 14, 1960,
pp. 14-15.

"Back to the Office" (Mittelholzer, MORNING AT THE OFFICE).
SUNDAY GLEANER, September 3, 1961, p. 14.

"West Indian Poetry." CARIBBEAN QUARTERLY, v. 7, no. 3,
December 1961, pp. 120-127.

[Review of] A HOUSE FOR MR. BISWAS, by V. S. Naipaul. CARIBBEAN
QUARTERLY, v. 7, no. 4, April 1962, pp. 217-219.

PAGE, MALCOLM

"West Indian Writers." NOVEL, v. 3, no. 2, Winter 1970,
pp. 167-172.

PANTIN, RAOUL

Panton, George

"The Ultimate Transient" (Naipaul, V. S., THE OVERCROWDED
    BARRACOON). CARIBBEAN CONTACT, v. 1, no. 2, January 1973,
    pp. 4, 23.

"Portrait of an Artist; What Makes Naipaul Run" (interview with
    V. S. Naipaul). CARIBBEAN CONTACT, v. 1, no. 6, May 1973,
    p. 15, 18, 19.

"We Are Still Being Betrayed" (interview with Walcott).
    CARIBBEAN CONTACT, part 1, v. 1, no. 7, July 1973, pp. 14, 16;
    part 2, v. 1, no. 8, August 1973, pp. 14,16.

"Writings of Two Young Poets" (Lee, VOCATIONS; Worrel).
    CARIBBEAN CONTACT, v. 3, no. 3, June 1975, p. 3.

PANTON, GEORGE (pseudonym of Cedric George Lindo and Hugh Panton
    Morrison)

"West Indian Writing." SUNDAY GLEANER, September 22, 1957, p.
    9.

"Short Stories--West Indian and English--And Poems." SUNDAY
    GLEANER, March 9, 1958, p. 11.

"Too Rich for Hollywood" (Mittelholzer, KAYWANA BLOOD). SUNDAY
    GLEANER, March 30, 1958, p. 11.

"Vic Reid Makes Triumphant Return." SUNDAY GLEANER, April 6,
    1958, p. 11.

"Pork Knockers of British Guiana" (Carew, BLACK MIDAS). SUNDAY
    GLEANER, May 4, 1958, p. 11.

[Review of] MIGUEL STREET, by V. S. Naipaul. SUNDAY GLEANER,
    November 1, 1959, p. 14.

"Through the Poet's Eye" (Collymore, COLLECTED POEMS). SUNDAY
    GLEANER, January 3, 1960, p. 14.

"The Middle-Class Miasma" (Salkey, ESCAPE TO AN AUTUMN PAVE-
    MENT). SUNDAY GLEANER, August 21, 1960, p. 14.

"B. G. Conundrum" (Harris, PALACE OF THE PEACOCK). SUNDAY
    GLEANER, October 2, 1960, p. 14.

"Review of] GUIANA BOY, by Lauchmonen. SUNDAY GLEANER, December
    4, 1960, p. 18.

Panton, George

"Jamaica Writers of Today." SUNDAY GLEANER, December 11, 1960,
    p. 18.

"The Romance of Jamaican History" (Reid, SIXTY-FIVE). SUNDAY
    GLEANER, December 25, 1960, p. 14.

"Angry Young West Indian" (Lamming, PLEASURES OF EXILE). SUNDAY
    GLEANER, February 19, 1961, p. 14.

"Have We Really Solved the Race Problem" (Dawes, THE LAST
    ENCHANTMENT; Hercules, WHERE THE HUMMINGBIRD FLIES). SUNDAY
    GLEANER, March 19, 1961, p. 14.

"A Real History of Jamaica" (Roy, BLACK ALBINO). SUNDAY
    GLEANER, April 16, 1961, pp. 14, 20.

[Review of] ELTONSBRODY, by Edgar Mittelholzer. SUNDAY GLEANER,
    May 7, 1961, p. 14.

"Social Problems of Independence" (Lamming, SEASON OF ADVEN-
    TURE; Harris, THE FAR JOURNEY OF OUDIN). SUNDAY GLEANER,
    November 5, 1961, p. 14.

[Review of] LAND OF THE LIVING, by John Hearne. SUNDAY
    GLEANER, November 26, 1961, p. 14.

"W.I. Writing Comes of Age" (Naipaul, V. S., HOUSE FOR MR.
    BISWAS). SUNDAY GLEANER, December 3, 1961, p. 14.

[Review of] LAUGH WITH LOUISE, by Louise Bennett. SUNDAY
    GLEANER, December 10, 1961, p. 14.

"Our Caribbean Brothers" (BIM). SUNDAY GLEANER, February 11,
    1962, p. 14.

"New Author--Jamaican" (Fraser, WOUNDS IN THE FLESH). SUNDAY
    GLEANER, April 1, 1962, p. 14.

"Tension ... Tragedy" (Mittelholzer, THUNDER RETURNING). SUNDAY
    GLEANER, April 15, 1962, p. 14.

"The Magic of Words" (Walcott, IN A GREEN NIGHT). SUNDAY
    GLEANER, May 13, 1962, p. 14.

"Bedward--In New Guise" (Wynter, THE HILLS OF HEBRON). SUNDAY
    GLEANER, July 22, 1962, p. 14.

Index of Critics and Reviewers

Panton, George

"Slavery's Greatest Damage" (Naipaul, V. S., THE MIDDLE PASSAGE).
   SUNDAY GLEANER, September 9, 1962, p. 14.

"Mystical W.I. Writer" (Harris, THE WHOLE ARMOUR). SUNDAY
   GLEANER, November 4, 1962, p. 14.

[Review of] THE LAST BARBARIAN, by Jan Carew. SUNDAY GLEANER,
   November 25, 1962, p. 14.

"Sequel to 'With Love'" (Braithwaite, PAID SERVANT). SUNDAY
   GLEANER, January 20, 1963, p. 14.

"Modern Jamaican Poetry" (Lucie-Smith, A TROPICAL CHILDHOOD).
   SUNDAY GLEANER, February 3, 1963, p. 14.

"Sex in the Tropics" (Nicole, DARK NOON). SUNDAY GLEANER,
   February 17, 1963, p. 14.

"BIM Magazine a Must for Those Interested in West Indian
   Writing." SGM, April 7, 1963, p. 10.

"Two W.I. Writers" (Harris, THE SECRET LADDER; Mittelholzer,
   A SWARTHY BOY). SGM, May 26, 1973, p. 13.

[Review of] A KIND OF HOMECOMING, by E. R. Braithwaite. SGM,
   July 7, 1963, p. 9.

"The Absence of an Old Age Cure." SGM, August 25, 1963, p. 10.

"New Caribbean Voices" (Williams, OTHER LEOPARDS; Anthony, THE
   GAMES WERE COMING). SUNDAY GLEANER, December 15, 1963, p.
   14.

"West Indian Writing of Today." SUNDAY GLEANER, January 26,
   1964, p. 4.

"Tragedy in the West Indies" (St. Omer, SYROP). SUNDAY GLEANER,
   February 2, 1964, p. 4.

"Not for the Squeamish" (Patterson, CHILDREN OF SISYPHUS).
   SUNDAY GLEANER, March 29, 1964, p. 4.

"Vivid Story of South Africa's Troubles" (Abrahams, A NIGHT OF
   THEIR OWN). SUNDAY GLEANER, April 4, 1964, p. 4.

"Hurricanes in Jamaica" (Salkey, HURRICANE). SUNDAY GLEANER,
   May 31, 1964, p. 4.

Panton, George

"Drop Pan--And All That" (Bennett, GOD THE STONE BREAKER).
     SUNDAY GLEANER, August 2, 1964, p. 4.

"Search for Identity" (Dathorne, THE SCHOLAR-MAN; Nicole, BLOOD
     AMYOT). SUNDAY GLEANER, September 27, 1964, p. 4.

"More Seeking by West Indians" (Naipaul, V. S., AN AREA OF
     DARKNESS: Harris, HEARTLAND). SUNDAY GLEANER, October 4,
     1964, p. 4.

"Major Poet" (Walcott, SELECTED POEMS). SUNDAY GLEANER, October
     18, 1964, p. 4.

"Bacchanal and Cane" (Khan, THE OBEAH MAN; Clarke, SURVIVORS
     OF THE CROSSING). SUNDAY GLEANER, November 1, 1964, p. 4.

"A Jamaican Childhood" (Lucie-Smith, CONFESSIONS AND HISTORIES).
     SUNDAY GLEANER, November 15, 1964, p. 4.

"Race Prejudice in Moscow" (Carew, MOSCOW IS NOT MY MECCA).
     SUNDAY GLEANER, November 29, 1964, p. 4.

"Little Plays for Little Children (Brathwaite, FOUR PLAYS FOR
     PRIMARY SCHOOLS). SUNDAY GLEANER, December 13, 1964, p. 4.

"Short Stories--West Indian and Others" (STORIES FROM THE
     CARIBBEAN). SUNDAY GLEANER, July 11, 1965, p. 4.

"W.I. Novels--And a Lecture on Them" (Anthony, THE YEAR IN SAN
     FERNANDO; Selvon, THE HOUSING LARK). SUNDAY GLEANER, August
     8, 1965, p. 4.

[Review of] AMONGST THISTLES AND THORNS, by Austin Clarke.
     SUNDAY GLEANER, August 22, 1965, p. 4.

"W.I. from Within and Without" (Lovelace, WHILE GODS ARE
     FALLING). SUNDAY GLEANER, September 5, 1965, p. 4.

[Review of] EARTHQUAKE, by Andrew Salkey. SUNDAY GLEANER,
     October 31, 1965, p. 4.

"Black and White in England" (Brathwaite, CHOICE OF STRAWS).
     SUNDAY GLEANER, November 7, 1965, p. 4.

[Review of] THE AMYOT CRIME, by Christopher Nicole. SUNDAY
     GLEANER, January 9, 1966, p. 4.

Panton, George

[Review of] THE THREE NOVELS OF ROGER MAIS. SUNDAY GLEANER,
May 8, 1966, p. 4.

"Salute to Guyana" (NEW WORLD QUARTERLY, Independence Issue).
SUNDAY GLEANER, May 29, 1966, p. 4.

[Review of] WHITE BOY, by Christopher Nicole. SUNDAY GLEANER,
June 12, 1966, p. 4.

"Drought in Jamaica" (Salkey, DROUGHT). SUNDAY GLEANER, July 3,
1966, p. 4.

[Review of] BROWN SUGAR, by J. B. Emtage. SUNDAY GLEANER, July
24, 1966, p. 4.

[Review of] THE CLOUD WITH THE SILVER LINING, by C. Everard
Palmer. SUNDAY GLEANER, September 25, 1966, p. 4.

"Our Country--Past and Future" (Abrahams, THIS ISLAND NOW; Rhys,
WIDE SARGASSO SEA). SUNDAY GLEANER, October 23, 1966, p. 4.

[Review of] WILD CONQUEST, by Peter Abrahams. SUNDAY GLEANER,
November 6, 1966, p. 4.

"Happy Goes the Lucky" (Nicole, KING CREOLE). SUNDAY GLEANER,
December 11, 1966, p. 4.

"Literary Event" (Bennett, JAMAICA LABRISH). SUNDAY GLEANER,
December 18, 1966, p. 4.

[Review of] RIGHTS OF PASSAGE, by Edward Brathwaite. SUNDAY
GLEANER, March 12, 1967, p. 4.

[Review of] GREEN DAYS BY THE RIVER, by Michael Anthony.
SUNDAY GLEANER, March 26, 1967, p. 4.

"For Young Jamaicans" (Reid, THE YOUNG WARRIORS). SUNDAY
GLEANER, May 7, 1967, p. 4.

"Jamaican Successor to Albert Camus" (Patterson, AN ABSENCE
OF RUINS). SUNDAY GLEANER, June 18, 1967, p. 4.

"The W.I. Scene" (Naipaul, V. S., THE MIMIC MEN; Salkey, RIOT).
SUNDAY GLEANER, June 18, 1967, p. 4.

[Review of] THE MEETING POINT, by Austin Clarke. SUNDAY
GLEANER, July 2, 1967, p. 4.

Panton, George

[Review of] THE WAITING ROOM, by Wilson Harris. SUNDAY
GLEANER, July 9, 1967, p. 4.

[Review of] ODALE'S CHOICE, by Edward Brathwaite. SUNDAY
GLEANER, November 12, 1967, p. 4.

"West Indian Satirist" (Naipaul, V. S., A FLAG ON THE ISLAND).
SUNDAY GLEANER, December 3, 1967, p. 4.

[Review of] A ROOM ON THE HILL, by Garth St. Omer. SUNDAY
GLEANER, March 3, 19 , p. 4.

"Slice of Trinidadian Rural Life" (Lovelace, THE SCHOOLMASTER).
SUNDAY GLEANER, April 14, 1968, p. 4.

"Jamaican Country Life--For Children" (Palmer, BIG DOG BITTER-
ROOT). SUNDAY GLEANER, August 4, 1968, p. 4.

[Reviews of] THE SELF-LOVER, by Christopher Nicole; SONG FOR
MUMU, by Lindsay Barrett. SUNDAY GLEANER, August 18, 1968,
p. 4.

[Review of] TUMATUMARI, by Wilson Harris. SUNDAY GLEANER,
October 13, 1968, p. 4.

"Excellent Writer from Dominica" (Rhys, TIGERS ARE BETTER-
LOOKING). SUNDAY GLEANER, November 17, 1968, p. 4.

[Review of] SHADES OF GREY, by Garth St. Omer. SUNDAY GLEANER,
January 19, 1969, p. 4.

[Review of] THE HUMMING-BIRD TREE, by Ian McDonald. SUNDAY
GLEANER, February 23, 1969, p. 4.

"Exciting Jamaican Thriller" (FEVERGRASS). SUNDAY GLEANER, April
20, 1969, p. 4.

"Love and the West Indian Migrant in London" (Salkey, ADVENTURES
OF CATTULLUS KELLY). SUNDAY GLEANER, May 18, 1969, p. 4.

"A Man and His Country" (St. Omer, NOR ANY COUNTRY). SUNDAY
GLEANER, June 8, 1969, p. 4.

"The Naked Truth" (Hutchinson, MAN FROM THE PEOPLE). SUNDAY
GLEANER, August 17, 1969, p. 4.

"Jamaica Becomes Involved with the Mafia and H-Bombs." SUNDAY

Index of Critics and Reviewers

Panton, George

GLEANER, April 26, 1970, p. 27.

[Review of] CRICK-CRACK MONKEY, by Merle Hodge. SUNDAY
GLEANER, May 24, 1970, p. 31.

[Review of] THE DEVIATOR, by Christopher Nicole. SUNDAY
GLEANER, July 26, 1970, p. 32.

[Review of] THE LEOPARD, by V. S. Reid. SUNDAY GLEANER,
February 27, 1971, p. 47.

"Another Self-Published West Indian Book" (Mahabir, THE CUTLASS
IS NOT FOR KILLING). SUNDAY GLEANER, March 7, 1971, p. 27.

"Poetry from Barbados" (Collymore, SELECTED POEMS). SUNDAY
GLEANER, April 4, 1971, p. 27

[Reviews of] THE HUMMINGBIRD PEOPLE, by C. Everard Palmer; THE
AGE OF THE RAINMAKERS, by Wilson Harris. SUNDAY GLEANER,
June 6, 1971, p. 29.

[Review of] OGOG, by Vera Bell. SUNDAY GLEANER, July 18, 1971,
p. 28.

"Life in a Vanishing Rural Jamaica" (Palmer, THE WOOING OF BEPPO
TATE). SUNDAY GLEANER, March 26, 1972, p. 37.

[Review of] TROPIC DEATH, by Eric Walrond. SUNDAY GLEANER,
July 2, 1972, p. 15.

[Review of] BLACK BAM AND THE MASQUERADERS, by Garth St. Omer.
SUNDAY GLEANER, August 20, 1972, p. 33.

"Entertaining Story of a Young Jamaican Boy" (D'Costa, SPRAT
MORRISON). SUNDAY GLEANER, December 10, 1972, p. 47.

[Review of] VOICES UNDER THE WINDOW, by John Hearne. SUNDAY
GLEANER, March 18, 1973, p. 35.

"Acclaim of a Poet" (Scott, UNCLE TIME). SUNDAY GLEANER,
January 6, 1974, p. 23.

"The Businessman Poet" (A. L. Hendriks). SUNDAY GLEANER, June
16, 1974, p. 21.

"The Arch Conservative Who Was Also a Pioneer (De Lisser).
SUNDAY GLEANER, July 14, 1974, p. 31

Paterson, James Hamilton

"Prolific Writer, Historian, Poet" (Sherlock). SUNDAY GLEANER, July 28, 1974, p. 27.

"Our Well-Known Well-Loved Poet" (Louise Bennett), SUNDAY GLEANER, August 11, 1974, p. 23.

"NEW DAY Man--A Trail Blazer" (Reid). SUNDAY GLEANER, September 29, 1974, p. 27.

"Dennis Scott--Prize-Winning Poet." SUNDAY GLEANER, October 13, 1974, p. 27.

"C. Everard Palmer, The Boy's Ideal Story-teller." SUNDAY GLEANER, November 3, 1974, p. 25.

"Edward Kamau Brathwaite, Poet, Historian and Playright." SUNDAY GLEANER, December 15, 1974, p. 27.

"John Hearne, Accurate Portrayer of the Middle Class." SUNDAY GLEANER, March 9, 1975, pp. 23-24.

"Roger Mais--Portrayer of an Inner Vision." SUNDAY GLEANER, March 16, 1975, p. 23.

"Peter Abrahams--Our Distinguished Immigrant." SUNDAY GLEANER, March 23, 1975, p. 23.

"Andrew Salkey: Versatile and Prolific." SUNDAY GLEANER, April 20, 1975, p. 23; April 27, 1975, p. 23.

"The Tennis-Playing Poet" (Morris). SUNDAY GLEANER, May 25, 1975, pp. 23, 31.

"V. S. Naipaul, The Most Famous West Indian Writer." SUNDAY GLEANER, June 22, 1975, pp. 23, 31.

"A True Caribbean Man" (Hopkinson). SUNDAY GLEANER, March 7, 1976, p. 8.

"The Poet Who Became a Biographer" (Brown). SUNDAY GLEANER, March 21, 1976, p. 8.

PATERSON, JAMES HAMILTON

"Hot Little Offshore Island" (Naipaul, V. S., THE LOSS OF EL DORADO), SUNDAY GUARDIAN (Trinidad), November 16, 1969, p. 5.

PAUL, DAVID

[Review of] SHADOWS MOVE AMONG THEM, by Edgar Mittelholzer. LISTENER, v. 45, 1951, p. 633.

[Review of] IN THE CASTLE OF MY SKIN, by George Lamming. LSO, March 15, 1953, p. 9.

[Review of] THE HILLS WERE JOYFUL TOGETHER, by Roger Mais. LSO, April 26, 1953, p. 9.

[Review of] THE LIFE AND DEATH OF SYLVIA, by Edgar Mittelholzer. LSO, May 10, 1953, p. 11.

"A Tragic Homecoming" (Abrahams, RETURN TO GOLI). LSO, June 21, 1953, p. 10.

"Two West Indians" (Lamming, OF AGE AND INNOCENCE; Selvon, TURN AGAIN TIGER). PUBLIC OPINION, January 3, 1959, p. 7.

PEARSE, ANDREW

"West Indian Themes." CARIBBEAN QUARTERLY, v. 2, no. 2, September 1950, pp. 12-23.

PENNANT, DOROTHY

"Anthony McNeill, He Writes Poetry of the Mindscape." SUNDAY GLEANER, January 12, 1975, p. 22.

PHELPS, GILBERT

[Review of] A SWARTHY BOY, by Edgar Mittelholzer. NEW STATESMAN, v. 65, March 1, 1963, p. 309.

PHELPS, KAREN

"Back to Childhood" (Anthony, SANDRA STREET AND OTHER STORIES). SUNDAY GUARDIAN (Trinidad), April 8, 1973, p. 7.

POLLINS, HAROLD

[Review of] THE PLEASURES OF EXILE, by George Lamming. RACE, v. 2, no. 1, November 1960, pp. 78-79.

POORE, CHARLES

Pope-Hennessey, James

"A Native's Return to the Caribbean World" (Naipaul, V. S., THE
MIDDLE PASSAGE). NYT, September 7, 1963, p. 17.

POPE-HENNESSEY, JAMES

"Return to the Caribbean" (Naipaul, V. S., THE MIDDLE PASSAGE).
LSO, July 29, 1962, p. 18.

PORTER, PETER

[Review of] ANOTHER LIFE, by Derek Walcott. LSO, August 5, 1973,
p. 28.

POTTER, DENNIS

"A Long Way from Home" (Naipaul, V. S., IN A FREE STATE). THE
TIMES (London), October 4, 1971, p. 15.

"The Writer and His Myth" (Naipaul, V. S., THE OVERCROWDED
BARRACOON). THE TIMES (London), December 4, 1972, p. 6.

POVEY, J. F.

[Review of] THE SCHOLAR-MAN, by O. R. Dathorne. BOOKS ABROAD,
v. 39, no. 4, Autumn 1965, p. 483.

POYNTING, JEREMY

"A Small Indian Voice in Guyana" (Sadeek), JCL, v. 6, no. 2,
December 1971, pp. 152-154.

POYSER, JOHN

[Review of] JONAH SIMPSON, by Andrew Salkey. THE TIMES (London),
September 30, 1969, p. 20.

PRESCOTT, ORVILLE

[Review of] SHADOWS MOVE AMONG THEM, by Edgar Mittelholzer.
NYT, September 14, 1951, p. 23.

[Review of] CHILDREN OF KAYWANA, by Edgar Mittelholzer. August
25, 1952, p. 23.

[Review of] IN THE CASTLE OF MY SKIN, by George Lamming. NYT,
October 27, 1953, p. 25.

Pyne-Timothy, Helen

[Review of] TELL FREEDOM, by Peter Abrahams. NYT, August 9, 1954, p. 15.

[Review of] A WREATH FOR UDOMO, by Peter Abrahams. NYT, May 25, 1956, p. 21.

"The Land of His Ancestors" (Naipaul, V. S., AN AREA OF DARKNESS). NYT, April 16, 1965, p. 17.

PRIEBE, RICHARD

"The Search for Community in the Novels of Claude McKay." SBL, v. 3, no. 2, Summer 1972, pp. 22-30.

PRITCHETT, V. S.

"A Barbados Village" (Lamming, IN THE CASTLE OF MY SKIN). NEW STATESMAN, v. 45, April 18, 1953.

[Review of] THE FACES OF LOVE, by John Hearne. NEW STATESMAN, v. 56, October 4, 1958, pp. 468-469.

[Review of] A WREATH FOR UDOMO, by Peter Abrahams. NEW STATESMAN, v. 56, October 4, 1958, pp. 468-469.

"The Heritage and Decline of Prospero" (Lamming, THE PLEASURES OF EXILE). NEW STATESMAN, v. 60, July 30, 1960.

"Climacteric" (Naipaul, V. S., MR. STONE AND THE KNIGHTS COMPANION). NEW STATESMAN, v. 65, May 31, 1963, pp. 831-832.

"Back to India" (Naipaul, V. S., AN AREA OF DARKNESS). NEW STATESMAN, v. 68, September 11, 1964, pp. 361-362.

"Crack-Up" (Naipaul, V. S., THE MIMIC MEN, A FLAG ON THE ISLAND). NYRB, v. 10, no. 7, 1968.

PRYCE-JONES, DAVID

[Review of] THE MIMIC MEN, by V. S. Naipaul. LONDON MAGAZINE, New Series, v. 7, no. 2, May 1967, pp. 82-84.

PYNE-TIMOTHY, HELEN

"Earl Lovelace: His View of Trinidad Society in WHILE GODS ARE FALLING and THE SCHOOLMASTER." NWQ, v. 4, no. 4, Cropover 1968, pp. 60-65.

Questel, Victor

QUESTEL, VICTOR

"Caliban's Circle of Death" (Lamming, WATER WITH BERRIES).
TAPIA, v. 2, no. 11, December 18, 1972, p. 15.

"Drama of the Streets" (Malik, BLACK-UP). TAPIA, v. 2, no. 13,
December 31, 1972, pp. 8-10.

"The Horns of Derek's Dilemma." TAPIA, v. 3, no. 12, March 25,
1973, pp. 4-5.

"Look and Listen" (Anthony, SANDRA STREET). TAPIA, v. 3, no. 32
32, August 12, 1973, p. 11.

"Poets Go Forth" (Brown, ON THE COAST). TAPIA, v. 3, no. 33,
August 19, 1973, pp. 6-7, 9.

"Literary Jackals on the Make" (Naipaul, S., THE CHIP-CHIP
GATHERERS). TAPIA, v. 3, no. 51, December 16, 1973, pp. 6-7.

"Walcott's Major Triumph" (ANOTHER LIFE). TAPIA, part 1, v. 3,
no. 51, December 23, 1973, pp. 6-7; part 2, v. 3, no. 52,
December 30, 1973, pp. 6-7.

[Review of] NO PAIN LIKE THIS BODY, by Harold Ladoo. KAIRI, no.
1, 1974.

"Towards Anancy Becoming One Total Person" (Salkey, ANANCY'S
SCORE). KAIRI, no. 2, 1974.

"Stripping of the Masks" (Gonzalez, THE LOVE SONG OF BOYSIE B
AND OTHER POEMS). TAPIA, v. 4, no. 10, March 1974, pp. 6-8.

"Suffering, Madness, Or an Early Death" (Ladoo, NO PAIN LIKE
THIS BODY). TAPIA, v. 4, no. 17, April 1974, pp. 5, 11.

"The Price of Selfhood" (Gonzalez, THE LOVE SONG OF BOYSIE B AND
OTHER POEMS). NEW VOICES, v. 2, no. 4, June 1974, pp. 11-14.

"DREAM ON MONKEY MOUNTAIN in Perspective." TAPIA, part 1, v. 4,
no. 35, September 1974, pp. 2-3; part 2, v. 4, no. 36, pp.
6-7; part 3, v. 4, no. 37, pp. 6-7; part 4, no. 37, pp. 6-7;
part 4, v. 4, no. 39, pp. 5, 8.

"Creole Poet in a Classical Castle" (Morris, THE POND). TAPIA,
v. 5, no. 11, March 1975, pp. 6-7.

Ramchand, Kenneth

"Their Tragic Destiny." TAPIA, v. 6, no. 20, May 1976, pp. 4, 11.

"UNCLE TIME: A Pointer to the Shape of Things to Come." TAPIA, v. 6, no. 26, June 27, 1976, pp. 6-7, 8.

"New Writing in the Caribbean" (Pantin, JOURNEY; LEE, VOCATION). TAPIA, v. 6, no. 36, September 5, 1976, pp. 5-7.

"Views of W.I. Writer Earl Lovelace" (interview). CARIBBEAN CONTACT, v. 5, no. 3, June 1977, pp. 15, 16.

[Review of] THE MAD WOMAN OF PAPINE, THE FRIEND, by Slade Hopkinson. CARIBBEAN CONTACT, v. 5, no. 4, July 1977, p. 3.

QUIGLY, ISABEL

[Review of] AN ISLAND IS A WORLD, by Samuel Selvon. SPECTATOR, v. 194, April 15, 1955, p. 480.

[Review of] VOICES UNDER THE WINDOW, by John Hearne. SPECTATOR, v. 195, September 16, 1955, p. 374.

RABASSA, GREGORY

[Review of] THE LOSS OF ELDORADO, by V. S. Naipaul. NYT, May 24, 1970, Section 7, p. 7.

RAGUNATH, N. S.

[Review of] FIREFLIES, by Shiva Naipaul. LITERARY CRITERION, v. 11, no. 2, Summer 1974, pp. 88-90.

RAMCHAND, KENNETH

"Decolonization in West Indian Literature." TRANSITION, v. 5, no. 22, 1965, pp. 48-49.

"The Myth of TO SIR WITH LOVE" (Braithwaite). VOICES, v. 1, no. 5, December 1965, pp. 13-20.

"BLACK LIGHTNING." PUBLIC OPINION, Roger Mais Supplement, June 10, 1966, p. 5.

"The Dislocated Image" (Harris), NWQ, Guyana Independence Issue, 1966, pp. 107-110.

Ramchand, Kenneth

"Dialect in West Indian Fiction." CARIBBEAN QUARTERLY, v. 14,
nos. 1 and 2, March-June 1968, pp. 27-42.

"The World of A HOUSE FOR MR. BISWAS." CARIBBEAN QUARTERLY, v.
15, no. 1, March 1969; pp. 60-72.

"The Artist in the Balm-yard: SEASON OF ADVENTURE." NWQ, v. 5,
nos. 1 and 2, Dead Season/Croptime, 1969, pp. 13-21.

"Obeah and the Supernatural in West Indian Literature." JAMAICA
JOURNAL, v. 3, no. 2, June 1969, pp. 52-54.

"The Art of Memory: Michael Anthony's THE YEAR IN SAN FERNANDO"
(with Paul Edwards). JCL, no. 7, July 1969, pp. 59-72.

"Terrified Consciousness." JCL, no. 7, July 1969, pp. 18-19.
Also appears as Chapter 13 in THE WEST INDIAN NOVEL AND ITS
BACKGROUND. London: Faber and Faber, 1970.

"Literature and Society: The Case of Roger Mais." CARIBBEAN
QUARTERLY, v. 15, no. 4, December 1969, pp. 23-30.

"Aborigines, Their Role in West Indian Literature." JAMAICA
JOURNAL, v. 3, no. 4, December 1969, pp. 51-54.
Also appears as "The Significance of the Aborigine in Wilson
Harris' Fiction." LITERARY HALF-YEARLY, v. 11, no. 2, 1970,
pp. 7-16.

"Claude McKay and BANANA BOTTOM." SOUTHERN REVIEW, v. 4, no. 1,
1970, pp. 53-66.

"Wilson Harris, Caribbean Genius." SUNDAY GLEANER, January 11,
1970, pp. 4, 18.

"The Negro and the English Language in the West Indies."
SAVACOU, v. 1, no. 1, June 1970, pp. 33-44.

"Concern for Criticism." CARIBBEAN QUARTERLY, v. 16, no. 2,
June 1970, pp. 51-60.
Also appears in LITERARY HALF-YEARLY, v. 11, no. 2, 1970,
pp. 151-161.

"In-Between" (THE ISLANDS IN BETWEEN), JCL, no. 9, July 1970,
pp. 126-127.

"The Writer Who Ran Away: Eric Walrond and TROPIC DEATH."
SAVACOU, no. 2, September 1970, pp. 67-75.

RAMRAJ, VICTOR

"History and the Novel: A Literary Critic's Approach." SAVACOU,
v. 1, nor. 5, June 1971, pp. 103-113.

"Before the People Became Popular...." CARIBBEAN QUARTERLY, v.
18, no. 4, 1972, pp. 70-73.

"Readings of 'Laventille'" (Walcott, THE CASTAWAY). TAPIA, v.
5, no. 50, December 1975, pp. 6-7.

"The Pounding in His Dark: Edward Brathwaite's Other Poetry"
(OTHER EXILES). TAPIA, v. 7, no. 1, January 2, 1977,
pp. 6-8.

"The All-Embracing Christlike Vision: Tone and Attitude in
THE MIMIC MEN." COMMON WEALTH: PAPERS DELIVERED AT THE
CONFERENCE OF COMMONWEALTH LITERATURE, AARHUS UNIVERSITY,
APRIL 26-30, 1971. Aarhus, Denmark: Aarhus University,
1971, pp. 125-134.

RAMSARAN, J. A.

"The Social Groundwork of Politics in Some West Indian Novels."
NEGRO DIGEST, v. 18, no. 10, 1969, pp. 71-77.

"The 'Twice-Born' Artist's Silent Revolution." BLACK WORLD,
v. 20, no. 7, 1971, pp. 58-67.

RAMSINGH, ASHOOK

"A Question of Creative Writing vs. Paul Theroux and V. S.
Naipaul's Autobiographers, Ganesh Ramsumair and Ralph Singh."
CORLIT, part 1, v. 1, no. 2, April 1974, pp. 22, 42-45, 49,
54; part 2, v. 1, no. 3, July 1974, pp. 49-50.

RANDALL, DUDLEY

[Review of] SELECTED POEMS, by Derek Walcott. NEGRO DIGEST, v.
14, no. 11, 1965, pp. 52-86.

RAPHAEL, FREDERICK

"The Latter Spring of Mr. Stone." SUNDAY GUARDIAN (Trinidad),
June 9, 1963, p. 15.

RAVEN, SIMON

Rawlins, Randolph

    [Review of] MR. STONE AND THE KNIGHTS COMPANION, by V. S.
       Naipaul. LSO, May 26, 1963, p. 21.

RAWLINS, RANDOLPH

    "Migrants with Manuscripts, Social Background of the West
       Indian Novel." BLACK ORPHEUS, no. 4, October 1958, pp. 46-
       50.

RAYMOND, JOHN

    [Review of] SHADOWS MOVE AMONG THEM, by Edgar Mittelholzer. NEW
       STATESMAN, v. 41, May 19, 1951, pp. 573-574.

REED, HENRY

    "Passage to India" (Naipaul, V. S., AN AREA OF DARKNESS).
       SPECTATOR, v. 213, October 2, 1964, p. 452.

REES, DAVID

    [Review of] A SWARTHY BOY, by Edgar Mittelholzer. SPECTATOR,
       v. 210, March 29, 1963.

REES, GORONWY

    [Review of] THE WILD COAST, by Jan Carew; OF AGE AND INNOCENCE,
       by George Lamming. LISTENER, v. 60, December 18, 1958, p. 1046.

REID, STANLEY

    "A Moving Interpretation of Local Tradition" (TI-JEAN AND HIS
       BROTHERS). LINK, v. 2, no. 2/3, p. 13.

REINDERS, ROBERT

    "A Black Briton Comes 'Home'; Claude McKay in England, 1920"
       (with Wayne Cooper). RACE, v. 9, no. 1, July 1967, pp. 67-
       81.
       Also appears in NEW BEACON REVIEWS: COLLECTION ONE (edited
       by John La Rose). London: New Beacon Books, 1968, pp. 3-
       21.

REINHARDT, JOHN E.

    [Review of] MINE BOY, by Peter Abrahams. PHYLON, v. 16, 1955,
       pp. 476-477.

RHODE, ERIC

[Review of] AN ABSENCE OF RUINS, by Orlando Patterson. NEW
STATESMAN, v. 73, April 7, 1967, pp. 477-478.

RICHARDSON, E. C.

"Abrahams New Novel Is a Must" (WREATH FOR UDOMO). SUNDAY
GUARDIAN (Trinidad), December 7, 1958, p. 22.

RICHARDSON, MAURICE

[Review of] AN ISLAND IS A WORLD, by Samuel Selvon. NEW
STATESMAN, v. 49, April 23, 1955, p. 586.

[Reviews of] A WREATH FOR UDOMO, by Peter Abrahams; STRANGER AT
THE GATE, by John Hearne. NEW STATESMAN, v. 51, May 12,
1956, pp. 543-544.

[Review of] THE LONELY LONDONERS, by Samuel Selvon. NEW
STATESMAN, v. 52, December 29, 1956, p. 846.

[Review of] MIGUEL STREET, by V. S. Naipaul. NEW STATESMAN, v.
57, May 2, 1959, p. 618.

[Review of] A QUALITY OF VIOLENCE, by Andrew Salkey. NEW
STATESMAN, v. 58, October 10, 1959, p. 487.

RICKARDS, COLIN

"Boom Time for West Indian Authors." SUNDAY GLEANER, March 5,
5, 1961, p. 14.

"New Novelist Chooses Mythical W.I. Island" (Ferguson, THE
VILLAGE OF LOVE: Mittelholzer, THUNDER RETURNING). SUNDAY
GUARDIAN (Trinidad), April 23, 1961, p. 4.

"Carew's Latest Not His Best" (THE LAST BARBARIAN). SUNDAY
GLEANER, August 6, 1961, p. 14.

"H. G. de Lisser Rides Again." SUNDAY GLEANER, September 17,
1961, p. 14.

"Mittelholzer on the Attack" (THE PILING OF CLOUDS). SUNDAY
GUARDIAN (Trinidad), December 17, 1961, p. 22.

"Bumper Year for West Indian Books." SUNDAY GLEANER, January

Ricks, Christopher

7, 1962, p. 14.

"New Jamaican Author Has Hint of Naipaul" (Fraser, WOUNDS IN
    THE FLESH). SUNDAY GUARDIAN (Trinidad), April 8, 1962, p.
    17.

"Brilliant First Novel" (Patterson, CHILDREN OF SISYPHUS).
    SUNDAY GLEANER, April 5, 1964, p. 4.

"Now Salkey Tries Children's Fiction (HURRICANE). SUNDAY
    GLEANER, July 5, 1964, p. 4.

"A Tribute to Edgar Mittelholzer." SUNDAY GLEANER, May 16,
    1965, pp. 4, 8.

"A Tribute to Edgar Mittelholzer." BIM, v. 11, no. 42, January-
    June 1966, pp. 98-105.

"Jan Carew to Return Home." SUNDAY GLEANER, June 19, 1966, p.
    4.

"A Most Original Talent" (Mais). SUNDAY GLEANER, March 26,
    1967, p. 4.

"Christopher Nicole, Mystery Man among W.I. Writers." SUNDAY
    GLEANER, March 16, 1969, pp. 4, 11.

"Caribbean Bookshelf" (Salkey, ADVENTURES OF CATULLUS KELLY;
    St. Omer, SHADES OF GRAY; Nicole, DEVIATOR, ELIMINATOR;
    Harris, PALACE OF THE PEACOCK). SUNDAY GLEANER, May 18,
    1969, p. 4.

RICKS, CHRISTOPHER

[Review of] GOOD MORNING MIDNIGHT, by Jean Rhys. NYRB, v. 15,
    no. 2, 1970.

RISDEN, WINNIFRED

[Review of] MASKS, by Edward Brathwaite. CARIBBEAN QUARTERLY,
    v. 14, nos. 1 and 2, March-June 1968, pp. 145-147.

ROACH, ERIC

"Shy, Young and Unknown" (Lovelace, WHILE GODS ARE FALLING).
    SUNDAY GUARDIAN (Trinidad), July 26, 1964, p. 6.

Index of Critics and Reviewers

Rodman, Selden

"MASKS--A Homecoming with a Taste of Aloes." SUNDAY GUARDIAN (Trinidad), October 12, 1968, p. 6.

"This Musical Fuses Both Traditions of Folk Legend" (TI-JEAN AND HIS BROTHERS). SUNDAY GUARDIAN (Trinidad), June 28, 1970, p. 11.

"Minty Alley Revisited." SUNDAY GUARDIAN (Trinidad), April 29, 1973, p. 6.

"Politics on a Tiny Island" (Thomas, RULER IN HIROONA). SUNDAY GUARDIAN (Trinidad), May 13, 1973, p. 6.

[Review of] HOUSE OF BLUE LIGHTENING, by Wilfred Cartey. SUNDAY GUARDIAN (Trinidad), September 16, 1973, p. 15.

ROBERTS, W. ADOLPHE

"The Art of Roger Mais." PUBLIC OPINION, July 14, 1951, p. 5.

"Caribbean Literature: The Transplanters and Imitators." WIR, v. 4, no. 31, February 7, 1953, p. 28.

"Caribbean Literature: The British Possessions." WIR, v. 4, no. 42, April 25, 1953, pp. 16-17.

"That Jamaica May Remember--Tom Redcam Founder of Our Literature." SUNDAY GLEANER, March 1, 1959, p. 8.

"Book Publishing in Jamaica." SUNDAY GLEANER, July 24, 1960, pp. 14, 23.

RODMAN, SELDEN

"A Search for a Place in the Sun (Abrahams, MINE BOY). NYT, June 12, 1955, Section 7, p. 5.

"Fugitives from the Sun" (Lamming, THE EMIGRANTS). NYT, July 24, 1955, Section 7, p. 16.

"Time of Decisions" (Selvon, TURN AGAIN TIGER). NYT, May 3, 1959, Section 7, p. 28.

"Catfish Row, Trinidad" (Naipaul, V. S., MIGUEL STREET). NYT, May 15, 1960, Section 7, p. 43.

[Review of] THE GULF, by Derek Walcott. NYT, October 11, 1970,

Rodman, Selden

    Section 7, p. 24.

    [Review of] DREAM ON MONKEY MOUNTAIN, by Derek Walcott. RRI,
    v. 1, no. 2, Winter 1972, pp. 158-160.

ROHLEHR, F. GORDON

    "Predestination, Frustration and Symbolic Darkness in Naipaul's
    A HOUSE FOR MR. BISWAS." CARIBBEAN QUARTERLY, v. 10, no. 1,
    1964, pp. 3-11.

    "The Ironic Approach, The Novels of V. S. Naipaul." THE ISLANDS
    IN BETWEEN (edited by Louis James). LONDON: Oxford Univer-
    sity Press, 1968, pp. 121-139.

    "Social Context of Sparrow's Calypsoes." TRINIDAD GUARDIAN, pa
    part 1, February 21, 1968, p. 10; part 2, February 22, p. 10;
    part 3, February 23, p. 10; part 4, February 24, p. 6; part
    5, February 25, p. 10; part 6, February 26, p. 6; part 7,
    February 27, p. 6.

    "CAM Comment, Gordon Rohlehr's 'Sparrow and the Language of
    Calypso.'" CARIBBEAN QUARTERLY, v. 14, nos. 1 and 2, March-
    June 1968, pp. 91-96.

    "Character and Rebellion in A HOUSE FOR MR. BISWAS." NWQ, v. 4,
    no. 4, Cropover 1968, pp. 66-72.

    "Calypso and Morality." MOKO, no. 6, January 1969, p. 5.

    [Review of] RIGHTS OF PASSAGE, MASKS, by Edward Brathwaite.
    MOKO, no. 12, April 9, 1969, p. 2.

    "Small Island Blues, A Short Review of the Novels of Garth
    St. Omer." VOICES, v. 2, no. 1, September-December 1969, p.
    22-28.

    "The Historian as Poet" (Brathwaite, ISLANDS). LITERARY HALF-
    YEARLY, v. 11, no. 2, 1970, pp. 171-178.

    "Sparrow and the Language of Calypso." SAVACOU, no. 2,
    September 1970, pp. 87-99.

    "Calypso and Politics." MOKO, no. 73, October 29, 1970, pp. 7-
    8, 14-18.

Rohlehr, F. Gordon

"History as Absurdity: Columbus to Castro." TAPIA, part 1,
    no. 11, November 1970, pp. 4-7; part 2, no. 12, December,
    pp. 5-6, 8, 16.
    Also appears in MOKO, part 1, no. 49, December 4, 1970,
    pp. 6-7; part 2, no. 50, December 11, pp. 6-7, 10; part 3,
    no. 51, December 25, pp. 7, 18.
    And in IS MASSA DAY DEAD (edited by Orde Coombs). New York:
    Doubleday, 1974, pp. 69-108.

[Review of] ISLANDS, by Edward Brathwaite. CARIBBEAN QUARTERLY,
    v. 16, no. 4, December 1970, pp. 29-35.

"Islands" (Brathwaite, ISLANDS, MASKS, RIGHTS OF PASSAGE).
    CARIBBEAN STUDIES, v. 10, no. 4, June 1971, pp. 173-202.

"West Indian Poetry, Some Problems of Assessment." TAPIA, no.
    20, August 29, 1971, pp. 11-14.
    Also appears in BIM, part 1, v. 14, no. 54, January-June
    1972, pp. 80-88; part 2, no. 55, July-December 1972, pp. 134-
    144.
    And as "Some Problems of Assessment: A Look at New
    Expressions in the Arts of the Contemporary Caribbean."
    CARIBBEAN QUARTERLY, v. 17, nos. 3 and 4, September-December
    1971, pp. 92-113.

"Afterthoughts." TAPIA, no. 23, December 26, 1971, pp. 8, 13.
    Also appears in BIM, v. 14, no. 56, January-June 1973, pp.
    227-232.

"Forty Years of Calypso." TAPIA, part 1, v. 2, no. 1,
    September 3, 1972, pp. 1-4; part 2, v. 2, no. 2, September
    17, pp. 4-5; part 3, v. 2, no. 3, October 8, pp. 6, 7.

"The Folk in Caribbean Literature." TAPIA, part 1, v. 2, no.
    11, December 17, 1972, pp. 7-8, 13-15; part 2, v. 2, no. 12,
    December 24, 1972, pp. 8, 9, 15.

"The Creative Writer and West Indian Society." KAIE, no. 11,
    August 1973, pp. 48-77.
    Also appears in TAPIA, part 1, v. 4, no. 31, August 1974,
    pp. 5-9; part 2, no. 33, August, pp. 6-7; part 3, v. 4, no.
    33, August, pp. 4-6; part 4, v. 4, no. 35, August, pp. 4-5,
    7.

"Blues for Eric Roach." TAPIA, v. 4, no. 17, April 1974, p. 2.

"A Carrion Time." TAPIA, v. 4, no. 24, June 1974, pp. 5-8, 11;

Ross, Alan

BIM, v. 15, no. 58, June 1975, pp. 92-109.

"In Search of Innocence; An Introduction to Ian McDonald's THE HUMMING-BIRD TREE." TAPIA, part 1, v. 4, no. 49, December 1974, pp. 5, 8; part 2, v. 4, no. 50, December, pp. 6-7; part 3, v. 4, no. 51, December, pp. 4, 9.

"Naipaul Joins the Chorus" (Rohlehr Interviewed by Lennox Grant). TAPIA, v. 5, no. 27, July 1975, pp. 6-7; v. 5, no. 28, July 1975, pp. 6-7.

ROSS, ALAN

"A Broad View of Cricket" (James, BEYOND A BOUNDARY). LSO, June 2, 1963, p. 19.

[Review of] MR. STONE AND THE KNIGHTS COMPANION, by V. S. Naipaul. LONDON MAGAZINE, New Series, v. 3, no. 5, August 1963, p. 88.

[Review of] THE CASTAWAY, by Derek Walcott. LONDON MAGAZINE, New Series, v. 5, no. 10, January 1966, pp. 88-89.

[Review of] WIDE SARGASSO SEA, by Jean Rhys. LONDON MAGAZINE, New Series, v. 6, no. 8, November 1966, pp. 99-101.

[Review of] THE FACES OF LOVE, by John Hearne. PUBLIC OPINION, May 4, 1957, p. 7.

"A Shaggy Mystic" (Naipaul, V. S., THE MYSTIC MASSEUR). PUBLIC OPINION, August 24, 1957, p. 7.

ROWE-EVANS, ADRIAN

"Other Freedoms" (Williams, OTHER LEOPARDS). TRANSITION, v. 3, no. 10, 1963, pp. 57-58.

"V. S. Naipaul" (interview). TRANSITION, v. 8, no. 40, 1971, pp. 56-62.

RUSSELL, D. W.

"The Dislocating Act of Memory: An Analysis of Wilson Harris' TUMATUMARI." WLWE, v. 13, November 1974, pp. 237-249.

ST. HILL, CHALMERS

Salkey, Andrew

[Review of] A TALE OF THREE PLACES, by Edgar Mittelholzer. BIM, v. 7, no. 25, July–December 1957, pp. 58–59.

[Review of] THE WEATHER FAMILY, by Edgar Mittelholzer. BIM, v. 8, no. 29, June–December 1959, p. 68.

[Review of] A TINKLING IN THE TWILIGHT, by Edgar Mittelholzer. BIM, v. 8, no. 30, January–June 1960, pp. 136–137.

[Review of] WATER WITH BERRIES, by George Lamming. BIM, v. 14, no. 55, July–December 1972, pp. 189–191.

[Review of] THOSE WHO EAT THE CASCADURA, by Samuel Selvon. BIM, v. 14, no. 55, July–December 1972, p. 188.

ST. JOHN, BRUCE

[Review of] THE EMIGRANTS, by George Lamming. BIM, v. 6, no. 22, June 1955, pp. 130–132.

ST. JOHN, ORFORD

"On Jamaican Poetry" (A TREASURY OF JAMAICAN POETRY). WIR, v. 2, no. 15, August 12, 1950, p. 17.

"A New West Indian Play" (Walcott, THE WINE OF THE COUNTRY). WIR, v. 1, no. 9, September 1956, p. 32.

"Perspective on FOCUS." WIR, v. 1, no. 11/12, December 1956, p. 83.

[Review of] IONE, by Derek Walcott. WIR, v. 2, no. 3, March 1957, pp. 47–48.

[Review of] TI-JEAN AND HIS BROTHERS, by Derek Walcott. WIR, v. 4, no. 4, April 1959, p. 57.

SALKEY, ANDREW

[Review of] THE PLAINS OF CARONI, by Samuel Selvon. MOKO, no. 45, November 6, 1970, p. 3.

"The Sieve of Tradition" (Harris, ASCENT TO OMAI), MOKO, no. 46, November 13, 1970, p. 9.

[Review of] THE HUMMING BIRD PEOPLE, by C. Everard Palmer. MOKO, no. 65, July 24, 1971, p. 9.

Salveson, Christopher

[Review of] ONE LOVE, by Audvil King. MOKO, no. 70, October 1, 1971, p. 11.

SALVESON, CHRISTOPHER

[Review of] THE SCHOLAR MAN, by O. R. Dathorne. NEW STATESMAN, v. 68, September 11, 1964, p. 366.

SAMPSON, ANTHONY

"An African Story" (Abrahams, A WREATH FOR UDOMO). LSO, May 6, 1956, p. 17.

SANDER, REINHARD

"Writing and Publishing in the West Indies; An Interview with George Lamming" (with Dean Beebe and Ian Munro). WLWE, no. 19, April 1971, pp. 17-22.

"A New West Indian Literary Magazine" (THE NEW VOICES), WLWE, v. 13, April 1974, pp. 123-125.

"The Homesickness of Michael Anthony; The Predicament of a West Indian Exile." LITERARY HALF-YEARLY, v. 16, no. 1, January 1975, pp. 95-124.

SANDFORD, ANTONIA

[Review of] THE LAST BARBARIAN, by Jan Carew. JLW, v. 4, no. 78, March 1961, p. 354.

SCANNELL, VERNON

[Review of] THE WOUNDED AND THE WORRIED, by Edgar Mittelholzer. LISTENER, v. 68, July 12, 1962, p. 73.

SCOTT, ANDREW P.

[Review of] THE PLAINS OF CARONI, by Samuel Selvon. WLWE, no. 19, April 1971, pp. 92-93.

SCOTT, DENNIS

"The Poems of Exile" (Brathwaite, RIGHTS OF PASSAGE). PUBLIC OPINION, March 31, 1967, p. 7.

"Walcott On Walcott" (interview). CARIBBEAN QUARTERLY, v. 14, nos. 1 and 2, March–June 1968, pp. 77–82.

"Bennett on Bennett" (interview). CARIBBEAN QUARTERLY, v. 14, nos. 1 and 2, March–June 1968, pp. 97–101.

"Novels of Wilson Harris Reveal Guyanese History." SUNDAY GLEANER, February 22, 1970, pp. 4, 10.

SCOTT, J. D.

[Review of] THE LIFE AND DEATH OF SYLVIA, by Edgar Mittelholzer. NEW STATESMAN, v. 45, May 30, 1953, p. 651.

SCOTT, PAUL

[Reviews of] GUIANA BOY, by Lauchmonen; SEASON OF ADVENTURE, by George Lamming. NEW STATESMAN, v. 60, October 29, 1960, pp. 664–666.

SEALY, CLIFFORD

"Talking About the Thirties" (interview with Alfred Mendes). VOICES, v. 1, no. 5, December 1965, pp. 3–7.

SEALY, KARL

[Review of] THE FAR JOURNEY OF OUDIN, by Wilson Harris. BIM, v. 9, no. 35, July–December 1962, pp. 223,224.

[Review of] THE HILLS OF HEBRON, by Sylvia Wynter. BIM, v. 9, no. 36, January–June 1963, p. 292.

[Review of] THE WOUNDED AND THE WORRIED, by Edgar Mittelholzer. BIM, v. 9, no. 36, January–June 1963, p. 293.

SELVON, SAMUEL

"A Note on Dialect." COMMON WEALTH: PAPERS DELIVERED AT THE CONFERENCE OF COMMONWEALTH LITERATURE, AARHUS UNIVERSITY, April 26–30, 1971. Aarhus, Denmark: Aarhus University, 1971, p. 124.

SEN, DILIP KIMAR

"An Indian Looks at W.I. Poetry; A Footnote to Caribbean Poetry Written in English." SUNDAY GLEANER, January 12, 1964, p. 4.

Seymour, Arthur J.

SEYMOUR, ARTHUR J.

[Review of] THE CHALLENGE OF OUR TIME, by J. E. C. McFarlane.
KYK-OVER-AL, v. 1, no. 1, December 1945, p. 41.

"Guianese Poetry." KYK-OVER-AL, v. 1, no. 2, June 1946, pp.
13-15.

"The Poetry of Egbert Martin (Leo)." KYK-OVER-AL, v. 1, no. 3,
December 1946, pp. 17-20.

"Sunlight and West Indian Poetry." KYK-OVER-AL, v. 1, no. 4,
June 1947, pp. 17-19.

"The Poetry of Walter Mac A. Lawrence." KYK-OVER-AL, v. 2,
no. 6, June 1948, pp. 35-38.

"The Poet of Guiana, Walter Mac A. Lawrence." KYK-OVER-AL, v.
2, no. 9, December 1949, pp. 19-20.

"Open Letter to West Indian Writers." KYK-OVER-AL, v. 2, no. 9,
December 1949, pp. 23-27.

"The Literary Adventure of the West Indies." KYK-OVER-AL, v. 2,
no. 10, April 1950, 40 pp.

"Nature Poetry in the West Indies." KYK-OVER-AL, v. 3, no. 11,
October 1950, pp. 39-47.

[Review of] FETISH, by Wilson Harris. KYK-OVER-AL, v. 3, no.
13, Year end 1951, p. 248.

"Preface to THE KYK-OVER-AL ANTHOLOGY OF WEST INDIAN POETRY."
KYK-OVER-AL, v. 4, no. 14, Mid-year 1952, 5 pp.

"West Indian Pen Portrait. Edgar Mittelholzer." KYK-OVER-AL,
v. 5, no. 15, Year end 1952, pp. 15-17.

[Review of] A BRIGHTER SUN, by Samuel Selvon. KYK-OVER-AL, v.
5, no. 15, Year end 1952, pp. 82-83.

"Memorial to Roger Mais: A Green Blade in Triumph." KYK-OVER-
AL, v. 6, no. 20, Mid-year 1955, pp. 147-170.

[Review of] ETERNITY TO SEASON, by Wilson Harris. BIM, v. 6,
no. 22, June 1955, pp. 133-135.

"An Introduction to the Novels of Edgar Mittelholzer." KYK-
OVER-AL, v. 8, no. 24, December 1958, pp. 60-74.

Index of Critics and Reviewers

Seymour, Arthur J.

"A Letter to John Hearne." KYK-OVER-AL, v. 8, no. 24, December 1958, pp. 78-81.

[Reviews of] THE LEOPARD, by V. S. Reid; THE MYSTIC MASSEUR, by V. S. Naipaul; BLACK MIDAS, by Jan Carew. KYK-OVER-AL, v. 8, no. 24, December 1958, pp. 83-87.

[Review of] OF AGE AND INNOCENCE, by George Lamming. KYK-OVER-AL, v. 9, no. 26, December 1959, pp. 52-55.

[Review of] LATTICED ECHOES, by Edgar Mittelholzer. KYK-OVER-AL, v. 9, no. 27, December 1960, pp. 134-137.

[Review of] PALACE OF THE PEACOCK, by Wilson Harris. KYK-OVER-AL, v. 9, no. 27, December 1960, pp. 142-144.

"From Ralegh to Carew, The Books of Guiana." KYK-OVER-AL, v. 9, no. 27, December 1960, pp. 74-82.

"The Novels of Wilson Harris." BIM, v. 10, no. 38, January-June 1964, pp. 139-141.

[Review of] A SWARTHY BOY, by Edgar Mittelholzer. BIM, v. 10, no. 38, January-June 1964, pp. 143-144.

"Edgar Mittelholzer the Preacher." KAIE, no. 1, October 1965, pp. 31-33.

"The Novel in the British Caribbean." BIM, part 1, v. 11, no. 42, January-June 1966, pp. 83-85; part 2, v. 11, no. 43, July-December 1966, pp. 176-180; part 3, v. 11, no. 44, January-June 1967, pp. 238-242; part 4, v. 12, no. 46, January-June 1968, pp. 75-80.

"The Novel in Guyana." KAIE, no. 4, July 1967, pp. 59-63.

"Poetry in Guyana" (with Ian McDonald). KAIE, no. 4, July 1967, pp. 64-66.

EDGAR MITTELHOLZER, THE MAN AND HIS WORK, THE 1967 EDGAR MITTELHOLZER LECTURES. Georgetown (Guyana), 1968, 53 pp.

"Introduction to Guyanese Writing." KAIE, no. 7, December 1971 (entire issue).

"A Note on Literature and Caribbean Society." KAIE, no. 8, December 1971, pp. 12-18.

Seymour-Smith, Martin

SEYMOUR-SMITH, MARTIN

> [Review of] THE MIMIC MEN, by V. S. Naipaul. SPECTATOR, v. 218,
> May 5, 1967, p. 528.

> [Review of] THE POMEGRANATE, by W. Adolphe Roberts. PUBLIC
> OPINION, March 22, 1941, pp. 8-9.

SHERLOCK, PHILLIP

> [Review of] NEW DAY, by V. S. Reid. CARIBBEAN QUARTERLY, v. 1,
> no. 1, 1949, pp. 31-32.

SHERRATT, ANN

> [Review of] THE HILLS OF HEBRON, by Sylvia Wynter. JLW, v. 7,
> October 1962, p. 324.

SHOWERS, PAUL

> [Review of] PAID SERVANT, by Edward Brathwaite. NYT, May 19,
> 1968, Section 7, p. 40.

SIMMONS, CLIFFORD

> "Negro Writers Enrich the English Language." SUNDAY GLEANER,
> May 1, 1966, p. 4.

SIMMONS, HAROLD

> "A West Indian Poet Fulfills His Promise" (Walcott, 25 POEMS).
> SUNDAY GLEANER, February 27, 1949, p. 7.

> [Review of] A TALE OF THREE PLACES, by Edgar Mittelholzer.
> PUBLIC OPINION, May 4, 1957, p. 7.

SINGH, K. NATWAR

> "Unhappy Pilgrim" (Naipaul, V. S., AN AREA OF DARKNESS). NYT,
> July 11, 1965, Section 7, p. 35.

SKELTON, ROBIN

> [Review of] A TROPICAL CHILDHOOD, by Edward Lucie-Smith.
> CRITICAL QUARTERLY, v. 3, Winter 1961, pp. 376-377.

SMITH, DONALD B.

Sparer, Joyce

[Review of] CARIBBEAN VOICES, v. 1 (edited by John Figueroa).
   RRI, v. 1, no. 1, Spring 1971, pp. 64-68.

SMITH, G. H.

   "Writing Is Drifting to the Doldrums." SUNDAY GLEANER,
      September 16, 1956, p. 8.

SMITH, ROBERT A.

   "Claude McKay: An Essay in Criticism." PHYLON, v. 9, 1948,
      pp. 270-273.

SMITH, STEVIE

   [Review of] THE HARROWING OF HUBERTUS, by Edgar Mittelholzer.
      LSO, February 21, 1954, p. 9.

   [Review of] MY BONES AND MY FLUTE, by Edgar Mittelholzer. LSO,
      October 23, 1955, p. 12.

SOLOMON, DENIS

   "Ape and Essence" (Walcott, DREAM ON MONKEY MOUNTAIN). TAPIA,
      no. 7, April 19, 1970, p. 6.

   "A House of Pitch Pine in a Land of Arrowroot" (Thomas, RULER
      IN HIROONA). TAPIA, v. 2, no. 8, November 26, 1972, p. 10.

   "Beginning of the End?" (Walcott, FRANKLIN, A TALE OF THE
      ISLANDS). TAPIA, v. 3, no. 16, April 22, 1973, pp. 2-3.

   "Divided by Class, United by Bacchanal" (Walcott, THE
      CHARLATAN). TAPIA, v. 3, no. 27, July 8, 1973, p. 6.

   "Liberation and Libido" (Walcott, THE JOKER OF SEVILLE). TAPIA,
      v. 4, no. 49, December 1974, p. 3.

SPARER, JOYCE; See Also ADLER, JOYCE SPARER

   "The Art of Wilson Harris." NEW BEACON REVIEWS, COLLECTION ONE
      (edited by John La Rose). London: New Beacon Books, 1968,
      pp. 22-30.

   [Review of] THE WAITING ROOM, by Wilson Harris. CARIBBEAN
      QUARTERLY, v. 14, nos. 1 and 2, March-June 1968, pp. 148-151.

Stade, George

"Attitudes towards 'Race' in Guyanese Literature." CARIBBEAN
STUDIES, v. 8, no. 2, July 1968, pp. 23-63.

STADE, GEORGE

[Review of] TIGERS ARE BETTER-LOOKING, by Jean Rhys. NYT,
October 20, 1974, Section 7, p. 5.

STAR, LEONIE

[Review of] NOR ANY COUNTRY, by Garth St. Omer. WLWE, no. 19,
April 1971, p. 92.

STERN, JAMES

"Days of Agony, Minutes of Fun" (Abrahams, TELL FREEDOM). NYT,
August 8, 1954, Section 7, p. 1.

[Review of] THE EMIGRANTS, by George Lamming. LONDON MAGAZINE,
v. 2, no. 5, May 1955, pp. 109-110.

"If Exiles Return" (Abrahams, A WREATH FOR UDOMO). NYT, May 20,
1956, Section 7, p. 5.

SUBRAMI

[Review of] GREEN DAYS BY THE RIVER, by Peter Abrahams. WLWE,
no. 19, April 1971, p. 84.

SUCH, PETER

[Review of] YESTERDAYS, by Harold Ladoo. TAMARACK REVIEW, no.
63, 1974, pp. 78-80

SULLIVAN, MARY

[Review of] TIGERS ARE BETTER-LOOKING, by Jean Rhys. LISTENER,
v. 79, April 25, 1968, p. 549.

SWAN, MICHAEL

[Review of] IN THE CASTLE OF MY SKIN, by George Lamming. LONDON
MAGAZINE, v. 1, no. 6, July 1954, pp. 92-98.

SWANN, TONY

"DRUMS AND COLOURS--Guts at Least" (Walcott). PUBLIC OPINION,

May 10, 1958, p. 7.

SWANZY, HENRY

[Review of] FLOTSAM, by Frank Collymore. BIM, v. 3, no. 9,
1948, pp. 77-79.

[Review of] HENRI CHRISTOPHE, by Derek Walcott. BIM, v. 5, no.
17, 1952, pp. 75-76.

"Caribbean Voices; Prolegomena to a West Indian Culture."
CARIBBEAN QUARTERLY, v. 1, no. 2, September 1949, pp. 21-28.
Reprinted in v. 8, no. 2, 1962, pp. 121-128.

SWIRE, MYRTHE

"E. R. Braithwaite, Controversial as Ever, But with Subdued
Anger." SUNDAY GLEANER, June 12, 1966, p. 4.

SYLVESTER, HARRY

"Changing Landscape in Barbados" (Lamming, IN THE CASTLE OF MY
SKIN). NYT, Section 7, November 1, 1953, p. 4.

SYMONS, JULIAN

[Review of] RIGHTS OF PASSAGE, by Edward Brathwaite. NEW
STATESMAN, v. 73, April 7, 1967, p. 479.

"Triumphant Portrait" (Naipaul, Shiva, THE CHIP-CHIP GATHERERS).
SUNDAY GUARDIAN (Trinidad), April 22, 1973, p. 7.

TAUBMAN, ROBERT

[Review of] THE MAD MAC MULLOCHS, THE PILING OF CLOUDS, by
Edgar Mittelholzer. NEW STATESMAN, v. 62, no. 1600, November
10, 1961, p. 714.

[Review of] THE WOUNDED AND THE WORRIED, by Edgar Mittelholzer.
NEW STATESMAN, v. 64, July 13, 1962, p. 53.

TAYLOR, CHET

[Review of] CARIBBEAN VOICES, by John Figueroa. CARIBBEAN
STUDIES, v. 11, no. 4, January 1972, pp. 115-120.

TEWARIE, BHOENDRADATT

Theroux, Paul

   "Review of KAIRI '76." TAPIA, v. 6, no. 51, December 19, 1976, p. 5.

THEROUX, PAUL

   V. S. NAIPAUL, AN INTRODUCTION TO HIS WORK. London: Heinemann, 1972.

   "An Intelligence from the Third World" (Naipaul, V. S., GUERRILLAS). NYT, November 16, 1975, Section 7, pp. 1-2.

THIEME, JOHN

   "V. S. Naipaul's Third World: A Not So Free State." JCL, v. 10, no. 1, August 1975, pp. 10-22.

THOMPSON, IVY

   "Who's Who in the West Indian Novel." CARIBBEAN CONTACT, v. 1, no. 5, April 1973, pp. 4, 18.

THORPE, MARJORIE

   "THE MIMIC MEN, A Study of Isolation." NWQ, v. 4, no. 4, Cropover 1968, pp. 55-59.

THWAITE, ANTHONY

   [Review of] A TROPICAL CHILDHOOD, by Edward Lucie-Smith. SPECTATOR, v. 207, November 3, 1961, p. 634.

   [Review of] NATIVES OF MY PERSON, by George Lamming. LSO, October 8, 1972, p. 39.

   [Review of] BLACK MARSDEN, by Wilson Harris. LSO, November 26, 1972, p. 35.

TINDALL, GILLIAN

   [Review of] TUMATUMARI, by Wilson Harris. NEW STATESMAN, v. 76, September 6, 1968, p. 292.

TODD, NEILA

   [Review of] KAIRI, NOW. NEW VOICES, v. 3, no. 5, 1975, pp. 35-38, 39.

Wade, Michael

TOMALIN, CLAIRE

[Review of] NOR ANY COUNTRY, by Garth St. Omer. LSO, May 4, 1969, p. 30.

[Review of] ANOTHER LIFE, by Derek Walcott. NEW STATESMAN, v. 88, December 20, 1974, p. 908.

TOYNBEE, PHILIP

"Two Languages" (Selvon, WAYS OF SUNLIGHT). LSO, January 19, 1958, p. 16.
Reprinted in PUBLIC OPINION, February 8, 1958, p. 7.

TYRWHITT, JANICE

"Clarke Closes In." TAMARACK REVIEW, no. 38, Winter 1966, pp. 89-91.

VANSITTART, PETER

[Review of] A SWARTHY BOY, by Edgar Mittelholzer. LSO, February 24, 1963, p. 22.

[Review of] THE HOUSING LARK, by Samuel Selvon. SPECTATOR, v. 214, March 26, 1965, p. 410.

[Review of] GREEN DAYS BY THE RIVER, by Michael Anthony. SPECTATOR, v. 218, February 3, 1967, p. 141.

VERNON, KAY

[Review of] THE CHILDREN OF SISYPHUS, by Orlando Patterson. FLAMBEAU, no. 1, June 1965, p. 30.

WADE, C. ALAN

"The Novelist as Historian" (Naipaul, V. S., THE LOSS OF EL DORADO). LITERARY HALF-YEARLY, v. 11, no. 2, 1970, pp. 179-184.

WADE, HENLING

"Derek Walcott to Us." SUNDAY GLEANER, November 1, 1970, p. 29.

WADE, MICHAEL

"The Novels of Peter Abrahams." CRITIQUE, v. 11, no. 1, 1968, pp. 82-95.

PETER ABRAHAMS. London: Evans, 1972.

WAGNER, GEOFREY

"Edgar Mittelholzer: Symptoms and Shadows." BIM, v. 9, no. 33, July-December 1961, pp. 29-34.

WAIN, JOHN

[Review of] OF TREES AND THE SEA, by Edgar Mittelholzer. LSO, May 6, 1956, p. 9.

"Outlander among London Savages" (Braithwaite, TO SIR WITH LOVE). NYT, May 1, 1960, Section 7, p. 6.

"Mother India" (Naipaul, V. S., AN AREA OF DARKNESS). LSO, September 13, 1964, p. 24.

[Review of] THE MIMIC MEN, by V. S. Naipaul. NYRB, v. 9, no. 7, 1967, pp. 33-35.

"Characters in the Sun" (Naipaul, V. S., A FLAG ON THE ISLAND). NYT, April 7, 1968, Section 7, p. 4.

WALCOTT, DEREK

"Society and the Artist." PUBLIC OPINION, May 4, 1957, p. 7.

"The Poetry of George Campbell." PUBLIC OPINION, July 20, 1957, p. 7.

"The Poetry of M. G. Smith." PUBLIC OPINION, July 27, 1957, p. 7.

"Some Jamaican Poets." PUBLIC OPINION, part 1, August 3, 1957, p. 7; part 2, August 10, p. 7.

"Neo-Realism Parallel Noted in W.I. Novels." SUNDAY GUARDIAN (Trinidad), April 24, 1960, p. 7.

"Barbados--A Culture All Its Own." SUNDAY GUARDIAN (Trinidad), June 26, 1960, p. 23.

"Need for a Little Theater in Port-Of-Spain." SUNDAY GUARDIAN (Trinidad), July 10, 1960, p. 22.

"Local Art Headed in Confident Direction." SUNDAY GUARDIAN (Trinidad), July 31, 1960, p. 6.

Index of Critics and Reviewers

Walcott, Derek

"Let's Have the Best in Creative Writing." SUNDAY GUARDIAN
(Trinidad), August 7, 1960, p. 6.

"At Last! New Hope for Exiled Artists." SUNDAY GUARDIAN
(Trinidad), August 21, 1960, p. 4.

"Author's Exile Bewilders" (Lamming, THE PLEASURES OF EXILE).
SUNDAY GUARDIAN (Trinidad), September 4, 1960, p. 4.

"New Novel by Dawes Sticks to Formula" (THE LAST ENCHANTMENT).
SUNDAY GUARDIAN (Trinidad), September 11, 1960, p. 5.

"Jamaica Government Moves to Aid Artists" (with Fitzroy Fraser).
SUNDAY GUARDIAN (Trinidad), September 18, 1960, p. 7.

[Review of] GUIANA BOY, by Lauchmonen. SUNDAY GUARDIAN
(Trinidad), October 2, 1960, p. 5.

"A Work of Power and Imagination" (Harris, THE PALACE OF THE
PEACOCK). SUNDAY GUARDIAN (Trinidad), October 16, 1960, p.
5.

"Reflections on the November Exhibition." SUNDAY GUARDIAN
(Trinidad), November 13, 1960, p. 7.

"Give Us More Stories" (Salkey, ed., WEST INDIAN STORIES).
SUNDAY GUARDIAN (Trinidad), November 27, 1960, p. 5.

"Council Exhibition Recalls Great Names in Ballet." SUNDAY
GUARDIAN (Trinidad), January 15, 1961, p. 7.

"Novel with an Awkward Sincerity" (Fergusson, THE VILLAGE OF
LOVE). SUNDAY GUARDIAN (Trinidad), March 26, 1961, p. 11.

"Old FOCUS Back--This Time with New Blood." SUNDAY GUARDIAN
(Trinidad), April 2, 1961, p. 4.

"Really Good W.I. Novel Needed Now" (Carew, THE LAST BARBARIAN).
SUNDAY GUARDIAN (Trinidad), April 30, 1961, p. 7.

"Novelist Hearne Possesses Neat Disciplined Style." SUNDAY
GUARDIAN (Trinidad), September 3, 1961, p. 7.

"Third Trinidadian Novelist Makes His Bow" (Khan, THE JUMBIE
BIRD). SUNDAY GUARDIAN (Trinidad), October 22, 1961, p. 5.

"A Story of the B. G. Bush" (Nicole, SHADOWS IN THE JUNGLE).

Walcott, Derek

SUNDAY GUARDIAN (Trinidad), October 29, 1961, p. 4.

[Review of] ZOHARA, by Geoffrey Drayton. SUNDAY GUARDIAN
(Trinidad), November 12, 1961, p. 26.

"Love and Anguish on a Tropic Island" (Hearne, LAND OF THE
LIVING). SUNDAY GUARDIAN (Trinidad), December 24, 1961, p.
7.

"Magazine Should Cost More" (BIM, no. 34), SUNDAY GUARDIAN
(Trinidad), February 4, 1962, p. 19.

"Calypsonian! Danger Lurks in Tin Pan Alley." SUNDAY GUARDIAN
(Trinidad), February 25, 1962, p. 23.

"Bringing Their Lessons Nearer Home." SUNDAY GUARDIAN
(Trinidad), March 25, 1962, p. 7.

"Jamaican Lucky Jim Nurses a Grudge" (Fraser, WOUNDS IN THE
FLESH). SUNDAY GUARDIAN (Trinidad), July 15, 1962, p. 9.

"History and Picong ..." (Naipaul, V. S., THE MIDDLE PASSAGE).
SUNDAY GUARDIAN (Trinidad), September 30, 1962, p. 9.

"Lazy at Times But Hones" (Figueroa, LOVE LEAPS HERE). SUNDAY
GUARDIAN (Trinidad), January 27, 1963, p. 5.

"Brasher BIM Can Win More Friends." SUNDAY GUARDIAN (Trinidad),
April 28, 1963, p. 4.

"The Action Is Panicky" (Selvon, I HEAR THUNDER). SUNDAY
GUARDIAN (Trinidad), May 5, 1963, p. 4.

"His Is the Pivotal One About Race" (Williams, OTHER LEOPARDS).
SUNDAY GUARDIAN (Trinidad), December 1, 1963, p. 23.

"Spiritual Purpose Lacking." SUNDAY GUARDIAN (Trinidad),
January 5, 1964, p. 3.

"A Dilemma Faces West Indian Artists." SUNDAY GUARDIAN
(Trinidad), January 12, 1964, p. 3.

"A New Jamaican Novelist" (Patterson, CHILDREN OF SISYPHUS).
SUNDAY GUARDIAN (Trinidad), May 17, 1964, p. 15.

"Too Much of the Wrong Subject" (Carter, POEMS OF RESISTANCE).
SUNDAY GUARDIAN (Trinidad), June 14, 1964, p. 6.

Walcott, Derek

"Vintage Mittelholzer" (A MORNING AT THE OFFICE). SUNDAY
GUARDIAN (Trinidad), June 21, 1964, p. 15.

"Mr. Naipaul's Passage to India" (AN AREA OF DARKNESS). SUNDAY
GUARDIAN (Trinidad), September 20, 1964, p. 4.

"Dialect and Dialectic" (Carew, MOSCOW IS NOT MY MECCA). SUNDAY
GUARDIAN (Trinidad), November 22, 1964, p. 18.

"The Theatre of Abuse." SUNDAY GUARDIAN (Trinidad), January 3,
1965, p. 4.

"Just the Way It Was" (Anthony, THE YEAR IN SAN FERNANDO).
SUNDAY GUARDIAN (Trinidad), March 14, 1965, p. 8.

"Return to Jamaica." TGM, part 1, April 4, 1965, pp. 6-7; part
2, April 11, 1965, pp. 6, 7-8.

[Review of] STORIES FROM THE CARIBBEAN (edited by Andrew Salkey).
TGM, May 9, 1965, pp. 2-9.

"Analyzing Wilson Harris." TGM, May 30, 1965, pp. 8, 14.

"Selvon Has Returned to the Old Form" (THE HOUSING LARK).
SUNDAY GUARDIAN (Trinidad), June 27, 1965, p. 7.

"Nobody Knows Their Names" (DISAPPOINTED GUESTS). SUNDAY
GUARDIAN (Trinidad), July 4, 1965, p. 7.

"Rice Is Bitter" (Lauchmonen, OLD THOM'S HARVEST). SUNDAY
GUARDIAN (Trinidad), July 11, 1965, p. 8.

"In Praise of Peasantry; The Poetry of E. M. Roach." SUNDAY
GUARDIAN (Trinidad), July 18, 1965, p. 9.

"Sentimental Journeys ..." (BIM, no. 41). SUNDAY GUARDIAN
(Trinidad), August 15, 1965, p. 7.

"Crisis of Conscience: Ban Ban Caliban Is the Cry." SUNDAY
GUARDIAN (Trinidad), August 22, 1965, p. 11.

"Leaving School." LONDON MAGAZINE, New Series, v. 5, no. 6,
September 1965, pp. 4-14.

"A Bajan Boyhood" (Clarke, AMONGST THISTLES AND THORNS).
SUNDAY GUARDIAN (Trinidad), September 5, 1965, p. 8.

Walcott, Derek

"Writing for Children" (Salkey, HURRICANE). TGM, part 1,
   January 23, 1966, p. 2; part 2, February 6, pp. 28-29; part
   3, February 13, p. 3.

"Voices" (VOICES, no. 5). TGM, February 20, 1966.

"The Explorer Is in Danger of Disappearing" (Harris, THE EYE OF
   THE SCARECROW). SUNDAY GUARDIAN (Trinidad), February 27,
   1966, p. 8.

"Tracking Mr. Wilson Harris." SUNDAY GUARDIAN (Trinidad), April
   24, 1966.

"West Indian Art Today." TGM, May 8, 1966, pp. 8-9.

"Tribute to a Master" (Harold Simmons). SUNDAY GUARDIAN
   (Trinidad), May 15, 1966, p. 9.

"Art in Guyana: Beware of Love Vines" (NEW WORLD, Guyana
   Independence Issue). SUNDAY GUARDIAN (Trinidad), May 29,
   1966, p. 9.

"Anthologies" (Dathorne, CARIBBEAN NARRATIVE). SUNDAY GUARDIAN
   (Trinidad), July 3, 1966, p. 6.

"Is Bad Verse Forgivable at a Certain Stage in Our Evolution?"
   (Figueroa, ed., CARIBBEAN VOICES, I). SUNDAY GUARDIAN
   (Trinidad), September 11, 1966, p. 5.

"BIM, Putting on the Style" (BIM, no. 43). SUNDAY GUARDIAN
   (Trinidad), September 18, 1966, p. 7.

"Beyond the Backyard." SUNDAY GUARDIAN (Trinidad), December 11,
   1966, pp. 11, 27.

"Fellowships." TGM, January 15, 1967, pp. 8-9.

"It's Our Own Kind of Artist Figure." SUNDAY GUARDIAN
   (Trinidad), February 5, 1967, p. 11.

"Another Kind of Sentimentality." TGM, February 12, 1967, pp.
   8-9.

"Tribal Flutes" (Brathwaite, RIGHTS OF PASSAGE). TGM, March 19,
   1967, pp. 2-3.

"Is V. S. Naipaul an Angry Young Man?" (THE MIMIC MEN). TGM,

Wall, Cheryl A.

August 6, 1967, pp. 8-9.

"The Gift of Comedy." TGM, October 22, 1967, pp. 2-3.

"Derek's Most West Indian Play" (TI-JEAN AND HIS BROTHERS).
    TGM, June 21, 1970, p. 7.

"Meanings." SAVACOU, no. 2, September 1970, pp. 45-51.

"The Muse of History." IS MASSA DAY DEAD? (edited by Orde
    Coombs). New York: Doubleday, 1974, pp. 1-27.

WALL, CHERYL A.

"Paris and Harlem: Two Culture Capitols" (McKay), PHYLON,
    v. 35, March 1974, pp. 64-73.

WALL, STEPHEN

[Review of] THE MEETING POINT, by Austin Clarke. LSO, May 7,
    1967, p. 27.

Review of SONG FOR MUMU, by Lindsay Barrett. LSO, December
    10, 1967, p. 28.

[Review of] TUMATUMARI, by Wilson Harris. LSO, September 15,
    1968, p. 29.

[Review of] THE ADVENTURES OF CATULLUS KELLY, by Andrew Salkey.
    LSO, February 9, 1969, p. 30.

[Review of] FIREFLIES, by Shiva Naipaul. LSO, November 15,
    1970, p. 31.

WALMSLEY, ANNE

[Review of] THE ISLANDS IN BETWEEN (edited by Louis James).
    BIM, v. 12, no. 48, January-June 1969, pp. 271-272.

"Dimensions of Song, A Comment on the Poetry of Derek Walcott
    and Edward Brathwaite." BIM, v. 13, no. 51, July-December
    1970, pp. 152-167.

WALROND, ERIC

[Review of] FOCUS. LL, v. 63, no. 147, 1949, pp. 174-177.

Waugh, Auberon

WALSH, WILLIAM

"Meeting Extremes" (Naipaul, V. S., AN AREA OF DARKNESS). JCL,
no. 1, September 1965, pp. 169-172.

"V. S. Naipaul: Mr. Biswas." LITERARY CRITERION, v. 10, no. 2,
Summer 1972, pp. 27-37.

V. S. NAIPAUL. Edinburgh: Oliver and Boyd, 1973.

WARDLE, IRVING

[Review of] THE JILKINGTON DRAMA, by Edgar Mittelholzer. LSO,
June 13, 1965, p. 21.

[Review of] THE EYE OF THE SCARECROW, by Wilson Harris. LSO,
November 28, 1965, p. 28.

WARDROPPER, BRUCE

[Review of] THE YEARBOOK OF THE POETRY LEAGUE OF JAMAICA PUBLIC
OPINION, November 29, 1941, p. 8.

WARNER, MAUREEN; See Also LEWIS, MAUREEN WARNER

"Cultural Confrontation, Disintegration and Syncretism in A
HOUSE FOR MR. BISWAS." CARIBBEAN QUARTERLY, v. 16, no. 4,
December 1970, pp. 70-79.

WARREN, VIRGINIA LEE

"Dynasty of Death" (Mittelholzer, CHILDREN OF KAYWANA). NYT,
September 2, 1952, Section 7, p. 29.

WATERHOUSE, KEITH

[Review of] ESCAPE TO AN AUTUMN PAVEMENT, by Andrew Salkey. NEW
STATESMAN, v. 60, July 9, 1960, p. 63.

WAUGH, AUBERON

"The Old Order Changeth Not" (Naipaul, Shiva, FIREFLIES)
SPECTATOR, v. 225, October 31, 1970, p. 526.

[Review of] IN A FREE STATE, by V. S. Naipaul. SPECTATOR, v.
227, October 9, 1971, p. 511.

Webster, Aimee

[Review of] BLACK MARSDEN, by Wilson Harris. SPECTATOR, v. 227,
December 23, 1972, pp. 1008-1009.

[Review of] THE CHIP-CHIP GATHERERS, by Shiva Naipaul.
SPECTATOR, v. 230, April 21, 1973, p. 494.

WEBSTER, AIMEE

"What Una Had to Say" (Marson). SUNDAY GLEANER, May 9, 1965,
p. 4.

WEST, PAUL

[Review of] THE AUTUMN EQUINOX, by John Hearne. NEW STATESMAN,
v. 58, November 14, 1959, p. 686.

WHITE, ANTHONY

[Review of] A MORNING AT THE OFFICE, by Edgar Mittelholzer. NEW
STATESMAN, v. 39, May 1950, p. 552.

WHITLEY, JOHN

"Naipaul's New Book" (IN A FREE STATE). SUNDAY GUARDIAN
(Trinidad), October 10, 1971, p. 7.

WICKHAM, JOHN

"A Look at Ourselves" (Walcott, THE SEA AT DAUPHIN). BIM,
v. 6, no. 22, June 1955, pp. 128-130.

[Review of] A WREATH FOR UDOMO, by Peter Abrahams. BIM, v. 7,
no. 25, July-December 1957, pp. 59-61.

"Lamming's Poetic Touch Felt in His SEASON OF ADVENTURE."
SUNDAY GUARDIAN (Trinidad), December 11, 1960, p. 36.

[Review of] SEASON OF ADVENTURE, by George Lamming. BIM, v. 9,
no. 33, July-December 1961, pp. 69-72.

[Review of] DREAM ON MONKEY MOUNTAIN, by Derek Walcott. BIM,
v. 12, no. 48, January-June 1969, pp. 267-268.

[Review of] SHADES OF GREY, by Garth St. Omer. BIM, v. 13, no.
49, July-December 1969, pp. 63-64.

[Review of] THE HUMMING BIRD TREE, by Ian McDonald. BIM, v. 13,

Williams, Cheryl

no. 49, July-December 1969, pp. 61-63.

"Derek Walcott, Poet and Dramatist." BAJAN, no. 197, January 1970, pp. 4, 6.

"West Indian Writing." BIM, v. 13, no. 50, January-June 1970, pp. 68-80.

[Review of] SHADES OF GREY, by Garth St. Omer. BAJAN, no. 199, April 1970, pp. 24-25.

[Review of] THE PLAINS OF CARONI, by Samuel Selvon. BIM, v. 13, no. 51, July-December 1970, pp. 191-192.

[Review of] MAN FROM THE PEOPLE, by Lionel Hutchinson. BIM, v. 13, no. 51, July-December 1970, pp. 192-193.

[Review of] TI-JEAN AND HIS BROTHERS, by Derek Walcott. BAJAN, no. 204, September 1970, pp. 22, 24, 25.

[Review of] FIREFLIES, by Shiva Naipaul. BAJAN, no. 209, February 1971, p. 12.

[Review of] MINTY ALLEY, by C. L. R. James. BIM, v. 14, no. 54, January-June 1972, pp. 111-113.

"Colly--A Profile." BAJAN, no. 231, January 1973, pp. 12, 14, 16-17.

[Review of] KAS-KAS (edited by Reinhard Sander and Ian Munro). BIM v. 14, no. 56, January-June 1973, pp. 243-245.

[Review of] SAW THE HOUSE IN HALF, by Oliver Jackman. BAJAN, no. 255, February 1975, p. 22.

[Review of] MOSES ASCENDING, by Samuel Selvon. BAJAN, no. 263, October 1975, p. 26.

WILDING, MICHAEL

[Review of] THE WAITING ROOM, by Wilson Harris. LONDON MAGAZINE, New Series, v. 7, no. 5, August 1967, p. 95.

WILLIAMS, CHERYL

"Eric Roach's Poetry." TAPIA, part 1, v. 4, no. 17, April 1974, pp. 3-4, 9; part 2, v. 4, no. 18, May 1974, pp. 5-8.

Williams, Daniel   Williams, Daniel

WILLIAMS, DANIEL

  [Review of] L'OUBLI, by E. McG. Keane. BIM, v. 4, no. 13, 1950,
     pp. 69-71

WILLIAMS, HUGO

  [Review of] IN A GREEN NIGHT, by Derek Walcott. LONDON
     MAGAZINE, New Series, v. 2, no. 4, July 1962, pp. 77-79.

WILLIAMSON, KARINA

  "Roger Mais: West Indian Novelist." JCL, no. 2, December 1966,
     pp. 138-147.

WILLIS, DAVID

  "A Compassionate Spectator" (Naipaul, V. S., MR. STONE AND THE
     KNIGHT COMPANION). SUNDAY GUARDIAN (Trinidad), January 10,
     1971, p. 9.

WILMOT, CYNTHIA

  "Two Shows--Two Artists" (Mais). PUBLIC OPINION, July 26, 1952,
     p. 5.

  [Review of] CACTUS VILLAGE, by William Ogilvie. PUBLIC OPINION,
     November 7, 1953, p. 5.

  [Review of] THE GHOST BANK, by William Ogilvie. PUBLIC OPINION,
     February 6, 1954, p. 5.

  "It Happened in a Tramcar" (Bennett, Louise). SUNDAY GLEANER,
     November 27, 1955, p. 5.

WILMOT, FRED

  "Memorial to Roger Mais: A Green Blade in Triumph." KYK-OVER-
     AL, v. 6, no. 20, Mid-year 1955, pp. 147-170.

WILSON, ANGUS

  [Review of] PLEASURES OF EXILE, by George Lamming. LSO, August
     28, 1960, p. 26.

  "Between Two Islands." LSO, April 30, 1967, p. 27.

Wyndham, Francis

WILSON, UNA

> "Let the Hills Be Joyful Together." SUNDAY GLEANER, August 2,
> 1953, p. 7.

WRIGHT, WINSTON G.

> Series of Articles on Mais. SUNDAY GLEANER, part 1, "Roger
> Mais--The Novelist," September 10, 1967, p. 4; part 2, "Roger
> Mais, His Way of Life," September 17, 1967, p. 4; part 3,
> "Songs and Music in the Work of Roger Mais," September 24, 1967,
> 1967, p. 4; part 4, "Roger Mais. Racy and Dramatic Style,"
> October 8, 1967, p. 4; part 5, "Major Element of Roger Mais'
> Work," October 15, 1967, pp. 4, 10.

WYNDHAM, FRANCIS

> [Review of] A MORNING AT THE OFFICE, by Edgar Mittelholzer.
> LSO, May 7, 1950, p. 7.

> [Review of] THE FACES OF LOVE, by John Hearne. LONDON MAGAZINE,
> v. 4, no. 8, August 1957, pp. 66-67.

> "The New West Indian Writers." BIM, v. 7, no. 28, January-June
> 1959, pp. 188-190.

> [Review of] TURN AGAIN TIGER, by Samuel Selvon. LONDON MAGAZINE
> MAGAZINE, v. 6, no. 3, March 1959, pp. 74-75.

> [Review of] MIGUEL STREET, by V. S. Naipaul. LONDON MAGAZINE,
> v. 6, no. 9, September 1959, pp. 80-81.

> "Introduction to Jean Rhys." LONDON MAGAZINE, v. 7, no. 1,
> January 1960, pp. 15-18.

> "Emergent Novelists" (Lamming, PLEASURES OF EXILE). SPECTATOR,
> v. 205, July 22, 1960.

> [Review of] SEASON OF ADVENTURE, by George Lamming. LSO,
> October 23, 1960, p. 22.

> [Review of] THE LAST BARBARIAN, by Jan Carew. LSO, March 26,
> 1961, p. 30.

> [Review of] A HOUSE FOR MR. BISWAS, by V. S. Naipaul. LONDON
> MAGAZINE, New Series, v. 1, no. 7, October 1961, pp. 90-93.

WYNTER, SYLVIA

"Strangers at the Gate, Caribbean Novelists in Search of
Identity." SUNDAY GLEANER, January 18, 1959, p. 14.

"The Instant Novel--Now," (Abrahams, THIS ISLAND NOW). NWQ,
v. 3, no. 3, 1967, pp. 78-81.

"We Must Learn to Sit Down Together and Talk About a Little
Culture; Reflections on West Indian Writing and Criticism."
JAMAICA JOURNAL, part 1, v. 2, no. 4, December 1968, pp. 23-
32; part 2, v. 3, no. 1, March 1969, pp. 27-42.

[Reviews of] GREEN DAYS BY THE RIVER; THE GAMES WERE COMING,
by Michael Anthony. CARIBBEAN STUDIES, v. 9, no. 4, January
1970, pp. 111-118.

"Novel and History, Plot and Plantation." SAVACOU, v. 1, no. 5,
June 1971, pp. 95-102.

"Creole Criticism--A Critique." NWQ, v. 5, no. 4, Cropover
1972, pp. 12-34.

"One Love--Rhetoric or Reality?--Aspects of Afro-Jamaicanism."
CARIBBEAN STUDIES, v. 12, no. 3, October 1972, pp. 64-97.

YARDE, GLORIA

"George Lamming--The Historical Imagination." LITERARY HALF-
YEARLY, v. 11, no. 2, 1970, pp. 35-45.

ZUCKERMAN, RUTH V. H.

[Review of] A NIGHT OF THEIR OWN, by Peter Abrahams. BOOKS
ABROAD, v. 40, no. 1, Winter 1966, p. 116.

[Review of] THIS ISLAND NOW, by Peter Abrahams. BOOKS ABROAD,
v. 41, no. 4, Autumn 1967, pp. 487-488.

Part III
Index of General Articles

1933

"The Literary Club Nuisance." BEACON, v. 2, no. 11, May, p. 1.
    Literary clubs are detrimental to artistic development in
Trinidad.

"A West Indian Literature." BEACON, v. 2, no. 12, June, pp.
2-3.
    The West Indies must break away from the English tradition
to achieve a literature of its own.

1937

"Wanted: Writers and Publishers." Una Marson. PUBLIC OPINION,
June 12, p. 6.
    "Lovers of literature, lovers of Jamaica, can we persuade
our thinkers to write, can we form a publishing company?"

1939

"The Literary Movement." H. P. Jacobs, PUBLIC OPINION, March 4,
p. 3.
    European education hampers the development of a body of
literature in the West Indies. "The error of the intellectuals lay in overlooking the creative significance of the
common people and in ignoring the neccesity for seeking new
forms of artistic expression." Discusses McDermot, de Lisser,
J. E. C. McFarlane, McKay.

"Poetry of Jamaica." PUBLIC OPINION, September 23, p. 4.
    Review of THE YEARBOOK OF THE JAMAICA POETRY LEAGUE, 1939,
finds much of the poetry good because it is sincere. Singles
out the work of Lindo, Hollar, Kent, Virtue, Evelyn Underhill.

1940

"Let Us Paraphrase." Roger Mais. PUBLIC OPINION, February 3,
p. 6.

An indictment of local poets (unnamed) who waste their
time recounting the obvious beauties of nature in an over-
zealous search for "local colour" and run the risk of becoming insular "not only in our expression, but in our concept."

"Where the Roots Lie." Roger Mais. PUBLIC OPINION, March 9,
p. 12.
Disparages the poor quality of contemporary Jamaican
poetry. "The real root of the trouble lies in ourselves. We
have fed ourselves upon the pap of inferiority,'till now
we have not got any real bones in our bodies, only gristle,
and not too much of that either."

1941

[Review of] THE YEARBOOK OF THE POETRY LEAGUE OF JAMAICA, 1941.
Bruce W. Wardropper, PUBLIC OPINION, November 29, p. 8.
"Index of certain weaknesses in Jamaican society. It
reveals a contempt ... for the solid work of reading,
studying and thinking."

1946

"Guianese Poetry." A. J. Seymour. KYK-OVER-AL, v. 1, no. 2,
pp. 13-15.
Infant days in the development of poetry in Guyana.

1947

"Sunlight and West Indian Poetry." A. J. Seymour. KYK-OVER-
AL, v. 1, no. 4, pp. 17-19.
General noncritical discussion of the poets from the
various islands.

1948

"Caribbean Voices--A Challenge to Jamaican Writers." Archie
Lindo. SUNDAY GLEANER, January 25, p. 9.
Reproduction in part of a BBC talk by Henry Swanzy
(January 11, 1948). Praises some of the Trinidadian and
Barbadian poets who were on the BBC program "Caribbean
Voices" in 1947, but finds the Jamaican contribution weak.

"The Jamaican Poets." Wycliffe Bennett. LL, v. 57, no. 128,
April, pp. 58-61.
Extols the poetic spirit of Jamaica as found in the

works of McDermot, McKay, Roberts, Virtue, Campbell, J. E. C. McFarlane.

"Caribbean Poetry." Roy Fuller. SUNDAY GLEANER, June 13, p. 9.
    Reproduction of a talk given on BBC "Caribbean Voices" (May 16, 1948). Finds that West Indian poetry lacks a tradition and is too derivative. Suggests that elements of a tradition could include nationalism, landscape, social organization. Discusses Telemaque, Lamming, C. L. Herbert, Campbell, Selvon, Sherlock.

"The Poetry League." Archie Lindo. SUNDAY GLEANER, September 19, p. 11.
    Accomplishments of the Poetry League of Jamaica after twenty·five years of existence.

"Poets Play Part in Jamaica's Life." Wycliffe Bennett. SUNDAY GLEANER, October 17, p. 6.
    Founding of the Poetry League of Jamaica (September 19, 1923) and some of its leading lights. Its purpose and philosophy.

"Is There a West Indian Literature?" Peter Blackman. LL, v. 59, no. 135, pp. 96-102. Also appears in SUNDAY GLEANER January 28, 1949, p. 7.
    Major reasons for the lack of a distinctive literature in the British West Indies include the debilitating effects of colonialism in which the people of African origin "could offer no lasting opposition to the dominant Western heritage as represented in the learning of Europe." A plea for a valid West Indian aesthetic.

1949

[Review of] FOCUS, edited by Edna Manley. CARIBBEAN QUARTERLY, v. 1, no. 1, April, pp. 32-34.
    Examines the selections by Campbell, Sherlock, Carberry, Ingram, Verity, M. G. Smith.

"Caribbean Voices, Prolegomena to a West Indian Culture." Henry Swanzy. CARIBBEAN QUARTERLY, v. 1, no. 2, September, pp. 21-28. Reprinted in CARIBBEAN QUARTERLY, v. 8, no. 2, 1962, pp. 121-128.

"We Want Books--But Do We Encourage Our Writers?" Una Marson. SUNDAY GLEANER, October 23, p. 7.
    "The truth is that it has not yet come home to the hearts

and minds of the people of this island that our status in the
way of nationhood is more to be enhanced by our literary
output than by rum and bananas."

"Open Letter to West Indian Writers." A. J. Seymour. KYK-OVER-
AL, v. 2, no. 9, December, pp. 23-27.
    The state of the art in the West Indies and hopes for the
future. "A West Indian writer can partly express, partly
create the values of his region."

"The Reality of Trespass." Wilson Harris. KYK-OVER-AL, v. 2,
no. 9, December, pp. 20-22.
    Some of the problems encountered by the American
writer.... "We who inherit the world still shirk the responsibility of a continual discovery to disclose the reality
of man's freedom or man's total collapse."

[Review of] FOCUS, edited by Edna Manley. Eric Walrond. LL,
v. 63, no. 147, pp. 174-177.
    Points out, with approval, the many Jamaican and West
Indian aspects of the poems and stories.

"The Literary Adventure of the West Indies. A. J. Seymour.
KYK-OVER-AL, v. 2, no. 10, April, entire issue, 40 pp.
    Synopsis of important events in the development of West
Indian literature. Historical background including com-
parison with other Commonwealth literatures, little reviews,
poetry, and novels. Discusses W. A. Roberts, McDermot,
Campbell, Collymore, Walcott, Vaughan, Telemaque, W. MacA,
Lawrence, Mais, Reid, Mendes, Mittelholzer.

"On Jamaican Poetry." Orford St. John. WIR, v. 2, no. 15,
August 12, p. 17.
    Reviews A TREASURY OF JAMAICAN POETRY (J. E. C. McFarlane,
ed.), finds it too conventional and not expressive of
Jamaica.

"Mr. McFarlane's Treasury." WIR, v. 2, no. 16, August 19, p. 9.
    Collection is mediocre. Better examples of West Indian
poetry exist which were not included in this anthology.

"Pioneer Books--A Literary Event." Esther Chapman. WIR, v. 2,
no. 20, September 16, p. 19.
    The publications of the Pioneer Press (14 JAMAICAN
SHORT STORIES, POETRY FOR CHILDREN, MAXIE MONGOOSE AND OTHER

STORIES, ANANCY STORIES AND DIALECT VERSE) are a "landmark in the literary history of Jamaica." Discusses first four books and finds fault with each.

"Daylight for New Writing." Clinton V. Black. PUBLIC OPINION, September 23, pp. 6-7.
On the founding of the Pioneer Press and its first four publications.

"Nature Poetry in the West Indies." A. J. Seymour. KYK-OVER-AL, v. 3, no. 11, October, pp. 39-47.
West Indian poets describing the landscapes of their islands. Includes Collymore, Sherlock, Vaughan, Carberry, M. G. Smith, K. Ingram, Una Marson.

"Ideas on a West Indian Culture." John Hearne. PUBLIC OPINION, October 14, p. 6.
The West Indies is part of Christian culture. "Lack of critics and the critical spirit threatens West Indian art and the development of its culture today as nothing else does." There is a danger in too much acceptance.

"Barren Treasury." John Hearne. PUBLIC OPINION, November 11, pp. 6, 8.
Criticizes offerings in A TREASURY OF JAMAICAN POETRY. Discusses the selections by Mais, Sherlock, Roberts, and Carberry.

"What is Poetry?" SUNDAY GLEANER, December 17, p. 10.
Critique of A TREASURY OF JAMAICAN POETRY. General praise although some outstanding poets have been omitted.

"The Contribution of the West Indian to Literature." E. McG. Keane. BIM, v. 4, no. 14, June, pp. 102-106.
The freshness of West Indian writing, and the need to break away from European culture.

"Some Books of West Indian Interest; More Pioneer Press Books." Esther Chapman. WIR, v. 3, no. 6, June, p. 16.
Takes strong exception to the volume of poetry by Redcam. Finds the other volumes in the series amateurish but admirable.

"West Indian Themes." Andrew C. Pearse. CARIBBEAN QUARTERLY, v. 2, no. 2, December-January, pp. 12-23.

Divides thirty-six short stories from BIM into groups by theme, i. e., folk life, middle-class, urban. Explores each group with special reference to stories by Ernest Carr, E. Walcott, E. D. Archibald, C. H. Hope, Clifford Sealy, Mendes, Hendriks, Karl Sealy, Forde, Selvon, Lamming, Cecil Gray.

"The Recitation of Poetry." Geoffrey Drayton. BIM, v. 4, no. 15, December, pp. 179-180.
   Argument for West Indians reading West Indian poetry, i.e., on the BBC "Caribbean Voices" radio program.

"Some Religious Attitudes in West Indian Poetry." E. McG. Keane. BIM, part 1, v. 4, no. 15, December, pp. 169-174; part 2, v. 4, no. 16, June, pp. 266-271
   Traces tendencies toward orthodox religion and towards nature in the poetry of Campbell, Seymour, Collymore, M. G. Smith, Walcott, Telemaque, Brian Scott, Daniel Williams, Carr, Lamming, and Carberry.

1952

"The West Indian Artist in the Contemporary World." Jan Carew. PHYLON, v. 13, pp. 136-140.
   A conversation with Guyanese artist Denis Williams. "For the West Indian man, his history begins in himself. His real heritage has been the memory of mankind...."

"The Critics Criticized." Roger Mais. PUBLIC OPINION, May 3, p. 5; May 17, p. 5.
   Art criticism in Jamaica.

"Preface to THE KYK-OVER-AL ANTHOLOGY OF WEST INDIAN POETRY." A. J. Seymour. KYK-OVER-AL, v. 4, no. 14, Mid-year, pp. 1-5.
   Discusses the pattern of a developing colonial literature. Purpose of the anthology is "a link between the people and their poets, preserving for the people the poems they have lost or never found, and furnishing the poets with an audience of a size and quality some have perhaps lacked, but certainly all would desire to have."

[Review of] THE KYK-OVER-AL ANTHOLOGY OF WEST INDIAN POETRY. A. F. Crichlow Matthews. BIM, v. 4, no. 16, June, pp. 298-299.
   Valuable collection though not fully representative of each poet.

"West Indian Nationalism, Poetry Like--'Cold Embers of a Spent Passion.'" Roger Mais. PUBLIC OPINION, July 12, p. 5.

A very critical review of THE KYK-OVER-AL ANTHOLOGY OF
WEST INDIAN POETRY.

"The West Indian Artist." Errol Hill. WIR, v. 4, no. 15,
August 9, pp. 13-14.
The lack of support for the artist in the West Indies
drives him to seek opportunities in England.

"Has Literature in Jamaica Died?" PUBLIC OPINION, August-
October.
A debate on the state of the art in Jamaica, with con-
tributions by Vera Bell, Carberry, Waite-Smith, and others.

"The Question of Form and Realism in the West Indian Artist."
Wilson Harris. KYK-OVER-AL, v. 4, no. 15, Year-end, pp. 23-
27.
The role of the West Indian artist is to explore the basic,
original, authentic rhythms of his people.

1953

"British West Indian Poets and Their Culture." Jan Carew.
PHYLON, v. 14, pp. 71-73.
The significance of West Indian Poetry as a true reflec-
tion of West Indian culture. The poetry of Harris, Carter,
Basil McFarlane.

"Thoughts on West Indian Poetry." Neville Dawes. PUBLIC
OPINION, January 3, p. 5.
The poetry of M. G. Smith, Lamming, and Walcott.

"Caribbean Literature: The Transplanters and Imitators." W.
Adolphe Roberts. WIR, v. 4, no. 31, February 7, p. 28.
The literature of a colony will be meagre and derivative
to the extent that the people are satisfied with their
condition.

"Caribbean Literature: The British Possessions." W. Adolphe
Roberts. WIR, v. 4, no. 42, April 25, pp. 16-17.
The development of a national literature. Discusses works
by McDermot, de Lisser, Mendes, James, Reid, McKay,
Mittelholzer, and Selvon.

"Born Yesterday." Kathleen McColgan. WIR, v. 4, no. 45, May
16, p. 17.
West Indian writers tend to dismiss the past in their
efforts to create their own individual expression.
Nationalism should not be the basis for literature.

1954

1954

"The Contribution of the West Indies to Poetry." Janheinz
Jahn. BIM, v. 6, no. 21, December, pp. 16-22.
    The unique features of Caribbean poetry are its African
elements.

1955

"'Africa' in West Indian Poetry." G. R. Coulthard. CARIBBEAN
QUARTERLY, v. 4, no. 1, January, pp. 5-13.
    Prevalent themes in Cuban and Haitian poetry, and in the
poems of McKay.

"Lamming, Selvon, and Some Trends in the West Indian Novel."
Stuart M. Hall. BIM, v. 6, no. 23, December, pp. 172-178.
    Examines the novels of Reid, Mittelholzer, Lamming,
Selvon, and Mais.

[Review of] LA LITERATURA DE LAS ANTILLAS INGLESAS, edited by
G. R. Coulthard. John Figueroa. BIM, v. 6, no. 23,
December, pp. 203-204.
    Describes and expands on Coulthard's method of criticism
by theme.

1956

"Writing Is Drifting to the Doldrums." G. H. Smith. SUNDAY
GLEANER, September 16, p. 8.
    The Jamaican government should offer monetary literary
prizes as incentives for writers and to encourage an atmos-
phere of appreciation.

"Honesty Needed in West Indian Writing." V. S. Naipaul. SUNDAY
GUARDIAN (Trinidad), October 28, p. 29.
    West Indian writing is in danger of being imitative. "I
am interested only in good writing from the West Indies.
Honest writing from people who really have something to say.
The academic university writer who is educated abroad is un-
usually open to infection from foreign 'isms' which it would
be folly to apply to the West Indies."

"Perspective on FOCUS." Orford St. John. WIR, v. 1, no. 11/12,
December, p. 83.
    Reviews FOCUS 1956, and finds the prose better than the
poetry. Particularly censorious of Campbell and Figueroa.
"This collection makes one wish Jamaican poets would realize

that music and imagery are more important ingredients of
poetry than frustration, intellectual posturing and noisily
chewed but undigested earth."

1957

"Some Thoughts on West Indian Writing." Peter Blackman.
 PRESENCE AFRICAINE, no. 14-15, pp. 296-300.
  Problems facing the West Indian writer in a colonial
  society.

"West Indian Writing." D. W. [Derek Walcott?]. PUBLIC OPINION.
 January 26, p. 7.
  "I think a great sea literature will eventually be written
 in the West Indies." Discusses Campbell and M. G. Smith.

"Literary Period Piece." George Cumper. PUBLIC OPINION,
 January 26, p. 7.
  A review of A LITERATURE IN THE MAKING (J. E. C. McFarlane
 McFarlane) in which the essays are found to be lacking in any
 real critical appraisal.

"An Anthology of Prose and Poetry." SUNDAY GLEANER, February
 17, p. 12.
  A review of SEED AND FLOWER, an anthology by the Ormsby
 family of Jamaica.

"Society and the Artist." Derek Walcott. PUBLIC OPINION, May
 4, p. 7.
  West Indian society forces the artist into exile.

"New World of the Caribbean." Bruce Hamilton. BIM, v. 7,
 no. 25, July-December, pp. 53-55.
  Evaluation of a series of radio broadcasts by Lamming.
 Stresses deemphasizing search for cultural identity.

"Sir Galahad and the Islands." Edward L. Brathwaite. BIM, v.
 7, no. 25, July-December, pp. 8-16.
  Also appears, with additional concluding note, under the
 same title in IOUANALOA, RECENT WRITING FROM ST. LUCIA.
 Castries, St. Lucia: Department of Extra-Mural Studies,
 1963.
  The West Indian writer as emigrant and as "folk" writer.
 Discusses Roach, Selvon, Lamming, Mittelholzer, Walcott, Mais,
 Owen Campbell.

"Some Jamaican Poets." Derek Walcott. PUBLIC OPINION, part 1,

1957

August 3, p. 7, part 2, August 10, p. 7.
The poems of J. E. C. McFarlane, Virtue, Carberry,
Sherlock, Basil McFarlane.

"West Indian Culture in England." WIR, v. 2, no. 9, September,
pp. 9-10.
Some negative remarks about the acclaim given in London
to West Indian drama.

"West Indian Writing." George Panton. SUNDAY GLEANER,
September 22, p. 9.
Reviews anthologies of poetry in KYK-OVER-AL, no. 22, and
BIM, v. 7. They give readers an opportunity to find out
about the literature from other islands.

"The New West Indies: Nationality and Literature." Gordon
Lewis. SUNDAY GLEANER, December 8, p. 8.
West Indian artists have the responsibility to express
and define the spirit of nationalism and create the integrity
of a cultural identity. Discusses Naipaul, Mittelholzer,
Walcott, and Selvon.

1958"

"Migrants with Manuscripts, Social Background of the West
Indian Novel." Randolph Rawlins. BLACK ORPHEUS, no. 4,
October, pp. 46-50.
Explores the reasons for the migration of West Indian
authors to London. Briefly discusses works of Mais, Reid,
Selvon, Lamming, de Boissiere, and C. L. R. James.

"The Negro Writer and His World." George Lamming. CARIBBEAN
QUARTERLY, v. 5, no. 2, February, pp. 109-115. Also appears
in PRESENCE AFRICAINE, nos. 8, 9, and 10.
Identifies some of the problems facing black writers and
the themes that unite them.

"Short Stories--West Indian and English--And Poems." George
Panton. SUNDAY GLEANER, March 9, p. 11.
Reviews BIM (January-June 1958). Urges increase in
circulation to prevent its extinction.

"Fresh Winds from the West." Kingsley Amis. SPECTATOR, v. 200,
May 2, pp. 565-566.
Emerging West Indian novelists: Carew, Reid, Mittelholzer,
Naipaul, and Selvon.

"Mirror to Our Nature." George Panton. SUNDAY GLEANER, May
     18, p. 11.
          Reviews "An Anthology of West Indian Poetry" in a special
     issue of CARIBBEAN QUARTERLY. Finds the collection
     inclusive, and that the main themes are nationalism and pride
     in being West Indian.

"The Regional Barrier." V. S. Naipaul. TLS, no. 2946, August
     15, pp. 37-38.
          Naipaul laments his lack of involvement with London life,
     and discusses the difficulties encountered there by a non-
     European writer.

"West Indian Writers." Esther Chapman. WIR, v. 3, no. 9,
     September, p. 15.
          Current popularity of West Indian writers is due to their
     novelty in Britain. Though the fad may pass, it will have
     given West Indian writers the exposure that they need.

1959

"The West Indian Novel of Immigration." G. R. Coulthard.
     PHYLON, v. 20, pp. 32-41.
          West Indian novels of immigration from a sociological as
     well as a literary viewpoint. Discusses Selvon's THE
     LONELY LONDONERS and Lamming's THE EMIGRANTS.

"Strangers at the Gate, Caribbean Novelists in Search of
     Identity." Sylvia Wynter. SUNDAY GLEANER, January 18, p. 14.
          Reprinted from THE TIMES BRITISH COLONIES REVIEW, Fourth
     Quarter, 1958. Explores the common themes of West Indian
     novelists whose characters "are men from a world where people
     are still directly involved in the job of taming their
     environments, in coming to terms with a heritage of cultural
     confusions." Discusses Mittelholzer, Selvon, Mais, Lamming,
     Hearne, Carew, and Naipaul.

"The New West Indian Writers." Francis Wyndham. BIM, v. 7,
     no. 28, January-June, pp. 188-190.
          West Indian writers are producing vigorous and original
     novels. Briefly discusses novels by Reid, Mittelholzer,
     Selvon, Lamming, Hearne, and Naipaul.

"The West Indian Novelists." Frank Collymore. BAJAN, v. 6,
     no. 7, March, pp. 20-21.
          Brief mention of Reid, Mittelholzer, Selvon, Lamming,
     Mais, Naipaul, and Drayton, in a general discussion of West

1959

    Indian novelists.

"Rejection of European Culture as a Theme in Caribbean Liter-
ature." G. R. Coulthard. CARIBBEAN QUARTERLY, v. 5, no. 4,
June, pp. 231-234.
    Deals with this theme primarily in the poetry of the
French-speaking Caribbean, and also in the poetry of Claude
McKay.

[Review of] BIM (v. 8, no. 29). George Panton. SUNDAY GLEANER,
August 9, p. 14.
    Finds the poetry very good, but the reviews too un-
critical.

1960

"Writing in the West Indies: A Survey." Frank Collymore.
TAMARACK REVIEW, no. 14, pp. 111-124.
    Brief history of the West Indies and of the development
of its literature from the early twentieth century. Concentrates on the influence of Europe, especially England, and on
the BBC radio program, Caribbean Voices. Mentions major
poets and novelists.

"The Controversial Tree of Time." Edward Brathwaite. BIM, v.
8, no. 30, January-June, pp. 104-114.
    The jungle of Guyana in the novels of Mittelholzer and the
poetry of Harris.

"Neo-realism Parallel Noted in W.I. Novels." Derek Walcott.
SUNDAY GUARDIAN (Trinidad), April 24, p. 7.
    Similarities in the novels of Lamming, Hearne, Selvon,
Mittelholzer, and Naipaul.

"Barbados--A Culture All Its Own." Derek Walcott. SUNDAY
GUARDIAN (Trinidad), June 26, p. 23.
    Literature and the arts in Barbados.

"The New West Indian Novelists." Edward Brathwaite. BIM, part
1, v. 8, no. 31, July-December, pp. 199-210; part 2, v. 8,
no. 32, January-June 1961, pp. 271-280.
    Brief historical overview of West Indian writing. In-
depth discussion of Mittelholzer, Reid, Selvon, Lamming,
Hearne, Naipaul, and Salkey.

"Need for a Little Theatre in Port-of-Spain." Derek Walcott.
SUNDAY GUARDIAN (Trinidad), July 10, p. 22.

One of many efforts to gain support and recognition for theater in Trinidad.

"Book Publishing in Jamaica." W. Adolphe Roberts. SUNDAY GLEANER, July 24, pp. 14, 23.
   The publications of the Pioneer Press and their success.

"Let's Have the Best in Creative Writing." Derek Walcott. SUNDAY GUARDIAN (Trinidad), August 7, p. 6.
   Quality of writing in latest BIM and OPUS issues.

"At Last? New Hope for Exiled Artists." Derek Walcott. SUNDAY GUARDIAN (Trinidad), August 21, p. 4.
   Scholarship offers by Trinidad government to West Indian artists to visit their homelands.

"Jamaica Government Moves to Aid Artists." Fitzroy Fraser and Derek Walcott. SUNDAY GUARDIAN (Trinidad), September 18, p. 7.
   Compares cultural programs of Jamaica and Trinidad.

"An 'Exile' Returns." SUNDAY GUARDIAN (Trinidad), September 25, p. 7.
   Profile of Naipaul who returned to Trinidad on a grant from the government.

"Reflections on the November Exhibition." Derek Walcott. SUNDAY GUARDIAN (Trinidad), November 13, p. 7.
   The state of West Indian art.

"Give Us More Stories." Derek Walcott. SUNDAY GUARDIAN (Trinidad), November 27, p. 5.
   A review of WEST INDIAN STORIES (edited by Andrew Salkey).

"From Ralegh to Carew, The Books of Guiana." A. J. Seymour. KYK-OVER-AL, v. 9, no. 27, December, pp. 74-82.
   Chronicles the historians, poets, and novelists, mostly from Guyana, who have described the Guyanese landscape.

"Jamaican Writers of Today." George Panton. SUNDAY GLEANER, December 11, p. 18.
   Reviews FOCUS: 1960 and finds that it contains a fair sampling of current Jamaican writing.

1961

[Review of] TAMARACK REVIEW, ISSUE 14. Edward Brathwaite. BIM,
v. 8, no. 32, January-June, pp. 288-289.
Finds the collection to be a true reflection of a West
Indian point of view.

[Review of] WEST INDIAN STORIES, edited by Andrew Salkey.
George Panton. SUNDAY GLEANER (Jamaica), January 15, p. 14.
A valuable collection because it shows the West Indian as
a particular type of person.

"Council Exhibition Recalls Great Names in Ballet." Derek
Walcott. SUNDAY GUARDIAN (Trinidad), January 15, p. 7.
Costume designs in theatre.

"Boom Time for West Indian Authors." Colin Rickards. SUNDAY
GLEANER, March 5, p. 14.
The success of West Indian authors in the British
publishing market. Includes a chart of sales to December
1960.

"Old 'FOCUS' Back--This Time with New Blood." Derek Walcott.
SUNDAY GUARDIAN (Trinidad), April 2, p. 4.
Derek Walcott reviews FOCUS IV.

"The West Indian Novelist ... a Footnote." Bill Carr. SUNDAY
GLEANER, April 23, pp. 14-20.
West Indian writing should not be seen in relationship
to politics or sociology.

"The Coloured Woman in Caribbean Poetry (1800-1960)." G. R.
Coulthard. RACE, v. 2, no. 2, May, pp. 53-61.
Affirmation of the beauty of the Black woman in poetry
of the Spanish, French, and British Caribbean. Discusses
George Campbell, W. Adolphe Roberts, and Claude McKay.

[Review of] WEST INDIAN STORIES, edited by Andrew Salkey.
Harold Marshall. BIM, v. 9, no. 33, July-December, pp. 72-
73.
This anthology lacks balance.

"West Indian Poetry." R. J. Owens. CARIBBEAN QUARTERLY, v. 7,
no. 3, December, pp. 120-127.
Discusses the contents of two anthologies of West Indian
poetry; KYK-OVER-AL, no. 22 and CARIBBEAN QUARTERLY, v. 5, no.
3, including poems by J. E. Clare McFarlane, Virtue,
Collymore, R. L. C. McFarlane, Sherlock, Walcott, Roach, and
M. G. Smith.

Index of Articles

1962

"Bumper Year for West Indian Books." Colin Rickards. SUNDAY
GLEANER, January 7, p. 14.
The publishing activities of West Indian writers in
London. Also reviews SHADOWS IN THE JUNGLE (Nicole).

"Magazine Should Cost More. Derek Walcott. SUNDAY GUARDIAN
(Trinidad). February 4, p. 19.
Reviews 34th number of BIM. Though the reviews in BIM
may be too benign, the importance of the magazine lies in
its publication of creative work from the West Indies.

"Caribbean Brothers." George Panton. SUNDAY GLEANER, February
11, p. 14.
Reviews BIM, no. 34 and notes similarities in the back-
grounds and education of the writers although they are all
from different islands.

"Calypsonians! Danger Lurks in Tin Pan Alley." Derek Walcott.
SUNDAY GUARDIAN (Trinidad). February 25, p. 23.
Calypso began as folk poetry and is in danger of losing
its creative vitality as it becomes commercialized.

"Bringing Their Lessons Nearer Home." Derek Walcott. SUNDAY
Guardian (Trinidad), March 25, p. 7.
Praises schoolbook series which includes selections from
West Indian writers.

[Review of] THEMES OF SONG, AN ANTHOLOGY OF GUIANESE POETRY.
A. N. Forde. BIM, v. 9, no. 35, July-December, pp. 224-225.
Collection is superficial and romantic.

"The Independence Anthology." Bill Carr. SUNDAY GLEANER,
August 5, p. 18.
Although it does not go deeply into explaining emerging
West Indian writing, this anthology should help to stimulate
a positive interest in local literature.

"The Caribbean Mixture, Variations and Fusions in Race and
Style." TLS, no. 3154, August 10, p. 578.
Discusses West Indian novelists and their uses of
language, but disparages the concept of a "school" of West
Indian writing. Naipaul, Lamming, Hearne, and Mittelholzer
are reviewed with a varying lack of enthusiasm.

"The Prospects of a National Theatre." Derek Walcott. SUNDAY

1963

GUARDIAN (Trinidad), August 26, pp. 105-106.
Problems of a national culture and the difficulties that
the new nations of the West Indies have in supporting their
artists.

"Anthology of 29 Poets; A Success." Janheinz Jahn. SUNDAY
GUARDIAN (Trinidad), September 9, p. 9.
Discusses the anthology BLACK ORPHEUS and what the
Germans think of Caribbean writing.

"Angry! Not Me, Says Selvon." Carl Douglas. SUNDAY GUARDIAN
(Trinidad), December 30, p. 12.
Interview with Selvon who talks about West Indians in
England and his own writing.

1963

"BIM Magazine a Must for Those Interested in West Indian
Writing." George Panton. SUNDAY GLEANER MAGAZINE, April 7,
p. 10.
Describes v. 9, no. 36 of BIM and praises its high standards.

"Brasher BIM Can Win More Friends." Derek Walcott. SUNDAY
GUARDIAN (Trinidad), April 28, p. 4.
Reviews BIM in terms of its commercial success and its
contribution to West Indian literature. Finds fault with
layout and contents.

"From the West Indies." John Harrison. BIM, v. 10, no. 37,
July-December, pp. 60-63.
Text of radio broadcast given in Suva, Fiji on the emer-
gence of the West Indian novel. Discusses Naipaul and
Fraser.

"Roots." Edward Brathwaite. BIM, v. 10, no. 37, July-December,
pp. 10-21.
Examines rootlessness in West Indian writers and the
return to an examination of West Indian society as exem-
plified in Naipaul's A HOUSE FOR MR. BISWAS. Also discusses
Selvon Lamming, Dawes, and Hearne.

"West Indian Writing " SUNDAY GLEANER MAGAZINE, October 13, p.
10.
Review of BIM, v. 10, no. 37 finds the stories readable
but not up to standard.

322

Index of Articles

"Reflections on the Novel in the British Caribbean." Bill Carr. QUEENS QUARTERLY, v. 70, Winter, pp. 585-597.
    One British Critic's view of West Indian novelists. Carr sees the questions of color and identity as motive forces behind the works of Reid, Dawes, Mittelholzer, Salkey, Lamming, Mais, and Hearne.

1964

"Spiritual Purpose Lacking." Derek.Walcott. SUNDAY GUARDIAN (Trinidad), January 5, p. 3.
    Censures Trinidad government for not offering support to its artists.

"A Dilemma Faces West Indian Artists." Derek Walcott. SUNDAY GUARDIAN (Trinidad), January 12, p. 3.
    The potential of the Caribbean lies in its art. West Indian artists must reject the fads and phases from other countries and create a style of their own.

"An Indian looks at West Indian Poetry, A Footnote to Caribbean Poetry Written in English." Dilip Dumar Sen (From Indian PEN Club, September 1963). SUNDAY GLEANER, January 12, p. 4.
    Discusses the nature poetry of McKay, Redcam, and J. E. C. McFarlane.

"West Indian Writing of Today." George Panton. SUNDAY GLEANER, January 26, p. 4.
    Review of BIM, v. 10, no. 3. The issue is highly recommended.

"Carnival: The Theatre of the Streets." Derek Walcott. SUNDAY GUARDIAN (Trinidad), February 9, p. 4.
    Carnival and calypso as artistic expression.

"The Outlook for a National Theatre." Derek Walcott. SUNDAY GUARDIAN (Trinidad), March 22, p. 16.
    Suggestions for the creation of a National Theatre and the types of contributions it could make.

"Africa in West Indian Literature." O. R. Dathorne. BLACK ORPHEUS, no. 16, October, pp. 24-53.
    Also appears as "The Theme of Africa in West Indian Literature" in PHYLON, v. 26, Fall 1965, pp. 255-276.
    The concepts of "Africa" expressed by various West Indian authors. Cicely Waite-Smith, McKay, Telemaque, Salkey,

1964

Lamming, Louise Bennett, Roach, Sherlock, Drayton, Campbell, de Lisser, Walcott, Bell, Carter, A. M. Clarke, Dathorne, Williams, Reid, Harris, Hearne, and Wynter are discussed.

"Literature of Latin America and the Caribbean." G. R. Coulthard CARIBBEAN QUARTERLY, v. 10, no. 4, December, pp. 46-54.
    Similarities in the themes explored by Latin American and Caribbean poets and novelists, particularly in those relating to the landscape, both natural and human.

1965

"Decolonization in West Indian Literature." Kenneth Ramchand. TRANSITION, v. 5, no. 22, pp. 48-49.
    The process of decolonization and the search for language and identity. Examples from the novels of de Lisser, McKay, E. R. Braithwaite, Selvon, Lamming, and Salkey.

"The Theatre of Abuse." Derek Walcott. SUNDAY GUARDIAN (Trinidad), January 8, p. 4.
    Review of a play by Leroi Jones. Dramatic language must do more than merely create verbal shocks if the playright is to use abuse effectively. Language must be controlled and creative.

"Home Is Where They Want to Be." C. L. R. James. SGM, February 14, pp. 4-5.
    Writers in exile, specifically Naipaul, Lamming, and Harris, should return to live in the West Indies, where they will reach their greatest potential by writing for their own people.

"The West Indian Novelist. Prelude and Context." Bill Carr. CARIBBEAN QUARTERLY, v. 11, nos. 1 and 2, March-June, pp. 71-84.
    An analysis of why Carr thinks West Indian writers are the way they are. Discusses Naipaul, Allfrey, and Lamming.

"Return to Jamaica." Derek Walcott. SGM, part 1, April 4, pp. 6-7, part 2, April 11, pp. 6, 7-8.
    Changes at the University, dance, and painting.

"The Pamphleteers. Natural Reformers in Our Society." SUNDAY GUARDIAN (Trinidad), April 25, pp. 4-5.
    Examines little magazines, privately printed books, VOICES, and the poetry contributions of Roger McTair and

Index of Articles

Eliot Bastien.

[Review of] STORIES FROM THE CARIBBEAN, edited by Andrew Salkey.
Derek Walcott. SGM, May 9, pp. 2-9.
   Comments on the freshness and originality of the stories,
and points out that the value of BBC Caribbean Voices Program
was in keeping stories in the oral tradition.

"A New Poet, Jamaican." Derek Walcott. SUNDAY GUARDIAN
(Trinidad), June 20, p. 6.
   Review of ON THIS MOUNTAIN, poems by A. L. Hendriks.
Discusses the poet's need for an audience and the relatively
few published West Indian poets (books) as compared to
novelists. Also discusses FOCUS group including Campbell,
Basil McFarlane, and M. G. Smith.

"Nobody Knows Their Names." Derek Walcott. SUNDAY GUARDIAN
(Trinidad), July 4, p. 7.
   Reviews DISAPPOINTED GUESTS, a collection of essays on the
experiences of West Indians in London with contributions by
Kenneth Ramchand, Mervyn Morris, and Eliot Bastien.

"Short Stories--West Indian and Others." SUNDAY GLEANER, July
11, p. 4.
   STORIES FROM THE CARIBBEAN (edited by Andrew Salkey) is
an anthology that appeals to all.

"Sentimental Journeys ...." Derek Walcott. SUNDAY GUARDIAN
(Trinidad), August 15, p. 7.
   Review of BIM no. 41. Finds the poetry anthology in this
issue "leisured and syrupy." Poetry by Brathwaite, Escoffery,
Slade Hopkinson, and Michael Foster.

"Crisis of Conscience: Ban Ban Caliban Is the Cry." Derek
Walcott. SUNDAY GUARDIAN (Trinidad), August 22, p. 11.
   The invitation to the Commonwealth Arts Festival in the
light of the recently imposed migration ban in Britain raises
the question of the artist's responsibility. "Race, which we
once experienced at home withdrew as a subject for art with
the gradual withdrawal of the proconsuls, but now we are
facing it anew."

"Language and Literature in Developing Countries." Jan Carew,
NWF, v. 1, no. 22, part 1, September, pp. 25-29; part 2, v.
1, no. 23, September, pp. 23-27.
   The effect of NEW DAY on attitudes towards dialect. The
problems of dialect. Progress report on the West Indian

novel of the people, including Mais, Patterson, and Wynter.

"Leaving School." Derek Walcott. LONDON MAGAZINE, New Series,
v. 5, September, pp. 4-14.
A prose account of Walcott's adolescence, more fully
developed in his later autobiographical poem ANOTHER LIFE.

"Images." V. S. Naipaul. NEW STATESMAN, September 24, v. 70,
p. 453.
In this review of COMMONWEALTH LITERATURE (edited by John
Press), Naipaul suggests that literature should not be used
as a political weapon: "... a country is ennobled by its
writers only if these writers are good."

"An Artist in Exile--From the West Indies." Jan Carew. NWF, v.
1, nos. 27 and 28, Novem ber, pp. 23-30.
The permanent state of exile of the West Indian, the
writer's alienation from his own society, and the misunder-
standings that arise between the artist and his society.
Discusses Mittelholzer.

"Talking About the Thirties." Clifford Sealy. VOICES, v. 1,
no. 5, December, pp. 3-7.
In this interview with Alfred Mendes, Mendes discusses
BANANA BOTTOM, influences on the novelists of the thirties
in Trinidad, impact of the Russian Revolution in terms of
colonialism, and the effect of THE BEACON.

1966

"Islands of Man, Reflections on the Emergence of a West Indian
Literature." Louis James. SOUTHERN REVIEW, v. 2, no. 2,
pp. 150-163.
Development of West Indian literature since 1950 is
examined in terms of the themes of rootlessness and lack of
identity. Reviews works by Denis Williams, Walcott,
Patterson, Mais, Naipaul, Harris, Mittelholzer, Reid,
Brathwaite, Scott, and Wayne Brown.

"Writing for Children." Derek Walcott. SGM, part 1,
January 23, p. 2; part 2, February 6, pp. 28-29; part 3,
February 13, p. 3.
Part One discusses children's books by Andrew Salkey.
Parts Two and Three discuss a Caribbean textbook publishing
project, and dialect versus standard English.

"The Prospect of a National Theatre." Derek Walcott. SUNDAY

GUARDIAN (Trinidad), March 6, p. 6.
Apart from the actual theatre building, a group of professional and experienced people are needed.

"Negro Writers Enrich the English Language." Clifford Simmons.
SUNDAY GLEANER, May 1, p. 4.
A book show at the first world Festival of Negro Art held at Dakar included many Caribbean writers.

"The West Indian People." George Lamming. NWQ, v. 2, no. 2, Croptime, pp. 63-74.
An eloquent plea for West Indian unity. Insights into the dilemmas facing colonized peoples.

"West Indian Art Today." Derek Walcott. SGM, May 8, pp. 8-9.
West Indian art reflects the humanism of the nineteenth century, but does not reflect a recognition of "New World" sensibility.

"There's No Bitterness in Our Literature." Carl Jacobs.
SUNDAY GUARDIAN (Trinidad), May 22, p. 9.
In this interview with Derek Walcott, Walcott discusses the creative process in poetry, the tragic-comic spirit in West Indian writing, and why there are more West Indian novelists than poets.

"Art in Guyana: Beware of Love Vines." Derek Walcott. SUNDAY GUARDIAN (Trinidad), May 29, p. 9.
Review of NEW WORLD, Guyana Independence Issue. "There is a great danger, not only in this publication, but in a lot of West Indian criticism, of crowning men with glory whose work has just begun."

"KYK-OVER-AL and the Radicals." Edward Brathwaite. NEW WORLD, Guyana Independence Issue, v. 2, no. 3, High Season, pp. 55-57.
An assessment of KYK in terms of its contributions to the growing radical spirit in the West Indies. This is primarily seen in the reviews and poetry by Wilson, Harris and Martin Carter.

"The Rhythm of Society and Landscape (Mittelholzer, Carew, Williams, Dathorne)." Wilfred Cartey. NEW WORLD, Guyana Independence Issue, v. 2, no. 3, High Season, pp. 97-104
Various presentations of Guyana, from within and from without, in the writings of these four novelists.

1966

"Young Trinidadian Poets." Derek Walcott. SUNDAY GUARDIAN
(Trinidad), June 19, p. 5.
A review of the novel THE FLAMING CIRCLE (Jagdip Maraj)
and of poetry by Judy Miles, Roger McTair, and Elliot Bastien
in VOICES.

"Anthologies." Derek Walcott. SUNDAY GUARDIAN (Trinidad) July
3, p. 6.
This review of CARIBBEAN NARRATIVE (edited by O. R.
Dathorne) discusses the comparative merits of West Indian
prose versus its poetry.

"Caribbean Readers and Writers." Margaret Blundell. BIM, v.
11, no. 43, July-December, pp. 163-167.
Laments lack of a West Indian reading public.

"The Novel in the British Caribbean." A. J. Seymour. BIM,
part 1, v. 11, no. 42, January-June, pp. 83-85; part 2,
v. 11, no. 43, July-December, pp. 176-180; part 3, v. 11,
no. 44, January-June 1967, pp. 238-242; part 4, v. 12,
no. 46, January-June 1967, pp. 75-80.
Major themes and writers, including, Reid, Mais, Hearne,
Mittelholzer, Naipaul, Dawes, Lamming, and de Boissiere.

"Our Poetry." George Panton. SUNDAY GLEANER, September 11, p.
4.
Reviews CARIBBEAN VOICES PART 1; finds the selection not
of high standard, and finds fault with the editor's introduction as not sufficiently explanatory.

"Is Bad Verse Forgivable at a Certain Stage in Our Evolution."
Derek Walcott. SUNDAY GUARDIAN (Trinidad), September 11,
p. 5.
Review of CARIBBEAN VOICES, Part 1. The generally poor
quality of the verse may be due to the rhetorical tradition
in which the writers were brought up.

"BIM, Putting on the Style." Derek Walcott. SUNDAY GUARDIAN
(Trinidad), September 18, p. 7.
Finds that BIM, no. 43, has an old-fashioned format and
that the criticism is generally weak. Discusses poetry of
Slade Hopkinson.

"Derek Walcott, a Self-Interview Raises Questions of Identity."
SUNDAY GUARDIAN (Trinidad), October 16, p. 7.
West Indian literature is "rich and diversified because
the writers are not part of a 'school.'"

1967

"Beyond the Backyard." Derek Walcott. SUNDAY GUARDIAN (Trinidad), December 11, pp. 11 and 27.
There are few West Indian plays about the middle class because the "writer finds it difficult to clarify the subtle transitions in stress when Trinidadian English and Trinidadian Trinidadian dialect are crossed. Playrights cannot believe what they make their characters recite."

1967

"Frank Collymore and the Miracle of BIM." Edward Baugh. NWQ, v. 3, nos. 1 and 2, pp. 129-133.
Traces the life of BIM and its founder, and the contributions of both to West Indian literature.

"Jazz and the West Indian Novel." Edward Brathwaite. BIM, part 1, v. 11, no. 44, January-June, pp. 275-284; part 2, v. 12, no. 45, pp. 39-51; part 3, v. 12, no. 46, pp. 115-126.
Using Jazz as an archetype of Negro expression in the New World, Brathwaite develops an aesthetic alternative for the West Indies. Selvon, Reid, Lamming, Louise Bennett, Dawes, Lovelace, Mittelholzer, Lorrimer, Alexander, Harris, Mais, Naipaul, Salkey, and Patterson, are evaluated in terms of this aesthetic.

"Fellowships." Derek Walcott. TGM, January 15, 1967, pp. 8-9.
Protest poetry in the West Indies, and in poetry by La Rose, McKay, Campbell, and Carter.

"It's Our Own Kind of Artist Figure." Derek Walcott. SUNDAY GUARDIAN (Trinidad), February 5, 1967, p. 11.
"Trinidad has evolved its own kind of artist figure. In the pan-man, the untrained musician, in the steel-band, an untrained orchestra, in the calypsonian, a kind of poet, in the carnival craftsman, a kind of sculptor." Suggests that all these art forms must be accommodated in a National Theatre Centre.

"Another Kind of Sentimentality." Derek Walcott. TGM, February 12, 1967, pp. 8-9.
Race as history and as the basic subject of West Indian plays. Discusses Naipaul.

"Why Is Our Theatre So Tame?" Derek Walcott. SUNDAY GUARDIAN (Trinidad), April 30, p. 8.
Theatre in the West Indies displays all the signs of provincialism. Only West Indian novelists have broken out

1967

of this mold.

"The Novel in Guyana." A. J. Seymour. KAIE, no. 4, July , pp. 59-63.
    The development of the novel in Guyana, and the major novelists with brief summaries of their works, including Mittelholzer, Harris, Carew, Lauchmonen, Dathorne, Nicole, Braithwaite, and Denis Williams.

"Poetry in Guyana." A. J. Seymour and Ian McDonald. KAIE, no. 4, July, pp. 64-66.
    The absence of written poetry,pre-Emancipation was mainly due to the confusion of languages to which the African was subjected. Explores the major thrust of the poetry, pre-1940 and predominant themes informing Guyanese poetry after 1940.

"Caribbean Anthologies." Paul Edwards. JCL, July, no. 3, pp. 120-122.
    Reviews of CARIBBEAN LITERATURE (Coulthard), CARIBBEAN NARRATIVE (Dathorne), WEST INDIAN NARRATIVE (Ramchand).

"West Indian Literature: Some Cheap Anthologies." Mervyn Morris. CARIBBEAN QUARTERLY, v. 13, no. 2, June, pp. 36-39.
    The respective merits of WEST INDIAN NARRATIVE, CARIBBEAN NARRATIVE, and CARIBBEAN LITERATURE, in terms of their use for schools.

"The Negro Poet and His Landscape." Gerald Moore. BLACK ORPHEUS, no. 22, August, pp. 33-44.
    Mostly African writers and their descriptions of the landscape, but also discusses Lamming, Walcott, and Harris.

"The Naked Footprint: An Inquiry Into Crusoe's Island." John Hearne. REL, v. 8, no. 4, October, pp. 97-107.
    Analysis of Defoe's ROBINSON CRUSOE in terms of economics, Western ethics, and the mercantile society. Gives an insight into Hearne's viewpoint and approach in his own work.

"The Gift of Comedy." Derek Walcott. TGM, October 22, pp. 2-3.
    "The tragedy is that our society, garish, shallow, and determined to be 'gay' wears a mask that is indistinguishable from weeping, and its poets and novelists grow more and more embittered by that fixed hysterical joy." Discusses Naipaul and Harris.

"Home from the Wars ... An Epitaph." John Hearne. JAMAICA
JOURNAL, v. 1, no. 1, December, pp. 82-84.
Some of the reasons why the West Indian writers went into
exile--"What the West Indian artist was seeking ... was a
system of relationships in which a man and his society were
complementary and in which generally accepted rituals had
been fashioned."

"West Indian Prose Fiction in the Sixties, A Survey." Edward
Brathwaite. CRITICAL SURVEY, v. 3, Winter, pp. 169-174.
Also appears in BIM, v. 12, no. 47, July-December 1968, pp.
157-165 and SUNDAY GLEANER, part 1, March 8, 1970, p. 27;
part 2, March 15, 1970, p. 27; part 3, March 22, 1970, p.
27; part 4, March 29, 1970, p. 27, and with additional
material in BLACK WORLD, v. 20, no. 11, September 1971, pp.
14-24.
The prose writers of the 1960s began to explore the
Caribbean consciousness. This exploration is shown in the
fiction of Harris, Lamming, Naipaul, Patterson, Anthony,
C. L. R. James, and Alfred Mendes.

1968

"Movement to Overcome Isolation of West Indian Artists."
Edward Brathwaite. SUNDAY GLEANER, February 4, pp. 4, 7.
Also appears under title "The Caribbean Artists Movement."
CARIBBEAN QUARTERLY, v. 14, nos. 1 and 2, March-June, pp.
57-59.
Beginnings of the Caribbean Artists Movement (CAM), and
the reasons for its formation.

"Social Context of Sparrow's Calypsoes." George Rohlehr.
TRINIDAD GUARDIAN, part 1, February 21, p. 10; part 2,
February 22, p. 10; part 3, February 23, p. 10; part 4,
February 24, p. 6; SUNDAY GUARDIAN (Trinidad), part 5,
February 25, p. 10; TRINIDAD GUARDIAN, part 6, February 26
p. 6; part 7, February 27, p. 6.
"It seems to me that there is in the spoken language
of Trinidad a potential of rhythmic organization which our
poets have not yet discovered. They [the Calypsonians]
uncover with amoral frankness the existential cynicism of
a people who make a gay music out of anarchy."

"Kent Conference on Caribbean Arts." Edward Brathwaite. SUNDAY
GLEANER, March 10, p. 10.
Describes CAM Conference on Caribbean Arts.

1968

"Towards a West Indian Criticism." Edward Baugh. CARIBBEAN
QUARTERLY, v. 14, nos. 1 and 2, March-June, pp. 140-144.
A critique of ISLANDS-IN-BETWEEN (edited by Louis James),
leads Baugh to examine the need for a literary criticism
by West Indians of their own literature.

"'Folk' Themes in West Indian Drama: An Analysis." Cecil Gray.
CARIBBEAN QUARTERLY, v. 14, nos. 1 and 2, March-June, pp.
102-109.
Divides 51 West Indian plays into various classifications:
Peasant, Urban, Lower Class, etc., and examines charac-
teristics of each type.

"The Unresolved Constitution." Wilson Harris. CARIBBEAN
QUARTERLY, v. 14, nos. 1 and 2, March--June, pp. 43-47.
The "art of memory" and the necessity of writers and
critics to probe into their "Historylessness."

"Dialect in West Indian Fiction." Kenneth Ramchand. CARIBBEAN
QUARTERLY, v. 14, nos. 1 and 2, March-June, pp. 27-42.
Also appears in his THE WEST INDIAN NOVEL AND ITS BACK-
GROUND. London: Faber and Faber, 1970, pp. 96-116.
Illustrates the various ways in which West Indian writers
have employed dialect and the ways in which they are ex-
ploring its possibilities. Works by De Lisser, Selvon,
Reid, Hearne, Mittelholzer, Harris, Lamming, Clarke, and
Carew, are discussed.

[Review of] THE ISLANDS IN BETWEEN, edited by Louis James.
Alex Gradussov. PUBLIC OPINION. June 28, p. 6.
Finds the essays generally good and that the book as a
whole provides a valuable starting point in the assessment
of writers in the English-speaking Caribbean.

"Comments on West Indian Writers." George Panton. SUNDAY
GLEANER, June 30, p. 4.
Reviews ISLANDS IN-BETWEEN. Finds serious omissions of
key West Indian authors (McKay, P. Marshall) and bibliographical errors, but otherwise it is a useful collection.

"Challenge to Caribbean Artists." Anon. SUNDAY GLEANER, part
1, September 29, p. 4; part 2, October 6, pp. 4, 8.
Self-appraisal and examination of purposes of CAM. The
2nd CAM Conference.

"The Theatre Workshop at the Crossroads." Derek Walcott. TGM,
September 29, pp. 10-11.

Index of Articles

Problems of audience and production on being forced to
vacate the Basement Theatre. "Art still, however loosely,
coheres the concept of a federation."

"Five-Island Tour." Derek Walcott. SUNDAY GUARDIAN (Trinidad),
November 3, p. 11.
  Walcott reports on the first tour of the Trinidad Theatre
Workshop.

"We Must Learn to Sit Down Together and Talk About a Little
Culture, Reflections on West Indian Writing and Criticism.
Part One, Part Two." Sylvia Wynter. JAMAICA JOURNAL, v. 2,
no. 4, December, pp. 23-32; v. 3, no. 1, March 1969, pp. 27-
42.
  Devastating attack on some critics of West Indian literature, notably Bill Carr, Louis James, and Wayne Brown. The
writer as rendered functionless by his society. In-depth
analyses of Naipaul, Lamming, Hearne, Mais, and Harris.

"Reflections on West Indian Literature." Edward Brathwaite.
SOUTHERN REVIEW, v. 3, no. 3, pp. 264-272.
  A review of THE ISLANDS IN-BETWEEN. In this review,
Brathwaite condemns the European standards used to measure
West Indian literature. Discusses some of the criteria
which should apply and the relationship of Africa to West
Indian literature.

"The Crisis of Black Identity in the West Indian Novel." Lloyd
W. Brown. CRITIQUE, v. 11, no. 3, pp. 97-112.
  "Experience of racial discovery" in the West Indian novel
and the attempt to deal with a unique cultural position, as
seen in the writings of Lamming, Reid, Clarke, Mais, Salkey,
and Carew.

[Review of] THE ISLANDS IN BETWEEN, edited by Louis James. Anne
Walmsley. BIM, v. 12, no. 48, January-June, pp. 267-68.
  While admitting the value of these essays, she suggests
that West Indian writing be judged on its own terms rather
than by European standards.

[Review of] THE SUN'S EYE, edited by Anne Walmsley. Mervyn
Morris. CARIBBEAN QUARTERLY, v. 15, no. 1, March, pp. 57-59.

"The Social Groundwork of Politics in Some West Indian Novels."
J. A. Ramsaran. NEGRO DIGEST, v. 18, no. 10, April, pp. 71-

77.
   The dichotomy of culture and the complex social composi-
tion as themes in the novels of Mittelholzer, Salkey, Naipaul,
Patterson, and Harris.

"West Indian Writers: Future of Individual." Daphne Archbold-
Rousseau. SUNDAY GUARDIAN (Trinidad), April 20, p. 10.
   The West Indian attempts to interpret his environment and
also to create his environment. She finds that current
writers no longer have common themes.

"The Unsteady Flame: A Short Account of Guianese Poetry." Ian
McDonald. NWF, part 1, v. 1, no. 17, June, pp. 20-22; part
2, v. 1, no. 18, July, pp. 24-25, part 3, v. 1, no. 19, July,
pp. 19-20.
   Brief outline of Guyanese poetry and its major themes.

"Obeah and the Supernatural in West Indian Literature."
Kenneth Ramchand. JAMAICA JOURNAL, v. 3, no. 2, June, pp.
52-54.
   Supernatural forces of good and evil in the works of
Naipaul, Mais, Khan, Wynter, and Patterson.

"An Introduction to Caribbean Literature." Anthony Derrick.
CARIBBEAN QUARTERLY v. 15, no. 2 and 3, June-September,
pp. 65-78.
   Political and social commitment of French and Spanish
Caribbean literature. The developing orientation towards
Africa in British West Indian literature. Works by McKay,
Campbell, Sherlock, Walcott, Lamming, Williams, Dathorne,
Naipaul, Brathwaite, and Mittelholzer.

"Discovering Literature in Trinidad: Two Experiences."
Includes "The Nineteen-Thirties," C. L. R. James, "Growing
Up with Writing: A Particular Experience." Michael Anthony.
JCL, no. 7, July, pp. 73-87. Also appears in SAVACOU, no. 2,
September 1970, pp. 54-66.
   Autobiographical essays. James discusses the intellectual
ferment during the 1930s, Anthony talks about his boyhood
and development as a writer.

"Dialect in West Indian Literature." R. B. Le Page. JCL, no.
7, July, pp. 1-7.
   Explains how dialects come into existence and explores
some of the problems facing the West Indian writer in his
attempts to be true to his own dialect and also communicate
effectively with his readers.

"Our Society Is Growing Not Flowering" (an interview with
Wilfred Cartey). Carl Jacobs. SUNDAY GUARDIAN (Trinidad),
July 20, p. 10.
     Although the postwar generation of West Indian writers
came at a time of ferment, a passive hopelessness is setting
in. Writers are not accepting their responsibility to
society.

"African---Afro-American Literary Relations; Basic Parallels."
Charles R. Larson. NEGRO DIGEST, November, v. 19, no. 1,
pp. 35-42.
     Negritude as a link between African and Afro-American
literature. Claude McKay in the forefront of this literary
awakening in America.

"Tropical English Literature." M. M. [Mervyn Morris?]. SUNDAY
GLEANER, December 14, p. 4.
     Reviews THE CHOSEN TONGUE (Gerald Moore) and finds the
author guilty of colonialism with the tendency to regard the
colonial as good as long as he remains in this position.

1970

"The European Factor in West Indian Literature." Arthur D.
Drayton. LITERARY HALF-YEARLY, v. 11, no. 1, pp. 71-94.
     Neo-colonialism and the effect of Europe on the West
Indies. He suggests that "The West Indian abroad can only
be claimed for our national literature if his work is
stamped with a West Indian interest." Proceeds to evaluate
West Indian authors according to this guideline. Discusses
C. L. R. James, Mittelholzer, Lamming, Anthony, Harris,
Naipaul, Selvon, McKay, Walcott, Brathwaite, Williams,
Carberry, Sherlock, Telemaque, Vaughn, Hendriks, Morris, de
Lisser, and Campbell.

"West Indian Writing." John Wickham. BIM, v. 13, no. 50,
January-June, pp. 68-80.
     From a lecture given at the Multi-Racial Centre at the
University of the West Indies, Cave Hill, on the search for
West Indian identity in the prose fiction of the 1950s. He
finds few solutions in the fiction of Mais, de Boissiere,
Mendes, James, Selvon, Lamming, and Naipaul.

[Review of] NEW BEACON REVIEWS: COLLECTION ONE, edited by
John La Rose. Mervyn Morris. BIM, v. 13, no. 50, January-
June, pp. 131-132.
     Discusses each of the four essays with approval.

1970

"West Indian Writings." Wayne Brown. SUNDAY GUARDIAN
(Trinidad), May 31, p. 17.
    Reviews NEW BEACON REVIEWS: COLLECTION ONE and briefly
describes essays, suggests a second collection.

"Concern for Criticism." Kenneth Ramchand. CARIBBEAN
QUARTERLY, v. 16, no. 2, June, pp. 51-60. Also appears in
LITERARY HALF-YEARLY, v. 11, no. 2, pp. 151-161.
    Finds that major pieces of West Indian literary criticism
(i.e., THE ISLANDS IN BETWEEN, THE CHOSEN TONGUE). lack
genuine critical analysis. Suggests that the job of the
critic is as pedagogue rather than as political/social
commentator.

"Creative Literature of the British West Indies during the
Period of Slavery." Edward Brathwaite. SAVACOU, v. 1, no.
1, June, pp. 46-73.
    Examines literature, mostly poetry, of the eighteenth and
nineteenth century written by slaves in the West Indies.

"History, Fable and Myth in the Caribbean and Guianas." Wilson
Harris. CARIBBEAN QUARTERLY, v. 16, no. 2, pp. 1-32, June.
    Explores the psychological roots of many of the arts of
the West Indies. Suggests that a philosophy of history lies
behind these art forms which include those of the Caribs
and Amerindians, as well as those brought from Africa.
Discusses writings of Edward Brathwaite.

"The First Generation of West Indian Novelists." Wayne Brown.
SUNDAY GUARDIAN (Trinidad), June 7, pp. 6 and 11.
    Introduction to the works of Naipaul, Lamming, Salkey,
and Selvon.

"The Politics of the Educators." Wayne Brown. SUNDAY
GUARDIAN (Trinidad), June 14, p. 6.
    An argument for teaching West Indian literature in primary
and secondary school.

"Trinidadian English." Wayne Brown. SUNDAY GUARDIAN (Trinidad),
June 21, p. 6.
    Language changes with the society. There is no "standard"
English since the various kinds of English spoken are all
dialects.

"West Indian Consciousness in West Indian Verse." Arthur
Drayton. JCL, no. 9, July, pp. 66-88.
    Development of poetry in the West Indies from the

Index of Articles

eighteenth century to the twentieth.

"Teaching Poetry in West Indian Schools." Wayne Brown. SUNDAY
GUARDIAN (Trinidad), July 12, p. 6.
    Suggestions on how to teach poetry in primary and
secondary schools and which poetry to teach.

"West Indian Writers Critically Examined." SUNDAY GLEANER,
July 19, p. 35.
    Reviews THE WEST INDIAN NOVEL AND ITS BACKGROUND
(Ramchand). Finds that the book sets pattern for high standards of criticism. Also favorably reviews SAVACOU, v. 1,
no. 1.

"Analyzing West Indian Writers." F. E. Brassington. SUNDAY
GUARDIAN (Trinidad), July 26, p. 6.
    Review of THE WEST INDIAN NOVEL AND ITS BACKGROUND, and
the relevance of Ramchand's work as a contribution to West
Indian scholarship.

"On Art, Artists and the People." Wayne Brown. SUNDAY
GUARDIAN (Trinidad), August 9, p. 10.
    Discusses the major schism and dialogue in West Indian
writing between those writers who feel that art has a moral
responsibility to the society, and those who feel that art
exists for itself. Discusses Wynter, Brathwaite, James,
Lovelace, Mais, in first group; Walcott, Naipaul, St. Omer,
Denis Williams, and Anthony, in second.

"The Little Magazine in the West Indies." Wayne Brown. SUNDAY
GUARDIAN (Trinidad), August 16, p. 9.
    Problems of little magazines. Reviews BIM, and the first
issue of SAVACOU.

"On West Indian Critics and Historians." Wayne Brown. SUNDAY
GUARDIAN (Trinidad), August 23, p. 17.
    Traditional forms will break down as the writer describes
a culture that is removed from the conditions that produced
those forms. The task of the West Indian critic is to identify these innovations.

"West Indian Literature of the Past Year." Wayne Brown. SUNDAY
GUARDIAN (Trinidad), August 30, p. 5.
    Discusses FEVER GRASS and CANDYWINE FEVER (Hearne,
Cargill). "What makes these books dangerous to us here in
the West Indies, no matter how entertaining they may be to
metropolitan audiences, is that they exploit, they use the

1970

prejudices of the metropolitan audiences to achieve their
effects." Also discusses THE GULF (Walcott), ISLANDS
(Brathwaite), ASCENT TO OMAI (Harris).

"Art in Its Widest Sense and Reconstruction." Wayne Brown.
TGM, August 30, pp. 12-13, 17.
The artist is not encouraged in West Indian society.
Suggestions for promoting the artist in Trinidad.

"Beneath the North Star: The Canadian Image in Black Literature." Lloyd W. Brown. DALHOUSIE REVIEW, v. 50, no. 3,
Autumn, pp. 317-329.
Canada is increasingly seen by Caribbean novelists as an
extension of American racial and economic values, rather than
as the haven it was formerly considered. Evaluates the works
of Paula Marshall and Austin Clarke.

"Caribbean Poetry in English--Some Problems." Louis James.
SAVACOU, no. 2, September, pp. 78-86.
Considers the problems of poetic voice, point of view,
and whether or not the poem works, and why, in West Indian
poetry. Discusses Brathwaite, Walcott, Bennett, Sherlock,
Carter, Carberry, Harris, E. McG. Keane, J. E. Clare
McFarlane.

"Ideas of Patriotism and National Dignity in Some Jamaican
Writings." Leo Oakley. JAMAICA JOURNAL, v. 4, no. 3, pp.
16-21, September. Also appears in SUNDAY GLEANER,
part 1, March 28, pp. 31, 34; part 2, April 4, p. 27; part 3,
April 11, p. 25, as "Patriotism, National Dignity in
Jamaican Writings."
The changing concept of patriotism in Jamaican poetry from
the early twentieth century to Independence. Discusses
Redcam, Mais Arthur Nicholas, Constance, Hollar J. E.
Clare McFarlane, Lena Kent, Vivian Virtue, George Campbell,
M. G. Smith, Victor Reid, Vera Bell, A. L. Hendriks, R. L.
C. McFarlane, Louise Bennett, and Basil McFarlane.

"Meanings." Derek Walcott. SAVACOU, no. 2, September, pp.
45-51.
Autobiographical essay on Walcott's plays, his development as a dramatist, his theatre company, and influences on
his art.

"Sparrow and the Language of Calypso." F. Gordon Rohlehr.
SAVACOU, no. 2, September, pp. 87-99.

Index of Articles

Analysis of Sparrow's calypsoes from the viewpoint of
the calypso as a barometer of society. Use of English in
West Indian speech rhythms. Discusses Naipaul.

"Timehri." Edward Brathwaite. SAVACOU, no. 2, September,
pp. 35-44. Also appears in IS MASSA DAY DEAD? New York:
Doubleday, 1974, pp. 29-44.
   Partially autobiographical presentation of Brathwaite's
own developing cultural awareness. Mestizo and Mulatto
creolization and the artistic and spiritual potentialities
of these aboriginal and folk cultures.

"Towards a Revolution in the Arts." Marina Maxwell. SAVACOU,
no. 2, September, pp. 19-32.
   Many West Indian writers and critics have not yet freed
themselves from neocolonialism, others are exploring alternative forms and looking to Third World aesthetic models.
Maxwell sees Carnival as the central artistic metaphor, and
discusses Brathwaite, Lindsay Barrett, Reid, Harris, and
Lamming.

"New West Indian Writers of the Past Year." Wayne Brown.
   SUNDAY GUARDIAN (Trinidad), September 6, p. 8
   Reviews Shiva Naipaul, Merle Hodge, and Faustin Charles.

"West Indian Poetry of the 1940's, Part 1." Wayne Brown.
   SUNDAY GUARDIAN (Trinidad), September 13, p. 9.
   Religion, nature, and love of the Mother Country are the
themes of early West Indian poetry. ". . . Alternatives
fulfilling the identical function in the psyche of the
poet." Poetry by Redcam and J. C. McFarlane.

"Poetry of the 1940's, Part 2: West Indian Poetry, the Turn
of the Decade." Wayne Brown. SUNDAY GUARDIAN (Trinidad),
September 20, p. 11.
   The poets responded to the new consciousness by utilizing
the themes of the common man, but often sentimentalized
those things that they could not deal with.

"Poetry of the 1940's, Part 3: 'The Dilemma.'" Wayne Brown.
   SUNDAY GUARDIAN (Trinidad), October 4, p. 11.
   "In the 1940's West Indian poetry tried for the first
time to come to grips with the slave and African past." Dis-
cusses McKay, Campbell, Sherlock, M. G. Smith, Herbert, and
Roach.

"Poetry of the 1940's, Part 5: The Mulatto Question." Wayne

1971

Brown. SUNDAY GUARDIAN (Trinidad), October 11, p. 11.
The cultural and racial split and its effect on the poetry
of Sherlock, Campbell, and Roach.

"Poetry of the 1940s, Part 7: Returning the Islands to Themselves." Wayne Brown. SUNDAY GUARDIAN (Trinidad), October
26, p. 16.
Though the poetry of the 1940s broke with past poetic
tradition in language, imagery, and theme, it failed by not
challenging the basic assumptions of the metropole.

"West Indian Writers." Malcolm Page. NOVEL, v. 3, no. 2,
Winter, pp. 167-172.
A survey of the West Indian novel since 1950. Ostensibly
reviewing ISLANDS-IN-BETWEEN and CARIBBEAN WRITERS: CRITICAL
ESSAYS (Van Sertima), Page finds little merit in either the
literature or the criticism.

"Long Awaited Collection of West Indian Poetry." SUNDAY
GLEANER, November 1, p. 29.
Reviews CARIBBEAN VOICES, v. 2 (edited by John Figueroa).
Praises collection but finds that the editor's comments may be
"overdoing the dissection of the medium."

"On Exile and the Dialect of the Tribe." Wayne Brown. SUNDAY
GUARDIAN (Trinidad), November 8, p. 19.
Effects of exile on the writer and on the society he
leaves behind. Use of language to reflect the society. Discusses James, Lamming, and Naipaul.

"Telling It Like It Is. The Poet in the West Indies." John
Hearne. SUNDAY GLEANER, November 8, p. 29.
Reviews CARIBBEAN VOICES, v. 2, and finds that the poets
reveal a "Melancholy of the bone, an intuition of essential
loneliness." Only Brathwaite, Walcott, Simpson and Lucie-
Smith have so far created an oeuvre, with Morris, Scott, and
McNeill as promising. Folk poetry and calypso are not really
poetry.

"Talking About Aesthetics Seriously!" Wayne Brown. SUNDAY
GUARDIAN (Trinidad), November 15, p. 15.
Against art as polemic. Aesthetics as efficiency, grace-
fulness and necessary to society and its expressions.

"The Possibilities for West Indian Writing." Wayne Brown.
SUNDAY GUARDIAN (Trinidad), November 22, p. 21.
Explores the various styles and viewpoints of Lamming,

340

Naipaul, Walcott, and Harris.

"History as Absurdity: Columbus to Castro." F. Gordon
   Rohlehr. TAPIA, part 1, no. 11, November 29, pp. 4-7; part
   2, no. 12, pp. 5-6, 8, 16.
      Subtitled "A Literary Critic's Approach to FROM COLUMBUS
   TO CASTRO and Other Miscellaneous Writings of Dr. Eric
   Williams," this essay severely criticizes Williams's work in
   terms of its validity and explores the possibilities of
   historiography in the West Indies. Comments on major themes
   in West Indian culture which affect both the historian and
   the creative writer.

"Little Magazine From St. Lucia." Wayne Brown. SUNDAY GUARDIAN
   (Trinidad), November 29, p. 15.
      Reviews first issue of LINK.

"The New Battleground, Parts 1 and 2." Wayne Brown. SUNDAY
   GUARDIAN (Trinidad), December 6, pp. 9, 20; December 13, pp.
   15 and 20.
      Reviews SAVACOU 2 and discusses the polarization between
   Eurocentred and Afro-centred viewpoints that is evident in
   the articles.

"Thinking About Commonwealth Literature." Wayne Brown. SUNDAY
   GUARDIAN (Trinidad), December 20, p. 10.
      The development of a national literature. Language
   as a common element in Commonwealth literature.

"For the Reviewer, A Time to Change." Wayne Brown. SUNDAY
   GUARDIAN (Trinidad), December 25, p. 13.
      The danger of becoming too nationalistic. "The changed
   role of the reviewer must be to constantly question the
   validity of arguments brought forward to support it, and at
   the same time to try to ensure that in the focussed attention
   on the works of this particular region the universality of
   human experience (and therefore of human art) is not denied."

"Interior of the Novel: Amerindian/European/African Relations."
   Wilson Harris. NATIONAL IDENTITY; PAPERS DELIVERED AT THE
   COMMONWEALTH LITERATURE CONFERENCE, UNIVERSITY OF QUEENSLAND,
   BRISBANE, 9th-15th AUGUST, 1968, edited by K. L. Goodwin.
   London: Heineman, 1971, pp. 138-147.
      The artist's purpose is to explore and invoke the
   "absences" and memories of human experience, to uncover the

<u>1971</u>

many layers that create the "presence."

"The Native Phenomenon." Wilson Harris. COMMON WEALTH; PAPERS
DELIVERED AT THE CONFERENCE OF COMMONWEALTH LITERATURE,
AARHUS UNIVERSITY, APRIL 26-30, 1971, edited by A. Rutherford.
Aarhus, Denmark: Aarhus University, 1971, pp. 144-150.
   Concepts of "The great chain of memory" and the "ritual
of bounty or conquest." These contrasting elements inform
the nature of creativity in terms of legend, myth, and his-
tory, and inform Harris' own writing.

"A Note on Dialect." Samuel Selvon. COMMON WEALTH; PAPERS
DELIVERED AT THE CONFERENCE OF COMMONWEALTH LITERATURE,
AARHUS UNIVERSITY, APRIL 26-30, 1971, p. 124.
   Brief note to the effect that the success of Selvon's
own work proves that writing in dialect is not frivolous and
can produce work of lasting value.

"The Writer Without a Society." Shiva Naipaul. COMMON WEALTH;
PAPERS DELIVERED AT THE CONFERENCE OF COMMONWEALTH LITERATURE,
AARHUS UNIVERSITY, APRIL 26-30, 1971, pp. 114-123.
   A damning and despairing picture of Trinidadian society.
The problems of a writer coming from this background and in
recognizing "that he has a duty to fulfill towards the
English language; and simultaneously he has another to the
West Indies."

"The Calypso Tradition in West Indian Literature." Lloyd W.
Brown. BAR, v. 2, no. 1 and 2, February, pp. 127-143.
   Elements of the Calypso which have been effectively
utilized by West Indian writers, notably Brathwaite, Lamming,
Walcott, Paula Marshall, Khan, Charles, and Selvon.

"Caribbean Literature in English: 1949-1970." R. M. Lacovia.
BAR, v. 2, no. 1 and 2, February, pp. 109-125.
   Relates themes in Caribbean literature to African cultural concepts. Concentrates on Naipaul and Brathwaite and
also discusses Reid, Lamming, Anthony, McKay, Mittelholzer,
and Hearne.

"Some Views on CARIBBEAN VOICES, v. 2." Mervyn Morris.
CARIBBEAN QUARTERLY, v. 17, no. 1, March, pp. 48-49.
   Praises the selections of poetry chosen for this anthology, but has some reservations about Figueroa's introduction. Find his appendix on language valuable.

342

"Foreward to Savacou no. 3/4--New Writing." Edward Brathwaite.
   SAVACOU, 3/4, March, pp. 5-9.
      New writing in the Caribbean reflects the writer's concern
   with his own society and a desire to help shape its direction.

[Review of] CARIBBEAN VOICES, edited by John Figueroa. Donald
   B. Smith. RRI, v. 1, no. 1, Spring, pp. 64-68.
      Discusses some West Indian themes found in the poetry.

"Writing and Publishing in the West Indies; An Interview with
   George Lamming." Ian Munro, Reinhard Sander, and Dean
   Beebe. WLWE, April, no. 19, pp. 17-22.
      Lamming talks about his own works and laments the lack of
   publishing outlets in the West Indies.

"West Indian Culture Still Being Defined, Part 1." Merle
   Hodge. SUNDAY GUARDIAN (Trinidad), April 4, p. 12.
      Education in the West Indies has not taught West Indians
   to look at their own culture. Discusses the cultural contributions that intellectuals and artists can make.

"The 'Twice-Born' Artist's Silent Revolution." J. A. Ramsaran.
   BLACK WORLD, v. 20, no. 7, June, pp. 58-67.
      Awareness of Africa in black poetry, particularly in the
   works of Walcott and Brathwaite.

"History and the Novel: A Literary Critic's Approach." Kenneth
   Ramchand. SAVACOU, v. 1, no. 5, June, pp. 103-113.
      Shows that a large number of West Indian novels are con-
   cerned with history. Uses NEW DAY to illustrate the pitfalls
   of the historical approach.

"Novel and History; Plot and Plantation." Sylvia Wynter.
   SAVACOU, v. 1, no. 5, pp. 95-102.
      Critique of NEW DAY and an economic interpretation of the
   place of the historical novel in the West Indies. Discusses
   Reid, Naipaul and de Lisser.

"Ferment in Local Writing." C. L. [Cedric Lindo?]. SUNDAY
   GLEANER, June 13, p. 29.
      Reviews SAVACOU 3/4 and finds it of interest to the
   sociologist. It expresses the new directions of the
   Caribbean.

"West Indian Poetry: Some Problems of Assesment." F. Gordon
   Rohlehr. TAPIA, no. 20, August, pp. 11-14. Also appears

1971

under same title in BIM, part 1, v. 14, no. 54, January-
June 1972, pp. 80-88; part 2, v. 14, no. 55, July-December,
pp. 134-144, 1972, and under title "Some Problems of Assessment: A Look at New Expressions in the Arts of the Contemporary Caribbean." CARIBBEAN QUARTERLY, v. 17, nos. 3 and
4, September-December 1971, pp. 92-113.
    Uses the anthology of new writing in SAVACOU 3/4 to
initiate a debate on West Indian aesthetics and literary
criticism. Discusses Malik, Questel, Gonzales, McTair, Roach,
McNeill, Jerry, Carter, Brathwaite, and Morris. Analyzes the
influence of Rastafarians and contemporary music on the new
West Indian poetry.

"West Indian Prose Fiction in the Sixties." Edward Brathwaite.
    BLACK WORLD, v. 20, no. 11, September, pp. 14-29.
    Similar to Brathwaite's article of the same title cited
under 1968, with the addition of the examination of the works
of St. Omer and Barrett.

"Caribbean Perspectives--The Creative Potential and the Quality
    of Life." Rex Nettleford. CARIBBEAN QUARTERLY, v. 17, nos.
    3 and 4, September, pp. 114-127.
    Naipaul and Harris as typifying certain West Indian
attitudes.

"A Way of Teaching: A Review of a Library Series--Heinemann
    Series." Cecil Gray. CARIBBEAN QUARTERLY, v. 17, nos. 3
    and 4, September, pp. 139-143.
    Review of Heinemann Caribbean Writers Series and the first
four books: THE YEAR IN SAN FERNANDO; CORENTYNE THUNDER;
MYSTIC MASSEUR; VOICES UNDER THE WINDOW; and the introductions
to them by L. James, Morris, and Ramchand.

"Afterthoughts." F. Gordon Rohlehr. TAPIA, no. 23, December
    26, pp. 8, 13. Also appears under same title in BIM, v. 14,
    no. 56, January-June 1973, pp. 227-230.
    Continues discussion begun in "West Indian Poetry, Some
Problems of Assessment." Includes Walcott, Mais, and
Lamming.

"Introduction to Guyanese Writing." A. J. Seymour. KAIE, no.
    7, December.
    Entire issue devoted to texts of a series of broadcasts
for schools on aspects of Guyanese writing.

"A Note on Literature and Caribbean Society." A. J. Seymour.
    KAIE, no. 8, December, pp. 12-18. Text of a lecture

delivered at CARIFESTA '71.

The artist in the Caribbean has a responsibility to his people as well as to his art. CARIFESTA's primary purpose is to create a forum for such a dialogue in which the artist can attempt to express fundamental issues for the West Indian. Discusses Naipaul.

1972

"English Caribbean Literature: A Brave New World." R. M. Lacovia. BLACK IMAGES, v. 1, no. 1, January, pp. 15-22.
    Slightly variant form of his article "Caribbean Literature in English" (BAR, v. 2, nos. 1 and 2, 1971, pp. 109-125).

"Creole Criticism--A Critique." Sylvia Wynter. NWQ, v. 5, no. 4, Cropover, pp. 12-34.
    Criticizes THE WEST INDIAN NOVEL AND ITS BACKGROUND and accuses Ramchand of attempting to deny the African heritage within Caribbean culture.

"The Personal Sense of a Society--Minority View: Aspects of the 'East Indian' Novel in the West Indies." Barrie Davies. STUDIES IN THE NOVEL, v. 4, no. 2, Summer, pp. 273-283.
    The East Indian ambience as the "means of apprehending the quality of a total society" is illustrated in the novels of Khan, Selvon, and Naipaul.

"West Indian Poetry in English, 1900-1970: A Selected Bibliography." S. O. Asein. BLACK IMAGES, v. 1, no. 2, Summer, pp. 12-15.
    Brief summary of development of West Indian poetry up to 1970. Bibliography includes anthologies, authors, periodical articles, and reviews.

[Review of] CARIBBEAN VOICES, edited by John Figueroa. C. R. Gray. BIM, v. 14, no. 55, July-December, pp. 182-185.
    A basic anthology of West Indian poetry. Finds that Figueroa does not adequately prove his introductory points on dialect.

"Forty Years of Calypso." F. Gordon Rohlehr. TAPIA, part 1, v. 2, no. 1, September 3, pp. 1-4; part 2, v. 2, no. 2, September 17, pp. 4-5; part 3, v. 2, no. 3, October 8, pp. 6-7.
    Evolution of the calypso form and its significance in terms of West Indian culture.

1972

"The Folk in Caribbean Literature." F. Gordon Rohlehr. TAPIA,
    part 1, v. 2, no. 11, December 17, pp. 7-8; 13-15; part 2,
    v. 2, no. 12, December 24, pp. 8, 9, 15.
        In-depth exploration of the writer's relationship to the
    folk. Proposes a more flexible, realistic approach to the
    concepts of folk and urban in West Indian society. Discusses
    Lamming, Selvon, Mais, Walcott, and Louise Bennett.

1973

"Dialect in West Indian Literature." Ismith Khan. THE BLACK
    WRITER IN AFRICA AND THE AMERICAS, edited by Lloyd W. Brown.
    Los Angeles: Hennessey and Ingalls, 1973, pp. 165-194.
        A plea to the West Indian writer to cast off colonial
    overlays and use his own language to reach the people.
    Analyzes some of the problems inherent in using dialect in
    writing.

"Some Speculations as to the Absence of Racialistic Vindictive-
    ness in West Indian Literature." Austin C. Clark. THE
    BLACK WRITER IN AFRICA AND THE AMERICAS, edited by Lloyd
    W. Brown. Los Angeles: Hennessey and Ingalls, 1973, pp.
    165-194.
        Takes West Indian writers at home to task for the lack
    of racial awareness in their works. Passive acceptance of
    colonialism, an attempt to imitate the master, and to promote
    the myth of "racial harmony," are primary reasons for the
    lack of emphasis on nationalism and on Africanization of basic
    models. West Indian writers in exile seem to have a greater
    awareness of black aesthetics and the racial situation.
    Naipaul, Walcott, Anthony, Brathwaite, and Lamming, illus-
    trate both sides of this situation.

[Review of] BREAKLIGHT: THE POETRY OF THE CARIBBEAN. Liz Gant.
    BLACK WORLD, v. 22, no. 3, January, pp. 81-85.
        This collection reflects the West Indian poet's discovery
    of his heritage and of other cultures.

"Tribute to Frank Collymore." SAVACOU, no. 7/8, January-June.
        Entire issue consists of essays and poems written about
    and for Collymore by fifty writers and critics. Also in-
    cludes selections from BIM.

"Who's Who in the West Indian Novel." Ivy Thompson. CARIBBEAN
    CONTACT, v. 1, no. 5, April, pp. 4, 18.
        Racial pride and black awareness in the novels of Lamming,
    Hearne, and Khan.